W9-DAA-020

OXFORD HISTORIES

SERIES ADVISERS
Geoff Eley, University of Michigan
Lyndal Roper, University of Oxford

Donald Bloxham is Professor of Modern History at Edinburgh University. An expert in the history of genocide and the punishment of genocide, he is the author of *Genocide on Trial* (2001), *The Holocaust: Critical Historical Approaches* (with Tony Kushner, 2005), and *The Great Game of Genocide: Imperialism, Nationalism, and the Destruction of the Ottoman Armenians* (2005), which won the 2007 Raphael Lemkin Award for Genocide Scholarship. He is also co-editor of the forthcoming *Oxford Handbook of Genocide Studies* (2009) and the monograph series *Zones of Violence*.

The Final Solution
A GENOCIDE

DONALD BLOXHAM

OXFORD
UNIVERSITY PRESS

OXFORD

UNIVERSITY PRESS

Great Clarendon Street, Oxford OX2 6DP

Oxford University Press is a department of the University of Oxford.
It furthers the University's objective of excellence in research, scholarship,
and education by publishing worldwide in

Oxford New York

Auckland Cape Town Dar es Salaam Hong Kong Karachi
Kuala Lumpur Madrid Melbourne Mexico City Nairobi
New Delhi Shanghai Taipei Toronto

With offices in

Argentina Austria Brazil Chile Czech Republic France Greece
Guatemala Hungary Italy Japan Poland Portugal Singapore
South Korea Switzerland Thailand Turkey Ukraine Vietnam

Oxford is a registered trade mark of Oxford University Press
in the UK and in certain other countries

Published in the United States
by Oxford University Press Inc., New York

© Donald Bloxham, 2009

British Library Cataloguing in Publication Data

Data available

Library of Congress Cataloging in Publication Data

Bloxham, Donald.
The final solution: a genocide / Donald Bloxham.
   p. cm.
Includes bibliographical references and index.
ISBN 978–0–19–955034–0 (pbk.)—ISBN 978–0–19–955033–3 (hardback)
1. Genocide—Germany—History—20th century. 2. Holocaust, Jewish (1939–1945)—Causes.
3. Jews—Government policy—Germany—History—20th century. 4. Genocide—Political aspects.
5. Genocide—Sociological aspects. 6. Germany—Ethnic relations—History—20th century.
7. Europe—Ethnic relations—History—20th century. I. Title.
HV6322.7.B57 2009
940.53'1811—dc22   2009023182

Typeset by Laserwords Private Limited, Chennai, India
Printed in Great Britain
on acid-free paper by
Clay Ltd., St Ives plc

ISBN 978–0–19–955033–3 (Hbk.)
ISBN 978–0–19–955034–0 (Pbk.)

1 3 5 7 9 10 8 6 4 2

PREFACE

A few years ago, I wrote a book with Tony Kushner called *The Holocaust: Critical Historical Approaches*. In 'my' half of the book I set out a series of critiques of the historiography of the perpetrators and perpetration of Nazi genocide, and tried to suggest some new avenues of enquiry. This book is an attempt to take up my own challenge, and write a history of the murder of the Jews in the light not just of other Nazi population policies, but of a modern European history of violence, and an increasingly sophisticated scholarship on genocide in human history. Those who have read my 2005 monograph *The Great Game of Genocide: Imperialism, Nationalism, and the Destruction of the Ottoman Armenians* will see certain continuities of analysis, particularly in my attempt to link broad geopolitics with cultural specificities and with the detail of historical contingency in the explanation of genocide and related forms of violence. I am most grateful to Christopher Wheeler of Oxford University Press for suggesting that I contemplate the project, and for his support and advice, and to Geoff Eley, one of the advisory editors to the Oxford Histories, for his encouragement.

The book was written almost entirely during the academic year 2007–8, which I spent at the Center for Advanced Holocaust Studies at the United States Holocaust Memorial Museum (USHMM) in Washington, DC. I was fortunate enough to be invited as the J. B. and Maurice C. Shapiro Senior Scholar-in-Residence for that year, for which privilege I thank the Shapiro family and Foundation, and the

USHMM. The resources of the institution and the help of its staff were vital in ensuring the project's completion.

Jürgen Matthäus is senior applied research scholar at the USHMM, and during the time I was there, he was incredibly generous with his time as interlocutor, reference-source, proofreader, and constructive critic, not to mention companion and host. He has read the entire book in draft form and if it has any merit, a large portion is his. This should not, of course, be taken to indicate that he agrees with all I have to say.

Mark Roseman became another good friend in the time we spent together at the USHMM, and offered much useful advice. Jennifer Cazenave, Martin Conway, Emil Kerenji, Tom Lawson, Dirk Moses, Devin Pendas, Jill Stephenson, and Scott Straus all looked at parts of the manuscript and provided welcome criticism. For their companionship and help during the period in which the book was written, I also thank Michal Aharony, Pertti Ahonen, Michlean Amir, Ferzina Banaji, Peter Black, Richard Breitman, David Brown, Suzanne Brown Fleming, Tracey Brown, Michael Bryant, Douglas Cairns, Holly Case, Andy Charlesworth, Frank Cogliano, Ron Coleman, Martin Dean, Enda Delaney, Robert Ehrenreich, Michael Gelb, Jennifer Hansen, Patricia Heberer, Fabian Hilfrich, Emil Kerenji, Tony Kushner, Mark Levene, Geoffrey McGargee, Jim McMillan, Christopher Probst, Colin Richmond, Traci Rucker, Julius Ruiz, Paul Shapiro, Martin Shuster, Vincent Slatt, Seumas Spark, Eric Steinhart, Alexa Stiller, Nick Terry, Paul Vincent, Caroline Waddell, and Joe White. To Cordelia Beattie go not only my thanks but also my love. Hans-Lukas Kiser, Ziya Meral, and Vladimir Solonari pushed relevant references in my direction. Special mention should go to Lisa Yavnai, head of the visiting scholars programme at the USHMM, who is a staunch friend and took great care of me in Washington. Without her support the year would have been much less enjoyable than it was.

Finally, I am once again in the debt of the Leverhulme Trust. The leave permitting me to go to Washington was founded by receipt of a Philip Leverhulme Prize. I hope that this book represents a reasonable part return on the Trust's investment of money and faith.

CONTENTS

LIST OF MAPS AND ILLUSTRATIONS

Maps

Illustrations

All images © United States Holocaust Memorial Museum, Washington, DC, apart from illustration 4, © Imperial War Museum, London.

GLOSSARY AND ABBREVIATIONS

Aktion Reinhard 'Operation Reinhard': the codename for the murder of the Jews of the Generalgouvernement

CDR Coalition pour la Défence de la Republique: Rwandan political party

Cheka [Vserossijskaya] Chrezvychajnaya Komissiya: The All-Russian Extraordinary Commission for Combating Counter-revolution and Sabotage

CUP Ittihad ve Terraki Cemiyeti: Committee of Union and Progress, ruling faction in the Ottoman Empire, 1908–18

Eichmann, Adolf Expert on 'Jewish affairs' within the SD and then, from 1939, within the Gestapo after it had been incorporated in the RSHA

Einsatzgruppen Special task forces of the Sicherheitspolizei (Security Police) and the SD

Gauleiter Nazi regional party leader

Generalgouvernement The area of central Poland occupied by Germany from 1939 but not annexed to the Reich; it expanded in late 1941 to include eastern Galicia

Generalkommissariat Weissruthenien German administrative unit for the Belarussian territories within the Reichskommissariat Ostland

Generalplan Ost Design for the ethnic-racial 're-ordering' of Germany' eastern territories, and for the settlement there of Germans

Gestapo Geheime Staatspolizei: Secret State Police

Gleichschaltung 'Coordination' of the state with Nazi personnel

Heydrich, Reinhard Head of the SD; from 1936 also head of the Sicherheitspolizei; from 1939 head of the RSHA; from 1941 Protector of Bohemia and Moravia

Himmler, Heinrich Head of the SS ('Reichsführer-SS') and, from 1936, all of the German police forces

HSSPF Höhere Schutzstaffeln- und Polizeiführer: Higher SS and Police Leader

IAMM Iskân-ı Aşâyir ve Muhacirin Müdiriyyeti: Directorate for the Settlement of Tribes and Immigrants, Ottoman Empire

IKL Inspektion der Konzentrationslager: Inspectorate of Concentration Camps

Kommandostab: 'executive administrative organization' of the Reichsführer-SS (Himmler)

Kriminalpolizei Reich detective police

MRNDD Mouvement Républicain National pour la Démocratie et le Développement: Rwandan political party

NKVD Narodnyi Komissariat Vnutrennikh Del: Soviet People's Commissariat of Internal Affairs

OGPU Ob'edinennoe Gosudarstvennoe Politicheskoe Upravleniye: All-Union State Political Administration

Ordnungspolizei Order Police

Ostministerium Eastern Ministry, under Alfred Rosenberg, incorporating the Reichskommissariat Ostland and the Reichskommissariat Ukraine

OUN Orhanizatsiya Ukrayinskyh Natsionalistiv: Organisation of Ukrainian Nationalists

POW prisoner of war

Reichskommissariat Ostland German administrative unit incorporating the Baltic states Lativia, Lithuania, and Estonia and the northern parts of Belarus

Reichskommissar Regional German state leadership position

Reichskommissariat Ukraine German administrative unit incorporating Ukraine, parts of eastern Poland, and southern Belarus

RKF Reichskommissariat für die Festigung des deutschen Volkstums: Reich Commissariat for the Strengthening of Ethnic German Nationhood, within the SS

Rosenberg, Alfred Nazi ideologue; from 1941 Minister for the Eastern Territories

RPF Rwandese Patriotic Front: a primarily Tutsi military force

RSHA Reichssicherheitshauptamt: Reich Security Head Office, with the SS, created in 1939 and incorporating the SD and the Sicherheitspolizei, the Security Police

SA Sturmabteilung: the brownshirted paramilitary Nazi 'stormtroopers'

SD Sicherheitsdienst: 'Security Service' of the SS, particularly concerned with intelligence

Sicherheitspolizei Security Police: the Gestapo and the Kriminalpolizei

SPD Sozialdemokratische Partei Deutschlands: German Social Democratic Party

SS Schutzstaffeln

SSPF Schutzstaffeln- und Polizeiführer: SS and Police Leader

T4 Codename for the 'adult euthanasia' campaign orchestrated through the Führer's Chancellery and run from 4 Tiergartenstrasse

UPA Ukrayinska Poustanska Armiya: Ukrainian Insurgent Army

USHMM United States Holocaust Memorial Museum

Volksdeutsche Ethnic Germans living beyond Germany's pre-1938 borders

Volksdeutsche Mittelstelle The SS 'Ethnic German Liaison Office'

Waffen-SS Armed SS, the military wing of the organization

Warthegau (Reichsgau Posen) An area of western Poland annexed to the Reich in 1939

Wehrmacht German armed forces in the Nazi period

Wisliceny, Dieter Eichmann's subordinate on the 'Jewish desk' of the Gestapo, within the RSHA

WVHA Wirtschafts-Verwaltungshautptamt: SS Business Administration Head Office

INTRODUCTION

Between 5,100,000 and 6,200,000 Jews were murdered during the Second World War, an episode the Nazis called the 'final solution of the Jewish question'. The world today knows it as the Holocaust. The subtitle I have chosen for this book—*A Genocide*—uses the indefinite article not to diminish the magnitude of the Holocaust but to encourage the reader to think of it as a particular example of a broader phenomenon. Like Germany, the state primarily responsible for the killing, the genocide of the Jews had both specific and more general characteristics. In order not to lose sight of its specific features, the evolution and dynamics of the final solution are at the centre of the book, but that is to the larger end of asking how and how far the Holocaust fits into broader patterns of the human past.

The history of the Holocaust is itself an international history, and international history always has a comparative dimension. Almost every European country lost some Jews. The Channel Islands' administration, composed of British subjects, was as culpable in turning over its tiny Jewish population as was the bureaucracy of the Netherlands with its much larger Jewish citizenry. Other regimes and societies in eastern Europe went further still, murdering Jews themselves, like Croatia, or surrendering them gladly, like Slovakia. Without tens of thousands of Latvian, Lithuanian, Belarusian, and Ukrainian collaborators, the German police would not have been able to murder anything like the number of Jews that they did in the occupied Soviet territories.

Though the primary agent of the genocide was Germany, the Holocaust was a multinational, multistate phenomenon. Despite the obviously imperial nature of the two most powerful states in Europe in the period, Germany and the USSR, the imprint of the nation-state system pioneered by Europe was clear in the way Germany's allies, satellites, and dominions participated in the Holocaust. Heightened concerns about territorial integrity, uninhibited internal sovereignty, and population homogeneity were intertwined with wartime alliance issues. Geopolitics, 'ethnopolitics', and straightforward politics were inextricable,[1] and together, they determined why, say, Romania could kill more Jews than any other non-German state but still finish the war with one of the largest remaining Jewish populations in Europe; or why France could eagerly deport Jews with less than full French citizenship to Auschwitz but convince even the chief of the SS that it was not worth the risk to Franco-German relations to give priority to doing the same to wholly French Jews.

If the Holocaust was in some sense a European process, it took place within the context of other European processes of murderous exclusion, geopolitical turmoil, and economic restructuring in the period. While Jews were the pre-eminent victims of mass murder, they were by no means the only ones, and Nazi Germany not the only perpetrator. State violence against domestic minorities; violence against indigenous peoples in European colonies outside Europe; violence against opponents of the economic order; violence against the socially marginal; violence in wartime that exceeded the limits established by international law: all of these were established characteristics of the world in which Nazism appeared. With the partial exception of the USSR during the 1930s, when victims were at first selected primarily on political grounds, most of the violence beyond the military battlefield was ethnic or 'racial' in colouring. And even Stalin's regime employed ethnic cleansing extensively before, during, and after the Second World War as it applied the logic of collective measures against allegedly treacherous populations.

Violence against civilians with increasing state direction had been intensifying and spreading northwards from southeastern Europe since around the last quarter of the nineteenth century, when it was also becoming more intense in Europe's colonies. Its incidence was a complex outcome of urbanization, industrialization, population growth, great power competition, economic insecurity, and new intellectual and cultural developments. Amid the faltering of the older dynastic land empires, from the late nineteenth to the mid-twentieth century, the east, centre, and southeast of Europe was reordered according to conflicting ideas of nationalism and the economic and political interests of various constellations of great powers. By the time of Hitler's ascent to power in 1933, the east and southeast of the continent at least was already populated with political elites that, in appropriate circumstances (generally war), were prepared to consolidate or expand their states with extreme violence. The more stable, established great powers to the northwest—France and Britain—had thitherto generally reserved their violence for the non-Western world where different cultural rules applied, but under stress there were signs that this could change, most notably with the developing doctrine of 'area bombing'.

The Second World War was only the third and most violent period of transnational and interethnic conflict in recent European history in which matters were violently brought to a head. The second was the period 1912–22, from the Balkan wars before the First World War to the Greco-Turkish war after it. Earlier still was the 'eastern crisis' of 1875–8, as new Balkan states emerged with the decline of the Ottoman Empire, which also lost territory to Russia in the Caucasus. Though smaller in scale than the other two periods of concerted violence, the eastern crisis shared many characteristics of the later conflicts and their aftermaths. It was a moment of the collapse of an empire in a particular region—the Ottoman imperium in Europe—and of accompanying ethnic cleansing as new borders were established. It heralded a number of inter- and intrastate conflicts that would only find resolution during the eras of the First and Second World Wars. It saw the establishment of intolerant new states obsessed with their own minority issues, a matter only exacerbated by another innovation of the time: the vexed question of international 'protection' for minorities.

The following major explosion in 1912–22 has tended to interest Western historians primarily because of the slaughter of the Western Front in 1914–18 and the cultural ramifications of the conflict in Germany, France, and Britain. Yet for the lineage of political violence and increasingly radical ethnopolitics traced in this book, as important are the collapse of the remainder of the Ottoman Empire, the wartime violence astride the Eastern front and in the Balkans, and the post-1918 dispensation of what had been the lands of the Austro-Hungarian empire and the western marches of the Russian empire. The anti-civilian violence of the time began with massive ethnic cleansing of Muslims in the Balkan wars of 1912–13, culminated in the first full-blown case of genocide in the period, that of the Ottoman Armenian and Assyrian Christians in 1915–16, and concluded with mutual ethnic cleansing between Greece and Turkey, and ethnic-cum-ideological conflict all the way up the old Romanov western borderlands.

If much of this eviction and slaughter was precipitated by war, geo-political change, and modern conceptions of ethnic and even racial difference, those patterns were superimposed onto older, religious dis-tinctions that themselves often corresponded with the fault-lines of historical economic and power hierarchies. The years surrounding the First World War saw Muslims and Christians murdering and expelling each other in huge numbers in the eastern Mediterranean region. In the lead-up to and during the Second World War itself, Jews were the primary target. Unequal physical and economic conflict continued between Christians and Muslims in Bulgaria, Yugoslavia, and Turkey, and between different Christian sects-become-nationalities in Poland and Ukraine and, again, Yugoslavia, with the conflict particularly pro-nounced between Orthodox Christians on one hand and Catholics and Protestants on the other hand. Nevertheless, in the first half of the century the newly politicized Muslim–Christian and Christian–Jewish dynamics proved the most extensively murderous even in this greater maelstrom of political violence. Religious belief itself was rarely the driv-ing force; instead, it was the cultural inheritance of collective identity bequeathed by religion and woven in the modern period into newer forms of political identity, whether extant or desired.

A critical period in the intensification of political opposition between population groups arrived when pre-existing hierarchies in ethno-religious relations broke down amid increased emancipation for Otto-man Christians and Europe's Jews from the mid-nineteenth century. (Large-scale Muslim–Jewish violence did not occur until the Jews had significant political power in the Middle East in the aftermath of the Second World War.) These developments were part of a wider series of changes as the whole continent continued to feel the aftershocks of the French Revolution in terms of the threat posed to the established state order by greater demands for equality and national liberation. The onset of heightened 'status anxiety' as systems of social domination disintegrated and were reordered is well illustrated by an example taken from the beginning of the approximate time frame with which this book is concerned, and involving all three religions. Under French colonial rule in Algeria, a distinction had traditionally been made between French citizens on one hand and both local Jews and Muslims on the other hand. In 1870, however, Algerian Jews were granted full French citizenship. Emancipation provoked increasing anti-Semitism on the part of both the French colonizers and the local Muslims. A more bloody illustration is the slaughter of tens of thousands of Jews by counter-revolutionary forces during the Russian civil war. Like many elsewhere in the continent, the murderers saw Jews as the instigators and beneficiaries of the Bolshevik Revolution, and Christian Europe as the victim.

What was the specificity of Nazism within this generally violent—and increasingly anti-Semitic—greater Europe? The question can be broken down into three related lines of enquiry. The first concerns the position of Germany within Europe and the nature of the German state; the second concerns the nature of Nazi racism and anti-Semitism; and the third concerns the extremity of Nazi Jewish policy. In each case, Nazi-German particularities are indeed identifiable, but they have frequently been exaggerated and can in many ways be integrated into European patterns.

On the matter of specific national history, Germany was more advanced than the other perpetrator states just mentioned. From its birth, it was also a major power, It was not created quite out of the same end-of-empire conditions that in east-central and southeastern Europe led small, insecure, newly emergent states and their increasingly weak erstwhile imperial masters to reach for the radical policies witnessed in, say, the former Ottoman territories during and after the First World War. Hitler's geopolitical aims were in fact a hybrid of the imperial-colonial designs of a great power and the irredentist expansionism of the young European nation-state, both of which had been retarded by Germany's defeat in 1918. They concerned the territorial spaces that had been such a battleground over recent generations. It was in these spaces to the east of Germany that a German diaspora lived along with the vast majority of the European Jews, and it was in these spaces that the genocide of Jews and others was mainly perpetrated. This brings us to the consideration of Nazi ideology.

Nazi Germany saw itself as a protector of a certain set of European values against the threat of cultural and political trends that had 'weakened' European civilization from the French Revolution onwards (doctrines of human equality such as democracy, socialism, and communism); against Jews and 'inferior eastern hordes' that provided an actual, physical, biological threat; and against the fusion of the political and biological enemy, the Soviet state. It is often said that the Nazis' highly developed theory of racism set their ideology qualitatively apart from those of other regimes. Yet recent history showed that one did not need such a theory in order to treat other peoples as collectively dangerous or disposable. As a legitimation for genocide, biological racism is only at the extreme of a continuum of exclusionary beliefs that have the potential to attribute malign characteristics to all members of another group. The philosopher Berel Lang captures a truth that is as applicable to the 'communist' Khmer Rouge genocide in Cambodia and the mass murder of various socio-political groups in late-twentieth-century Latin America as it is to the Armenian genocide or the Holocaust, when he states that in many cases

> the perpetrators' justification for genocide often cites the responsibility of the targeted group, claiming that its decisions or actions have caused harm or represent a danger to others. But even the semblance of evidence for these claims is usually lacking, and a stronger objection still is that on this justification, the targeted group is held responsible for dispositions or conduct for which [individuals within the group] are not in fact responsible . . . This is one reason, it seems clear, why the language of genocide so frequently turns to medical or biological metaphors[2]

The German architects of genocide had not only practical historical precedents of group destruction on which to draw, but also a series of ideas established across Europe about 'inner enemies', ethnic fifth columns, and the particular, peculiar influence allegedly wielded by Jews. It is true that there was a strong element of contingency—in the rise of Nazism to power—in Germany leading the assault on Europe's Jews, but it is much less historically 'surprising' that large expanses of the continent turned on their Jews at that period of great historical flux. There is a sense in which the Nazis' *racial* stigmatization of Jews was only a more elaborate and far-reaching pseudo-theoretical basis for an attack on a people regarded by many Europeans as 'different' in a *different* way to other minorities. That conception of special difference emerged from medieval Christian culture and was associated with the putatively subversive, conspiratorial nature of Jews—even, in some cases, Jews who had converted to Christianity. The significance of the special difference was greatly heightened by the crises of modernity, and given extra emphasis by the intellectual developments of modernity, but it was not original to modernity. Biological racists though the key Nazi leaders undoubtedly were, the reason Jews were pursued with a zeal that set the 'final solution' apart even from other Nazi genocides was this 'special difference', which was cultural and political as much as 'racial' in its justification for action. We turn, therefore, from the supposed specificity of Nazi ideology to that of the implementation of genocide.

The final solution clearly owed its supranational dimensions to the different way in which the 'Jewish threat' was perceived relative to other minority 'problems' that were more directly territorial in nature. Nevertheless, the final solution went through a series of phases of development common to other genocides—like every other genocide, there was no inevitability to its occurrence, whatever the underlying consistencies in Hitler's thinking. Nazi policy began with a desire to force Jews to emigrate from German soil in the 1930s, and mutated from 1939 into a scheme to deport Jews to specific, isolated destinations. As with other murderous regimes, it was in the course of territorial expansion and military conflict, with Poland, but particularly with the Soviet Union, that the progression occurred from ethnic cleansing to outright genocide. In other words, however unrelated Nazi anti-Semitism was to actual power-political relations, the transition to genocide most assuredly did require some genuine interactivity with forces that existed independently of the Nazi world-view.

Nazi policy also existed in a two-way relationship with Germany's allies and collaborators. In their interactions with, say, Romanian and Lithuanian nationalists at the outset of the war against the Soviet Union in summer 1941, German personnel were sometimes given a policy guide in extremism, as at brief but seminal moments non-Germans showed how murder could be expanded in scope. Moreover, the readiness of the Croatian, Romanian, and Slovak governments to surrender their Jewish nationals to Germany in autumn 1941 ushered in a more fully European dimension to a German murder process which until that point was focused on the Soviet lands under direct German control. Conversely, as the war changed its course, the agendas of other European states restrained even mighty Germany's murderous designs, less out of humanitarian concern than for opportunistic reasons of European nation-statecraft. 'Europe' could be a decelerator of genocide as well as an accelerator.

Despite the categorical quality of its name, the final solution was not a matter of pure ideology transformed, unmediated, into action. It was an evolving policy that, like any other policy, adapted to circumstance, inopportune, and opportune, at both the tactical and strategic levels. New and more radical variants of the policy were layered on pre-existing designs, but did not always entirely supplant them, and never supplanted them immediately. The evolution of the policy *never* stopped, which is the problem with the many studies of the Holocaust that have focused upon identifying moments when 'the decision' was made—moments at which the fullest, continent-wide genocidal intent crystallized, after which the template of the 'final, final solution' was established, its course determined.

For those Jews under direct Nazi rule, meaning German Jews or the many more native to the lands of Germany's eastern empire, there was an approximately linear murder process, if by that we mean a phase of increasingly indiscriminate killing, followed by a sustained peak phase of organized killing. In the USSR the process began in summer–autumn 1941. In Poland it began in spring 1942. In both places it was largely concluded by autumn 1943. The murder of almost all the Soviet and Polish Jews was the heart of the genocide, and was over well before the war was concluded. It occurred where most Jews lived and accounted for perhaps five out of six Jewish victims of the Nazis. The approximate linearity of the process should not, however, suggest that the perpetrators acted in unison like some monolithic machine turned on after a grand decision and left to run its course, automaton-like, until its work was complete. The process required constant promptings, urgings, and recalibrations from a number of different German actors and interest groups.

Beyond the Nazi empire, still other interests and stimuli came into the picture, and these rendered the evolving pattern of genocide much less linear. The vision of the final solution as a genuinely international, continent-wide process relies upon deportations from Germany's allies, satellites, and dominions across Europe. Yet all these separate pro-grammes, including the huge Hungarian deportation of 1944, were to degrees incomplete in scope and unpredictable in incidence, remaining contingent on the state of the war or interstate relations.

There is no doubt that after a point Hitler would happily have had every Jew on the continent murdered, but this does not mean that all Jews everywhere were considered an equal priority, nor that Hitler himself was always central to or even always involved in decisions to pursue new categories of Jew, or Jews in untouched places. Removing Jews from territory required for the future German empire (primarily Poland and the USSR as well as greater Germany itself) was more important than the ongoing presence of Jews in, say, Romania. In Nazi eyes the latter remained, to a certain extent, 'Romania's Jewish problem'. The distinction can partly be explained by the fact that only a few German personnel had a great investment in pressing independent states on Jewish policy, whereas a much larger number of Germans depended for their positions of power in the Nazi structure on being radical on racial matters within their own territorial spheres of control. In short, and recalling that the final solution evolved archaeologically, layer upon layer, the undoubted European breadth of genocidal aspiration beyond a certain time in policy development did not fully supplant the territorially bounded logic of the final solution in its earlier incarnations, when getting Jews out of German-ruled territory was the primary goal.

Accordingly, even as the most extreme genocide, the murder of the Jews retained some of the shape of other genocides.

The final solution also developed in tandem with other Nazi mass murders. Like other extremely violent regimes, the Nazis had a multiplicity of targets: during the First World War, the Ottoman Empire's demographic policies concerned not just Armenians and Assyrians but Greeks, other, smaller Christian groups, and even non-Turkish Muslim populations; the Croatian Ustaša regime murdered Serbs, Jews, and Muslims; beyond greater Europe of that period, we might also reflect on Cambodia under the Khmer Rouge, when 'pale' city-dwellers were murdered alongside Vietnamese, Buddhist monks, Muslims, and anyone considered politically suspect.

As for Germany, by the invasion of the Soviet Union in 1941, it had been killing its mentally and physically ill citizens in their tens of thousands for a year and a half. The personnel and technology from this so-called euthanasia campaign were vital in the later murder of Jews in gas chambers. By some estimates two million ethnic Poles died under German occupation. Around 3.3 million Soviet prisoners of war were killed or died in German custody for reasons that had everything to do with their being considered 'subhuman Slavs'. Many millions more eastern Europeans died—perhaps 11 million non-Jewish Soviet non-combatant citizens alone—as a result of German war-making techniques, requisitioning, or outright murder, often at the hands of the soldiers and police who killed Jews. Drawn from that multitude, but also from Germany's western European dominions, were very large numbers of forced labourers who perished under German exploitation. The total number of labourers brought to Germany was at least 13 million. At least 200,000 Romanies ('Gypsies') were murdered, as well. This is an incomplete list of Nazi crimes, none of which were pursued with quite the same zeal as the Jewish genocide, but each of which had personnel, technical, functional, or conceptual connections with the final solution.

A search for parallels with the final solution at the levels of intensity and systematic ruthlessness requires the historian to look outside the frame of greater Europe in the early twentieth century. In seeking the sort of mindset that leads to the remorseless pursuit of 'enemies', the Khmer

Rouge, responsible for the murder of up to 2 million Cambodians out of a population of about 8 million in 1975–8, deserves our attention. In comparing speed in mass murder, as well as the Rwandan genocide, with up to 800,000 deaths in three months, we might also look to East Pakistan in 1971, where at least several hundred thousand Bengalis were murdered in 267 days, as the state attempted to crush demands for regional autonomy; moreover, an estimated ten million Bengalis fled to neighbouring India. Depending on the detail and intelligence of the comparison, raising such parallels is either a useful exercise in the conceptualization of genocide as a global phenomenon, a set of stimulating suggestions for a research agenda, or an unhelpful conflation of episodes from different cultural and political contexts.[3]

Much of this volume concentrates on a limited period and place for reasons of scale and practicality, but also to enhance its explanatory value. The focus on one transnational region shaped by varying but related and intersecting political cultures and national histories permits more detailed, useful comparison of when and why genocide occurs, when and why it does not, and where and why certain groups are victimized more or less than others. The aim is to go beyond the simple comparative history of different genocidal phenomena, which has characterized much of the political science scholarship, and to look at interrelations between cases of genocide and the polities that perpetrate genocide.

The regional approach is not, however, as helpful in explaining the *internal* dynamics of mass murder—its organization, the varying motivations of its perpetrators, and even its scale and intensity. As some of the insights of social psychology, political science, and sociology suggest about the comparative study of humans in social and political structures, not all aspects of genocide are equally conditioned by particular cultural or ideological factors, despite celebrated claims to the contrary.[4] Atrocities committed by states, for instance, will share some characteristics with atrocities committed by other states, irrespective of when and where, because of the way states exercise organizational powers, secure legitimacy, and implement the means of coercion. Atrocities committed by large numbers of people working together will have some shared characteristics wherever and whenever committed, by dint of commonalities in individual behaviour in social situations and under the influence of social and political power. A more directly comparative approach of the structure and organization of the final solution with other instances of genocide helps identify what was specifically 'Nazi', or 'German' about the way in which so many people could be brought to kill.

The three central parts of this book seek to blend analysis of the internal dynamics of the final solution, consideration of other Nazi racial policies, and the broader context of other genocides. Part I establishes the international context, Part II discusses the context of Nazi-German population policy as a whole, and Part III uses an explicitly comparative approach to shed light on participation in Nazi genocide. They seek to answer the following ten questions in turn, each of which is subsidiary to the larger question about where the Holocaust stands within human history:

1 Why was Europe such a volatile place by the early twentieth century?
2 Why were minorities in general so stigmatized?
3 Why were Jews in particular so stigmatized?
4 Why were some states more restrained than others towards minorities?
5 Under what conditions did repression transform itself into genocide?
6 How far did Nazi ideology fit into established European patterns?
7 How far did Nazi violence fit into established European patterns?
8 How was Nazi genocide shaped by the population policies of other states?
9 What was the relationship between different Nazi population policies?
10 How and why did so many people take part in Nazi genocide?

Now is an appropriate time to reconsider the final solution along these lines. While all historiographies are dynamic, we have reached a plateau in our understanding of Nazi policy after incorporating revelations from eastern European archives opened after the Cold War. Such new documents as surface today tend to alter our comprehension in nuanced and incremental ways rather than in any revolutionary fashion. At the same time, as a result of diverse theoretical and disciplinary approaches, there is a lively discussion about where we place the final solution in relation to other strands of history. Unfortunately, there is a disjuncture, a failure of communication, between the empirically grounded work and the theoretically orientated scholarship.[5] This book, with its combined focuses on Nazi policy, international history, and comparative history, hopes to transcend the divide.

Recently reignited debates have discussed whether Nazi extermination policies should be seen in the light of Europe's imperial crimes of race and pursuit of space outside Europe. More established lines of thought place the emphasis more strictly on intra-European developments such as the political and cultural legacy of the First World War, or Germany's complex relationships with Jews and anti-Semitism. The closing part of this book—Part IV—deals with some of the interpretative debates, and places the present book within an unfolding body of thinking on the Holocaust. It is not primarily concerned with the 'ordinary' characteristics of the historiography, meaning those features common to the sophisticated scholarship of any major historical event, such as: the increasingly detailed focus on individual regions or institutions; the relationship between ideological intention and circumstantial contingency; or the deployment of, say, gender-based analysis.[6] The emphasis instead is on what makes Holocaust historiography different. As Part IV's title, 'Civilisation and the Holocaust', suggests, the emphasis is on the changing ways in which scholars have situated this colossal event in our understanding of human history, be that German history, European history, occidental history, or modern history.

Given the breadth of the issues addressed in the book, the cited source material is mainly the accumulated, published scholarship plus select primary documentation. Yet such understanding as is evinced of the dynamics of the Holocaust has been shaped by a wider knowledge of the primary sources bequeathed by the perpetrators. The opening section of the book comprises a series of documents selected from the vast source-base of murder, to offer a glimpse of the materials on which all interpretations must rest. It also considers some influential representations of the final solution in order to question the understanding—or perhaps the caricature—of the Holocaust that has achieved popular currency.

It is a book about perpetrators, perpetration, and the milieux that produce both. Relatively little will be read about the numerous victim groups themselves, except insofar as the interaction of victims with states and other groups contributed to the dynamics of persecution and murder. Those books on Nazi genocide that pride themselves on 'integrated history', on bringing out the voices of the victims, only tend to do so for select groups, primarily Jews.[7] It would be beyond the physical capacity of the book to consider the myriad genocides, ethnic cleansings, and other murders described in these pages from the diverse perspectives of tens of millions of victims of different backgrounds. But that does not signify a lack of interest in those victims as human beings. Indeed, the intellectual purpose of looking at the full range of people and peoples killed and expelled for political reasons in the broadest sense in and around the Nazi period is complemented by a conviction that recognition of their often-undescribed fates is itself a moral statement.

DOCUMENTARY TRACES

Anti-Semitism

In parts of interwar Europe this advertisement for an exhibition of artworks would not have seemed unduly strange or offensive:

> Headquarters of 'The Nationalist' newspaper . . . Visit the exhibition of drawings [by] ION. Open from July 1 to August 1, 1923. Free entrance. Any good Romanian must visit this exhibition which has kosher pieces nicely described, such as: epileptic rabbis, criminal-talmudic scenes and many and diverse types of kike. N.B. Entrance is 1 lei for dogs and kikes.[1]

The advertisement appeared in 1923 in Iaşi, Romania. Eighteen years later, in late June 1941, as Romania was embarking on a war alongside Nazi Germany against the USSR, some 4,000 Jews ('kikes') were murdered in Iaşi on the grounds of a spurious security threat. The accusation was that the Jews were in league with the Bolshevik power over the nearby Soviet border. Romanian forces went on to murder far larger numbers of Jews in the territory they temporarily took from the USSR.

Of course it would be wrong to draw a firm and direct line from the atmosphere of the interwar period to the slaughter of the war years. That is also true for Nazi anti-Semitism; indeed it is true always and everywhere in the uncertain progression from prejudice to genocide. And it should be remembered that 'Ion's' exhibition was sponsored by a self-confessed nationalist organization that by today's standards would stand on the political far right. But the circulation, unashamed, in the public sphere, of such violent and contemptuous

Figure 1. Romanian poster.

language (not to mention the images to which they refer) reminds us that extreme nationalists were not in short supply in interwar Romania, and that verbally and symbolically abusing Jews was not an unrespectable thing to do. Some nationalists went far further, agitating for the deportation of Romania's Jews well before the war began. We also know that during the interwar period the Romanian government itself was increasingly involved in the economic marginalization of Jews, including their outright expropriation. Violent anti-Semitic language fed off this environment but also reinforced it.

The advertisement invokes images of Jewish religious life: rabbis, the Talmud. This shows the enduring significance of religious difference in stimulating anti-Jewish thought, and the convenience for propaganda purposes of the most obvious symbols of Jewish separateness. Yet while Romanian anti-Semitism of the late nineteenth and early twentieth centuries, like its Polish equivalent, owed a debt to the stereotypes established in Christian civilization, it was not simply a continuation of Christian Jew-hatred. Like all nationalisms, Romanian nationalism was a modern phenomenon with some new ideas about ordering society and economy and uniting and defining the limits of the national community—that which Germans called the *Volksgemeinschaft*.

Creating 'ethnic consciousness', which meant defining the individual with members of the same community and against 'aliens', was not just a matter of ideology or emotion. It could be fostered in very material ways, as the following rationing notice from Romania in autumn 1942 reminds us:

Office of the Mayor of Roman. Food distribution service. . . . Sugar for the month of October will be distributed as follows:

Christians 500 grams per person

Jews 100 grams per person

Gypsies 200 grams per person

Jews will receive the sugar from these stores: David Avram, Principatele Unite St.; Iosif Marcu, Mare St. Gypsies will receive the sugar from the Ilie Nastase store, 11 Banat St.[2]

The anti-Semitic aspect of Romanian nationalism, as of other European nationalisms, had been encouraged by one of the most significant events in the modern development of European anti-Semitism: the Russian revolution. The idea that Jews stood behind the revolution was also embraced by Adolf Hitler and his movement.

The poster in Figure 2 appeared in or around 1935 in a series entitled 'Theory of Heredity and Racial Hygiene', published by the Publisher for National Literature, Stuttgart. It is entitled 'The relationship between Jews and Freemasons'. The text at the top states: 'World politics—World revolution.' That at the bottom reads 'Freemasonry is an international organization beholden to Jewry, with the political goal of establishing Jewish domination through world-wide revolution.' The map, embellished with Masonic symbols, illustrates where revolutions took place in Europe from the French Revolution in 1789 through the Bolshevik Revolution of 1917 into Germany itself in 1919 after the defeat in the First World War.

The introduction of Freemasons to the picture, like 'Gypsies' (Romanies), reminds us that nationalists rarely have just one enemy, and that European history has produced many 'out-groups'. For Romania, for instance, the neighbouring, competing, Hungarian state was a huge threat, and the Hungarian people were seen as extensions of this threat in contested claims over territory. Hungarian nationalists felt the same in reverse. The Nazi world-view perceived enemies everywhere; but, as the poster reminds us, Jews were the ultimate enemy, supposedly exploiting and manipulating all others.

Expansion

For Germany, invading the USSR in 1941 was not just about fighting communism and 'the Jews'. More traditional imperial considerations accompanied the recent ideological obsessions.

> **Without colonial supplement, the German living space is too small to guarantee an undisturbed, secure and lasting food supply for our people. Therefore the demand for a colonial possession as part of an empire is one founded on economic need, and the attitude of other powers to this demand is simply incomprehensible.**

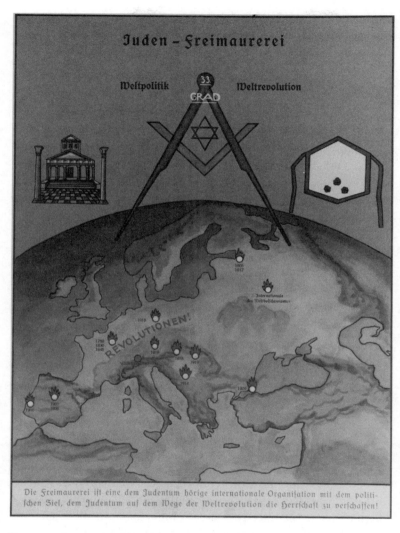

Figure 2. Poster on Jews and Freemasons with a map of revolutions.

Thus ran one of the 'weekly slogans' of the National Socialist German Workers' Party—the NSDAP, or Nazi party—in August 1938. The source of the quotation was Adolf Hitler. His words were printed immediately beneath a map of Africa, which featured three highlighted areas on the southwestern fringe of the continent and one on the eastern side, denoting Germany's colonies before they were removed in the peace settlement after the First World War. The focus on Africa was, by 1938, misleading, and references to it were generally used as a Nazi bargaining chip to justify other revisions of the Versailles settlement. One of Hitler's favourite themes was the hypocrisy of the victors of 1918, which enjoyed huge formal and informal empires while denying Germany the same. He echoed influential trends both in interwar opinion and in the rhetoric of Imperial Germany, which by the end of the nineteenth century felt itself hemmed in by established powers that had already secured their place in the global hierarchy.

Hitler nevertheless knew that in wartime overseas colonies were vulnerable outposts whose defence could overextend the imperial power: in his words, they were not remotely 'secure'. Since the ability to wage war was central to Nazi ideology, colonial possessions needed to be more defensible, which meant they needed to be closer to Germany. Hitler also knew that colonies were not always economically beneficial, for he frequently referred to Britain's unusual ability to run an empire profitably. As the slogan tells us, he was interested in food supply—livestock and particularly agriculture—to sustain Germany in peacetime, but most importantly in war. In 1938, Hitler's eyes were on eastern Europe, just as they had been early in the previous decade when he wrote *Mein Kampf*.

Aimé Césaire, mentor of the anti-colonial theorist Frantz Fanon, was one of the first to formulate the verdict that Nazi Germany did to Europe what Europeans had been doing to Africans and others for a long time.[3] The judgement has since become a commonplace in the scholarship of genocide and colonialism. If evidence is needed to support it, the colossal brutality of German actions in 'German southwest Africa' (approximately the territory of today's Namibia) and 'German east Africa' (approximately Tanzania) at the turn of the twentieth century provide a good deal of the substantiation.

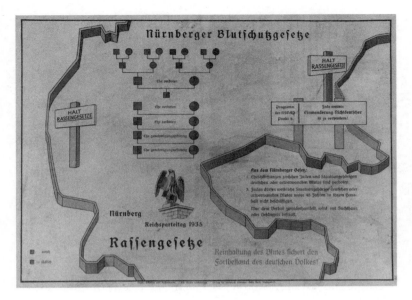

Figure 3. Poster on the Nuremberg law for the protection of blood and honour on a stylized map of Germany.

At the same time as casting avaricious eyes on the east, Nazi Germany feared precisely the contact with easterners that imperial expansion would bring. The concern itself was not novel; like Nazi colonialism, Nazi racism did not spring from nowhere, even if it attained new extremes of systematization and virulence. To some degree, every colonial power, including the USA in the Philippines and Japan in southeast Asia, was preoccupied with 'miscegenation' and the risks dominion posed to the 'superior' culture and 'blood' of the dominators. Situated on the boundary between eastern and western Europe, the German racists saw themselves as the frontline defence of Western culture against Eastern 'infection'. The Nazi empire would have the shape of one of the traditional dynastic European empires as it expanded into territory adjacent to Germany, but the empire was built with the mindset of the settler-colonialist in Africa or the Americas. Blood and boundaries of the literal and the figurative sort were bound together, as we can see from the poster in Figure 3, produced in or shortly after

1935, again by the 'Publisher for National Literature' in Stuttgart in their series 'Theory of Heredity and Racial Hygiene'.

The poster is entitled 'The Nuremberg Law for the Protection of Blood and German Honour'. It is a stylized map of the then borders of Germany, onto which is imposed a schematic of the forbidden degrees of marriage between 'Aryans' and 'non-Aryans', point eight of the Nazi party programme (opposing immigration of non-Aryans into Germany), and the text of the 1935 'blood protection' law. The text at the bottom reads: 'maintaining the purity of blood ensures the survival of the German people.'

Like the Romanian advertisement, and Hitler's imperialist pronouncement, the poster was not some secret party document. It was circulated in public with the intention of educating the people and mobilizing them around an ideal. The easily available knowledge of Nazism's imperial ambitions and its phobias about blood purity meant it was equally easy to deduce that German expansion would bring 'racial' dilemmas. How would Nazi Germany deal with future subject populations in its colonies? Even if it only adopted similar levels of harshness and exploitation to those deployed by other European states in their colonies, the picture was very grim. The rhetoric of Germany's leaders as it embarked on the colonial project suggested something worse still. Here is a genuinely secret pronouncement by Heinrich Himmler, chief of the SS, speaking at a meeting of SS leaders in Posen (Poznán) on 4 November 1943.

> One basic principle must be the absolute rule for the SS man: we must be honest, decent, loyal, and comradely to members of our own blood and to nobody else . . . Whether nations live in prosperity or perish interests me only in so far as we need them as slaves for our *Kultur*; otherwise, it is of no interest to me. Whether 10,000 Russian females fall down from exhaustion while digging an anti-tank ditch interests me only in so far as the anti-tank ditch is finished for Germany. . . . It is a crime against our own blood to worry about them. . . . Our concern, our duty, is our people and our blood. It is for them that we must provide and plan, work and fight, nothing else. . . .

If the peace is a final one, we shall be able to tackle our great work of the future. We shall colonize. . . . It must be a matter of course that the most copious breeding should be from this racial elite of the German people. In twenty to thirty years we must really be able to provide the whole of Europe with its ruling class. If the SS together with the farmers, and we together with our friend Backe [Minister of Agriculture], then run the colony in the east on a grand scale, without any restraint, without any question of tradition but with nerve and revolutionary impetus, we shall in twenty years push the national boundary 500 kilometres eastwards.

Today I have asked the Führer that the SS, if we have fulfilled our task and our duty by the end of the war, should have the privilege of holding Germany's most easterly frontier as a defence frontier. . . . We shall impose our laws on the east. We shall charge ahead and push our way forward little by little to the Urals. I hope that our generation will successfully bring it about that every age-group has fought in the east, and that every one of our divisions spends a winter in the east every second or third year. Then we shall never grow soft. . . . Thus we will create the conditions for the whole Germanic people and the whole of Europe, controlled, ordered and led by us, for the Germanic people, to be able, in generations to come, to stand the test in her battles of destiny against Asia, which will certainly break out again. . . . Then, when the mass of humanity of $1-1\frac{1}{2}$ milliards lines up against us, the Germanic people, numbering, I hope, 250–300 millions, and the other European peoples, making a total of 600–700 millions . . . must stand the test in its vital struggle against Asia. It would be an evil day if the Germanic people did not survive it. It would be the end of beauty and of *Kultur*, of the creative power of this earth.

Beyond the obvious callousness, the pride in harshness as an expression of correct 'racial consciousness', Himmler's terrifying vision illuminates the dynamics of Nazism. The movement's leaders had a vision of creation, as befitted a 'cultured people': cultivating and building on the colonized land, encouraging the numerical expansion of the 'Germanic peoples' and ensuring their fitness and well being. This constructive vision was the complement to, the mirror image of, the destructive vision that was all-too-apparent in Himmler's speech. Even after the anticipated victory in the Second World War, the largest and most destructive conflict in human history, Himmler was keenly speculating about future struggle on an even greater scale. Nazism was a ceaselessly dynamic system that needed conflict, enemies, and 'inferiors' to justify its own ideology, and would always find more people to fight and kill. Some of these potential victims were still within Germany, and had Nazism prevailed in war, there would certainly have been an intensified assault on Germans who were considered genetically or ethnically inadequate. Shortly before the speech, Himmler had been appointed Minister of the Interior as well as chief of the SS, which gave the most radical organization in the Third Reich greater control of domestic 'population policy' just as it enjoyed dominance in that area in Germany's dominions. It is doubtful that Nazism was actually a utopian ideology, as it is common now to call it, because in a utopia there are no enemies.

The significance of looking forwards, of moving on to future battles, is particularly pointed given the timing of the speech. In all the discussion of enemies in the cited section of the address, the ultimate enemy, the Jews, are notable by their absence. They had been mentioned earlier in the speech, but, vitally, in the past tense. Concerning what Himmler called 'the Jewish evacuation programme, the extermination of the Jewish people', he had affirmed:

> This is a glorious page in our history and one that has never been written and can never be written. For we know how difficult we would have made it for ourselves, if, on top of the bombing raids, the burdens and the deprivations of war, we still had Jews today in every town as secret saboteurs, agitators and troublemakers. We would now probably have reached the 1916–17 stage when the Jews were still part of the body of the German nation. . . . We had the moral right, we had the duty to our people, to destroy this people which wanted to destroy us. All in all, we can say that we have fulfilled this most difficult duty for the love of our people.[4]

Here and in other speeches afterwards Himmler referred to the successful murder of the Jews in Germany and the German-occupied territories, which had been almost entirely completed by the time of this speech in autumn 1943.[5] For him, at least, the destruction of the Jews under German rule—the 'inner enemy', the 'saboteurs, agitators and troublemakers' who had allegedly brought Germany to its knees from within in the First World War—was the main object of the 'final solution'. As we shall see more extensively later in this book, even though the genocide took on fully European dimensions, spreading, if generally only partly, to states allied to Germany or controlled but not annexed by it, 'cleansing' German domestic and imperial territory of the 'inner enemy' was the main German priority.

Orchestration

The 'final solution of the Jewish question' is the best-documented genocide in history. The sheer scale of the evidence means that whatever we do not know, we can be certain that organizing and implementing genocide was highly complex and involved a huge number of disparate people and agencies. Yet no historian wishes just to reveal complexity; he or she wants to make meaningful generalizations about 'how things were'. Theories of 'the perpetrator' abound, as if there were only one type of perpetrator, and these often result from generalizing from one group of perpetrators or one class of documents to the whole process and nature of genocide.

Even the superficially simple act of describing the Nazi-German machinery of destruction can itself imply something about the 'essence' of the system. One of the most striking rooms in the permanent Holocaust exhibition of London's Imperial War Museum concerns the 'bureaucracy of murder'. Three of the four walls of the space are covered with an organogram showing how a huge and intricate web of officialdom within and beyond Germany was involved in the organization of genocide. (The fourth wall concerns information about the final solution.) The sole artefact within the room is a typewriter on a small table. The obvious message of this powerful minimalist evocation of the Nazi state is the centrality of the administrator. The absence of any human being in the display suggests the impersonality of the activity involved in orchestrating murder. It hints that anyone could be behind the desk.

Figure 4. Imperial War Museum photo (of 'final solution' exhibition).

Other similar interpretations are more explicit about the message they seek to transmit. Writing in a journal designed for American school history teachers, one historian claimed that

> after teaching about the Holocaust for more than ten years, I have found one document which more than any other source illustrates the all-pervasive, destructive force that was National Socialism. The insidious, administrative language used here is a concrete, dramatic example of how an entire cast of civil servants could become active participants in the extermination process.[6]

A summary of the document also occupies a pivotal place in Zygmunt Bauman's *Modernity and the Holocaust*, a book centrally responsible for the understanding of the final solution as a cold bureaucratic crime perpetrated according to standard administrative principles.[7]

> Secret Reich Matter, Berlin, June 5, 1942 [Willy Just to Walther Rauff] Changes for special vehicles now in service at Kulmhof (Chelmno) and for those now being built.
>
> Since December 1941, ninety-seven thousand have been processed by the three vehicles in service, with no major incidents. In the light of observations made so far, however, the following technical changes are needed.
>
> The van's normal load is usually nine per square yard. In Saurer vehicles, which are very spacious, maximum use of space is impossible, not because of any potential overload, but because loading to full capacity would affect the vehicle's stability. So reduction of the load space seems necessary. It must be reduced by a yard absolutely, instead of trying to solve the problem, as hitherto, by reducing the number of pieces loaded. Besides, this extends the operating time, as the empty void must also be filled with carbon monoxide. On the other hand, if the load space is reduced, and the vehicle is packed solid, the operating time can be considerably shortened. The manufacturers told us during a discussion that reducing the size of the van's rear would throw it badly off balance. The front axle, they claim, would be overloaded. In fact, the balance is automatically restored, because the merchandise aboard displays during the operation a natural tendency to rush to the rear doors, and is mainly

found lying there at the end of the operation. So the front axle is not overloaded.

The lighting must be better protected than now. The lamps must be enclosed in a steel grid to prevent their being damaged. Lights could be eliminated, since they are apparently never used. However, it has been observed that when the doors are shut, the load always presses against them as soon as darkness sets in. This is because the load naturally rushes toward the light when darkness sets in, which makes closing the doors difficult. Also, because of the alarming nature of darkness, screaming always occurs when the doors are closed. It would, therefore, be useful to light the lamp before and during the first moments of the operation.

For easy cleaning of the vehicle, there must be a sealed drain in the middle of the floor. The drainage hole's cover, eight to twelve inches in diameter, would be equipped with a slanting trap, so that fluids can drain off during the operation. During cleaning, the drain can be used to evacuate large pieces of dirt.

The document was from a dispatcher and welder for the SS motor pool to the head of the office of technical affairs in charge of vehicles for the SS's 'security police'. Without referring to human beings, it describes the continuing technical innovation and the gathering of practical experience involved in mass murder by gas at one of a number of Nazi killing institutions—Chełmno, in western Poland, where the method of murder was the 'gas van'. Experimentation; learning-by-doing; dehumanization of the victims; the professionalization of killing: all these were central to Nazi genocide, but they were not its totality. Nor is it possible to say that administrative amorality, the cold rationality of the blinkered bureaucrat, was *the essence* of genocide. How, for instance, is this chilling document to be reconciled with the equally chilling but distinctly impassioned, highly ideological, indeed Manichean tone of Himmler's speech?

A reflection on the dates at which Bauman's book and the article in *The History Teacher* appeared reveals how all such interpretations are influenced by the time in which they are conceived. One appeared in 1989, the other in 1990, just as the Cold War was ending, but before scholars had had the opportunity to research and expose the mass of Nazi documentation that became available with new access to archives of former Eastern bloc states. Those new findings shaped new interpretations of the Holocaust. They underlined quite how much of the killing was done at close range, not from desks in Berlin or with the aid of impersonal killing mechanisms like gas vans and gas chambers. They also underlined that genocide was not decided from on high and implemented by obedient, unreflective automata, but was a matter of initiative and innovation among German personnel with an active engagement in mass murder.

Rather than replacing Bauman's model with another with its own flaws, however, the important conclusion is that that few documents 'speak for themselves', and no one representation can adequately capture the essence of the past, for there is never only one essence. Let us imagine what our conception would be of the Ottoman Empire's genocide of its Armenian Christian population during the First World War if we relied overly upon the following document.

Aleppo, Syria, September 29, 1915

The deportation of Armenians from their homes by the Turkish Government has continued with a persistence and perfection of plan . . . as indicated by the accompanying tables of 'Movement by Railway' [see Table 1 on p. 30], showing the number arriving by rail from interior stations up to and including August 31 last to be 32,751. In addition thereto it is estimated that at least 100,000 others have arrived afoot. And such a condition as these unfortunates are in, especially those coming afoot . . . that careful estimates place the number of survivors at only 15 per cent. of those originally deported. On this basis the number of those surviving even this far being less than 150,000 up to September 21, there seems to have been about 1,000,000 persons lost up to this date.[8]

Clearly the final solution was not the only genocide that utilized technology and public administration, though as Germany was a more advanced state than the Ottoman Empire, the bureaucratic and technological input to the murder of the Jews was greater than that to the murder of the Armenians. The use of the Ottoman railway and the other communications mechanisms of a modern state such as the telegraph

Table 1. Deportation of Armenians Movement by Railway from Interior to Aleppo City

Date	Adults	Children	Station
July 31, 1915	241	47	Achi-Koyounli
August 3	206	250	Katma
" 3	200	71	Achi-Koyounli
" 4	525	315	Katma
" 4	546	256	Ser-Arab-Pounar
" 5	290	180	Katma
" 6	505	162	Ser-Arab-Pounar
" 7	316	134	Djerablisse
" 8	138	250	Katma
" 8	542	255	Achi-Koyounli
" 9	140	200	Katma
" 11	505	195	"
" 12	1,400	600	"
" 12	442	55	Achi-Koyounli
" 15	1,060	550	Katma
" 15	708	95	Achi-Koyounli
" 17	117	30	Ras-el-Ain
" 18	649	140	Achi-Koyounli
" 19	350	250	Katma
" 20	670	395	"
" 23	1,240	900	"
" 26	500	300	"
" 28	500	300	"
" 31	239	—	Ras-el-Ain
Totals	12,029	5,930	
Add to July 30	6,891	1,331	
	18,920	7,261	
Add 25% for those who paid fares	4,755	1,815	
Grand Totals	23,675	9,076	

Total number adults and children 32,751, by railway only.[9]

system has been key to the efforts of some Armenian scholars to equate the Armenian genocide with the Holocaust.[10] The quest for a sort of total equivalency between different historical episodes is something peculiar to genocide studies, and the unhelpful character of such an exercise is particularly well illustrated in this instance. Not only was the Armenian genocide generally a rather low-technology affair despite the limited use of the railway (as the report above explained when accounting for the terrific mortality of those far greater numbers arriving 'afoot' in Aleppo), the 'model' of the 'hi-tech', bureaucratic final solution that it seeks to approximate itself does not reflect significant aspects of the genocide of the Jews. There are similarities as well as differences between the two episodes in terms of overall motivation, dynamics, and orchestration, as there are between any instances of genocide. Getting beyond caricatures and embracing both similarities and differences is one step towards ascertaining where the Holocaust sits in the patterns of the past. The next step, as I shall try to illustrate in the rest of this book, is to move beyond the straightforward comparative study of different instances of genocide, and to place them in relation to each other within the context of wider and deeper historical processes of change.

PART I A EUROPEAN HISTORY OF VIOLENCE

❝ Without a country you have no name, no identity, no voice, no rights, no membership in the brotherhood of nations—you remain just the bastards of humanity. Soldiers without a flag, Jews in a world of Gentiles, you will win neither trust nor protection. **❞**

Giuseppe Mazzini

CHAPTER 1
EUROPE ON THE BRINK

Introduction: Dominance and Destruction in European Ethnic Relations

At the dawn of the twentieth century Europe seemed at the peak of its powers. The partition of Africa from the 1880s underlined its technical and organizational superiority, and Africa was only an example of direct annexation. Informal influence extended to all corners of the world. Within the continent, with the exception of France, populations were rocketing. From 1800 to 1900 most countries had experienced growth of at least 100 per cent, and this encouraged urbanization, especially after the emancipation of the serfs in the Austrian and Russian empires in 1848 and 1861 allowed more people to leave the land. Extra labour power fuelled industrialization, particularly in the north, and increasingly in western Russia. The demographic trends necessitated social reform. Improved public health increased population and productivity.

Yet all was by no means well. In rural regions of Europe, growth swiftly meant overpopulation. The depressions of 1873–96 were a predominantly rural problem, upsetting traditional patterns of life, as the price of agricultural commodities plummeted relative to manufactures because of improved industrial technique and cheap grain imports from the USA. If some countryfolk saw opportunity in leaving the land for the cities, many others were forced into the move. Social discontent was being more stridently expressed as more social groups were represented in politics. Philosophers and avant-garde artists and writers focused on the uncertainties of life amid rapid change. In keeping with Gustav Le Bon's fashionable *Psychologie des foules* of 1895, many intellectuals felt the 'massification' of society would strangle creativity, that wider democracy would encourage demagoguery and populism. Rootlessness, alienation, and disorientation were feared as results of urbanization, industrial modernity, and intensified secularism. The watchword 'degeneration' could stand for anything from the demise of social stratification to the destruction of traditional culture to the dilution of 'racial value'.[1]

A few more sensitive souls even began to reflect on the legacy of European imperialism. The British political commentator Wilfred Scawen Blunt wrote in 1900 that

> All the nations of Europe are making the same hell on earth in China, massacring and pillaging and raping in the captured cities as outrageously as in the Middle Ages. The Emperor of Germany gives the word for slaughter and the Pope looks on and approves. In South Africa our troops are burning farms under Kitchener's command and the Queen and the two houses of Parliament and the bench of bishops thank God publicly and vote money for the work. The Americans are spending fifty millions a year on slaughtering Filipinos; the King of the Belgians has invested his whole fortune on the Congo, where he is brutalising the natives to fill his pockets . . . The whole white race is revelling openly in violence as though it never pretended to be Christian. God's equal curses on them all! So ends the famous nineteenth century into which we were so proud to have been born.[2]

Depending which part of Europe is examined, there were more or fewer signs of a system under pressure. Specific illustrations were provided by the 1905 revolution in Russia and a coup in Istanbul in 1908. More general indicators included the fall of laissez-faire commerce and the diplomatic strains between major powers in the heat of international industrial competition, multilateral armament, and the rampant expansion that left precious few parts of the world as neutral buffers between the European states. From the Iberian peninsula to the western provinces of the Russian empire, southward through the Caucasus, into Ottoman Turkey and back up into the Balkans, not only different states, but different ideas about organizing the relationship between people, economy, and the state were in burgeoning conflict.

The landmass was given a conceptual unity by the interconnected European state system, comprised broadly of nation-states to the north-west and dynastic, multinational empires to the east and southeast. The lands within it shared proximity, if to varying degrees, to the intellectual and cultural developments that had shaped socio-political change in the system, as expressed most obviously by the British industrial revolution and the French political revolution. Finally, the lands were bound together at some deep cultural level by the interface of the three great monotheistic religions: Judaism, Christianity, and Islam. As the nineteenth century progressed into the twentieth, relations between Jews, Christians, and Muslims grew increasingly murderous, even as the religions themselves were losing their grip on human minds, because they became entangled with the changing dynamic of the most basic of all political issues, encapsulated in Lenin's famous rhetorical question '*kto kogo?*': 'who-whom?'; more specifically, who dominates whom?[3]

Of all the forces unleashed by urbanization, industrialization, population growth, improved literacy, and ideas of emancipation, the one that acquired most venom in the final analysis was that of nationalities. Nationality questions were products of arguments about the relationship between peoples of a particular ethnic group, their loyalty, and sovereignty over the land on which they lived. Jews, Ukrainians, Macedonians, Armenians, the Irish, 'ethnic Germans', to name but a few, had the dubious privilege of being subjects of a question. A question demanded an answer, a solution, and none of these questions would be answered without blood being shed. Those peoples suffering the most tended to live in the most contested places, and they suffered most when identities and power balances were in greatest flux around them.

This part of the book considers the patterns and interlinkages of the increasingly violent 'solutions' to ethno-national problems in 'greater Europe' in approximately 1875–1949. As such, it pays less attention than is traditional in narratives of the time to social questions. This is not to downplay the significance of such themes: indeed, periodic reference to the intersection of ethno-religious and socio-economic conflict illustrates that it is often impossible to understand one without reference to the other.

The grand narrative of the last quarter of the nineteenth century and the first half of the twentieth begins with the end of the dynastic empires—the Ottoman-Turkish; the Romanov-Russian; and the Habsburg-Austro-Hungarian—under the pressure of European modernization and war, and the emergence in their place of smaller and more ethnically-homogeneous nation-states whose names reflected the majority national population: Poland as the land of the Poles, and so on. Whatever the hopes of the midwives to the new Europe, the early life of each new state, and in some cases its very birth was characterized by intergroup violence perpetrated in the quest for ethnic dominance within a territory.

Early state life was heavily influenced by the second phase in our grand narrative: the intrusion at different times of two new imperial forms, one very modern, one modernizing very quickly, into the spaces left by the collapse of the dynastic empires: the Nazi and Soviet states. However lethal Soviet policies were, Nazism was more congruent with the existing tendencies of nationalism in the region, and the 'final solution of the Jewish question' unfortunately accorded with the desires of many nationalists who shared little of the rest of the Nazi agenda. As well as being a coercive presence Nazism was thus a facilitating force for other exclusivist tendencies across the continent.

We should not view as inevitable the triumph of the national idea as the European map emerged after the First World War, or as it is today. The emergence of each nation-state, and the shape it took, depended upon a range of factors, particularly the attitudes of major powers. Some of these powers were themselves dynastic empires, meaning it is facile simply to juxtapose empire and nation as categories of actor or as characteristic of different historical epochs:[4] even the most significant political development of the nineteenth century, the emergence of the unified Germany of 1870, owed much to strategic Russian support. Of the other great powers, the one consistently influential arbiter of national boundaries and nationality questions across our period was Great Britain, which was not even on the continental landmass. The murders committed for land and domination reflect the *interaction* of various states and of proto-state movements of different forms and strengths, as each tried to further its agenda.

Ethnic dominance within a bounded territory was the basic, non-negotiable goal of all emerging nationalists. It also became a goal of some of the older imperial elites as their imperia came under threat and pressure to modernize. Securing ethnic dominance involved the suppression of competing nationalities and the removal of their members from positions of political, administrative, and economic prominence. A further, ideal outcome for many nationalists and 'nationalizing' imperial elites was complete *ethnic exclusivity*, a perfect fit between national territory and ethnic population in the nation-state. Exclusivity could only be achieved by *ethnic destruction*, comprising ethnic cleansing (meaning eviction of a group from a territory to secure that territory for the group on whose behalf the perpetrators purported to act) or genocide (taken here to mean the physical destruction of a large portion of a group in a limited or unlimited territory with the intention of destroying that group's collective existence). However, contrary to the accumulated history of ideas of racism and ethno-nationalism which often passes for explanation of genocide, the pure, abstract logic of ideology was rarely enough on its own to push even extremists into ethnic cleansing or mass murder, the most straightforward methods of achieving exclusivity. Were this not the case, then genocide and ethnic cleansing would have been even more common in the period in question than they were. How and how far the utopian goal of exclusivity was pursued depended upon the course of events. Indeed, how far the malign trends in the high culture and intellectual life of modern Europe gained popular and political purchase in the affected states was as much to do with geopolitical and economic fortune, and institutional arrangements, as with the force of ideas.

Forms of discrimination, including forced assimilation of minorities by language policy, or expropriation, sporadic violence, and restrictions on entry into key professions, became de rigueur during peacetime in many different states. Even though such measures of domination might ultimately have provided some psychological and practical preparation for removal measures during, say, wartime, they were ends in themselves and certainly not simply or even deliberately a prelude to ethnic destruction. Discriminatory policies up to and including equivalents of the Nazi 'Aryanization' of state and economy were standard practice in parts of Europe, consistent with contemporaneous notions of the very logic of independent statehood. Genocide and ethnic cleansing were different, because they were often triggered by interstate conflict rather than simply internal political agendas, and because they generally had ramifications beyond state borders in terms of regional destabilization, mass refugee movement, and even the opinion of the outside world, which was not always an inconsequential matter for would-be perpetrators. There is no necessary contradiction at all between a state and its majority population enthusiastically excluding, say, Jews or Greeks from its economy but balking at murdering them.

Both policies of dominance and destruction are ideal types, and in practice there could be slippage in both directions from one to the other, as there could be slippage between the two forms of destruction, ethnic cleansing and genocide. Nevertheless, the distinction remains analytically important. To one degree or another most of our Europe was discriminatory, but it was still possible during times of stability for most individual members of every single ethnic group on the continent to live in relative peace, even if that was peace with socio-economic disadvantage or outright humiliation. The same is true even for the archetypal victims, the Jews, even in hotbeds of traditional anti-Semitism such as nineteenth-century Ukraine and Romania.[5] Ethnic destruction, on the other hand, made exemption the exception rather than the rule, and at stake at the very least was the loss of home and homeland.

Moreover, in Europe in the period in question, whole *societies* tended to be implicated in systems of domination, whereas it was *states* or the elites of would-be states that more often contemplated destruction at crisis moments. (This sets Europe apart somewhat from, for instance, its colonies, where the settler societies could provide the driving force behind genocide.) The majority of the dominant population was complicit in bolstering the hierarchy through everyday cultural expressions of dominance down to such seemingly minor but symbolically significant practices as derogatory jokes. At moments of particular tension, the maintenance of or challenge to the hierarchy might 'require' violence, in the form of, say, ethnic riot or pogrom, where elements of the dominant group might provide the lead from political or personal motives. This violence, however extreme, was generally transitory and irregular, depending upon local conditions and only—if at all—tacit acceptance by the state. But when states, or political movements gifted effective sovereign power (such as the Ustaša regime in Second World War Croatia), threw their weight behind destruction, many more individuals were brought into the perpetration of violence in a more systematic and enduring way.

State and societal violence could be complementary rather than opposed, but there is something about the very logic of the state in the crisis period under consideration that particularly promoted genocide because of its *dual* benefits to the perpetrating regime. Genocide was *one* logical expression of the political drive that sought to minimize heterogeneity even among ethnic majorities, changing 'peasants into Frenchmen' or Anatolian Sunnis into Turks, by way of creating the critical mass of unified demographic strength necessary for states to establish themselves, and then to repel others or expand.[6] Genocide or ethnic cleansing served the purposes of removing 'problem' groups *while simultaneously* sharpening and rendering more exclusive the identity of the majority. The strength of this point is not reduced by the fact that important if generally proportionally small societal constituencies provided additional impulses for some genocides at some points. Nor is it reduced by the observation that many ordinary people from many genocidal regimes participated in the crime when it was underway. Nor does the argument ignore the motivational power of the material benefits of genocide for the majority population: indeed, byproducts like property theft from the victims were an important means of further binding the beneficiaries to each other and the regime.

Our Europe does provide substantiation for some conceptual half-way house between more demotic and more statist interpretations of intergroup violence. Some of the most vicious incidences of mass murder that we will encounter in these pages occurred when established state authority had been destroyed and there was sustained, often multilateral competition for hegemony between groups with aspirations to formal post-conflict influence. The Russian civil war was such a case, but also the conflict ensuing as Ottoman authority collapsed in Anatolia during the second half of the First World War, and the situation in the Ukraine and eastern Poland in the Second World War after Nazi Germany lost control and before the Soviet Union gained control. Nevertheless, whatever the spiralling violence in these situations of lawlessness, many of the social cleavages which widened to cavernous dimensions had previously been exacerbated by state policy. Moreover, extreme, general social polarization was, again, as much the result as the cause of conflict. In anarchic situations, it became essential to align for self-preservation as the most radical elements on all sides set the political tone.

Whatever the weight to be given to societal impulses for extreme violence, for most of our period and across most of our area, the state was a fact of life. So too was its highly significant capacity to arbitrate violence by and against peoples under its control. That meant restricting violence or unleashing it in the most destructive manner.

Exceptional Minorities and Changing Stereotypes

Minorities were becoming increasingly vulnerable throughout the period. At a time of fragmenting empires and proliferating nation-states, Jews were particularly exposed as a stateless, trans-state minority. Their plight was also experienced by the Romanies, who equally lacked a protective homeland.

Historically concentrated in the Balkans, where they experienced centuries of enslavement in the Romanian lands, Romanies had fled the Ottoman advance of the fifteenth century, heading into central and western Europe. There they faced the accusation of being Ottoman spies—a calumny that would endure into the Second World War when they were cast as enemy agents by both Germany and the defeated France. As Jews had been accused of poisoning wells in premodern Europe, Romanies had been accused of being plague carriers. Like Jews, too, because of their difference to the surrounding populations, Romanies were some of the longest standing objects of official attempts to 'normalize' them as states expanded their power and tried to rationalize their rule. From the early seventeenth century in Spain through the eighteenth century in the Habsburg empire and elsewhere, Romanies were subjected to forced sedentarization and prohibitions on traditional clothing and language. In the nineteenth and twentieth centuries, many states, including pre-Nazi Germany, passed discriminatory laws against them.

Unlike Romanies, however, Jews were increasingly stigmatized as somehow gaining extraordinary power from their peculiar status. At best, their cosmopolitanism and their proverbial cross-border commercial and cultural links simply came sharply into perspective as ethnically delineated nation-states emerged into the world and its economy. At worst, such cosmopolitanism was held to signify a higher loyalty which, since it was unquantifiable in terms of a Jewish state, must be clandestine and threatening. The inflation of the 'Jewish problem' to the point where, unlike other minority 'problems', it was not just a question of the Jewish presence in one discrete territory meant increasing without limit potential anti-Semitic 'grievances' and Jewish 'provocations'. Eventually it also 'required' an 'international solution'.

Traditionally, as a tolerated monotheistic religious minority, the experience of Jews in Europe bore some similarity to that of Christians (and Jews) in the Muslim Ottoman Empire. Toleration also meant contempt and periodic exposure to violence from the 'morally superior' religious majority. Jews' relations with surrounding populations had historically been shaped by the canard that sees them as murderers of Jesus, though strict Christian theology only criticized them for rejecting his revelation. The most damaging allegations developed in medieval Christendom, and concerned 'usury' (profitable moneylending), the ritual murder of Christian children, profanation of the host, and other methods of undermining Christianity.[7] The precariousness of traditional Jewish life in Europe had been illustrated by expulsion from Spain in 1492 and Portugal in 1497, and earlier from England, France, Germany, and Lithuania. Yet even as a more secular age held out the promise of a harmonious future in the west and centre of the continent, pogroms with religious ingredients continued into the twentieth century in parts of eastern Europe. Even as Europe modernized, anti-Jewish stereotypes remained, based in part on the simple, continued existence of Jewish communities with their own traditions in the midst of non-Jews.

The stereotype of Jews as usurers lay ironically in the socio-economic arrangements imposed on Jews in pre-modern times. Traditional Christian prohibitions on the profitable lending of money meant

Jewish moneylenders fulfilled an important financial role in economies increasingly based on investment, just as Jews had been barred from land ownership and the 'honourable' professions Christians found to their taste.[8] Christians were in a similar position in the Ottoman Empire, and were victims of much the same stereotype. Providing services to the agricultural or pastoral populations around them, and often caught between landlord and peasant, the Jews were frequently blamed by the latter for the exploitation from which the former benefited. Over time, they were also increasingly centred in the cities of eastern and central Europe—again, seemingly separated from the 'organic' communities around them. Beyond financial and commercial functions, Jews had historical specialisms in spheres in which the surrounding population lacked either desire or aptitude, such as medicine and metallurgy. For all these things they might be admired, feared, or hated. The ensuing economic, social, and political stereotypes would survive when the concrete historical explanations had been forgotten.[9]

While emerging modern forms of rationalism—pre-eminently liberalism—promoted greater Jewish integration and social mobility in western and central Europe, they gave a new inflection to anti-Jewish thought. In some eyes, the more assimilated the Jews were, the more insidiously and effectively their imaginary collective ethno-religious agenda of dominance was being carried out. As Jews were gaining greater formal emancipation in Germany, the Habsburg empire from the formation of the Dual Monarchy in 1867, or western Russia at various points, they would often simultaneously be depicted as the agents and beneficiaries of disruptive change, particularly by conservative political parties seeking to rally constituencies affected by depression and dislocated by urbanization, or churches struggling with the impact of liberalism. After all, Jews were relatively prominent in undertakings particularly associated with the onset of a disturbing modernity, such as journalism, the arts, and the liberal professions.[10] Jews who had abandoned their faith altogether could still be seen as bearers of a 'Jewish tradition' with a different perspective on the surrounding world: these have been dubbed the 'non-Jewish Jews'.[11] The historian of capitalism Werner Sombart was by no means alone in identifying Jews in particular with the spread of the new economic order; some of the prime Jewish movers in his depiction were secular, which gave grist to the mill of anti-Semites pronouncing on the insidious role of 'hidden Jews'.[12] At the same time, in places where Jews were not assimilated by the late nineteenth century—broadly, in the east—a supposed subversive Jewish agenda came to be associated either with the west in the form of 'pro-Jewish' diplomatic pressure or with internal left-wing revolutionaries who sought to destroy the old order altogether. All across the continent, Jews could be blamed in one way or another for the upheavals of the age, irrespective of the often detrimental impact modernization had on their actual lives.

The change in the real and perceived status of Jews as they gained greater social equality had as violent an outcome as the equivalent process for Ottoman Christians. For nationalists seeking ethnic dominance within their borders, the spectre of Jewish economic power was among their chief targets. The actions of these nationalists, and the actions of the late Ottoman state against various Christian groups, included boycott, expropriation, discrimination, and terror. At some point, however, perceptions of Jewish economic power became indistinguishable from notions of increasing Jewish political power, because of the new significance of moneylending and middleman activities in increasingly capitalistic economies, and because those very functions often brought with them contacts beyond state borders which could be depicted as suspicious. There were some very prominent symbols of the putative relationship between Jews, capitalistic modernization, and supranational power. Concerning the Rothschild family, the economist Karl Polanyi once wrote of the 'metaphysical extraterritoriality of a Jewish bankers' dynasty'. For Polanyi, the significance of such a dynasty was its ability to command 'the confidence of national statesmen and of the international investor alike',[13] but for anti-Semites preoccupied with alleged Jewish conspiracies the Rothschilds had a very different significance.

One manifestation of putative Jewish *political* power above all terrified Europe's nationalists and religious conservatives alike. The Bolshevik Revolution, one of the disparate children of the Enlightenment, was alleged to embody the rise of the Jews as a parasitic political force, and with the emergence of the Bolshevik state emerged also the desire to strike bodily at the Jews in qualitatively and quantitatively new ways. Fear of 'Judeo-Bolshevik' political domination led to the huge Jewish massacres of the Russian civil war; the association of Jews with Soviet rule stimulated Rumanians, Ukrainians, and Lithuanians to murder Jews en masse in 1941; and war with the USSR prompted Nazi Germany to murder all the Jews they could lay their hands on.

Of course, within the deep cultural framework that determined the peculiar status of Jews, and the recent circumstances of Europe's modernization that gave a new inflection to anti-Jewishness, Nazism contributed one further element: 'biological racism'—the idea of genetically inherited difference. Racism was not original to Nazism but Nazism was exceptional in systematizing it and promoting it so determinedly to the centre of a state's agenda. Building on intellectual developments beginning in the seventeenth century and culminating in the late nineteenth century, pseudoscientific differentiation between human 'subspecies' stemming from perversions of genuine scientific insight into genetics and biological classification gave a new colouring to older but more inchoate assumptions of civilizational superiority and difference.[14]

As an extension of scientific differentiation between whole human groups came differentiation between members of particular groups. This was based on the truth that some individuals were clearly born less physically or mentally able than others. 'Progress' might create the capacity to ease the life conditions of the less able, but it might also mean creating the conditions under which such people never came into the world in the first place, or others were 'eased on their way' out of it—a notion of a 'positive' death that had hitherto had no place in Christian culture.[15]

The doctrine of 'eugenics' that emerged in the late nineteenth century was not only embraced by racists and 'social Darwinists' seeking to improve the human stock, but also by members of the political left as they sought to reconcile their secular understanding of human equality with the manifest inequality of heredity. Eugenics was practised most extensively in the most advanced societies, including Britain, Scandinavia, Germany, and the USA, where forced sterilization of the 'unfit' was accepted state practice. In Britain Churchill was an enthusiastic proponent as Home Secretary before the First World War.[16] Again, some eugenic ideas and practices had been developed in the colonies: 'hereditary criminality' and asocial behaviour had a long pedigree in

British India, for instance. Meanwhile, many of the states that had suffered in the First World War spent the interwar period anxiously surveying their depleted people resources and turning to one degree or another to natalist policies designed to enhance the 'desirable' population—this was the 'positive' compliment to the negative eugenic practice of sterilization. Eugenics and racism—the very modern preoccupation with the vitality and purity of peoples—provided one of the many routes by which Europe's violence in the world beyond was imported into the continent itself.

The Order of Europe's Empires on the Eve of Modernity

As far as the rest of the world was concerned, even the basic claim to universality springing from Enlightenment Europe—the discovery of rational principles for autonomous human morality and thus for the general regulation of human affairs—looked like just the last in a long line of presumptuous western claims. It emerged from an occident that harked back to the equally pretentious Greece and Rome for its models of civilization.[17] The intolerance of that European civilization once it had recovered from the fall of the Roman Empire was evinced in the central Middle Ages in the campaigns of the emergent power centre of Catholic Rome internally against 'heretics' (notably Cathars), lepers, and Jews, and externally against Muslims and, again, Jews in the Crusades.[18] The sword of Christian Europe in the later medieval period had been the Spanish state. Its suspicion of its Jews was paralleled by its hostility towards the Muslim 'Moors': immediately both had been driven from Spain at the end of the fifteenth century, the battle of civilizations was exported to the continent of South America, with Columbus the emblem. The impact of the Enlightenment did little to combat ideas of European exceptionalism informing expansion into the outside world: quite the opposite, as the mushrooming nineteenth century 'civilizing mission' attested. Reason itself could be used as an index of superiority in a world at the mercy of technologically advanced westerners.

Imperial expansion almost always entailed violence, but the greatest violence was generally reserved for those areas at the greatest physical and therefore cultural distance from the imperial core territories. A key question was whether new territory was earmarked for settlement, and thus the removal of the local people, or for the economic exploitation of that people.

More complex issues of population management faced the rulers of the dynastic European empires which expanded from the early modern period to incorporate adjacent territories in central, eastern, and southeastern Europe and in the Eurasian rimlands along Russia's expanding border. Each dynastic empire allowed degrees of decentralization and cultural independence for subject populations, but each had a territorial core and a ruling people holding the senior political, administrative, and military posts. The situation in the Ottoman Empire has already been touched upon; Slavs were below Germans and Magyars in the Habsburg empire; non-Russian Slavs, other Christian populations, and Muslims were below Great Russians in the Russian empire. As each empire expanded, members of the core people, or other groups deemed sufficiently reliable or different to the new additional populations, were sometimes dispatched to break up demographic concentrations of subject peoples, and to defend border regions. While further mixing already multiethnic regions, such policies entrenched a correlation between power relations and cultural difference.

The Russian and Ottoman empires in particular used demographic engineering as a way of breaking up 'troublesome' population groups or removing them from sensitive areas such as borders or communications routes. In the mid-nineteenth century, the Romanovs and the Ottomans actually agreed to the transfer of particular Muslim groups from the Russian Caucasus into Ottoman territory. An interesting variant on imperial demographic engineering was created in the western provinces of the expanding Russian empire at the end of the eighteenth century as it partitioned Poland: the 'Pale of Settlement', where Catherine the Great and her successors segregated the Jews.

Each empire used particular population groups for particular functions. We know that aspects of the traditional economic dispensation for Europe's Jews and non-Muslim Ottomans were perpetuated into the modern period. Jews were disproportionately represented in financial and commercial functions in the Habsburg lands, since they were considered by the Austrian and Hungarian nobility to be a loyal minority with no territorial ambitions. This situation obtained until the end of the empire, despite the development of increasingly virulent anti-Semitism in late imperial Vienna; and it is possible to go so far as to talk of a Magyar–Jewish symbiosis that lasted until the First World War.[19] As for the Ottoman Empire, as it was incorporated into the burgeoning global economy from the early nineteenth century, Christians filled important intermediary roles in relation to the outside world, which owed much to their language skills and their religious confraternity with the European powers.

Ethnic Germans enjoyed social and economic dominance in the Baltic region of the Russian empire. German agricultural labourers and those with particular commercial and technical skills also settled in the lower Volga region, in Volhynia, and around the Black Sea (Bessarabia and Bukovina) at the invitation of Catherine the Great and her successors. Jews were sometimes and in some places allowed by the Tsars to deploy their commercial and financial skills, though they were also the victim of repeated attacks based precisely on those characteristics.

Overall, in the dynastic empires there was a hierarchical demographic order, and frequently the perpetuation of partial ethnic divisions of labour. Though often established by coercion, the hierarchies 'worked' while the empires in question were in the ascendant. As the empires were challenged, their hierarchies were challenged and either violently overturned or violently consolidated. The legacy of hierarchies and divisions outlasted the empires and would provide some of the main grievances upon which leaders of subject peoples acted as they expressed new forms of collective consciousness.

The French Revolution: National and Religious Emancipation

The most significant challenge to the established dynastic order was also the most significant political manifestation of Enlightenment ideas in the eighteenth century: the French Revolution. Such, at least, was the revolutionaries' own account of it, though at least as important in stimulating change was the discrediting of the *Ancien Régime* by repeated military defeats at the hands of a better organized Great Britain. Judging by attitudes towards Jews, the early revolutionaries certainly provided some grounds to substantiate their own enlightenment. In 1791 France became the first regime to institute legal near-equality for all citizens, regardless of faith. The other states that would follow this lead to varying degrees only did so over the course of several decades, and more out of reasons of pragmatism or administrative uniformity than of principle, and then often more in theory than reality.

Restoration France maintained many of the tenets of emancipation, to the dismay of the not insignificant representatives of political Catholicism. Hence, through the last decade of the nineteenth century, when their unusual freedom betrayed the Jews amid accusations that they were exploiting the country for their own ends, an international Jewish solidarity movement flourished in France. The movement pressed for the improvement of conditions of Jews in the Ottoman Empire and its successor states as well as propounding the French imperial 'mission civilatrice'.[20] The idea of full Jewish emancipation would always remain bound together with 'French revolutionary values' for many central and eastern Europeans.

Emancipation tied to the values of revolutionary universalism those Jews who could convince themselves there was no contradiction between their faith, traditions, and social structure and full adherence to the revolutionary project. Yet the sort of emancipation at stake was not an unalloyed blessing. If the 'emancipation contract' meant greater acceptance of Jews, it also required that Jews compromise their distinctiveness, subjecting themselves fully to the state, without mediating agencies and intervening duties. Liberal emancipation may have been good for individual Jews, and it may have been eagerly embraced by many German as well as French Jews, but as it was framed within the European state system it was not good for Judaism as a religion and social system, and indeed sought to remove the very 'difference' of Jews except perhaps in private conviction.

The many changes wrought by the revolutionaries within France were enough to terrify the conservative elites of the other European states. The revolutionary attempt to create a new order, when married with political disturbances in the Low Countries, Sweden, Switzerland, and Ireland in the 1790s, created a fear of general revolution, which in turn suggested to some observers a hidden international subversive organization. Hitler would later see the hidden hand of world Jewry operating behind the French Revolution as well as the Bolshevik Revolution. In the formulations of contemporaries such as Edinburgh University's John Robison and Abbé Augustin Barruel the enemies were not Jews but rather Freemasons (the 'Illuminati' or 'Illuminés'), but their supposed perfidious agenda was very similar and the accusation provided a cultural template into which Jews could easily fit later on. Thus Barruel: 'From the Sophisters of Impiety and Rebellion, arose the Sophisters of Impiety and Anarchy. These latter conspire not only against Christ and his altars, but against every religion natural or revealed: not only against kings, but against every government, against all civil society.' And Robison:

> The Illuminati . . . intended to root out all religion and ordinary morality, and even to break the bonds of domestic life. . . . Hence it has arisen that the French aimed, in the very beginning, at overturning the whole world. . . . The revolutionary societies were early formed, and were working in secret before the opening of the National Assembly, and the whole nation changed again, and again, as if by beat of drums.[21]

Beyond the conspiracy theorists, the most startling feature of the Revolution for outsiders was the way that these godless men were able to rally so many people to their cause in the form of the *levée en masse*—the *national* conscription policy that later allowed Napoleon to defeat the smaller, professional armies of the other powers. As an extension, onlookers feared Napoleon's exhortation to the subject peoples of other empires to liberate themselves—his sponsorship of what we would now call *nationalism*. Another matter was of less immediate concern to those trying to close the Pandora's box of the Revolution, but was nonetheless a stark illustration of the murderous potential of a modern revolutionary movement when its agenda was threatened. That was the earlier massacre of at the very least 117,000 people in the Vendée region of west-central France in 1794, as this largely peasant population rose up against the centrally imposed regime owing to local grievances but encouraged by clerical and monarchical reaction.[22]

Napoleon went on to betray the stated principles of 1789. His empire was based more on coercion than consent. Yet his imposed constitutions raised the possibility, even if only theoretical, of greater governmental accountability to the people, while his administrative reforms introduced greater rationality into the practices of the state machinery, and boosted nascent processes of industrialization in and beyond France. The introduction of greater taxation and conscription in his domains expanded the role of the state in the social domain. His consolidation of many small German principalities created some of the preconditions for greater German unity. Meanwhile, defeated polities were quite capable of learning the lessons of French success, as Prussia did with its military and administrative modernization after 1806. And the rhetoric of national liberation left a powerful imprint, initially in rejection of the legitimacy of French rule itself, but later, too, in opposition to the continental 'restoration' imposed by Europe's crowned heads in 1815. As the revolutionaries had come to define themselves and their France against the hostile, non-French, outside world, so Napoleon's subject peoples defined themselves in contrast to French rule.

The Napoleonic impact and legacy illustrated an enduring truth about nationalism. In theory, it was a liberal notion, a corollary of Enlightenment ideas of individual autonomy derived from reason rather than tradition. As liberalism related to individual freedom, subject only to the rule of rational law, nationalism related to the right of 'self-determination' of separate peoples in 'nation-states'. Nationalism as a system of political organization theoretically presupposed popular participation in political life. In practice however, as nationalisms developed in Europe, they rarely allowed internal pluralism or external tolerance. Some traditional elites resisted nationalism and encouraged violence in reaction. Others exploited nationalism's mobilizing potential as a means—like copying British industrialization—to enhance state military power, while restricting its emancipatory and egalitarian connotations. Into the latter category would fall particularly the proponents of the romantic nationalisms emerging in the nineteenth century.

The romantic idea of nationalism—of a distinct national people shaped by language, geography, and culture, with a shared history and destiny—started to crystallize during the Napoleonic period. The word *Volkstum*, connoting an ethnic community, suggests German ownership of the concept, but many other nationalities found equivalents, and the developing German political tradition incorporated more liberal conceptions of nationalism as well. Romanticism was shaped in reaction to socio-economic change, to 'French revolutionary values', and to the mechanistic understanding of society emerging from British utilitarian thought. Yet it was not conservative, rather neo-conservative. It was not a rejection of the political project of forging the nation. In its belief in a mythologized past, and thus a significant future, the idea that a people was not an inert collection of individuals, but a subject of history, an agent of change with a common will transcending individuals, it provided a powerful legitimation for the nation-state in the present.

It has become fashionable to distinguish between more inclusive civic nationalisms based on shared values in the west of the continent and more atavistic and essentialist nationalisms based on ethnicity in the centre and east, to which romantic forms of nationalism bear a close relation. Yet to the extent that western nationalisms tended to be more stable, this reflects the happier circumstances in which France and England developed over earlier centuries, with relatively constant populations, borders, and (before 1789 in France) political institutions, as opposed to those nationalisms emerging from the eastern empires. Besides, both France and Britain had undergone some processes of coercive ethnoreligious homogenization in earlier centuries, and no modern nation remained untouched by romantic notions of origin. Further, both France and Britain were guided into the twentieth century by distinctly monocultural liberalisms.[23] More developed parliamentary systems with expanding franchises and a plurality of elites were no guarantee against intolerance of 'difference' from whatever was the prescribed norm.

At least as important in determining the bellicosity and chauvinism of any nation was the sense of security it felt in the world and its state of economic well being. Depressions did nothing at all to enhance intergroup relations. (One scholar wrote of the 1873–96 depressions, in a way equally true of the 1930s, that 'anti-Semitism rose as the stock market fell'.[24]) It is better to think of civic and ethnic nationalisms as ideal types, with all states having a variable mixture of each over time, and civic nationalism possessing its own homogenizing tendencies even if these are not necessarily or explicitly ethnic.[25] We are also on safe ground in saying that as Europe's *fin-de-siècle* identity crisis descended, elites from all nation-states, national communities, and imperial core peoples became more ruthless in adhering to the fashionable tenets of 'social Darwinism' in international affairs—the belief that Charles Darwin's work on natural selection in the plant and animal kingdoms provided an analogy for competition for survival between peoples. Moreover, those selfsame elites not infrequently found that playing on the language and symbols of popular legitimacy was successful, with public support for at least limited wars (or wars that it was hoped would be limited) and imperial expansion, irrespective of the variety of nationalism theorists have attributed to their countries.

But this is to get ahead of ourselves, for even as France and a waking Germany were working out the balance of their national identities, the demise of none of the dynastic empires was preordained. Each tried, with varying degrees of success, to reform its structures to adjust to the forces associated with the French Revolution, the challenges of western European technological and economic advance, and the demands of subject peoples. With wiser leadership than prevailed in the crisis culminating in the First World War, the Habsburg imperium would have endured in some form for a considerable time: the war was at least as important in radicalizing subject nationalisms in the Habsburg empire as in providing an opportunity for national liberation.[26] As for Russia, Lenin was correct in saying war was the mother of revolution: without the First World War, the 1917 revolutions would have been unthinkable. Alone of the three empires, it is questionable to what extent the Ottoman Empire could have survived the nineteenth century without British support.

Imperial Reform and the Spread of Nationalism

Imperial reform itself had unforeseen consequences for intergroup relations. Across the landmass, the drive for greater economic productivity, administrative regularity, and military efficiency required the state to penetrate more deeply into the lives of its subjects. Attempts at expanding education went alongside regularizing taxation, extending conscription within communities and to communities hitherto exempt, and improving communications for the flow of commerce, the ease of troop transportation, and the swifter pacification of troublesome peripheries. States needed greater information than ever before about the location, make-up, economic function, and perceived 'loyalty' of their populations. The expansion of state power also meant the expansion of the state's perception of how far it could reshape the body politic.[27]

Greater taxation and conscription could arouse popular enmity against the state, while improved transportation and education, particularly in cities and among the growing if often still embryonic middle classes, meant the circulation of innovative ideas of all sorts, not simply those conducive to the strengthening of the empires. More people came into contact with their own wider linguistic communities, furthering the development of collective consciousness. Large towns and cities were particularly important in this process, as urbanization expanded and changed their demographic composition. The standardization of revived or reinvented national languages through the nineteenth century promoted 'print nationalism', as consumers of newly written histories and of the growing number of newspapers could see themselves as part of a broader community of interest—one much wider than their village, town, or province—that was tied together through reading about, and thus in some way experiencing, common imagined pasts and presents. Part of this process was also the more frequent encounter with an increasingly assertive state, and therefore with representatives of the dominant imperial peoples who spoke the language of state transaction, not the local vernacular.[28]

Language became arguably the key marker of national difference, an indicator not just of cultural contrast, but of the inferiority, dominance, or threat posed by 'others'. It was also a focus of attention for political elites once independence had been achieved, and even in independent states of long-standing such as France. The standardization of language and the attack on dialect were important to the project of 'forging the nation', and showed how elite-driven the process could be.[29] Indeed, there was considerable functional value to encouraging sentiments of unity on cultural grounds, given the obvious socio-economic disparities within (as well as between) national peoples. Late-nineteenth-century

Germany provides an obvious example of how the pursuit of collective objectives, such as linguistic 'Germanization' of Poles on the eastern borders and Frenchmen in the west, and empire-building in the colonies, were used to build national unity and divert attention from the obvious social tensions stemming from the rise of the organized working class. The assault on political Catholicism known as the *Kulturkampf* was an integrative move aimed at entrenching central sovereignty and enforcing a common identity and, therefore, loyalty.

The *Kulturkampf* and the reactions to it illustrate the continuing cultural influence of religion, and not just in stigmatizing Jews. The secularization accelerated by the Enlightenment meant religion was removed further from the levers of direct political power, and that bourgeois or aristocratic nationalists acquired the social power of the priesthood. But syncretic nationalism incorporated religion as a marker of belonging, while private faith remained a potent focus for mobilization of the masses. Particular churches remained bastions of national or regional identity: the Catholic Church in Poland, Slovakia, Croatia, Austria, and Lithuania; different Orthodox churches in Russia, Serbia, Greece, Bulgaria, and Ukraine; Lutheranism in Prussia and Finland, Calvinism in Hungary; Hussitism among the Czechs.

While in theory religion and language as markers of ethnicity were not the immutable barriers that 'race' in the pseudoscientific conception of the late nineteenth century was, in practice the boundaries were far from porous. In the empires, individual members of ethnoreligious groups had historically tended to marry within those same groups rather than across group boundaries. Gaining technical proficiency in another language did not automatically confer the 'proper' accent or idiomatic fluency, as Yiddish-speaking immigrants to *fin-de-siècle* Vienna would testify, and it certainly did not mean entry into kinship networks. There was decided slippage between conceptions of ethnic and 'racial' difference.[30]

From the imperial perspective, or the perspective of new nation-states with large minorities like Germany, the growing nationalist consciousness within subject peoples presented an obvious dilemma. Not all were in the same position of power that permitted Germany to force its integrative agenda on Poles. The Habsburg empire, or at least the more tolerant Austrian half of it, went furthest from the later nineteenth century towards accommodating the developing aspirations of its subject peoples through such measures as language and education reforms. It was home to the development of some of the more humane ideas then in circulation for the coexistence of different nationalities in a federal structure.[31] Austrian policies found some posthumous reward in the relative moderation of Czech nationalist policy towards ethnic Germans and other minorities in the interwar period. By contrast, Slovak and Romanian nationalists would prove significantly less tolerant of Hungarians in light of the vigorous Magyarization programmes of the late nineteenth century, and would also attack Jews on the basis that their status in the empire made them co-responsible for Magyarization. (Whatever the relative merits of the Habsburg empire, when in 1914 it was confronted with the most serious challenge to its authority, by the upstart Serbian state, it proved amply capable of murderous vengefulness.[32])

Throughout its existence, and beyond into the Soviet period, the Russian empire was particularly noteworthy for the fluctuations in its population policy. One of many voltes-faces was performed by Alexander III after the assassination of the relatively liberal Alexander II by 'Populist' revolutionaries in 1881. Alexander's assassination resulted in a series of pogroms against Russia's Jewish population, who were held collectively responsible by many elements of Russian society. (Atheistic Jews were over-represented in Populist ranks, as in other radical circles, because of the hardship experienced by the population under the status quo.[33]) The assassination also precipitated anti-Jewish laws, including tight limits on the number of Jews who could enter state schools and universities. Meanwhile, a continued drive for modernization and centralization went hand in hand across the provinces with general if uneven campaigns of linguistic Russification and repression from the 1880s.

In the nineteenth century, under pressure from Balkan Christian nationalism and Russian military advance, Ottoman policy towards non-Muslim populations also flowed back and forth along the two axes ranging from greater integration to greater discrimination and from toleration of separateness to forced assimilation. In the mid-century *Tanzimat* period, reforms of the religious *millet* structure enabled greater inter-religious equality, as a means to keep Christians within the empire. The reform decrees of 1839 and 1856 improved the lot of Christians and Jews on paper. But the attempt to modernize without removing the traditional system of confessional organization (where the Orthodox, Catholic, Armenian, and Jewish communities had some self-governing autonomy) backfired, because subject Christian nationalisms developed along the cleavages of the old religious framework. Besides, the external sponsorship of reforms for Christians and Jews, particularly by Britain and France, caused tremendous resentment among the Ottoman elite and many ordinary Muslims. The erosion of the established ethnoreligious hierarchy had gone quite far enough. A new course was heralded in light of the 'eastern crisis' of 1875–8. It is no accident that this seminal event occurred in the European empire most exposed by Europe's modernization race.[34]

The Eastern Crisis

The eastern crisis provides a point of departure for examining the intertwined geopolitical and demographic concerns of both great powers and smaller nationalities that would so shape all of Europe in the following decades. From then until 1914, while the world focused on Christian victims of Ottoman massacre in Bosnia-Herzegovina and Bulgaria, Muslims were in fact the primary victims of violence in the eastern Mediterranean at the hands of Christian states and substate actors. As Serbia, Montenegro, Romania, and part of Bulgaria achieved full independence from Istanbul, and as Bosnia, Herzegovina, and other parts of Bulgaria gained extensive autonomy, hundreds of thousands of Muslims were expelled from these former Ottoman domains, with many others murdered in the process. To them may be added perhaps two and a half million more Muslims from the North Caucasus, expelled or fleeing in the face of Russian policy: the flood from the Caucasus had begun in earnest around the time of the Crimean War of 1854–6, but was greatly augmented during the 1877–8 Ottoman–Russian war as Russia expanded at Ottoman expense, and continued until 1914.

The eastern crisis was precipitated by little more than a tax revolt in Herzegovina, but the wider context was vital. The 1873 Vienna stock market crash that brought on the European depression coincided with poor harvests, drought, and famine in the Ottoman domains. The crash meant that the debt-ridden empire, which could no longer avail itself of foreign loans, tried to raise capital domestically by increasing taxes. The tax-farmers in the Balkans further squeezed the predominantly Christian peasantry, which was already suffering environmental hardships. Nationalist agitators stirred the ensuing revolt and found some willing support among the population, though neither the nationalist element nor the scale of popular participation should be overplayed.[35] The Catholics amongst the agitators had been encouraged by recent Austro-Hungarian overtures, while Orthodox Serbian agitators were encouraged by Serbia, which cast avaricious eyes on Bosnia, and enjoyed geopolitical and 'pan-Slavic' Russian support. Swiftly the crisis achieved regional dimensions, as Russia backed Serbia unsuccessfully in a military campaign and then decided to do the job itself, causing great concern to Austria–Hungary, Germany, and Britain over the balance of power. The involvement of the Powers gave the insurgents the opportunity to avenge themselves against members of a group associated with the subordination of the Christian majority populations.

In Turkish ethnic memory the suffering and dislocation experienced at the time of the eastern crisis is known as the *sökümü*, the disaster or 'unweaving'.[36] For its part the 1877–8 Russian war radicalized a generation of future Ottoman leaders. The unweaving: that poignant term encapsulates much of the tragedy of greater Europe in the twentieth century. For if what has elsewhere been called the 'unmixing' of peoples began in earnest in central and eastern Europe around the First World War,[37] by then the process was well underway in former Ottomania. The eastern crisis brought the end of most of the empire in Europe, and was marked not by 'old-fashioned barbarity', but by a very modern form of violence: ethnic cleansing. Though not all Bulgarian or Bosnian Muslims would die or flee, the point of the violence was to reverse the ethnic power balance and pave the way for Christian ethnic dominance in the future.

As important for our analysis as the ethnic violence of the eastern crisis was the way it was resolved—or rather deferred—by the 1878 Treaty of Berlin. First, in his chairmanship of the peace conference, Bismarck subtly helped rebut Russia and further the German rapprochement with

Austria–Hungary after the Austro-Prussian war of 1866—a process aided by his tactical winding-down of the *Kulturkampf*, except in the Polish areas of eastern Germany. The eastern crisis crystallized Bismarck's aspiration to entrench Germanic rather than Slavic political and economic influence in southeastern and east-central Europe, which coincided with a growing German interest in ethnic German populations in eastern Europe. Russian frustrations pushed that state into closer alignment with France, a relationship that would in circular fashion contribute to the later German sense of encirclement, as the alliance blocs began to solidify before the First World War.[38]

Second, Britain succeeded in reducing both the territory Russia had gained on the Ottoman border and that which Russia had allocated to Bulgaria at the abortive treaty of San Stefano earlier in 1878. Macedonia was accordingly restored to Ottoman control. In a move designed simultaneously to justify keeping the eastern Anatolian border regions under Ottoman authority, and to illustrate concern for the Christians of eastern Anatolia (who had undergone much hardship during the 1877–8 war and in the decades before, especially at the hands of Muslim refugees from Russia), Britain pressed Istanbul to concede reforms for the Armenian population of the area. Britain even considered suggesting what would later become a staple international solution to minority problems: a sort of population transfer, moving as many Armenians as possible into a few provinces where, as an outright demographic majority, they could be subject to a special regime.[39]

Even though Ottoman territorial losses to Russia had been reduced, it would remain an article of faith for the generation of leaders that brought the Empire into the First World War to regain the 'lost territories' of 1878—Kars, Ardahan, and Batum. And, far from protecting Armenians, the Armenian clauses in the Berlin Treaty left them exposed to enduring Ottoman accusations of treachery for appealing to an external power, like Bulgaria before. The reform clauses made no practical difference, as was shown by the impunity with which massacres of 80,000–100,000 Armenians were perpetrated in 1894–6.[40] As external impositions, the 'reforms' merely made Istanbul mistrust Britain almost as much as Russia, since both states were seen as giving Ottoman Christians power by proxy. Infringements of Ottoman internal sovereignty were increasingly seen as just as injurious as removal of territory, and the Empire was shortly to experience one of the greatest infringements of that sovereignty, in the form of the 'Ottoman Public Debt Administration' of 1881. This institution arrogated same Ottoman tax-raising powers to Paris and London in light of Istanbul's default on the loans raised over previous decades to fund Ottoman military campaigns and reforms.

The eastern crisis convinced the Istanbul elite of the hopelessness of trying to incorporate its non-Muslim populations by inclusive reform. It speeded the new Sultan, Abdülhamid II, down the road of 'pan-Islamism' (really pan-Sunniism), a neo-conservative doctrine in which Christians would be returned to their 'rightful', subordinate status. The massacres of 1894–6 were a means of putting the Armenians in their place—an extremely violent measure of ethnic dominance rather than, yet, exclusivity—and of warning them against future appeals to the Christian powers. They also showed that Istanbul had learned the lesson of the ethnic majoritarianism that had won the Balkan nations their independence: rather than the abortive British design of creating predominantly Armenian provinces in eastern Anatolia, massacres, forced conversions, and the strategic settlement of new Balkan Muslim refugees into the region reduced the concentration of Christians with a view to securing the lands within the Empire. Though the Empire awaited the secularizing revolution of the Committee of Union and Progress, it was already becoming a 'nationalizing state',[41] seeking to preserve the primacy of the Muslims—*millet-i hâkime*, or the dominant *millet*—by incremental demographic measures against competing groups.

One final effect of the Berlin Treaty was to leave Bulgaria with a sense of unfulfilled nationhood, an obsession with the San Stefano boundaries and the regaining of its 'rightful' territory in Macedonia. Bulgaria was equally preoccupied with acquiring Dobruja, which had been gifted by Russia to Romania in 1878 as Russia sought to mollify Romania after annexing Bessarabia after the 1877–8 war. The twin obsessions would be the driving force in Bulgarian foreign policy through to the Second World War, the main explanation for its alliance choices and one of the main reasons for the revanchist shift in internal population policy that the era of the world wars brought.

Minorities and the Limits of Sovereign Independence

The major disappointment greeting the elites of new nation-states like Bulgaria was the realization that statehood came with constraints imposed by great powers. This is not to say that all fell obediently into the subordinate roles desired of them. Particularly where different spheres of influence met, lesser states could play the powers against each another. Nevertheless, the battle for statehood was only the beginning, and was succeeded by continuing battles for genuine independence, for internal consolidation, and, thereafter, possibly for expansion. Hungry for resources, land, and prestige, the distance was short to the point where such small states themselves behaved like the 'imperial nations'[42] from which they had been liberated.

Romania, for instance, gained full independence from the Ottomans in 1878 after decades of increasingly autonomous status. It then found itself facing the very problems of internal intervention in state-minority relations that infuriated Istanbul from 1878 in its dealings with the Armenians. In the mid-nineteenth century, Romania's traditionally small Jewish population had swelled with refugees from persecution in Russia and Poland. These immigrants filled much-needed commercial roles when the nascent state was opened to foreign trade in 1829, but as a result they were sometimes subjected to the pogroms that had characterized Romanian-Jewish history, and to official discrimination denying them citizenship rights on religious grounds. Some nationalists suggested the presence of this 'foreign' community was suffocating any potential indigenous bourgeoisie. The refrain stressed the need to develop a 'national economy', as the German theorist Friedrich List called it, as he rejected the British laissez-faire model.

The matter of civil equality for Romanian Jews had first been raised in 1858, at the moment when Romanian autonomy was internationally guaranteed, as an extension of the equality that had been established two years previously in the Ottoman Empire. With full Romanian independence in 1878, and against the backdrop of persecution, the powers insisted as a sop to their own consciences that full citizenship be extended to non-Christians. But Romanian nationalists only saw in the move confirmation that Jews were in league with the outside world against the nation.[43] Though the minority stipulation also applied to Romanian Muslims, it remained a symbol of 'Jewish power', which to some degree it was (in the sense that French and German Jewish organizations had pressed for it), if with none of the sinister quality attributed to it. The anti-Semitic interpretation was given spurious substance by the fact that Bismarck's influential financial advisor, the Jewish banker Gerschon von Bleichröder, was instrumental in persuading Bismarck to press the minority issue, and benefited personally from the German economic penetration of independent Romania, by gaining a commanding stake in its oil industry.[44] Thus for Romania, as for the Ottoman Empire, and for Serbia and Montenegro, which were also subjected to the minorities treaties, the economic development of the country, the future of the dominant ethnic group, and the relationship of the state to the outside world were bound together with the question of its minorities.

The illusion of preponderant Jewish power would not be shattered by the detail that the outside world lifted barely a finger to protest at the non-implementation of the constitutional clauses on non-Christians, as Romania proceeded to implement its policies of ethnic dominance. Why did the powers, who had effectively set themselves up as guardians of Romanian and Ottoman minorities, not act as those minorities were abused and even massacred? First, they were not united. Second, attitudes towards minorities were always a flexible part of grand strategy. Discontented minorities could be either a focal point in themselves for the interventionist or irredentist goals of neighbouring states with some ethnic affinity or a cause of internal disturbance which might trigger external intervention by a larger power. Either eventuality might lead to interstate warfare, the avoidance of which was the main concern of statesmen interested in regional stability. Thus considerable latitude had traditionally been allowed for governmental violence against minorities provided it did not appear set to trigger interstate conflict.[45]

Eastern Continuities

For the Balkan states and the great powers, the final stage of the 'eastern question' that the eastern crisis introduced foretold the drawn-out

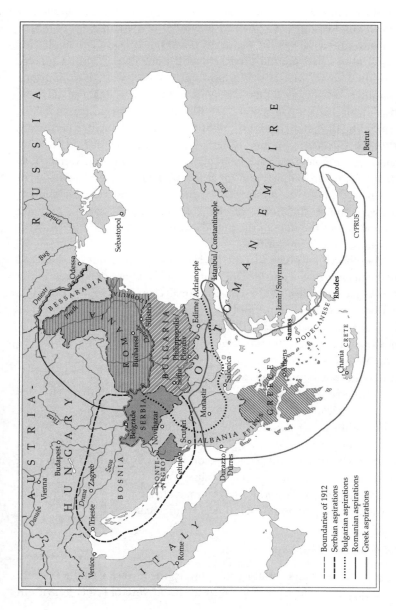

Map 1. The Balkans

Boundaries of 1912
Serbian aspirations
Bulgarian aspirations
Romanian aspirations
Greek aspirations

problems of the collapse of the Habsburg empire. The odd impression conveyed by much Western scholarship on this period is that the 43 years between the Franco-Prussian war and the First World War were years of European peace. This is only true if we ignore the eastern Mediterranean, while a glance at European violence in Africa would qualify out of existence any notion of a pacific epoch. In fact the Serbian–Bulgarian War of 1885, the Greco-Turkish War of 1897, the Macedonian Ilinden Uprising of 1903, the Italian-Turkish or 'Tripolitanian' war of 1911–12, and the two Balkan Wars of 1912–13 were all accompanied by often extensive violence against civilians. Each had distinctly ethnic aspects, coloured by religious sentiment: the Ottoman leaders of the resistance to Italy in Tripoli rallied their side with incitements to jihad—holy war—while the Christian states in the first Balkan war of 1912 declared themselves to be in crusade against Ottoman rule. The regional significance of these conflicts was such that in Serbia the First World War was sometimes referred to as the third Balkan war.

Of all of the Balkan conflicts, the most violent were the wars of 1912–13. The first involved Bulgaria, Serbia, Montenegro, and Greece allying against the Ottoman Empire and securing most of the territory of Macedonia and Thrace, with Bulgaria the greatest beneficiary as it sought to restore the San Stefano borders. The second war involved Bulgaria's erstwhile allies turning against it, and dividing up Macedonia amongst themselves, while the Ottoman Empire took advantage of the situation to recover eastern Thrace up to Edirne/Adrianople. Thereafter, the new possessors of Macedonia started forcibly assimilating the land and its people: in Aegean Macedonia place names were Hellenized, and the name Macedonia and the Macedonian language were banned; Serbian Macedonia was dubbed 'southern Serbia'.

During the Balkan wars, ethnic groups on the 'wrong' side of any border were used alternately as recruiting grounds for irregular warfare and targets for collective reprisals. 'Alien' populations in lands coveted or conquered by the participants were subjected to massacre, ethnic cleansing, terror, and forced conversion or assimilation by way of con-solidation of the conqueror's control. Many soldiers swapped sides to join their ethnic brethren. These wars were conducted 'at the high noon of mass ethnic nationalism, undertaken by states bent on shaping their territories in accordance with maximalist—and often fantastically exaggerated—claims of ethnic demography and committed to moulding their heterogeneous populations into relatively homogeneous national wholes'.[46] Nevertheless, we should not ascribe the extreme violence to popular passions unleashed. Public sentiment was manipulated by nationalist elites seeking to inculcate nationalism in their often apolitical countrymen, while much of the killing was, again, done by paramilitary forces often operating with their own local agendas.[47] In any case, Muslim civilians were again the primary—but by no means the only—victims of the massive violence, with tens of thousands of deaths and as many as 400,000 fleeing into Ottoman Anatolia.

The wars marked the end of any vestige of inter-religious pluralism in the Ottoman Empire, and the beginning of an even more intense obsession with the ethnic make-up of the remaining lands. A new organization, the Directorate for the Settlement of Tribes and Immigrants, was established within the Interior Ministry to settle Muslim refugees. In a further systematization of Abdülhamid's policy of strategic Muslim refugee settlement, the Directorate developed plans for the targeted deportations of non-Muslim groups from areas of concentration, where they constituted threatening pluralities or even majorities, in order to ensure Turkic-Muslim ethnic dominance in Anatolia. Even some non-Sunni and non-Turkish groups were scheduled for relocation, since the recent secession from the Empire of predominantly Muslim Albania pushed the new ruling faction in the Ottoman government, the Committee of Union and Progress (CUP), into suspicion of even some of their co-religionists.

Many of the CUP members were atheists anyway, and believers in social Darwinism and sociological positivism—the idea that human problems were susceptible to scientific quantification, analysis, and solution.[48] By any standards, they were modern men. Most of them hailed from the lands lost or under imminent threat in 1912–13, and accordingly were highly sensitized to the issues at stake. While their prime goal was to save the Empire, they were increasingly adopting the means and mindsets of ethnonationalists. They were also in the process of trying to coerce the state administration into line with party ideology.[49]

In the aftermath of the Balkan wars, a new practice was introduced into European diplomacy and population politics: a population exchange in the interests of mutual ethnic homogenization, as agreed between erstwhile combatants. This was mandated by the Ottoman Empire and Bulgaria. It accommodated the new post-1913 boundaries that marked the expulsion of the Ottomans from all of Europe bar their sliver of Thrace. In actuality, the exchange was merely a retrospective legitimation of a fait accompli.[50] All that was really left to do was to sort out property claims, which was an integral component of ethnic cleansing in pursuit of the 'national economy' so desired by ethnonationalists. Indeed, the Balkan wars also brought intensified policies of ethnic dominance against ethnic groups not involved in the conflict. An extensive boycott of Greek businesses along the Ottoman Aegean coast also affected Armenians, as the government attempted to stimulate the development of a Turkic-Muslim bourgeoisie by removal of the Christian competition.

Ethnic Tensions in Wider Europe

The impulse to ensure ethnic dominance was not restricted to the Ottoman lands, though the Balkan wars made the Ottoman case more violent. In the spirit of the times, 1912 also saw Polish boycotts of Jewish businesses. During the coming world war, Russia would adopt similar policies towards some of its Jews and ethnic Germans as part of an early and incomplete process of 'nationalizing' the empire.[51] Elsewhere in Europe, if this was not a time of warfare and ethnic cleansing, it certainly was a time of mass population movement. In the decades prior to the First World War, as European and Caucasian Muslims were driven into the remaining Ottoman lands of Anatolia, central and eastern Europe saw the internal movement of some five million Christian refugees, including Slovenes, Slovaks, Croats, and Germans, leaving the mixed lands of their birth.

The arrival of many refugees in Germany, plus the influx there from the end of the nineteenth century of more than a million foreign workers, particularly Poles and Ruthenes, enhanced German anti-Slav chauvinism.[52] These numbers were augmented by more than two and a half million Jews leaving the western Russian lands and Habsburg

Galicia. The deeper causes of the Jewish exodus lay with socio-economic factors, including the changes accompanying the modernization programmes which, together with urbanization, squeezed out many Jewish artisans and small tradesmen. Yet the pogroms after the assassination of Alexander II added numbers and urgency to the flight westwards, and furthered the willingness of many Jews to embrace their own form of integral nationalism—Zionism, the movement for the establishment of a Jewish home in Palestine—in the quest for safe domicile.[53]

Refugee and migrant movement stimulated greater discrimination against Jews in the immigration policies of intended destinations, including Germany, Britain, and the USA, and prompted rhetoric of the damage immigrants would do to national identity in the host countries. Each recipient state was concerned that arrivals be assimilable and of 'good racial stock', to use the contemporary terminology. Accordingly, Romanies seeking to emigrate faced a more difficult task than any. In 1885 they were forbidden entry altogether to the USA.

The arrival of eastern European Jews discomfited some of the western Jewish communities, which were on the whole more assimilated. Western Jewish populations evinced feelings of cultural superiority and anxiety that the newcomers might upset the delicate modus vivendi established under the 'enlightenment contract' in these more stable and developed states. In France, Germany, and Austria the visibility of the Jews as a community was increased by the influx of eastern migrants into the towns and cities, where Jews were already highly represented relative to their total national numbers.

The vulnerability of the Jewish migrants did little to allay suspicions of the hidden power of the Jews that was strengthened by the 1878 minorities treaties and the 1881 assassination of the Tsar. Pogroms in 1903–6 in the Ukraine had as a motive resentment of the commercial position of some Jews at a time of economic downturn, but the proliferation of pogroms around October 1905 can only be attributed to the liberalizing Russian 'revolution' of that moment, where, once again, Jews were held to be revolutionaries undermining the old order for their own benefit. After 1905, an increasing number of monarchist organizations with Russian ethnonationalist tendencies came into being. Most notable was the Union of the Russian People, which enjoyed Nicholas II's support, and which was involved with the militias collectively known as the Black Hundreds that perpetrated extensive attacks on Jewish communities. The revolutionary year was also notable for the increased popularity of a forgery that had been created by reactionary anti-Semites in the late nineteenth century and was first published in 1903. The *Protocols of the Learned Elders of Zion* purported to be an instruction manual for worldwide Jewish conspirators in using any and every means of subversion against national systems.[54]

Resentful anxiety and envy over politicized ethnic status hierarchies exploded elsewhere in the fraught circumstances of 1905. Russians were assailed in Lithuania, as were ethnic German landlords and pastors in Latvia and Estonia. This was a time at which 'pan-German' activists were taking an intensified interest in, and pressing for the protection of, ethnic Germans in Russia and elsewhere. Baltic German notables themselves were seeking to attract ethnic German farmers from elsewhere in eastern Europe as a counterbalance to the increasingly assertive Baltic peoples. Azeris in Baku in Russian Azerbaijan attacked the city's Armenians, who were disproportionately significant in the skilled labour market, among leftist political parties, and in positions of economic importance.[55] Such expressions of socio-economic-cum-ethnic antipathy would be given a massive impetus amid world war, the collapse of two more empires, and further revolution in Russia. The war itself brought home to Europe a conflict between major states that had hitherto been expressed only as imperial competition on the soil of Africa and Asia.

CHAPTER 2
THE FIRST WORLD WAR ERA

Introduction: The First World War and its Legacies of Violence

The immediate origin of the First World War in the Balkans is one of the best-known tales of modern history. A small, new nation-state—Serbia—with irredentist aims in a neighbouring territory—Bosnia—provoked a dynastic power—the Habsburg empire—that had itself recently annexed the contested territory from a rival empire—the Ottoman. For the major continental powers drawn into the dispute between Serbia and Austria–Hungary after the assassination of Franz Ferdinand in Sarajevo, victory might mean strategic territorial expansion. Each cast eyes on nearby territory, whether it be French designs on 'recovering' Alsace-Lorraine from Germany, Russian designs on Constantinople, Bukovina, and Austrian Galicia, the Ottoman quest to restore the 'lost territories' of 1878, or German aspirations to annex a 'frontier strip' of territory from the west of Tsarist Poland or resource-rich land in Belgium and Luxemburg.[1] Most of these aims, if achieved, would have resulted in demographic engineering of some degree. Nevertheless, for these great powers the First World War was not primarily a war about ethnic consolidation or expanded formal empire in Europe.

No matter how it ended, the war began for the continental balance of power, greater political and economic influence within Europe, and greater access to markets and resources without. The exception among the major combatants was the weaker Ottoman Empire. For the Committee of Union and Progress (CUP) the war was mainly a fight for independence: an opportunity to remove the burden of external intervention in the form of the extraterritoriality agreements, the Public Debt Administration, and the latest Armenian reform plan that had been foisted onto the empire at the close of the Balkan wars.

The contrast was marked between the Ottoman war experience and that of the more advanced war machines of the northwestern nation-states. The disparity was not in the quantity of violence but in its quality. Britain and France fought against Germany primarily in pitched battles on the Western Front. There, with the exception of a flurry of war crimes committed by the German army in Belgium and northern France in the early race to assumed victory, the massive slaughter of the flower of their youth was conducted almost entirely within the laws of war as developed between urbane Europeans out of pragmatism and cultural fraternity. The very fact that the rules of Western civilization permitted the massacres of tens of thousands per day at Verdun, the Somme, and Passchendaele surely goes a good distance to explaining the stunning cultural impact of the war on its participant states.[2]

The war confirmed the potential of the nation-state to mobilize its citizenry, and, for the most part, confirmed the appeal of national-ism over socialism or other forms of internationalism. An impressive historiography illustrates the trauma of the battlefront experience in cheapening human life, shaping the generation that fought the war and the generation that came after, and introducing more radical forms of politics and new political communities that rejected liberalism as a basis for collective life. In so far as the emphasis in this strand of scholarship is also placed on the mechanized killing and dehumanizing effects of trench warfare, its ramifications are clearly intended to extend to the industrialized murder of Auschwitz.[3] The particular approach of these accounts, however, downplays less dramatic but equally significant forms of killing, such as the British blockade of Germany. Studies of the impact of the Western Front are by definition based on the experience of the three northwestern states, with their advanced, urbanized industrial societies, participatory politics, and civil societies. They are not repres-entative of the experiences of other states and peoples. The established strand of interpretation is necessary in helping to explain subsequent German aggression, British appeasement, and French collaboration in the Second World War, but must be complemented by additional lineages of political violence for a fuller understanding of genocide in 1939–45.

A focus on the dynastic empires during and immediately after their collapse illuminates many things. In the Ottoman case, it highlights the first full case of genocide in greater Europe in the modern period, along with associated policies of demographic engineering. The lessons of continuing ethnic cleansing around the eastern Mediterranean were heeded by nationalists and great power system-managers elsewhere. In the Russian case, it illustrates the wartime radicalization of German territorial ambition in the east. That ambition went hand-in-hand with notions of bringing imperial 'order' to an 'inferior' region. To this central European chauvinism the Bolshevik Revolution then generated an additional violent, counter-revolutionary urge of massive anti-Semitic potential, providing the target for the developing European right-wing movements, and prolonging the ravages of war in an area of competing national and cross-cutting class-based movements. In the case of eastern Europe as a whole, a focus on the former Habsburg, Romanov, and Ottoman domains is a focus on the area where genocide happened in the Second World War. This was no mere coincidence of geographies. The fragmentation and reordering of the region from the Baltic Sea to the Black Sea and from Russia to the western German border tells us much about who—besides Germans—killed whom and why, during the Second World War, and provides a major context for Nazi colonial policies.

Irredentism, Ethnic Insurgency, and State Paranoia

Most of the lesser participants in the First World War had emerged from the retreating Ottoman and Habsburg empires. For them, the issues involved in going to war in 1914–18 and 1939–45 respectively were more similar than they were for the greatest protagonists. In both conflicts, new land and some of its human occupants composed the primary stake for these less powerful states (alongside fear of the loss of their newfound independence), and their allegiance could be purchased on promise of the reward at the postwar reckoning. In their alliance choices in the First World War, Serbia, Bulgaria, Greece, and Romania all gave priority to the quest for adjacent territory. Italy did too, with respect to Dalmatia and Albania, though in its pretensions to great power status and dominance of the eastern Mediterranean, it also craved African land and much the same territory on the Turkish coast that Greece sought in fulfilment of its own *megali idea*, the vision of a greater state incorporating the Orthodox population of western Anatolia.

The great powers not only exploited the expansionist ambitions of smaller states (often cynically, giving false promises to Italy and Romania), they also stoked the fires of ethnonationalism and state paranoia in their attempts to attack weak points in the opposing alliance. The maritime empires were targeted in their colonies, and the land empires were targeted through their subject nationalities, with the intimation of liberation in return for rebellion—though Germany also supported left-wing revolutionary groups in Russia. Germany appealed to Ukrainian nationalists, Georgian Christians, and Jews within the Russian empire, and the Republican Irish; together with the Ottoman Empire, Germany sought to incite the Muslims of the Caucasus, central Asia, and India; Britain appealed to Arab nationalism; France maintained links with Lebanese and Syrian Christians and some Armenian and Greek nationalists; Russia exploited the aspirations of Czechs, and, in Ottoman territory, of Armenians, Kurds, and Assyrian Christians; almost everyone played on Polish nationalism. Most of the attempts at stimulating insurgency had very limited results, as the prospective cannon fodder on the ground proved less enthusiastic for self-sacrifice than their nationalist leaders and the fantasies of émigrés predicted.

Of all attempts to exploit minority sentiment, the most variable involved the Jews. Because of the power attributed to Jews, their loyalty was a subject of particular interest to both warring sides. Russia, especially its anti-Semitic military leadership, feared Jewish leftists of various persuasions and Jewish allegiance to the Habsburgs and to Germany, whence Jews had found safe haven over the previous decades. This suspicion was only reinforced by proclamations and appeals to Russia's Jews from the central powers' supreme command, endorsed by the German-Jewish 'Committee for the Liberation of the Jews of Russia'. The combination of established anti-Semitism, proximate 'provocation', and the state's desires to remove Jews from economic positions and to remove putatively hostile elements from newly conquered territory helps explain why, from late 1914, troops from the Russian army and its Cossack regiments, and members of the local populations, were allowed to massacre large numbers of Jews in the Galician and Bukovinan territories taken from the Habsburg empire. In a pattern that would become common in ensuing years, the imaginary Jewish fifth column was also blamed for Russian military failures.[4]

Germany itself was seeing a surge in anti-Semitism at the time. The immediate background was the 1912 Reichstag elections, which had seen significant gains by the Left, and were accordingly interpreted by many German conservatives as a victory for Judaism. They were dubbed the 'Judenwahlen', or 'Jewish elections'. In wartime itself, the notion that Jews were profiteering and hiding from battle while Germans perished led to the 'Judenzählung', or 'Jew-count', of 1916—a census, supported by most mainstream political parties, to establish the relative proportions of Jews and non-Jews at the front. Its findings of no significant discrepancy were concealed during the conflict, allowing cynical rumours to circulate that it had uncovered precisely what the anti-Semites predicted. Polish Jews conscripted for work in the German war economy became obvious targets for this wave of hatred, which succeeded in early 1918 in prompting the authorities to close the German border to the group.

There was a third variation on the theme of Jewish power. The attempt to maintain 'international Jewish support' for the Allied war effort was ultimately behind the British offer of what the dispersed Jews could never hope to achieve in Europe. That was a Jewish national home in the Ottoman Palestinian territory Britain had earmarked for postwar control.[5]

If Jews were alternately victims and 'beneficiaries' of a paranoia itself alternating between anti-Semitism and its twin, philo-Semitism, the greatest immediate losers of the ill-fated obsession with insurgency were the Armenians. The Ottoman 'Assyrian' Christians (Süryani and Asuri) came a close second.[6] As Germany and the Ottomans used Muslim 'self-defence' groups in the Caucasus to cause problems in the Russian military rear, so Russia tried to stimulate minorities behind Ottoman lines, using special armed units of Russian Armenian subjects to appeal to the Anatolian Armenian communities. Like all other such policies, this met with only slight success, but it fed pre-existing, chauvinist views of concentrated minority populations serving as the focus of external irredentist claims or great power manipulation. The Russian insurgency policy dovetailed precisely with the existing Ottoman suspicion of the Christian populations' associations with the Entente powers, and helped confirm the CUP's own view that these groups had no place in the Anatolian future.

The Armenian and Assyrian Genocides

Up to a point, CUP population policy in the First World War mirrored that of the Tsars and the Habsburgs. After a series of localized 'pacification' measures in their shared border regions from the outset of the war (measures bloodier than those deployed by Germany against suspected *francs-tireurs* in France and Belgium at the time), and incursions into enemy territory, each regime radicalized its policies in spring 1915 as the war situation became critical. As the Entente attempted to invade the Ottoman Empire at the Gallipoli peninsula, and Russia likewise through eastern Anatolia, and as a new offensive of the central powers opened on the Eastern Front, both states began to deport hundreds of thousands of members of 'suspect' minorities from behind their lines. The fear of ethnic fifth columns who would join with advancing enemy forces found expression in the Tsarist deportation not only of perhaps a million Jews from Russian and formerly Habsburg territory, but of Volhynian and other ethnic Germans (dubbed 'colonists' because of their earlier settlement patterns), Poles, Latvians, and Lithuanians, as well as Chinese and Koreans, and of Muslims in the Caucasus and central Asia.[7] At about the time the major Armenian deportations began, the Russian authorities in the Caucasus considered deporting all of the Muslims of Kars and Batum — the Ottoman 'lost territories' — as a security measure. The Austro-Hungarian authorities contributed to the overall picture of coercive population movement by forcibly resettling Ruthenes when they re-took Galicia, on suspicion that they were pro-Russian.

One important explanation of why Russian Caucasus policy did not become genocidal in 1915 stresses that, in contrast to the later Bolshevik leadership, Russia was under an older-style managerial authoritarian regime, characterized by bureaucratic checks-and-balances, and more traditional precepts of population management.[8] The imperial disposition did not, however, prevent the Russian massacre of large numbers of Kyrgyz in Central Asia the following year as the Muslim population rose up in rejection of the increasingly desperate Tsarist conscription policy: by some estimates 100,000 people in total were killed by the army or perished under the conditions of 'Urkun' (the 'exodus') as they fled towards China. Whatever the precise balance of issues within Russia, a comparative glance at the Ottoman Empire in 1915 reveals that the CUP was certainly less institutionally bound and further down the road of ethnonationalism. The faction had risen violently to power, and had an insecure hold on its authority and a determination to penetrate and control the Ottoman state according to its own political and ethnic priorities. Unlike Russia, the civilian leadership of the Ottoman empire was more ideological radical than the military. The CUP had a paramilitary arm—the 'Special Organization'—which had served both to coerce political opponents and to terrorize the Aegean Greek population before the war, and which would now be one of the main instruments used in the murder of the Armenians.

It soon became clear that what was happening to the Armenians and Assyrians was qualitatively different from anything happening elsewhere at the time. It was different because these Christian groups were being targeted almost in their entirety and with the intention of permanent removal: on 17 June, CUP Interior Minister Talât averred the intention to use cover of war to finish for good with the Empire's 'inner enemies', thereby removing forever the problems of external diplomatic interference.[9] It was different because the deportation destinations of the deserts of Syria and Iraq were not remotely fit for habitation by large numbers of people from a temperate mountainous plateau. At the beginning of May 1915 the Ottoman leadership had considered simply forcing Armenians over the Russian border,[10] but this idea was dismissed because it was feared that the Armenians would join Russian ranks and return with invading forces. So the deportation had to be arranged in such a way that the deportees would neither return nor remain an external threat, which meant keeping them within Ottoman control in an area where they would inevitably experience massive loss of life.

The situation was also different to other simultaneous atrocities and movements of peoples because, where massacres did not occur in situ, which they did for most of the Assyrians and for Armenian men of fighting age, the deportees were systematically massacred en route. Women, children, and the elderly were attacked by paramilitaries, some army units, and elements of the surrounding Muslim population as they were forced into the deserts, with kidnap for sexual slavery or acculturation as Muslims the only alternative to murder during the march or at the desert destinations. In the deserts, a further round of massacres in the summer of 1916 finished off most survivors. The victim groups were targeted for ethnic destruction rather than the earlier policy of ethnic domination. The small number of survivors would be so enfeebled and isolated as to be irrelevant as a collective. Perhaps 300,000 Assyrians and up to 1.2 million Armenians, out of a population of two million, were killed.

Contrary to CUP propaganda, the property of the deportees was not kept safely, nor were the deportees remunerated. Some of the proceeds of legalized state theft went straight into the pockets of corrupt officials, some to local landowners and bigwigs, and some to provide for the Muslim refugees fleeing wartime Russian measures in the Caucasus, and the victims of ethnic cleansing in the Balkan wars. In this capital transfer, we see genocide also paved the way for the complete fulfilment of the established policy of ethnic domination through expropriation.

There was more, in the form of another series of Ottoman policies of ethnic dominance as opposed to outright excision. Owing only partly to wartime upheaval, up to one-third of the Anatolian population of more than 17 million people migrated internally or were subject to 'relocation'. Circassians, Albanian, Bosnian and Georgian Muslims, Kurds, 'Gypsies', and some Jews and Arab groups were moved around the Empire, during and after the war, for purposes of assimilation and in some cases, punishment, though none were so comprehensively dislocated as the Armenians, and none subject to the same near-total murder.[11] For instance, approximately 300,000 Muslim Kurds were deported westwards through Anatolia in 1917 and settled in Turkish areas in order to assimilate them. Under the orchestration of the Directorate for the Settlement of Tribes and Immigrants, a 'io per cent rule' operated, whereby non-Turkish populations were not allowed to exceed that proportion of the local population.

It bears repeating that the Armenian and Assyrian genocides were extreme measures even by the standards of the time. Yet for consideration of violent ethnopolitics in the era of the world wars, CUP policy is highly relevant. It illustrates the fusion of geopolitical, ethnic, and economic considerations in strategic design, and the fallacy of any attempt to pinpoint one or other of the three factors as somehow decisive on its own. Moreover, it shows the range of population policies available to sufficiently radicalized states at moments of crisis and licence. Policies ranged from outright genocide of populations deemed too dangerous or unassimilable, through more-or-less coercive assimilation of populations considered sufficiently culturally similar or malleable, to material provision for the well being of members of the 'core people' and their settlement in newly 'secured' areas.

In the aftermath of genocide, the fluctuations of the Russi-an–Ottoman front and the ensuing collapse of state rule in Anatolia brought the region to a point of anarchy in 1916–17. In this situation, a bewildering array of ethnic groups, cross-cutting in allegiance with political doctrines and great powers, fought an entirely criminal set of small wars against each other. Aspects of the situation were replicated to the north of the Black Sea.

'Ethnic' Revolution and Counter-revolution in Eastern and Central Europe

To the north, the unravelling of the Russian and Habsburg empires began around 1915, with German and then later Bolshevik designs for the region providing competing imperial models for the vacated space. The fluidity of the central powers' Eastern Front meant that huge areas from Poland eastwards were temporarily depopulated and their infrastructure devastated, rendering them more susceptible to economic crisis, intergroup antagonism, and the sort of socio-economic restructuring that any new imperial imposition would entail.

Germany occupied much of Poland from summer 1915. Anti-Slavism was clearly present in German attitudes: this was, after all, a war in which Germanic *Kultur* was supposedly at stake. Accordingly, Russian prisoners of war were treated worse than western Europeans, and the Russian army's destruction of German settlements brought German responses in kind in Russian Poland. Large numbers of people thought sympathetic to Russia were driven out of areas of German control. Nevertheless, despite German forced labour programmes, which brought tens of thousands of Poles as well as Jews into Germany, despite extensive war requisitioning, and despite a clear sense of superiority, German occupation policies as a whole towards Poles were somewhat restrained; there was a desire to extend formal and informal influence without alienating Poland during war. This would have changed had Germany prevailed in the conflict and been able to implement its plans for seizing western Poland almost up to Warsaw, removing the indigenous rural population and replacing them with a 'reliable' frontier population of ethnic Germans from Germany itself and from throughout eastern Europe.[12]

To the northeast, in and around Lithuania, German attitudes were different because of the early expectation that the territory would return to Russia and the later expectation that it might be thoroughly absorbed into the German sphere. In the Baltic the old ethnic German communities were supposed to play a Germanizing role and provide the basis for the developing German claims to the area. As in Poland, some Lithuanian Jews welcomed the German arrival, but while the anti-Semitism of the German military leadership did not bring physical persecution, it did bring discrimination. Jews were a target in the restructuring of a local economy in German interests. However, they were only part of the picture in the eyes of an occupier who perceived 'the east' according to established conceptions as primitive, dirty, disease-ridden, unhealthily ethnically mixed, and in desperate need of Germanic order.[13] Many German soldiers returned from the Eastern Front with an increased conviction of their own superiority, while the tradition of academic experts pondering Germany's past and future relations with the 'Russian east' was given a great boost.[14]

The Bolshevik revolution of October 1917 presented the opportunity for a radical expansion of German imperial goals and lent a new ideological twist to international relations north of the Black Sea. As a result of initial refusal to accept German demands for the 'independence' of Poland and Lithuania (which Germany already occupied), the Bolsheviks were obliged to accept the peace treaty of Brest-Litovsk in March 1918, by which they also ceded the territories of present-day Ukraine and Belarus. Fertile and rich in natural resources, the control of these huge territories would have decisively influenced the continental balance in Germany's favour over the longer term. As it was, German forces had to retire after the armistice of November 1918.

It is one of history's great ironies that in the interests of destabilizing Russia, Germany helped smuggle Lenin into the country in 1917 and financed the Bolsheviks, only to become their most radical antagonist in the coming generation. In a continental war where the 'fifth column' had become a subject of such intense paranoia and propaganda, irrespective of reality, the Bolsheviks were an 'internal enemy' that actually did succeed. The Bolshevik coup introduced an element not seen in European politics since the French Revolution: a regime whose very ideology threatened the established order of states, whatever the precise balance of power among the traditional regimes.

Like 1789, the Bolshevik Revolution too could be seen through the prism of its emancipatory consequences for Jews. This seemed to follow from the stereotype of Jews as left-wing subversives, as embodied in their representation in the Russian 'Populist' movement and its successor, the Socialist Revolutionary Party; in the socialist Jewish workers' organization the 'Bund'; and in the ranks and leadership of the Russian Social Democratic Party that spawned both Bolsheviks and Mensheviks.[15] The association of Jews and revolutionaries also seemed to follow from the anti-Christianity and internationalism of the Bolsheviks, and was heavily played upon by the 'White' Russian forces as they tried to orchestrate resistance against the revolutionaries. It fed into deeper cultural traditions that had for many centuries depicted Jews as conspiratorial subversives.[16]

In February 1918, Kaiser Wilhelm II of Germany declared that the 'Russian people [are] at the mercy of the revenge of the Jews, who are allied with all Jews of the world.' In endorsing covert paramilitary action against the Jew-Bolsheviks in the Baltic he said the campaign had an immediate precedent: 'analogy Turks in Armenia'.[17] Less extreme men than Wilhelm II subscribed to the same associations. American military intelligence was little short of obsessed with the notion of the Jewish domination of the Bolshevik movement, Lenin the puppet of Trotsky and a host of other concealed Jews. Stimulated in part by the German connection, a number of agents spent the early postwar years seeking to prove the existence of the international Jewish conspiracy.[18] In 1920 Winston Churchill alluded to 'the international Soviet of the Russian and Polish Jew'; and one of the underlying logics of his support of a Jewish state in Palestine was that encouraging Jewish nationalism would wean Jews off Bolshevism.[19] The *Protocols of the Learned Elders of Zion* gained a very broad readership in the immediate post-revolutionary years, encouraged by counter-revolutionary forces, and was translated into western European languages from 1919–20. Its exposure as a forgery in 1921 did not reverse its earlier impact. In other words there was a significant body of opinion across the world that Bolshevism was not just a socio-political revolution; it was also somehow an *ethnic revolution* that had brought the Jewish fifth column to unprecedented political power.

The threat to the established global economic and power system from the avowedly internationalist Bolshevism was something on which all other powers could agree. At points, most of them, Japan included, sought to support counter-revolutionary forces in Russia with men, materiel, and money. International intervention and opposition in turn provided the paranoiac stimulant and the opportunity for repeated Bolshevik assaults on 'class enemies' and internal 'subversives', including whole populations like the Terek and Don Cossacks. Meanwhile, the Bolshevik doctrine of exporting revolution provided the powers in Europe and beyond with a parallel set of fears and an enduring incentive to destroy the Bolshevik regime.

The first war against Bolshevism in Europe in 1918–22 can be divided into three conceptual theatres of battle: beyond the Romanov shatterzone; within that shatterzone; and places in which international and internal armed forces interacted. The first sphere involved central Europe, and the three defeated states of Germany, Austria, and Hungary, each of which was exposed to varying levels of communist revolutionary threat. By far the most serious threat transpired in Hungary, where, uniquely, between March and August 1919 a communist government was established under the leadership of Béla Kun as the previous, liberal Károlyi regime collapsed under the weight of the massive territorial concessions demanded by the Entente. Part of Kun's manifesto was the reacquisition of some of these lands, showing that nationalism could also be used as a vessel for far-left politics. The communists were then defeated by Romanian invasion, which allowed Bucharest to annex Transylvania with its large Romanian population. A communist rising in Austria in November 1918 was instantly repressed. The 'Spartacist' uprising in Berlin at the beginning of 1919 was crushed with only slightly more difficulty by the forces available to the German Social Democratic Chancellor Ebert, which included the right-wing paramilitaries of the *Freikorps*. With their new-found legitimacy, these forces then moved on to Munich to destroy the brief and unstable 'communist republic of Bavaria'.

Though of varying degrees of gravity, the communist risings all raised the spectre of an enemy within, to go alongside the hostile outside world that had left Austria, Hungary, and Germany so diminished in defeat. The internal enemy was instantly judaified, both for familiar reasons and because of the relatively high proportion of Jews in communist leadership positions, including Rosa Luxemburg, Kurt Eisner in Bavaria, and Kun himself (pointedly dubbed 'Béla Cohen' by Churchill), as well as in non-revolutionary Social Democrat parties. The prominent female role in the same movements further persuaded right-wing conservatives and extremists of the extent of degeneration within their society. It was from radicalized elements within different shades of the political Right, ranging from proto-fascists to monarchical conservatives, that a genuinely international counter-revolutionary movement emerged from 1918 onwards.

The counter-revolutionary international was loosely federated, but marked by structural similarities, personal contacts, and collaboration across national lines. It included some Russian émigré anti-Bolsheviks,[20] but most members were defined not just by anti-communism and anti-Semitism but by anti-Slavism, as would become evident in the vicious conduct of its paramilitaries around the same time in fighting over national boundaries between Germany and Poland in Upper Silesia, and Austria and Yugoslavia in Carinthia and Styria. (Austria and Hungary also fought over the Burgenland.) Figureheads of the movement included Adm. Miklós Horthy, the Regent of Hungary from 1920, and the influential and notoriously anti-Semitic Gen. Erich Ludendorff. The actual commanders and the rank-and-file, organized in various paramilitary outfits, of which the *Freikorps* are only the most notorious, combined two age cohorts that would together provide most of the drive for the later Nazi movement. The first cohort were those with first-hand experience of the First World War, particularly middle-ranking officers such as captains and lieutenants, who would be of the age for senior military leadership in the next World War. The second cohort were those born too late to serve—the so-called 'war-youth generation'. Both generations could express their frustrations at German defeat, and the younger generation could prove itself in a situation where the laws of war did not exist. Everywhere, their violence was disproportionately directed towards Jews, but while in Germany and Austria after the crushing of the communist risings it was restricted to individual murders, such as the assassination of Foreign Minister Walther Rathenau in 1922, with the wide license provided in post-Béla Kun Hungary, the death toll of enemies under the 'White Terror' reached at least 1,500.[21]

The Baltic States, particularly Latvia, provided the theatre where the external war against Bolshevism fused most thoroughly with local dynamics. Within former Romanov territory, the German defeat gave the opportunity either for the Bolsheviks to re-expand or for the inhabitants of the westerly territories to achieve self-rule. In the Baltic, the British permitted German forces to remain into 1919 to bolster local resistance against the Red Army. The most enthusiastic for this task were a combination of far-right-wingers, adventurers, unemployed ex-soldiers, and landless labourers seeking their own piece of Baltic land. Included were elements of the German Eighth Army and volunteers from Germany itself, who viewed their mission as an extension of the German domestic fight against the Left. In their number were many future Nazis including Rudolf Höss, the future *Kommandant* of Auschwitz. These men were constituted as *Freikorps* units and were reinforced by the *Baltische Landeswehr*, which was composed largely of local ethnic Germans. Their own agenda was to defeat Bolshevism and then install German-dominated regimes in the Baltic. They succeeded in the first aim but were ordered to disband before they could attain the second, leaving them to propound another version of the 'stab in the back' tale that so many of their compatriots were already telling to explain away the defeat of 1918. The violence entailed in their actions was colossal and generally indiscriminate. While suffering around 30,000 fatalities themselves, by one estimate they killed up to 100,000 opponents and civilians.[22]

To the south of the Baltic States, the dynamics of communist–anti-communist war inside the western Romanov shatterzone blended with the wars of nationalists for contested territory. A major territorial victor of the transition from Romanov to Bolshevik empire was Romania, which, in addition to gaining Transylvania from Hungary, and Dobruja from Bulgaria, reacquired Bessarabia and Bukovina. In 1919 Ukrainian nationalists enjoyed a brief period of sovereignty, fighting Bolshevik and counter-revolutionary 'White Russian' forces to entrench independence, and fighting Polish forces for contested territory. Losing to Poland over eastern Galicia and Volhynia, in April 1920 Ukrainian forces then allied with Poland against the Bolsheviks. Fluctuating fortunes in the Bolshevik–Polish conflict combined with the more decisive defeat of the Ukrainians to produce a Bolshevik–Polish peace treaty in March 1921 in which Ukrainian territory was divided between the two signatory powers. Poland also gained Vilnius at Lithuanian expense in 1922.

Relative peace in the west by 1922 allowed the Bolsheviks to focus on defeating the disparate internal counter-revolutionary forces, thus bringing to an end one of the most vicious and criminal conflicts of the world war era. As well as hundreds of thousands of military deaths on each 'side', and countless civilian deaths from privation, Bolshevik forces murdered tens of thousands of 'class enemies'. The 'Whites' murdered large numbers of communists, but the 'Volunteer Army' of Gen. Anton Denikin in particular reserved its greatest atrocities for the Jewish populations of the western and southwestern territories in which they had their support base. Ukrainian and Polish nationalist forces and various peasant factions also participated in the slaughter of

Jews, for whom the overall death toll reached at least 50,000. Though a (relatively small) number of Jews were murdered by communists, this did not shake the conviction of the nationalists and counter-revolutionaries about Judeo-Bolshevism, which was intertwined with accusations that the Jews were German agents. The depth of anti-Semitic conviction is illustrated by the fact that no top-down policy or formalized orders seem to have existed for the killing of Jews across a huge territory; it was a common political instinct to take revenge on Jews for the revolution and remove them so that they could not assume socio-political superiority. There were elements of pogrom here, if on a massive scale, but beyond its intrinsic significance, the often systematic murder of Jews in 1917–19 is noteworthy because the primary agents were now official militaries and organized militias.[23]

Continuing Ethnic Warfare in the Caucasus and Anatolia

The peripheries that the Bolsheviks had most difficulty 'pacifying' after the civil war were the North Caucasus and Central Asia. In the former, the 'de-Cossackization' campaign continued, if with decreasing intensity, while the population of the mountainous region provided much the same difficulties as they had for the Tsars over the previous one hundred and fifty years. Chechnya in particular was the site of a massive and bloody assault by the Red Army as late as 1925.[24]

The southern Caucasus was at the intersection of the shatterzones of the Romanov and Ottoman empires, and provided the stage for similar patterns of intergroup violence during the temporary weakness of major regional powers as did the Ukraine and the Baltic states. The peoples of the region experienced a brief independence between the end of Tsarist dominion and the imposition of Bolshevik rule on one hand and between the Ottoman defeat and the nationalist Turkish resurgence under Kemal on the other hand. They took advantage of this time to establish states, fight amongst themselves over border territory, and ethnically cleanse any such territory of other ethnoreligious groups, with Armenia and Azerbaijan particularly culpable. The Turkish advance into the Caucasus in 1920, which ended such arguments and resulted in the recovery of the 'lost territories' of 1878, looked very like a continuation of the earlier genocide in its violence against the Caucasian Armenians.

There had been two stimuli to Kemal's movement, and both indicated the ongoing influence of great powers from beyond the region. One stimulus was the 1919 Greek occupation of Smyrna/Izmir and its hinterlands on the western Anatolia coast, which was supported by Britain as a means of pre-empting Italian claims on the area. The other was the Allied-dictated treaty of Sèvres in 1920, which formalized the extension of the Greek state into western Anatolia and stipulated the creation in huge areas of eastern Anatolia of an independent Armenia and Kurdistan. Had not Kemal's rise forced a radical revision of the settlement, ethnic cleansing of Muslims, sponsored by Britain, France, and the USA, would have been a predictable result of the treaty, which gave regions with strong Muslim majorities to Armenia and Greece in the interests of defensibility, communications, and resources.[25]

Britain sought to use the Greek forces on the ground in a failed bid to destroy the burgeoning Kemalist resistance to its imperial division of Anatolia. The net result was a vicious ethnic war in Anatolia in 1921–2, in which both Greek and Turkish forces targeted civilians extensively and hundreds of thousands perished. Having survived the world war with only a relatively small number of deportations from sensitive coastal regions, which was attributable to Greece's neutrality until 1917, the Anatolian Greek Orthodox population was now cast as the next in a long line of fifth columns of an external power. Much of it was driven away with the defeated Greek armies.

Unmixing Europe's Christians and Muslims

The process of ethnic cleansing was completed and made mutual as Greece and Turkey built on the prewar Ottoman–Bulgarian precedent of exchange. This was now an internationally mandated affair, however. The formalized exchange agreement, approved by all of the signatories to the 1923 Lausanne peace treaty that guaranteed Turkey's new borders, was partly recognition of the reality on the ground. Yet the refugee movement continued until around 1926 and until some 1.25 million

Ottoman subjects of the orthodox faith and 356,000 Greek Muslims had traded countries. Because of the tensions between Greece and Turkey, the appalling conditions under which so many passed both ways across the Aegean, and the lack of resources to cater for the refugees' arrival 'home', the exercise bore no relationship to the controlled process it was supposed to be.[26]

The suffering of the resettled 'Greeks' and 'Turks' predictably did not feature in British advocacy of later population exchanges. Nor did that of the approximately 280,000 people exchanged at the same time by Greece and Bulgaria over western Thrace, nor again that of the inhabitants of Aegean Macedonia, where the settling of Ottoman Greek refugees became part of the ongoing Athenian policy of Hellenization. And barely mentioned then or later were the 10,000–15,000 Dönme, expelled by Greece to Turkey from their native Salonica. The Dönme were a pacific group of followers of the messianic Jewish rabbi Shabtai Tzvi, and they maintained many of the outward signs of Islam while retaining some of their own religious practices and remaining endogamous. They were expelled as Muslims and because Greece wished to rid itself of a significant non-Greek economic element in an important former Ottoman cosmopolitan commercial centre it sought to 'nationalize'.

As the most influential great power, Britain saw the Lausanne exchange as a convenient way to wash its hands of a catastrophe of its own making, particularly as it was starting to think of moving back towards a position of friendship with Turkey as a regional bulwark against Bolshevism. The Greek–Bulgarian exchange was a way of compensating Greece and punishing Bulgaria for their respective wartime allegiances, for Woodrow Wilson's original intention had been to award western Thrace to Bulgaria owing to Bulgarian ethnic predominance there. This obstruction of Wilson's plan for national self-determination provides but one illustration of how the politics of the international system continued to shape the destinies of weaker states and minorities, and to channel what many then thought of as the inevitable force of nationalism. The horrific nature of Turkey's 'wars of independence', as the 1914–22 conflicts were called from within, was conveniently downplayed as Kemal foreswore any further territorial expansion that might disrupt the international system.

The new Republican regime applied itself to the task of consolidating Turkish rule internally in Anatolia in a series of increasingly violent programmes of forced assimilation and 'pacification' directed towards the Kurds. The Kemalists also illustrated the intolerance of their brand of secular nationalism by rounding in their turn on the Dönme. Famed for their commercialism and international ties, the Dönme had been initially supportive of the CUP's coup and modernizing project in the days before Salonica passed from Ottoman to Greek hands. Now they faced the same suspicion of their cosmopolitanism that the Ottomans had reserved for the Armenians and Greeks and the Europeans still had for the Jews.[27]

Turkey was the first loser in the First World War to revise the postwar settlement, and the Lausanne settlement was a validation of its previous developmental violence, and carte blanche to do whatever it wanted within Anatolia. Many a German nationalist admired Kemal's achievements, not least of which was the removal of disloyal internal minorities who had tried to 'stab Turkey in the back'. As far as many even within the political mainstream were concerned, Turkey had simply prevailed in a fight to the death between rival nationalisms in Anatolia. While a dwindling band of humanitarians still sought to provide for Armenian refugees, to others the Darwinian lesson of conflict between peoples was obvious. Unless the 'Jewish question' was solved by a 'bloody clash', 'the German people will end up just like the Armenians', opined one man in 1924, having recently seen his native Austria stripped of its empire and his adopted Germany driven out of eastern Europe. That man was Adolf Hitler.[28] And the idea that the great power constellation might even condone forms of ethnic cleansing that favoured friends or victors served as a precedent of massive population engineering not only for Winston Churchill when he advocated in the Second World War a 'clean sweep' of the minorities issues that plagued interwar nationalists and international relations, but also for Italian fascists, future nationalist leaders such as Israel's David Ben Gurion, and liberals such as the Czech Edvard Beneš. The mass population redistribution of the First World War also provided a precedent for demographic planners in the Nazi empire.[29]

Genocide and population exchange all but ended nearly two thousand years of Christian existence in Anatolia, or Asia Minor. That is the major story told today of these events. For the few hundred thousand Christians who remained, primarily in larger cities and particularly Istanbul, life was characterized by continuing socio-economic discrimination and the occasional pogrom. In the face of these pressures, mass emigration reduced the Christian population to its current, tiny size of a few thousand. Yet there is an equally important obverse to the excision of the Ottoman Christians. The population exchange, on the back of the eastern crisis and the Balkan wars, also ended the greater part of Muslim existence in Europe. All that was now left was the ethnic Albanian population, and groups of Turkic Muslims and of Slavs who had earlier converted to Islam, predominantly in Bulgaria and Bosnia. Like the Greek Orthodox in Turkey, the Bulgarian Muslims would continue throughout the twentieth century to experience harassment and to be 'encouraged' to migrate, while both Albanians and 'Bosniaks' would be targeted for ethnic cleansing during the murderous dissolution of the former Yugoslavia in the 1990s.

To the Future: Whither the Jews in the New Europe?

With Europe largely divested of one of its two most important and long-standing ethno-religious 'others', the Muslims, what of the second, the Jews? When would modern Europe as a whole achieve what King Ferdinand II had achieved in Spain by 1492? The fate of the Jews would be sealed in a much shorter span than the two or so generations it had taken to remove so many of the Muslims. It would not happen yet, because the pieces on the European board had temporarily settled as the Bolsheviks stabilized Russia and the finalized peace treaties determined the east European order. The extirpation of the Jews required the radicalization and licence of renewed world war, and the imperative provided by Nazi Germany, which would find accomplices among peoples who felt their national integrity under threat, or who were bidding for sovereign independence and saw Jews as one of the major obstacles to achieving it.

During the Second World War the Nazis' accessory states would progress to one degree or another from the policies of ethnic dominance to those of ethnic exclusivity. In the interwar period, the majority of states in Europe, irrespective of their future allegiances in the world war, pursued policies of ethnic dominance against a range of groups, with Jews generally but not always the common factor. Indeed, it is another of the peculiarities of the period that the same states that had so vigorously expelled Muslims and rejected Ottoman rule would be less murderous towards their Jewish minorities than would former Habsburg and Romanov states to the north.

Bulgaria, Bosnia, Albania, Greece, Serbia, and even Turkey itself were *relatively* less dangerous places to be a Jew than elsewhere in interwar Europe, though their Jews were still victims of a general xenophobia. In interwar Greece, for instance, the major outburst of anti-Semitism was a pogrom in Salonika in 1931, but that should be seen in the broader context of Greek attempts to entrench ethnic dominance in this recently acquired city.[30] Nazi rule or influence during war changed the picture to a greater or lesser degree as, in different ways, did Italian rule or influence. Greece and Serbia lost all control of state policy under Nazi occupation, but in Bulgaria, Albania, and Bosnia local attitudes plainly continued to influence events.

Why should there be differences in attitudes towards Jews between the Ottoman successor states and the Habsburg and Romanov successor states? First, the traditional (pre-1908) Ottoman religious framework continued to influence patterns of intergroup interaction in the successor states, so that Jews who had converted to Islam or to Christianity were not seen as alien in the way they would be in Nazi Germany, with its racial conception of Jewishness. Indeed, converts were to be protected in the name of the national body. Second, in the perception of at least some Balkan Christians, Jews had shared their subservience under the Ottomans rather than 'controlling' or 'exploiting' them; for the remaining Balkan Muslims, Jews simply did not occupy the same cultural position that they did for Christians. The exception to these crude generalizations is Romania—but there, as we have already hinted, the 'Jewish problem' in its modern form was one imported to the state *after* its de facto secession from Ottomania had begun, by the mid-nineteenth century arrival of Russian Jewish refugees.

In the former Romanov lands, the Judeo-Bolshevik stereotype held firm, as it did further west. In the former Habsburg lands, Jews found themselves spread across an array of smaller nation-states whose nationalists saw them as supporters and beneficiaries of the previous

Austrian and Hungarian dominion. The evidence these chauvinists needed to confirm the assumption was to be found in the Jewish grief for the end of the empire, and the speed with which Zionist committees in each new country went with the tide of the times in pressing new state and the Entente alike for recognition of Jews as a separate nationality with nationality rights.[31] Even among the former Habsburg ruling peoples, Jews were increasingly cast as anathema, and not just because of the 'communist threat'. In Hungary, the swingeing territorial losses of 1918–19 left the proportionately magnified Jewish minority exposed in an otherwise much more ethnically homogeneous state, subject to radicalized Magyar opinion now going down a 'Christian-nationalist' route.[32] The situation was similar in the small post-imperial state of Austria, which was the recipient of tens of thousands of Orthodox Jewish refugees from Poland and civil war Russia.

Under empire it had been possible to have a split identity: Jewish 'nationality'; Habsburg patriotism; and some adaptation to whatever was the local culture. In the nation-state, this possibility would dwindle to non-existence.[33] But putting faith in the guarantee of the capricious international system as a substitute for a more consistent and proximate imperial authority was to put faith in a chimera.

CHAPTER 3
ETHNOPOLITICS, GEOPOLITICS, AND THE RETURN TO WAR

Introduction: The Paris Dispensation

Unlike the shattering of the Ottoman and Romanov empires, the end of the Habsburg empire was more of a controlled dissolution into nation-states. This result was key to the geopolitical designs of the victorious powers, and the more so as swathes of the western marches of the Russian empire were reabsorbed by the Bolsheviks. Britain had wanted to sustain the Habsburg empire because of its worries about German and Russian influence in a series of smaller and weaker states. It was foiled by the centrifugal forces within the empire itself and by the competition between Lenin and Wilson to promote 'national self-determination'. Even so, in 1918 boundary decisions were not simply made on the basis of the pursuit of ethnic majority. The principle was qualified by the requisites of stability as understood by the victors: namely stability angled to their interests.

The settlement entailed the containment of the two major revisionist powers, Soviet Russia and Germany, in the 'lands between'[1] the two by the creation of a row of (it was hoped) democratic, capitalist buffer nation-states from north to south. Austria was decisively relegated to minor power status, so that Austrian revisionism could only be seriously expressed through the medium of pan-Germanism, wherein Germany would be the dominant power. This was certainly the path that many Austrian nationalists took in their immediate enthusiasm for political union with Germany, giving the lie to the postwar myth that Austria was Germany's 'first victim'.[2] Czechoslovakia and Poland stood in the centre between Germany and the USSR, with Czechoslovakia, Yugoslavia, and Romania together (the 'Little Entente') also seeking to contain the revisionist aspirations of Hungary.

The territorial arrangements of Versailles necessitated consideration of the 'viability' of each new state in terms of resources, defence, and communications. Where viability and majoritarianism conflicted, as in the 'Danzig corridor' and the question of Polish access to the Baltic Sea across an area of predominantly German population in Western Prussia, or where ethnic ownership was simply contested, as in Alsace, or as in the land that Hungary lost to each of the Little Entente states, adjudications over sovereignty tended predictably to go against the defeated states, creating irredenta in the process. Elsewhere, Bulgaria still cast covetous eyes on Greek Thrace and Serbian Macedonia. Bulgaria's location, and its revisionist agenda, pushed it into Italy's orbit, for, uniquely among the victors, in the postwar settlement Italy ignored the gains that it had made to the north, in Istria, Trieste, Trentino, and the South Tyrol, to bemoan its failure to achieve Albania, Dalmatia, and parts of western Anatolia. Rectifying the 'mutilated peace' and establishing dominance in the Mediterranean became the main goal of Italian foreign policy after 1919, and was an instrumental factor in the Italian Fascists' rise to power.

The peacemakers were aware of the potential for disgruntled minorities to upset the peace, just as they knew that in the minute ethnic patchwork of the region each state would inherit substantial minorities, however boundaries were set. Population transfer was not *yet* considered acceptable in the heart of Europe in the way it was for Turks and Balkan-dwellers. Nevertheless, the Allied boundary-makers clearly hoped migration would defuse the issue as they stipulated that minority inhabitants of the post-1918 states should leave their new state within a year if they were unhappy. Some 10 million people indeed got on the move, whether voluntarily or not, but the remaining 'national minorities' still comprised 25 to 30 million people, up to a quarter of the combined population of the new states created.

To be labelled a 'minority' was a matter of power as much as size. The name Czechoslovakia did not reveal that the state contained more Germans than Slovaks. Yugoslavia, or 'The kingdom of the Serbs,

Croats, and Slovenes', as it was first called, was also much more than that, as the Bosnian Muslims, Montenegrins, Macedonians, Jews, and Romanies within it might have testified. But power–political tensions also existed between the titular, *de jure* dominant national groups of these two state experiments in ethnic pluralism. The make-up of the state bureaucracies and political and military elite, and in the Czech case the economic elite too, indicated that Serbs and Czechs were the dominant groups within their respective states, and this impression was not lost on the Croats and Slovaks, some of whose nationalists felt they had emerged from one sort of subordination into another.[3] As with the multinational empires of old, the potential was there for both states to be undermined by manipulation of their ethnic divisions.

As for the minorities 'proper', their continued dwelling in the places of their birth should not be taken to signal contentment with the new geopolitical arrangement. It simply shows that ordinary people had priorities other than ethnic homogenization, just as later on many South Tirolean ethnic Germans preferred to remain *in situ* rather than go 'home' to Hitler's Reich. For such minorities, the powers built on the ill-fated precedent of 1878: the guarantees for protection of minority rights on language, religion, and communal institutions, supposedly to be enforced by the new League of Nations. The first treaty was signed in June 1919 by Poland. Czechoslovakia, Yugoslavia, Romania, Greece, Austria, Bulgaria, Hungary, and Turkey all subsequently signed up because they had to. Italy did not have to sign, so, even if 'minority protection' had really meant much, there was no formal recourse over the Italianization policies enacted against the Slavs coming under its control from 1919 on the Adriatic coast.

'Protection' and 'transfer' were different 'solutions', but both worked from the principle of the minority as the problem. If the treaties were in the medium term to provide a measure of cultural self-determination for minorities in states dominated by 'different' ethnic groups, in the longer term they were only a transitional measure, designed to soften and render peaceful the absorption of the minorities into majority culture, towards the wider end of stability. This was, in effect, a general application to all national minorities of the emancipation dilemma that had faced the Jews from 1789. And though the consequences of the minorities' response varied from place to place, the dilemma was not just restricted to minorities in new states: to take the example of Britain, which maintained at least some of its liberal-democratic credentials throughout the period, the belief that anti-Semitism had its roots in the persistence of Jewish 'difference' endured. Britain's restrictive interwar refugee policy was concerned not to create a 'minority issue at home', as was Britain's determination from 1939 to 1945 not to be seen to be fighting a war on behalf of the Jews.[4]

Policies of Ethnic Dominance in the Interwar Period

Whatever the efforts of some on the League of Nations' Minority Commission, infringements of the treaties were treated tolerantly because the treaties were only a means to an end.[5] This was how Britain, as a major potential enforcer of the League, viewed forced assimilation in Greece, Bulgaria, and Yugoslavia. The same went for shades of minority unrest in the Arab 'mandate' territories taken from the Ottomans, and in Turkey itself.[6] Of the remaining, harassed Greek population of Istanbul, the British consul in Ankara reflected to the Foreign Office in 1928 that 'the problem is comparable, in its minor sphere and minor reactions, to those of Upper Silesia, [and] the Polish corridor . . ., which, I believe it to be the view of His Majesty's Government, can only find an ultimate solution, if left, undisturbed, to the operation of time and natural forces'.[7] The events in Upper Silesia euphemistically described as 'natural forces' had firstly entailed violent clashes from 1918 between Polish and German forces in this contested border region, and then, when the territory was formally assigned to Poland, vigorous attempts at the 'Polonization' of the Germans that remained. Poland was also engaged periodically throughout the interwar period in its southeastern regions (Chełm, Volhynia, and eastern Galicia) in repression of Ukrainian insurgents and Polonization and modernization campaigns, albeit interspersed with mollifying cultural concessions. It used internal deportation as a means of consolidating national control.[8]

If the minority treaties frequently remained unenforced, they still elicited resentment from the states in question as an infringement of sovereignty. Not every state was intolerant to the same degree. Poland,

Romania, and Yugoslavia were instantly as resentful of the Versailles minorities treaties as they were of certain minorities, Czechoslovakia much less so. Indeed, in the interwar years Czechoslovakian citizens were permitted to choose their own nationality on censuses rather than submitting to pseudo-objective impositions based on their language and culture. Nevertheless, while the Czech Germans were not generally subjected to the same threats and abuse as elsewhere in east-central Europe, Germans were decidedly second-class citizens.

Jews were accorded exceptional attention by many of Europe's ethnonationalists. For Hungarian nationalists, who in their reduced territory no longer needed the Jews to bolster their numerical and economic strength, the notion of making special efforts to protect the cultural status of its Jews in the aftermath of the Béla Kun regime seemed a perverse joke. Romania, having just expanded by its own military efforts to incorporate Bessarabia, Bukovina, Transylvania, and Dobruja, was even less happy than earlier to be told how to deal with the many Jews, Russians, Ukrainians, ethnic Germans, and Bulgarians living in these places. The state having doubled in size, Romania's minority population also increased from a pre-1914 proportion of about 8 per cent to about 28 per cent. In Jewish policy alone it spent much of the interwar period indulging in harsh measures in both its new eastern and western territories on the grounds of the Jews' alleged sympathy for Soviet and Hungarian rule, respectively. In October 1942, at the height of the Holocaust, the then Romanian leader, Ion Antonescu, would accuse the 'Yids' of having conspired with Britain and the USA to dictate the peace terms after the First World War. He would also observe that his own predecessor, Ion Brătianu, had been obliged to grant civil rights to Jews in 1878, which 'compromised the Romanian economy and the purity of our race'.[9]

After more than a hundred years of partition, Polish nationalists were similarly displeased to encounter limits on their sovereignty, and the more so where this concerned 'effete' Jews, who had not earned their national rights by fighting, and who had relied on the distinctly underhand channels of international diplomacy.[10] In states like these marked by profound anti-Bolshevism, the notion of international Jewish power was almost a *sine qua non*. Both beliefs furthered the established perception of Jewish 'difference' as somehow different to other forms of ethnic difference—a phenomenon that has been dubbed 'allosemitism'.[11]

The concept of assimilation into the majority ethnic group was open to varying interpretations.[12] In 1896 Norway had developed one of the most straightforward and extreme methods of assimilating its Romany population: a law empowered the state to remove Romany children from their parents and place them in state institutions, paralleling Australia's policy towards its aboriginal population. For most states, alongside some reallocation of land-ownership, and in extreme cases internal deportation, standardizing use of the majority language and educational control were key methods in 'nationalizing' minorities once the dust of the 1918–23 border disputes had settled. But such policies could actually exacerbate what they were supposed to remove. Romanian education policy angered the Romanian ethnic Germans just as Romanians in the Habsburg empire had earlier reacted nationalistically to Magyarization; French interwar language policy in Alsace had led many resentful Alsatians to embrace reconnection to Germany just as Prusso-German policies from the 1870s had stimulated nationalism among ethnic Poles in eastern Germany and just as Polish interwar policy in eastern Poland stimulated Ukrainian nationalism. Nevertheless, the theory of assimilation presupposed different populations were somehow sufficiently similar to be dissolved into the majority. Polish nationalists, for instance, believed Belarussians or Lithuanians could be merged into the national body, as Turkey believed of its Kurds, Romania of its Hungarians, and Bulgarians of its 'Pomaks'—Slavic converts to Islam. But Jews in Poland, like Ottoman Armenians or 'Turks' in Bulgaria, seemed at one further remove from the 'core people'.

Jews had served as a convenient counterpart to Polish ethnic-national identity in its modern phase of construction from the 1880s onwards. Independent Poland saw a wave of pogroms, and some of the interwar governments continued to instrumentalize the anti-Semitism of extreme right-wing groups for their own power-political ends.[13] From the mid-1930s, particularly after Józef Piłsudski's death paved the way for greater political influence for more radical anti-Semites, the Polish regime seriously entertained thoughts of the deportation of Jews to

Madagascar as part of its own attempt to achieve 'great power' status by empire-building in Africa. The desire to force Jews to emigrate was openly and frequently expressed, which is why Zionism was sometimes encouraged.[14]

Despite having granted Jews nominal citizenship, Romanian nationalists also considered deportation well before the war. Given the local hostility in both countries, it is entirely unsurprising that their large Jewish populations simply could not see Romanian or Polish nationality as a viable political identity, and so in overwhelming numbers responded to censuses by recording their nationality as 'Jewish'.[15] It is an open question as to what would have happened to the Polish and Romanian Jews without the intervention of the Second World War, just as it is regarding the Ottoman Armenians absent the First World War, but the likelihood that all three scenarios would have entailed ever greater socio-economic marginalization and increasing pressure to emigrate must be very high indeed.

As in Poland and Romania, a convergence of political, socio-economic, and international factors in the interwar period drove most of the states that emerged between 1878 and 1923 to become even less tolerant of minorities than they were at the outset. With the exception of Czechoslovakia (and Finland), with its more advanced industrial and urban society, every single country exchanged its democratic trappings for right-wing authoritarian regimes of the sort that prevailed in Portugal, or in Spain after Generalissimo Franco's defeat of the Republic. The Balkan states and Romania gained monarchical dictatorships; the east-central European states developed forms of 'praesidial dictatorship'. For most countries in the region, developing and strengthening the state in the name of the state's titular people took priority over any political pluralism, insofar as that notion even had any purchase amongst nationalist elites socialized to autocratic systems and often surprised at how statehood had descended upon them so suddenly.[16] Besides, many of these elites were themselves aristocrats who shared the assumption of right-wingers elsewhere that liberal democracy prepared the soil in which socialism, the deadly enemy of nationalism, could flourish. Among the populations of the emergent states, even some political radicals were prepared to accept national emancipation as the first step to individual emancipation, and many were prepared to accept the former *instead* of the latter.

With monocultural authoritarian statism came the further development of means of central surveillance and control of the population. The simple gathering of demographic information, for instance, was not in itself sinister, but some of the purposes to which census information could be deployed might be. Moreover, encouraged by eugenics movements using the scientific language of biological determinism in a Darwinian world, states across the board became more deeply involved in social reform, public health, and reproductive issues as they sought to improve both the 'quality' and well being of their titular national group, and its absolute and relative numbers. The influential 1926 work of the later Romanian Iuliu Moldovan, entitled *Biopolitica*—biopolitics—neatly sums up the way that state action sought to regulate populations on ever more levels of life.[17] In such organic conceptions of the state, it was not unusual for executive offices of state to dress their roles in biological metaphor, with, for instance, regular or political police forces deployed to safeguard the 'health of the national body' by quelling threats to its social and political framework. This was as true in comparatively liberal Weimar Germany as further east. Under Weimar as elsewhere, Romanies and other 'anti-social' elements would increasingly come under the microscope of the institutions of surveillance.[18]

State bureaucracies became the most active supporters of statism, and not just out of aggrandizing self-interest. The demographic composition of the bureaucracies that were now strengthened and extended had been one of the main focuses of grievance amongst subordinate nationalities in the late imperial period. Now in the new states these bureaucracies, like the armies, were not merely neutral executive bodies for the state policies of the titular people, but one of the most prominent expressions of its new and separate identity, and one of the guarantors of its 'organic integrity'. In the pre-existing state of Germany, the strong continuity in military and bureaucracy from the imperial regime through the Weimar Republic meant both saw themselves as embodiment and guardian of national interest, and saw the Weimar regime as transient and illegitimate, much in the way that elements of the Spanish army regarded the Popular Front regime in 1936, and that the Turkish military has viewed various governments over succeeding generations. It is no accident that purging bureaucracies of suspect elements was such a significant part of nationalist programmes everywhere.

Economic Crisis and Geopolitical Change

Almost all of the new states were afflicted by grievous economic problems, which were worsened, but not caused, by the Great Depression of the early 1930s. The Depression itself hit hardest in the industrialized states, including most obviously Germany, which was still coming to terms with the economic effects of the peace settlement. In Germany, depression helped provide the conditions for the overthrow of the Weimar Republic by the Nazi party, aided and supported—and, in the case of the Brüning and Papen administrations from 1930 onwards, even anticipated—by large swathes of the conservative political, bureaucratic, industrial, and military elite, for whom the regime instituted after the defeat in 1918 was both the very evidence of German humiliation and the antithesis of Germanic values.

In contrast to Germany, most of the new eastern European states had predominantly agrarian economies, many overpopulated in terms of their capacity to provide for their populations at more than a subsistence level. Their populations could not generate surplus capital for investment, nor provide much of a market for manufactured goods, as the wilting industry in the formerly Russian parts of Poland proved after 1919. The erstwhile Habsburg provinces emerged from an enclosed economic bloc, where economic functions had been divided between provinces, into the full glare of integration into the world economy. To say conditions were unpropitious would be an understatement. The very geopolitical functions the new states were supposed to fulfil—containment of the defeated powers—meant economic incorporation with their natural regional trading partners would be stymied from the outset by resentments and fear of external control. The international economy tended to subordinate less-developed exporters of raw materials to more advanced exporters of manufactured goods, as shown by the late Ottoman experience at the hands of the European powers. Nationalist ideology would not allow that.

Where else to look? The USSR remained largely self-enclosed. Despite their efforts, Britain and France proved incapable either of inducing much political cooperation between the new states (with the temporary exception of the Little Entente members, who had their own territorial reasons) or of providing the necessary economic partnership, since both were undergoing their own economic difficulties and increasingly traded within the protective confines of their colonial empires. In the medium term, isolation left each new state easier prey to the sort of economic penetration that had characterized pre-First World War designs for a German dominated 'Mitteleuropa' (as in Germany's 1936 trade agreement with Yugoslavia), and later to Hitlerian political expansion. The Depression-era restriction of western European trade actually forced Germany to look eastwards economically as well as 'racially'. In the shorter term, eastern European isolation expressed itself through autarky, or 'economic nationalism'—a route that Germany and Austria tried to take together from 1931, as the two attempted to form a customs union, in an approximate precursor of the 'Anschluss' that would occur under Hitler in 1938, and an approximate repeat of their rapprochement during the depression of the 1870s. There was a close but not inevitable relationship between the ideology of economic nationalism and the imperative to ensure ethnic control of the economy.[19]

In the quest for 'economic emancipation' to ward off 'economic colonization', Romania passed a series of laws limiting foreign ownership. Suspiciously 'cosmopolitan' minorities also fell victim to such logic. Jews and some Ukrainians with economic influence were targeted in the drive to expand the small Romanian bourgeoisie in a process openly called 'Romanianization', while, like the Polish interwar regime, the radicalized Magyar elite also sought to marginalize Jews with the aim of achieving ethnic economic control. A few years later, Slovakia also pursued 'Slovakianization' of its economy, or 'Christianization', as it was also known.[20] As well as providing a European context for German 'Aryanization' in the 1930s and for Austrian anti-Jewish economic policy from even before the 'Anschluss', each programme also mirrored aspects of Republican Turkish policy from the 1920s to the 1950s. One of the peaks of Turkish economic discrimination came in 1942 in the form of *Varlık Vergisi*, a 'property tax' aimed at the remaining Greeks, Armenians, Jews,

Figure 5. Vandalized Jewish goods store (Eckstein) in Bratislava.

and Dönme.[21] It does not take a great comparative leap to see the similarity with the *Judenvermögensabgabe*, or 'Jewish capital levy', deployed in the aftermath of 'Kristallnacht' in 1938 Germany, or the other special taxes, fines, and 'contributions' imposed on Jewish communities from Rome to Minsk to northern France during the Second World War.[22]

The great stock market crash of 1929–31, the fall of the largest eastern European bank, the Austrian *Creditanstalt*, and then the world depression only confirmed eastern Europe's ethnonationalists in their mistrust of the international system that had simultaneously sought to thrust bourgeois democracy, minority protection, and the free market onto them. It was not the Nazis alone who saw Jews presiding over and benefiting from those alien impositions, and the impression of a Jewish conspiracy was ironically only furthered by the efforts of some international Jewish organizations to help their eastern European brethren through the crisis years.[23] The assault on democracy, laissez-faire economics, and minorities was collective and supranational. It was Germany, however, that spearheaded the attack first on the interwar system and then on Europe's Jews.

The Collapse of the International System

German rearmament from 1935 and the army's occupation of the demilitarized Rhineland in 1936 were conducted in defiance of the Versailles treaty terms, as was Italy's 1935 invasion of Abyssinia. Rearmament was the first move in Germany's attempt to rejoin the ranks of the great powers. The state expenditure and economic direction involved in stimulating military production and other public works was also a means to expand employment and stimulate productivity in the short term, entrenching the Nazis in power and gaining Hitler unprecedented personal popularity. But rearmament would create its own dynamic, not only because it pushed the other great powers in the same direction, but also because an economy increasingly geared to war would soon have to go to war or suffer domestically from its own distortions. Similarly, the products foregone in the pursuit of rearmament could be acquired by conquest, as could the materials required to sustain conquest. This was clear to Hitler if to few others at the time—the Allies and his own generals included—as in 1936 he established the office for the Four Year Plan under Hermann Göring, with the express purpose of making the country ready for war within that time span.

The gradual crystallization of Hitler's long-standing desire for expansionist war in the east and a reckoning with France in the west did not take place in isolation. The year 1934 had witnessed a change of direction in international communist policy as the Comintern reacted to the rise of fascism in Europe by urging all antifascist groups to unite in 'popular fronts'. During that year the French socialist party under André Léon Blum came to lead a coalition including the Communist Party and the Radical Party. In May 1936, the Popular Front won a parliamentary majority, and Blum began to preside over a new government. He was the first socialist, and the first Jew, to become Prime Minister of the country; of course in Hitler's mind, as in that of the wide array of antisocialist

French forces in the fractious Third Republic, Blum's twin identities were anything but incidental. During these developments, in May 1935, France and the USSR signed a defensive alliance, which was mirrored in the establishment the following year of the German–Italian Axis.

The year 1936 also saw the beginning of the Spanish civil war, as nationalist elements within the army turned against the newly formed popular front regime. Shortly afterwards, Germany, Italy, and Japan formally agreed to act together to stop communist expansion. Increasing Nazi penetration of the established German state machinery from 1936 in the medium of new, more overtly ideologized institutions like the Four Year Plan office, and in the unification of the SS and German police, had parallels in Soviet policy. Stalin's regime began to purge its bureaucracy and intensified attacks on 'internal enemies', including members of 'suspect' nationalities, in preparation for some form of war in Europe and Southeast Asia that Stalin himself saw as inevitable.

But ideology alone, or at least *Ideology* in the sense of something alien to the traditional, pre-1914 mental world of Europe's statesmen, while certainly necessary, was insufficient. World war, from the point of view of its main instigator, was also about *expansion and power as traditionally conceived*: geopolitics and geo-economics. From the perspective of Germany's future western opponents too, it was only when territorial revision began in earnest that war would be joined. The formal addition to Germany of Austria in the 'Anschluss' of March 1938 began the process of territorial revision. It gravely disturbed the outside world, but did not fundamentally alter the geopolitics of the Versailles settlement because Austria had leaned some way towards Germany from 1919, and there was at least some external recognition of the ethnic confraternity of the two states. The stakes were different in Germany's relations to non-Germanic states like Czechoslovakia.

The demographic distribution of the post-1918 settlement meant Germany became an upholder of the minority clauses, manipulating the 'minority question' in the interwar period, by protesting to the League of Nations on behalf of ethnic Germans in Czechoslovakia and Poland.[24] In accordance with the Munich agreement of October 1938,

Hitler and the local Nazi leader Konrad Henlein contrived to detach the Sudetenland from Czechoslovakia after roiling the Czech German population. Slovakia became autonomous. Hitler also unsuccessfully demanded that Danzig be returned to Germany. Five months later, playing on Czech–Slovak divisions, Hitler and the Hungarians cajoled and threatened Slovak leaders into declaring formal independence, though the Slovak state that emerged under the presidency of the Catholic priest Jozef Tiso was dependent on German support. German pressure simultaneously resulted in the incorporation of the Czech lands into the 'Third Reich' as the 'Protectorate of Bohemia and Moravia'. The predators Hungary and Poland took advantage of Munich to hack pieces off the Czechoslovak carcass. Italy did likewise in invading Albania, to take the first step in rectifying the 'mutilated peace'.

So it was not the continuing abuse of minorities that discredited the minorities treaties, but rather the abuse of the treaties in the pursuit of territorial revisionism by a major power. 'Munich' sounded the death-knell of minority 'protection' in central Europe and the embrace by the Allies of the Balkan precedent of population transfer. In the first instance the device was proposed as a last-ditch bid to avoid war (though without much consideration of the plight of the populations concerned). In 1939 it dawned on Britain that Germany might be appeased by a population exchange for Danzig, West Prussia or Upper Silesia.[25] Hitler's refusal ironically furthered a chain of developments that would result in the postwar expulsion of the 12 million or so ethnic Germans living in east-central Europe, which was the largest single forced population movement in European history, plus a series of smaller exchanges and evictions of other minorities in the region.[26] It would take the 1939 Nazi–Soviet partition of Poland, the other great central European buffer erected in 1918 between the two, to precipitate all-out war, but the line Britain and France drew in the sand over Poland was a result of the lessons learned from Munich. Fittingly, 1938 was the year to which Beneš and Churchill would later refer in justification of the German expulsions, which were also the final stage of the unweaving of the Habsburg empire.

Excursus: Solving Ethnic Questions from Outside the Axis Alliance

More needs to be said on the expulsion of the ethnic Germans, first to illustrate the scale of the *continuing* unweaving and homogenization process even after Hitler's Holocaust. Second, to illustrate the contingent interaction of the unweaving with the prevailing international environment and power constellation—in this case, great powers prepared to countenance mass ethnic cleansing as a swift route to international stability and German containment. After both world wars, the Allies desired a Germany restricted in territory and eastern influence, but this was increasingly seen as impossible so long as the boundaries *imposed by the Allies to the ends of their own dominance* placed large ethnic German populations outside Germany. Since Germany was not allowed to expand, the ethnic Germans had to be removed. This narrative should give pause to those who contend the ethnic Germans were expelled solely because of their complicity in Nazi rule. (Many *were* complicit, and more benefited, though many also suffered because of Nazi demographic engineering.) It is simply incorrect, though the fact and nature of Nazi rule were the catalyst for the expulsion, and made it more violent than it might otherwise have been: at least 500,000 ethnic Germans perished, and possibly many more.[27]

While Czechoslovakia deserves some credit for trying to make multiethnicity work in the interwar period, elsewhere ethnic Germans were seen as just as problematic as any minority on the basis of their 'difference' and, relatedly, of their economic roles in some places. The eviction of more than 200,000 ethnic Germans from Hungary from 1945, conducted by many of the same Hungarian personnel who had helped deport Jews in 1944, had been envisaged as early as 1934 by the then regent Adm. Miklós Horthy as part of a reciprocal exchange, and had been discussed with the Nazis during the war.[28] Hungary also used the end of the war to divest itself of some of its Slovaks, and the move was reciprocated.

As to Poland, and as the experiences of Germans in Upper Silesia in the interwar period suggest, one might contend that the eviction of the Germans was only the last and largest chapter in a battle begun in the

1870s over ethnopolitical ownership of what were now Poland's western borderlands. It is hard to imagine many Polish nationalists mourning the loss of their ethnic Germans through expulsion (or that of their Jews through murder). Indeed, the nationalist organizations that had sprung up in reaction to imperial German cultural policies were instrumental in the eviction of the Germans.[29]

What the Polish nationalists did mourn was the loss of huge numbers of ethnic Poles under Soviet and German rule in 1939–45, and also in one of the lesser known tales of ethnic violence in the Second World War era: the Polish–Ukrainian conflict that emerged over the long-standing issue of dominance in the old Habsburg–Romanov border territories. From early 1943 a 'homogenization' process had been conducted on the changing Polish–Ukrainian borders in Volhynia and eastern Galicia, by local participants at first, though with heavy Soviet involvement at the war's end. Poles were the chief victims during the war itself, though many Ukrainians acted according to the memory of Warsaw's policy during Poland's interwar rule over the western Ukraine.[30] From later in 1943 through to the end of the world war, mutual violence, on a scale similar to that to be dubbed 'genocide' in the Yugoslav disintegration of the 1990s, resulted in up to 100,000 deaths in the two communities and some 1.4 million expulsions.[31]

The postwar communist Warsaw regime used internal deportation westward as its means of dispersing the remnant of Ukrainians, the easier to assimilate them. The overall result was the forcible resettlement of some 94 per cent of Poles in what became Soviet Ukraine and 95 per cent of Ukrainians in what became Poland. With the additional loss to the USSR of areas of heavy Lithuanian and Belorussian population in the east from 1945, the Polish population became almost entirely ethnically Polish. Millions of these Poles in turn were internal refugees from the now-Soviet east, and many of them found accommodation in the properties vacated by Poland's ethnic Germans.

Beyond central Europe, the rhetoric of troublesome minorities who had, perforce, to be dealt with gave sustenance to the ethnic designs of the Greek nationalists who, during the civil war (1946–9), justified their assault on dissident Macedonians by labelling them 'Sudetens of the Balkans'.[32] Some 150,000 Pomaks were also ushered out of Bulgaria at the end of the war. In the ensuing years, in another former Ottoman province, Palestine, the nascent Israeli state forced the dispersal of large numbers of Arabs and went on to deny them the right to return. In and around Palestine, Arab Muslims objected not only to the influx of a European population, but to the unprecedented imposition of Jews as rulers of Muslims. Within Yugoslavia, in Fiume/Rijeka (which Italy had taken in 1924), Dalmatia (occupied by Italy during the Second World War), and Istria (allocated to Italy in 1919), 200,000 or more Italians fled a calculated campaign of terror and subsequent discrimination in 1945–60, at the outset of which up to 10,000 were killed by locals or by Marshal Tito's partisan forces, which were also responsible for revenge killings of Germans, Hungarians, and Croatian militia members.

The other main agent of ethnic cleansing in Europe from outside Axis ranks was the USSR. The Stalinist regime was remarkably brutal, but its relationship to ethnicity was highly complex, and only deliberately murderous at specific points. The Soviet political purges of the late 1930s, with their more than 800,000 executions, were the most extensive direct killing actions of the regime. The 'dekulakization' campaign of 1929–32 featured relatively few executions, and the majority of the approximately 2.5 million deportees were moved only within their own region or *raion*. Nevertheless, because of the conditions for those who were deported, death tolls of kulaks run into the lower hundreds of thousands. These 'rich peasants', some of whom had resisted Bolshevik policy in the civil war era, were seen as obstacles to the collectivization of the rural economy. Many were sent to labour camps or deported with their families for 'special settlement' in central Asia, the Urals, Siberia, and elsewhere. Both dekulakization and the purges had some ethnicized characteristics, particularly as far as they extended to individual members of 'diaspora peoples', who would continue to be objects of suspicion—Germans, Finns, and Poles, for instance.[33] Yet while the Soviet regime was happy on occasion to label national peoples pejoratively, this did not necessarily mean that those peoples would be targeted 'as such' (in the language of the UN genocide convention) or in their entirety. Circumstances were important in determining the extent of Soviet collective action against subject populations defined along ethnic or national lines, as the famines of 1931–3 and a series of deportations in the Second World War era illustrated.

The Soviet regime inherited many of the problems of imperial management from its Tsarist predecessor, but its threat perception was greatly enhanced by the experience of the Russian civil war. The civil war had illustrated the reliance of the urban areas, which contained the Bolsheviks' working-class constituency, on agricultural regions like the Kuban in the North Caucasus, and the Ukraine. The significance of these border regions as breadbaskets of empire also explains why imperial Germany had sought to expand so far eastwards during the First World War. Both the Ukraine and the Kuban, with its large Cossack population had, as we have already seen, provided extensive resistance during the civil war. Both, in addition to the vital livestock-raising lands of Kazakhstan, fell victim to the famines that engulfed some six million people, as the regime forced collectivization onto the countryside, and imposed huge, unattainable quotas of livestock and grain while preventing the peasants from leaving the land. In all areas the regime was guilty of imposing conditions that would clearly bring suffering and mass death, yet in the Ukraine the deaths became arguably more a deliberate consequence than a by-product. Stalin gradually came to see the deaths and dislocation as a way of breaking the peasant majority as a whole, which he viewed as the backbone of the powerful Ukrainian nationalist movement and thus an impediment to the construction of the Soviet order in this economically and geopolitically crucial area.[34]

A related Soviet paranoia emerging from the civil war concerned external regimes and their putative—and, in some cases, real—influence among subject populations. During the Second World War, as this security concern reached new heights, Soviet deportation practices extended to removing select populations from sensitive regions, though without a desire to ethnically homogenize the areas cleared in the process. Ethnically based Soviet deportations in the period affected around 3 million people. The first total ethnic deportation was of the Far Eastern Koreans in 1937. The largest deported group in absolute terms was the ethnic German population of the Volga region and elsewhere (around 750,000), deported into the interior in the face of advancing German troops in 1941. The largest deportations in relative terms concerned the smaller, often Islamic nationalities deported after the German retreat in 1943–4 from the Caucasus and the Crimea—other areas of traditional resistance to Romanov and Bolshevik rule—on allegations of collaboration.[35]

There was no general attempt to murder the deportees, though at a minimum scores of thousands died under conditions of transit, and some at particularly inhospitable destinations, which not all destinations were; the Soviet Secret State police (NKVD) also sometimes conducted massacres during round-ups. Ultimately, as political circumstances changed—the war ended and, most importantly, 'de-Stalinization' arrived—deportations could be reversed. That was the case with most of the deported nations, though notably not the Crimean Tatars, Meskhetian Turks, nor, less surprisingly, the Volga Germans.

One counter-factual suggestion emerging from these deliberations is to imagine how intolerant European behaviour towards the large and scattered ethnic German diaspora would have been before 1945 had the German state itself not been a huge, forbidding presence. The rise of the Third Reich undoubtedly forced moderation in the treatment of ethnic Germans in countries allied to or fearful of Germany, though it had had the opposite effect among Germany's outright opponents. What is certain is that when Germany had been the hegemonic great power in the region, it had ruthlessly encouraged ethnic hatred both as a means to its own political ends and as an ideological end in itself. Let us return, then, to the narrative of the years of European conflict up to and during the world war.

Ethnic Destruction in the Second World War: The Beginnings, 1938–40

While expanding its own nation-state-based empire directly, Germany, like Italy, allied with the Balkan and east-central European losers of the post-1918 settlement to reverse the prevailing balance of power in each region. In establishing alliances and puppet regimes, Hitler and Mussolini played on all of the ethnic resentments already stimulated from the days of imperial modernization onwards. Sometimes these dynamics needed vigorous agitation, as in Czechoslovakia; sometimes less, as in the first stages of the dismemberment of Yugoslavia in 1941, or the encouragement of Bulgarian and Hungarian irredentism.

Even before war, Nazi racism radiated outwards to influence the policies of smaller states, and emboldened extreme nationalists and proto-fascists in other countries. Bulgaria was particularly concerned to ingratiate itself with the major revisionist power, which goes a long way to explaining its adoption of anti-Semitic legislation from 1940. Inter alia, this banned Jews from public service and imposed economic restrictions. The legislation was phrased in religious rather than racist terms, however, illustrating Bulgaria's continuing debt to the Ottoman *millet* system. It should also be seen in the context of indigenous measures since the mid-1930s to 'Bulgarianize' all minority names and force particular modes of dress onto minorities.

Between 1938 and 1941 Slovakia and Hungary progressed from anti-Jewish laws based on religious definitions to closer approximations to the racist Nazi Nuremberg Laws, reversing the emancipation Jews had enjoyed since 1867. Italian laws copied aspects of earlier German legislation, forbidding marriage between Jews and non-Jews and removing Jewish teachers from public schools. Poland, then enjoying reasonable relations with Germany, also showed the knock-on effects of the Nuremberg laws as its own anti-Semitic parties took advantage of the atmosphere to pressure the government to further restrict the rights and commercial and professional opportunities of Jews in 1937–8.[36]

Jewish policy in Poland was soon taken out of Polish hands, however, as Germany and the other major revisionist power, the USSR, together applied the *coup de grâce* to the interwar international system by invasion and partition. The executioner's axe was the infamous Molotov–Ribbentrop pact of August 1939, which divided eastern Europe into German and Soviet spheres of influence, and secretly arranged for the partition of most of the former Romanov and Habsburg land therein. The following months saw the Soviet annexation of Latvia, Lithuania, Estonia, and eastern Poland, while Germany took control of large tracts of western and central Poland. The defeat of France in 1940 then allowed Germany and the USSR to dictate the reduction of Romania, as the USSR regained Bessarabia and northern Bukovina, and Germany's supplicants, Hungary and Bulgaria, respectively retook northern Transylvania and southern Dobruja. The USSR then completed the restoration of most of the state's pre-Versailles borders by invading Finland.

Summary population engineering followed swiftly on these developments. As we shall see in greater detail in the following chapters, Germany set to work reordering the population of Poland into strips of ethnically homogeneous territory, isolating the Jewish population in preparation for an as yet undefined final solution, and systematically murdering the Polish political and social elite. Some 128,000 western Poles were transferred into the Soviet zone in 1940, with Moscow's agreement.[37] The USSR began its own form of demographic engineering, deporting up to 600,000 people from its areas of pre-1939 Poland as a means of removing political opposition and class obstacles in order to smooth the path for communist rule. Other deportations from the Baltic states Bessarabia and Bukovina also remained in principle assaults on 'class' and 'social' enemies, and were thus selective if large in scale.[38]

The Lesser Axis Powers in the Balkans[39]

Beyond Poland, a de facto population exchange occurred as some 100,000 Romanians were obliged to leave Hungarian northern Transylvania to 'make space' for a similar number who left Romanian southern Transylvania. Having learnt the lessons of the border settlement and population exchange with Greece in the mid-1920s, Bulgaria followed up its successful territorial revisionism with the more formal 1940 'exchange' of 100,000 Romanians and 61,000 Bulgarians around the new Dobruja boundaries. Romania agreed as a way of limiting its own territorial losses.[40]

The Dobruja episode gives us a clue about the dynamics of ethnic policy among Germany's allies. They are dynamics that we have encountered earlier in the shatterzones of the dynastic empires: the desire to create demographic fait accompli in newly acquired territory—particularly territory to which some historical claim was made—in order to secure that territory for the future. The expulsion of minorities was made all the easier at these times of flux because the minority inhabitants of new territories often did not have citizenship of the titular nation extended to them anyway, so there was much less of an issue of sovereignty involved for the expellers, and less of whatever residual historical sense of compatriotism towards fellow citizens.

Some similarities to the above pattern would characterize the behaviour of Hungary, Bulgaria, and Romania when they laid claim to disputed territories from 1940–1 onwards, as Yugoslavia and Greece fell to Germany in April 1941 and then Germany invaded the USSR in June. Where Jews resided in contested areas, they were particularly likely to suffer the most extreme of fates given the premium put by Germany on an increasingly radical and Europe-wide solution to the Jewish question. Nevertheless, whatever the level of indigenous anti-Semitisms, the specifically Jewish factor of ethnic policy was often of only secondary significance to the greater goal of national consolidation and expansion. Hungarians, Bulgarians, and Romanians only acquiesced in Nazi demographic goals when and insofar as it suited their nationalist agenda. Much the same went for the large number of proto-fascist and national-secessionist volunteers who joined the armed (Waffen) SS.[41]

The outbreak of the German–Soviet war provided the opportunity for Hungary to expel Jews from the areas previously gained from Slovakia into the German-conquered Ukraine. Hungarians did not deport Jews from the areas they occupied in Yugoslavia. They did, however, on occasion attack these Jews in a way that they did not domestically, as in the murder of thousands of Jews and Serbs in the city of Novi Sad in January 1942.

Bulgaria did not deport Jews of Bulgarian nationality. In 1943 it did deport to German control, and subsequent death, more than 11,000 non-Bulgarian Jews from the Macedonian territories it had annexed from Yugoslavia and the Thracian territories taken from Greece in 1941 during its third bid to restore the San Stefano boundaries of 1878. At least as important for Bulgarian goals in these territories were the harsh policies enacted against Greeks and Macedonians. Like Hungary, Bulgaria was happy to exploit Jewish men for forced labour, and to avail itself of the opportunity to expropriate Jews and remove them from key positions in the capital's economy: it deported some 20,000 from Sofia to the provinces during 1943. It should be reiterated that in 'old Bulgaria', as within the boundaries of post-1920 Hungary, these expropriations were pursuant to ethnic domination not ethnic destruction, though the postwar Bulgarian regime was not distraught when most of the Bulgarian Jewish population left for Palestine/Israel. Jews of Hungarian nationality were not so fortunate, as German occupation from March 1944 co-opted part of the Hungarian administration, including some very willing Magyar ethnic-cleansers, into surrendering more than 500,000, most to die at Auschwitz-Birkenau. Around one thousand Romanies were likewise deported.[42]

The Second World War chapter of Romania's national story began differently to that of Hungary or Bulgaria, but developed some similarities. Romania emerged from the conflict as the greatest murderer of Jews in Europe after Nazi Germany. In the region of 270,000 Jews under Romanian control died as a result of Romanian and German measures. Simultaneously, the vast majority of the Jewish population of the 'old' Romanian lands of Moldavia and Wallachia—around 375,000 people—survived the war because of a series of decisions made in Bucharest from the second half of 1942 onwards.

The great Romanian territorial losses of 1940 caused a similar trauma to that experienced by Hungary in 1919–20. The result was the fall of the existing government, the rise of a more extreme one, and an explosion of xenophobia and anti-Semitism. In September 1940 King Carol II was obliged to abdicate after the loss of northern Transylvania; the 'National Legionary State' was declared under right-wing radicals from the military under Ion Antonescu and the fascist Iron Guard, only for the Iron Guard to fail in an attempted seizure of total power in January 1941, and to be removed from power altogether. The National Legionary State passed a tranche of anti-Semitic laws in its short months of existence, and the Iron Guard murdered a number of Jews. Though not quite as rabidly extreme, the succeeding Antonescu regime nevertheless entirely associated Jews with the Bolshevik regime that had retaken Bessarabia and northern Bukovina and had deported many thousands of Romanians, and it blamed Jews for Romania's earlier reluctance to draw closer to Nazi Germany. Tempted now by Hitler, and having months since lost any faith in Britain, Romania's leaders decided that alliance with Germany in the coming war with the USSR was the obvious path to regaining the eastern territories.

If Bulgaria learned its demographic lessons in the First World War era, Romania learned them as a result of 1940. Like the late CUP–Ottoman state with its Directorate for the Settlement of Tribes and Immigrants, Romania's experience of interstate population exchange was swiftly translated into designs for the internal ethnic reordering of the state. The State Undersecretariat of Colonization and Evacuated Populations was established in September 1940 to manage the population exchange with Bulgaria. It was reorganized in May 1941 to manage 'Aryanization', colonization projects, and the general 'Romanianization' of the state.[43]

Antonescu's administration, guided by its chief ideologue, foreign minister and deputy prime minister Mihai Antonescu, planned a step-by-step removal of Jews from the economy and then, very probably, society. Without the fully fledged Nazi racial imperative this needed only to progress at a rate dictated by other national priorities. There was a desire for immediate and outright removal of Jews in order to secure the land only for those territories seized back from the USSR upon the invasion in June 1941, and later, from August 1941, for adjacent Ukrainian territories between the Dniester and the Bug rivers ('Transnistria'). As Mihai Antonescu said in July 1941 of the continuing cleansing of Bessarabia and northern Bukovina, 'in all our history there has never been a more appropriate, more complete, more far-reaching, more free moment for total ethnic liberation.' 'Liberation' from the Jews was to be followed by removal or forced assimilation of all the other non-Romanian populations of Bessarabia, northern Bukovina, and Transnistria, and then, at a later date, possibly the deportation of all Romanian Jews into German hands.

The escalation to outright mass murder was not automatic. Romania would have been equally happy to evict Jews over the Dniester from the newly (re)acquired territory, but the problem was that Jewish refugees fled and were dumped into territory recently overrun by the rapidly advancing German forces. In June and July, the SS and police killing squads operating immediately in the rear of the Wehrmacht in the southern USSR were focusing only on select political and 'racial' targets, and had to keep up with the military. The influx of Romanian Jews behind the lines was considered an unbearable security risk, so, while the killing squads murdered some 20,000 of the refugees, in the second half of July 1941 the Wehrmacht sent many thousands more back into Bessarabia. As Romania acquired Transnistria the following month, it also acquired 200,000 Ukrainian Jews to add to the Jewish population it could not expel.

Over the following several months the Romanian army took matters into its own hands as, with police units and the assistance of local Romanian, Ukrainian, and ethnic German civilians, it slaughtered scores of thousands of Jews, and incarcerated similar numbers in improvised camps and ghettos in Transnistria, where the death toll from cold, disease, and privation was massive. Along with the murder, the securing of the land through 'nationalization' proceeded apace: three-quarters of the farmland taken from Jews by the Romanian government was in territories outside the 1940 boundaries.[44] Some of the violence spilled just inside 'old Romania', as with the Iaşi pogrom of late June 1941, when 4,000 Jews were murdered on grounds of a spurious security threat. Some deportations of Jews from old Romania did take place, mostly from southern Bukovina, adjacent to the territory recently recovered from the USSR. Less discriminating still were the deportations of up to 26,000 Romanies from throughout Romania into Transnistria, where seven thousand were massacred and thousands more died of illness, cold, or hunger.[45]

Why were most Jews in old Romania not deported? National *amour propre* is part of the explanation: Romania resented German racial condescension and the feeling of being treated like a minor ally; Hungary and Italy had not had to surrender their Jews on German terms and Germany had done nothing to redress Romanian grievances about the Hungarian seizure of northern Transylvania. There was also an increasing belief that even as Germany was failing to equip its ally properly, many thousands of Romanian soldiers were dying for German ends in Russia. Domestic ethnonational priorities are another part of the explanation: Germany had increasingly been using the ethnic German population of greater Romania as a wedge to influence Romanian policy; removal of Jews would strengthen the already significant economic role of these ethnic Germans, and might lead to German claims for a protectorate in southern Transylvania. Each of these concerns was amplified in the aftermath of the major German defeat at Stalingrad at the end of 1942. Towards the end of the war Romanian anti-Semitism worked to save Jews, who were seen as having influence among the likely victorious Allies.[46]

Fascist Italy: Mediterranean Imperialism and Ethnic Policy

Germany's major European ally, Italy, had far less of an anti-Semitic tradition than Romania, and a much more assimilated Jewish population. Left to its own devices, fascist Jewish policy was a classic expression of ethnic dominance rather than destruction—Mussolini said its intention was to 'discriminate not persecute'. Italy did not deport its own Jewish nationals as a matter of policy—though some Italians were involved in round-ups of Jews and in denunciations—and it provided something of a haven for some Jews in its wartime occupation zones in southeastern France, western Yugoslavia ('Dalmatia'), and western Greece. These actions are partly testament to the lesser significance of Italian anti-Semitism, but they owed less to any particular Italian benevolence than to matters of national pride, a refusal to be dictated to by German priorities, and a sort of sovereignty battle amongst allies increasingly distrustful of one another in their adjacent occupation zones.

Rome had other, more pressing priorities in the geopolitical and economic spheres, racist as Mussolini and his Fascists were. Accordingly, insofar as Italy opposed the extremities of the proto-fascist Croat Ustaša policy during the war—a reaction shared at times even by the local German military—this was more out of fear of its destabilizing effect on a region the Axis was keen to keep pacified. The stance might also justify Italy further encroaching on Yugoslavian territory. In any case, Italy could scarcely be opposed to the general thrust of the Ustaša agenda since, up to 1941, as part of its interwar policy of upsetting the Balkan order, it had played host to the movement's leader, Ante Pavelić, alongside pro-Bulgarian Macedonian terrorists with other extremist agendas. In exchange for continuing Italian support, Pavelić had agreed that Italy could annexe Dalmatia, which it did as the Axis defeated Yugoslavia.

As with every other state, Italy's expansionist agenda was underpinned by a sense of ethnic antagonism and hierarchy. As with every other imperialist of the period, the formal empire Italy sought would have grave implications not just for local economic structures but also for the local demographic order. A foretaste of what would have transpired had Italy consolidated its European empire may be gained from the deportation of Slovenians from their former capital, Ljubljana, as Italy sought to penetrate deeply into its new Dalmatian territory and cement control of that important metropole immediately on the border with the German occupation zone. In the interwar period, along with Japan, Italy had been the most ruthless imperialist power, confronting obstacles to the establishment of the African part of its Mediterranean empire with huge and indiscriminate violence. Some of this violence was imported to the European domains Rome claimed during the Second World War (the coastal regions and islands of the Adriatic, Ionian, and Aegean seas), most notably in Greece, where Italy took a fulsome part in the brutal Axis anti-insurgency campaign against Greek partisan forces. Within its Greek zone of occupation Italy played the common game of ethnic divide-and-rule in its deployment of the Vlach minority (a partly secessionist population speaking a Latin-Romanian dialect) in this campaign, which frequently involved the total destruction of 'suspect' Greek settlements. Italy was also thoroughly implicated in the draconian system of wartime economic organization that brought starvation to scores of thousands of Greeks.

The 'Jewish question' intersected in varying ways with Italy's imperial aims. In places where Italy simply sought to entrench control and enrich itself, such as the Ionian islands, the Italians expropriated the Jews in precisely the way so many other Europeans were doing. In Salonika, within the German zone of Greece, things were different. Prior to its deportation by the Nazis, the 50,000-strong Jewish population, comprising the majority of Greek Jewry, was, despite earlier Greek efforts at establishing a 'national economy', still at the commercial hub of the city as it had been in Ottoman times. Since Italy aspired to controlling Salonika and using it for its own ends in a similar regional capacity to its old Ottoman one, and since a number of Italian interests were represented there by Jews, Italy fought hard not just to protect

Salonikan Jews of Italian nationality but also these select native Jewish contacts. As with all of its hubristic wartime designs, this one fell apart as Italy turned against Mussolini and surrendered to the Allies in September 1943, prompting Germany to occupy not just the former Italian occupation zones but northern Italy itself, and then to deport to Auschwitz nearly 8,000 Italian Jews. More than 40,000 Jews nevertheless survived in Italy owing to official and private assistance.[47]

Dependent Allies: Slovakia and Croatia

Moving from Germany's more independent allies to its more subordinate partners, Slovakia and Croatia, we arrive at two polities that only came into existence in 1939 and 1941, respectively. Both were dependent on Germany, and in the Croatian case Italy too, and yet both retained independence in many matters of internal policy, including ethnic policy. Both ultimately participated of their own volition in the Holocaust, but in very different ways. Few Jews were killed on Slovak soil, but it became the first state outside of direct German control to agree to the deportation of its Jews. Some 59,000 were deported, almost all to their deaths at Auschwitz. In the 'Independent State of Croatia', though 7,000 Jews were deported to Auschwitz, most of the remaining 32,000 Jewish victims were murdered in indigenous concentration camps. If Romania murdered the largest absolute number of Jews beyond Germany, the Croatian Ustaša regime killed the largest number of Jews relative to those under its control. And Jews were not even the main target. Alongside Yugoslav Muslims, the regime killed nearly as many Romanies (28,000) as Jews; but the primary objects of Croatia's race laws and victims of racial murder were Serbs, depicted in Ustaša rhetoric as both inferior and oppressive when the boot had been on the other foot in the interwar years. The regime killed up to 330,000 Serbs in a policy designed to remove them entirely from a greater Croatia by massacre, forced dispersal, and forced conversion to Catholicism.

The Ustaša regime brought instability and violence to all peoples under its sway, though its polarization of society brought it supporters, as did the prospect of plunder from its many victims. In fact the Ustaša movement was not a monolithic organization but rather a coalition of

Figure 6. Serbs and Gypsies rounded up for internment (Jasenovac, Croatia).

extremist Catholic nationalists whose agendas did not always cohere. The brutality of their politics encouraged both armed resistance and responses in kind in the form of Serbian royalist-nationalist partisans, the Četniks, who carried out revenge massacres of Croats, as well as killing some Jews and Muslims, particularly Albanians. Serbs also fell victim to atrocities by Bosnian Muslims, a number of whom formed their own Waffen-SS regiment. (In terms of absolute numbers, Muslims suffered fewer deaths than Croats, and many fewer than Serbs in wartime Yugoslavia.) Added to the mix were Tito's communist partisans, who fought against Četniks, Ustaša, and German and Italian forces, thereby encouraging further the ruthless anti-insurgency violence of the main Axis powers. The situation was yet further complicated by the way the warring Yugoslav factions fitted into the uneasy imperial cooperation of Germany and Italy: many Croat nationalists resented the loss of Dalmatia to Italy, and actively undermined Italian authority in its zone;

in turn, this encouraged the Italians to further contacts with the Četniks. The overall result was to turn Croatia into a chaotic charnel house for much of the war, with very little of the internal stability that might be achieved by other allies of the Nazis.[48]

Despite the common genocidal outcomes, there are clear differences between the Slovakian and Croatian polities. Rather like the wartime Romanian regime after the suppression of the Iron Guard, the Slovakian regime had more national legitimacy than its Croatian counterpart, and could claim to be more representative of the Slovak people. For longer than Antonescu, Tiso had to coexist in power and accommodate some of the agenda of an extremist, proto-fascist faction—the Hlinka Guard, an organization headed by the Prime Minister, Tuka, and one enjoying considerable German support until 1942. In the Hlinka Guard's view, Slovakia's '*židovská otázka*', or 'Jewish question', had to be solved by immediate bodily removal. This was not initially the view of Tiso's Catholics. For them, ethnic domination was what was desired. Where Jews had been the masters before, under Magyar and then Czech rule, they would now be made to serve the Slovak people, and this was to be achieved by discriminatory legislation on social, economic, and professional life. That 'Slovakization' accelerated as the regime drew closer to Nazi Germany is not itself evidence of a move to a more radical solution; it simply shows that the Slovak state wished to ensure it rather than Germany profited from the expropriation of the Jews.

The only initial exception to the logic of Slovak domination as opposed to extirpation again had some of the territorial logic into which other eastern European nationalists wove their Jewish policy. This was the deportation of some Jews into the territory that Hungary took from Slovakia (Subcarpathien Rus) around the time of the Munich agreement. Tiso found the scapegoat for this national humiliation in the Jews, whom it was always suspected were Hungarian sympathizers. In November 1938, spurred on by the Hlinka Guard, and by violent paramilitary units of ethnic Germans, Tiso decided to prevent any Jews in the soon-to-be ceded territories from coming into Slovakia, whether or not they were of Slovakian citizenship. The logic was that Jews had wanted Hungarian sovereignty so should be forced to accept it. Swiftly this decision was followed by the idea of expelling a large number of Jews of foreign nationality into the same no-man's land, except insofar as their removal damaged the Slovak economy. About 7,500 Jews altogether were involved, though many ultimately returned to Slovakia because of Hungarian refusal to take them. The result of the episode was, first, to create an apparatus for dealing specifically with Jews (a 'central office for the solution of the Jewish problem in Slovakia' was established to coordinate the policy), second, to create a precedent for eviction, and third, to illustrate that eviction might rebound without the cooperation of the recipient state.

To draw a straight line from the events of November 1938 to the 1942 deportations to Auschwitz would be wrong. Without the input of the German policy advisor on the Jewish question, Dieter Wisliceny, who had been dispatched by the SS's Reich Security Head Office in August 1940, it is unlikely Slovakia would have deported its own Jewish nationals. Radicalization occurred partly from the economic immiseration of the Jewish population that was the logical result of Slovakization policy. As in Germany in the later 1930s, creating a large number of unemployed and impoverished Jews in the interests of the national economy created a burden on the state. It led to some Jews being placed into forced labour camps, thereby further dislocating the Jewish community. Deportation to German control for supposed labour in Poland, as Germany portrayed it, was as much as anything a way of solving this self-created problem. Wisliceny and the German Foreign Office were vital in the policy's crystallization, less in forcing it than suggesting and facilitating it.

For most in the administration, Tiso included, the important thing about the deportations was that the Jews would not return this time. What would actually happen to them was a secondary consideration. Tiso and his colleagues possibly were not aware of the precise fate lying in wait for the Jews, for at the time of the deportation decision in March 1942 the name Auschwitz did not have the resonance it later acquired. Yet neither did they really care, and those officials desirous of enquiring recognized that the deportees would die in the immediate or medium term depending on their physical state.

All 56,000 of the Slovakian Jews deported with Slovak acquiescence were taken in 1942. This left 18,648 Jews in the country, either in forced labour camps or, the vast majority (16,000), with some form of exemption. The Tiso regime's growing reluctance to deport the remnant after 1942 was certainly encouraged by Germany's military failures and a concern for Slovakia's place in the postwar world, while such Catholic opposition as there was in the country at large stemmed substantially from concern for Jewish converts to Christianity and Jews in mixed marriages. With the German occupation of Slovakia from summer 1944 in light of the Slovak uprising, the Hungarian pattern of the same period was followed on a smaller scale. German units, with assistance from Hlinka Guard elements, deported 8,000 more Jews to Auschwitz and 4,300 to other camps, and killed more than a thousand Romanies.[49]

Vichy France: The Non-combatant Collaborator

France was obviously a much more stable and long-established nation-state. Nevertheless, defeat and partial occupation in 1940 brought internal tensions to the fore—between population groups, but primarily between different ideas of what sort of country France should be. The Catholic political influence that manifested itself as the Vichy government in the 'national revolution' was the right wing that inherited the mantle of the anti-revolutionary tradition and of the authors of the infamous Dreyfus affair in the 1890s. The Vichy regime in the unoccupied south, which was nominally neutral but de facto subordinate to Germany in its provision of wartime materiel and labour power, clearly partook of anti-Semitism, yet of a different form to that of the Nazis. Manifestations of ethnic dominance, namely the infamous anti-Jewish legislation, the *statuts*, and the French 'Aryanization' policy, derived from domestic conservative tradition. The internment and deportation of mostly foreign Jews to the extermination camps was more an expression of straightforward collaborationism.[50]

France's deportation of more than 56,000 non-French Jews (out of a total of around 135,000, mostly refugees from Germany or eastern Europe), 8,000 French children of non-French Jews, 8,000 naturalized Jews, and 1,500 Jews born in Algeria presents a seeming historical paradox. The energy with which these people were rounded up by primarily French police and administrators has long and rightly held the attention of scholars of the subject. From the French perspective, this ruthless collaborationism was a way of filling (sometimes overfilling) deportation quotas while not deporting Jews of 'true' French nationality. The motivations for the distinction were twofold: the now-familiar determination not to compromise national sovereignty and its prerogatives, and the less familiar aim of not agitating sympathetic gentiles, of whom there were not a few, judging by the number of Jews who survived the war in hiding.

Tellingly, French deportation policies served to preserve in some form the contract between nation-state and citizen that the original French revolutionaries had bequeathed to the world, and simultaneously to illustrate the harsh logic of *any* nationalist morality, wherein the distinction between citizen and non-citizen was all-important. The point should not be pressed too far, for by 1944 Vichy Prime Minister Pierre Laval gave up even on the attempt to protect French Jews, when he had earlier done so quite vigorously. Nevertheless, because Nazi Germany was defeated when it was, of a prewar French Jewish population of 195,000, 16,500 Jewish citizens as formally defined and 'only' 6,500 Jews born in France to French Jews were passed into German hands and thus to their deaths.[51]

Peoples under Nazi Control: Collaboration and Protection

The final category of polities fell under direct Nazi control and to one degree or another lost their sovereignty. Those in the north and the west of the continent experienced generally less disruption and brutality than those to the east, though, as the war progressed, German requisitioning of materiel and forced labourers intensified everywhere, and growing resistance across the continent was met with increasingly unfettered violence. The northern and western states benefited from their perceived higher levels of civilization and 'racial value'. Like France, most also had the good fortune of relative historical stability, longevity, advanced civil society and representative political structures, and greater ethnic homogeneity. None would be immune from some internal fracturing along political and in some cases ethnic lines—Belgium, for instance, experienced hostility between its Flemish and Walloon populations—and each would produce some collaborators acting from motives ranging from political conviction to greed. But the main ethnic question confronting each state was how far it would collaborate with Germany in deporting its Jews eastwards. No citizen of these countries was forcibly coerced into getting his own hands dirty in the business of racist murder, but quite a few did.

In May 1940 Belgium came under German military control, and the Netherlands and Luxembourg came under German civilian administration. Most of the small Jewish population of Luxembourg fled the country for unoccupied France in 1940–1. The German military took on responsibility for the deportation of Belgium's Jews. It succeeded in deporting some 25,000 of a prewar population of 65,000–70,000, most of whom were foreign, many stateless. Most of these 25,000 died at Auschwitz. A further 25,000 hid amongst the Belgian population. The Dutch civil service was heavily implicated in the deportation to their deaths of at least 102,000 Jews of a prewar population of 140,000. Its level of collaboration with the Nazi authorities may be explained more by the particular constellation of German SS personnel in that country compared to, say, France, than by a peculiarly Dutch official disposition to rigour and obedience.[52]

To the north, Denmark was occupied in April 1940. Because it offered no resistance, and because Hitler considered the Danes fellow 'nordics', Denmark was treated very leniently, and substantially allowed to administer itself. These factors, plus a distinct lack of indigenous anti-Semitism, and perhaps also the milder attitudes of some of the senior Nazis in Denmark, combined to ensure that of the prewar Jewish population of around 7,500, only 100 died. In autumn 1943 some nearly 5,000 Copenhagen Jews were ferried to the safety of neutral Sweden by a combination of popular local initiative and Danish state assistance.

In contrast, Norway did resist the German attack of April 1940, and was accordingly subject to more extensive German control. German forces found some indigenous collaborators to help with the round-up of the Jews but also encountered some vocal opposition to deportations. In consequence of these divergent responses, of 1,700 Jews living in Norway in 1940 some 760 Jews were deported, most to die at Auschwitz, while 900 were helped to escape to Sweden by the underground movement.

The remaining Scandinavian country, Finland, was a co-belligerent of Nazi Germany but not an actual Axis member. It deported no Jews during the Second World War.

Peoples under Nazi Control: Indigenous Motives for Murder

In eastern Europe, German rule meant the destruction and remodelling of existing infrastructures in the sole interests of Nazi economic and racial policy. It entailed a much more thoroughgoing attempt than the First World War effort of bringing 'Germanic order' to this underdeveloped, 'inferior', and ethnically mixed region. The Slavic populations there were held in degrees of contempt ranging to the genocidal.

Poland was treated with a combination of racism and simple vengefulness stemming from its failure to obey Hitler's demands over Danzig in 1938. Those parts of Poland not incorporated into the 'Reich' were ruled directly by a German civil administration, where Poles were allowed no senior roles, even as collaborators. Polish policemen were used, however, under German supervision as auxiliaries in the rounding-up of Jews and for innumerable menial occupation tasks. In the areas of Poland taken from the USSR, by contrast, Poles were allowed some senior administrative positions; equally after subjection to Soviet rule, many eastern Poles objected less to the possibility of collaboration with Germany. Later in the war, many eastern Poles were deployed to combat a frustrated Ukrainian nationalist movement.

Germany had previously contributed fulsomely to exacerbating Polish–Ukrainian ethnopolitical enmity. Like Italy with its harbouring of Balkan terrorists, Germany had fostered prewar ties with the Organization of Ukrainian Nationalists (OUN), which wrongly viewed Germany as the power most likely to pave the way to independent Ukrainian statehood. In Nazi-ruled Poland, a number of administrative positions were given to Ukrainians as part of the policy of ethnic divide-and-rule.

The territory of Ukraine was transferred from Soviet to Nazi hands by the German invasion of June 1941, along with Belarus and the Baltic States to the north. The collaborators the lands provided in the Holocaust outnumbered the German personnel in these territories many times over. In Lithuania these men would do the bulk of the killing, and would be exported southward for the same task. In Ukraine and Belarus, the indigenous population did proportionately less of the shooting, but they facilitated it by policing ghettos, assisting deportations, and locating escaped and hidden Jews.

A broad spectrum of motives promoted collaboration in occupation and genocide. Beyond venal or mundane incentives — the quest, say, for loot, or the power status that an official capacity brought — additional motivations were provided in the east over those available in western Europe: greater threat and compulsion, consistent with the German attitude towards the population as a whole. The German occupiers furthered the element of terror by promoting some of the most radical anti-communist and racist elements to positions of political seniority, such as the Lithuanian Activists' Front (*Lietuvtu Aktyvistu Frontas*; LAF). These factors underscore the quite uncommon courage required of that proportionally small but still significant number of non-Jews who aided Jews and others. Moreover, on the historical rather than ethical level, whatever the precise motives for collaboration in murder, a distinction should be drawn between such deeds, however horrific, and more independent murdering of Jews on one's own account. Independent indigenous policies of murdering Jews tended to develop when the 'Jewish question' fitted into overlapping nationalist dynamics, which may explain why Belarus, with no strong nationalist tradition or movement, produced many collaborators but few pogroms outside of the more predominantly Polish western areas.

The other lands taken from the USSR had very divergent historical attitudes to their Jews. Lithuanian–Jewish relations were traditionally much more cordial than Ukrainian–Jewish ones, despite interwar 'Lithuanianization' policies. Unlike the LAF, the puppet civilian Lithuanian 'Provisional Government' installed by Germany generally supported 'only' classic measures of ethnic dominance against Jews — expropriation and segregation — rather than destruction.[53] What the lands did have in common was more extensive nationalist sentiment than in Belarus. Further all had lost their independence at various points to the Soviet Union, as had the eastern territories of Poland in 1939, and they had experienced the privations, persecutions, deportations, and summary economic reordering associated with Soviet rule and particularly the extremely violent Soviet withdrawal. Together, these factors suggest why in June–July 1941 Latvia, Lithuania, 'western Ukraine', and parts of the northeast of Poland (most infamously the town of Jedwabne[54]) experienced a wave of locally organized massacres with the arrival of German forces. In Lithuania, massacres occurred even before German control was established. In each instance, prior Soviet rule and its hardships were equated with the political ascendancy of Jews.

It is not necessary by this stage to detail the usual anti-Semitic inflations of a core of perfectly explicable reality. The proportional overrepresentation of Jews in the local communist parties and in the ranks of the NKVD cannot be denied, nor that many Jews welcomed the arrival of Soviet forces; but nor can the fact that Jews suffered more than most groups from Soviet economic restructuring and the deportation of 'bourgeois elements'. Ultimately, what was at issue was not the actual number of Jews involved in communist rule, but the historical association of Jews with Bolshevism (*zhydo-bolshevyzm* in Ukrainian) and the fact that any Jews at all should find themselves in positions of political authority in lands where this had not historically been the case.[55] Also present, perhaps, was a desire to create the false impression that Jews had been the only collaborators with Soviet rule. At a time of the absence of state authority, and then its arrival in the form of licentious Nazi rule, any number of imaginary scores could be settled in a way that recalls both 1905 and 1918. A further proximate stimulant for some of the Ukrainian massacres was the discovery in NKVD prisons of the corpses of thousands of prisoners murdered immediately prior to the Soviet retreat.[56]

At the same time, where a different ethnicity could be held scapegoat for ethnonational humiliation, committed nationalists and some ordinary civilians were prepared to vent their spleen in the corresponding direction. For independent Lithuania, as for Ukraine, Poland had been as great an imperial threat as the USSR. The most painful reminder of historical Polish dominance was the larger Polish population of the historic 'Lithuanian' capital Vilnius, the city that had been annexed by Poland in 1922. Though Vilnius also had a large Jewish population, which was instantly targeted by Germany and its Lithuanian auxiliaries, its Jews were not generally attacked on Lithuanian initiative in June 1941, in contrast to events in the other major Lithuanian city of Kaunas where

3,800 were so murdered from 23 to 27 June. In Vilnius it was the Polish population that was targeted according to a long-standing Lithuanian nationalist agenda. This took the form of some massacres, and many more evictions. Germany played its part, deporting many thousands of Poles for forced labour. The USSR completed the 'de-polonization' of Vilnius after the war.[57]

What was true for Vilnius was true for the whole of the 'western Ukraine', which Poland had ruled and which still had a large Polish population. Notwithstanding the 12,000 or so Jews murdered on local initiative in the area, and the mutual Ukrainian–Moldavian violence of the Second World War, much more important in the eyes of the OUN for the longer term prospects of a Ukrainian state were Polish–Ukrainian relations. Indeed, there were large tracts of western Ukraine such as Volhynia where, despite the collaboration of thousands with the SS in the German final solution, anti-Semitism did not generally erupt into pogroms, but where Ukrainian anti-Polish violence reached terrible proportions.

One faction of the OUN (the 'Bandera' faction), through its proxy the UPA or Ukrainian Insurgent Army, was the chief agent of the murder and ethnic cleansing of Poles and the only organization to pursue total removal of the Poles. It began to realize this agenda after the German defeat at Stalingrad at the end of 1942. It was the most radical Ukrainian nationalist organization, one that had risen to dominance through its destruction of rival OUN factions and the accompanying murder of thousands of fellow Ukrainians. This was only possible because the German and Soviet occupations had decapitated Ukrainian as well as Polish civil and political society. Its leaders were veterans of the 1918–19 Polish-Ukrainian war, and many of its recruits had spent time in the Polish interwar concentration camp used to pacify eastern Poland. The prediction on which their policy of ethnic pre-emption was based was that if Germany were defeated, Poland would look to re-expand to its prewar boundaries, with all the consequences that had brought with it before for Ukrainian national identity. Such was precisely the plan of the Polish 'Home Army.'

The terrible truth of how the UPA partisans were hardened to their task of killing Poles lies in the history of OUN's earlier collaboration with Germany. Ukrainian nationalists composed a large proportion of the 12,000 Ukrainian auxiliaries who aided Germany in the final solution of the Jewish question in 1941–2. Those who actually killed numbered probably in the low thousands, but many more were involved in the preparations for murder. Rather than being drawn to this task through anti-Semitism, undoubtedly anti-Semitic though many were, their motivation for collaboration had been to further the nationalist cause. The Germans had other ideas, and the Ukrainians ended up simply as foot soldiers in the killing of 200,000 Volhynian Jews, almost the entire prewar population. Some of the Ukrainians learned anti-Semitism on the job. All learned the skills and brutality needed later for organizing the slaughter of Poles.[58]

To Germany

Without the UPA, the LAF, the Ustaša, and innumerable other agents, the Holocaust would not have achieved the dimensions it did. The multifarious murders committed by non-Germans are significant principally because they indicate that whatever the new quality and quantity of horror Germany imposed on Europe, the continent was already a place where extreme collective violence was an accepted measure of resolving identity crises. Their secondary significance is that on occasion they signalled to Germany what was possible: the scale of murder by Lithuanian personnel around the end of June outstripped that of the German police; and on 19 August, Hitler observed of Romania's genocidal policies that Antonescu's regime was showing the way in its radicalism.[59]

The Third Reich was a product of the continent as well as the most destructive shaper of it. Nazi racial policy was geared not just to Hitler's peculiar obsession with the Jews, but to a host of other biopolitical and geopolitical concerns that would have been entirely recognizable to millions of nationalists in and beyond Germany. Nevertheless, the Third Reich was the chief driver of war and the reshaping of Europe, so the question remains: why Germany?

PART II GERMANY AND THE FINAL SOLUTION

“ Since the French Revolution the world has been drifting with increasing speed towards a new conflict, whose most extreme solution is Bolshevism, but whose content and goal is the removal of those social strata that have given leadership to humanity up to the present, and their replacement by international Jewry. ”
Adolf Hitler, memorandum on the establishment of the Four Year Plan, 1936

CHAPTER 4
NAZISM AND GERMANY

Introduction: Legacies of the First World War and Versailles

Why Germany? Why Germany what? If the question is why did
Germany do everything in its power to revise Versailles, with its
diminution of German territory and sovereignty, the answer is that is
what any state in the European system would have done in its place,
sooner or later. Nazism was not needed for revisionism, as hosts of
quotidian nationalists in Germany and elsewhere could testify. Some
expansion had been supported across the spectrum of German politicians
in 1914. Gustav Stresemann had endorsed the annexation of Belgium
during the First World War and spent much of his time as Weimar
foreign minister pressing the issues of the eastern borders and the ethnic
Germans in the territories of what was now western Poland. After 1918,
revisionism was one of the few things on which most Germans in the
fractious Weimar Republic could agree. For most politicized Germans
beyond the 'Weimar Coalition' around the Social Democratic Party
(SPD), 'Weimar' itself was a target for revision.

The loss of territory to France rankled throughout the German
population, but not nearly so much as the losses to Poland. A German
cultural tradition had looked eastwards since the medieval settlement of
the Teutons in the Baltic, and while modern Germany was not born
of the end of empire in eastern Europe, its aspirations and chauvinisms
were predominantly orientated towards the region. The First World
War had provided concrete recent experience of eastern empire and
consolidated a sense of superiority over the Slavs. Moreover, Germany
had not been defeated in the east, and its leaders shared with the

USSR a sense that the post-Habsburg states of east-central Europe were inauthentic Allied puppets—the Soviet Foreign Minister Molotov famously describing Poland as the 'monstrous bastard of Versailles'.

There were many other connections between Germany and the imperial shatterzones. One was the ethnic Germans, or *Volksdeutsche*, living in the newly created states, including the former western Habsburg metropol of Austria, which provided a disproportionate number of Nazis. The most famous Austrian German is Hitler himself. Hitler was politically socialized in the increasingly xenophobic environment of late-imperial Vienna where he came to see the empire's multinationality as the source of its weakness, learned pan-German nationalism and, from the example of the city's mayor Karl Lueger, the political value of anti-Semitism as a uniting force. The other *Volksdeutsche* elsewhere in the former Habsburg lands and in the former Russian empire would provide a focus and the personnel for some of the most radical nationalist movements of the Weimar years. In 1930 the Nazi party established its own foreign organization (*Auslandsorganisation*) to disseminate propaganda through the diaspora communities. The *Volksdeutsche* were highly represented in the ranks of the most murderous SS regiments.[1]

There is merit to the judgement that Germany was either treated too harshly or not harshly enough at Versailles: too severely for it not to seek revision; too leniently to prevent it achieving revision, particularly after Allied troops pulled out of the Rhineland in 1930, so relinquishing any real opportunity for enforcement of the provisions of the Versailles treaty. After the war against Napoleon some of the sting had been taken from that defeat by incorporating in the settlement some of the desires of France's new leaders. No such negotiation took place with Germany, because the strength of public sentiment forced British and French leaders to go further than some advisors thought prudent. The impact of the Versailles '*Diktat*' had much the same galvanizing effect on German revanchism as the announcement of the Trianon terms on Hungary and the Sèvres terms in pre-Kemalist 1920 Turkey, and served similarly to discredit the governing regime that had been established in the immediate aftermath of defeat. But in contrast to the position in Anatolia, the Allies had the will and the means to impose their plans on Germany (and Hungary), including continuation of the murderous wartime blockade until July 1919 to ensure German acquiescence. While military demobilization was forced onto Germany, the desire amongst parts of its population to reverse the war's outcome meant that 'cultural demobilization',[2] the shedding of wartime mindsets, did not occur to the extent it did in France and Britain.

Within Germany, the idea that Germany had not lost on the battlefield, but instead had been betrayed by enemies within was both irksome and comforting. The huge popular investment in warfare would not allow a simple admission of defeat. For Germany's traditional, conservative elites and the radical Right, propagating the 'stab in the back' myth was safer politics than examining the reality of the war record. The myth was the obverse side of the burgeoning myth of the 'community of the front'—a supposed microcosm of the national community, characterized by sacrifice and heroism.[3] The twin myths of solidarity and betrayal consolidated the effect of the German war propaganda that had depicted imminent victory late into 1918 and laid the blame for inadequate German wartime economic organization at the door of Jewish profiteers. Both sustained the idea that the 'real Germany' was not a loser in the Darwinian struggle, and that what was needed for a German reassertion was an attack on 'internal' as well as 'external' enemies.

The notion Germany had not been defeated in battle disregarded allied successes in 1918, and increasing rates of German desertion, but more importantly it obscured the truth of 'total war'. Germany lost because ultimately it could not compete in a long-drawn-out war of attrition where industrial and financial power and sheer weight of manpower—all three boosted on the Allied side by US entry—were as important as battlefield tactics, and where its civilian population suffered grievously through the British blockade and Germany's lack of self-sufficiency, which in turn contributed to the revolutionary mood in the country in 1918. Nonetheless, beneath the rhetorical evasions, some of the lessons of defeat *were* learned. What is really important is how in the minds of the future Nazi leadership and other important German elites these 'actual' lessons were *compounded* with others emerging from the paranoia, self-deceits, and intensified ethnonationalism of the period.

Unity of state and society, security of resource, and speed of conquest: these were the war lessons Germany's future leaders learned. Unity, the ability to mobilize the entire population in the national project, was the *raison d'être* of the nation-state. While Nazism saw the state only as a vehicle for the ethnic community, and the Nazi movement as the expression of the people's will, in power the Nazis were obsessed with the state's readiness for war. Pursuing resource independence in the form of autarky was not only a useful policy during the Great Depression; it would provide the material basis for the war effort, to maintain war production and sustain the population's morale and keep it at fighting strength.[4]

Unity and resource supply had distinct human corollaries. Unity in the Nazi view meant unity of the racially desirable, politically aligned, and physically and mentally healthy, including ethnic Germans from beyond German frontiers. Those found wanting in the first two categories needed to be purged in the interests of security and purity, and because the purge itself would further unite and discipline the desirable masses. Those found wanting in the third category needed to be purged to improve the stock of the population and to remove an unproductive drain on its resources.

Autarky necessitated territorial expansion within Europe, since Germany had failed to provide for itself during the First World War, and had not been able to rely on the dubious economic benefits of its overseas colonies because of the blockade. One of the main tasks of the Office of the Four Year Plan from 1936 was to procure resources in order to forestall a repeat of the earlier experience. The expansion this procurement entailed dovetailed with Hitler's desire for 'living space' and resources to support the future German empire, and with the more traditional imperial ambitions of many influential Germans beyond Hitler's circle. As Nazi plans developed, eastward expansion was to incorporate the industries of the Czech and western Polish lands and the vital agricultural soil of the Ukraine and western Russia, over which so much blood had been spilled in the collectivization famines occurring in the years immediately prior to the Nazi accession. Historically, Europe west of the Elbe River had relied on grain produced to its east, just as the region was vital for the Russian empire and then the USSR. And while the two anti-Versailles states had re-established this supply relationship in the interwar period out of common interest, if Hitler were ultimately to fight the USSR, the grain would have to be taken by force. The subsistence needs of the peoples of those lands, already viewed as racially inferior, and so appropriate for exploitation or expulsion, would not interfere with the prime purpose of providing for the German people and its war effort. Racist, strategic, and economic principles would be mutually reinforcing because they were all elements of the world-view of the warmonger.

Considerations about resources were related to operational speed. Probably from the end of 1934, Hitler had formulated intentions but not concrete plans to invade the Allied-created bulwark of Czechoslovakia—which ultimately proved unnecessary—then attack France, and Britain if it saw fit to join a continental war again. As his ideas developed, an attack on the USSR was next, and, finally, even the USA, the power whose entry into the conflict in 1917 seemed to have tipped the balance. (War with the other Versailles bulwark of Poland in 1939 occurred to secure Germany's eastern flank before attacking westward.) In a classic example of learning the lessons of the last war rather than the next, western Europe was seen as the real challenge, because the central powers had won in the 'degenerate' Slavic east in the First World War. Now the former Russian empire, which had supposedly only been sustained down to 1917 by its Germanic elites, was ruled by the even more incompetent Bolsheviks, whom it was assumed would collapse under the pressure of total war like their Tsarist predecessors. Germany thus developed weapons systems primarily for use in the west.

The quest for swift victory in the east raised the matter of 'pacificatory violence'. The spectre that had haunted Germany's generals since the Franco-Prussian war of 1870, gaining in intensity with native resistance to Germany's colonial campaigns, and then with Belgian resistance at Liège and Louvain during the 1914–18 war, was partisan warfare conducted behind German lines and/or by fighters indistinguishable from the surrounding population. Anxiety about the threat to military operations and supply lines and the prospect of a civilian population complicit in resistance also illuminates the behaviour of a number of German officers in the Russian–Ottoman campaign in 1914–15.

The military's acquiescence in the Armenian genocide as a result of 'insurrection hysteria', and its perpetration of mass slaughter in the Herero and Maji-Maji wars at the beginning of the century were ominous precedents for the army's war with the USSR. But the invasion of the Soviet Union lay well into an unpredictable future.

If the question is why Germany chose Nazism as opposed to a less extreme revisionist option, the answer is more locally contingent. The fall of Weimar may have been likely, given the economic consequences of depression, the lingering psychological effects of inflation, and the powerful political forces opposed to Weimar's survival. By 1930, Weimar democracy had effectively ended, with Brüning and successive chancellors relying on emergency powers arrogated to President Hindenburg in order to circumvent the fractious parliament. But the fall of Weimar is not the same as the rise of Nazism. Beyond economic crisis, Nazism's success was due to Hitler's political talents and charisma; the electoral system in Weimar and the political factionalism it encouraged; doctrinal divisions on the Left; the appeal of parts of the Nazi manifesto; and the agenda of members of Germany's conservative political elite who believed they could exploit and control Hitler.

Hitler achieved power constitutionally, though not by gaining a majority of the popular vote. From its 2 per cent showing in 1928 the Nazi share of the vote rose to its peak in summer 1932 (37.2%), but, despite the terror tactics of the Nazi stormtroopers (SA), it fell markedly by the autumn, by which time the party was in some internal disarray. A backroom deal gave Hitler the Chancellorship in January 1933. Despite the intensification of the SA's terror campaign and the arbitrary incarceration of opponents, the Reichstag elections of 5 March gave only a narrow victory to Hitler's coalition government and no majority for the Nazi party. But it was victory nonetheless and thereafter other political parties were banned and, on Hindenburg's death in 1934, Hitler was free to seize the Presidency, fusing leadership of state and government in his person.

The likes of Franz von Papen (Chancellor for six months in 1932) and Alfred Hugenberg (leader of the DNVP, the German National People's Party) underestimated Hitler, and paved his way to total power by permitting him the chancellorship on the assumption he would be a useful ally. Mussolini had also been ushered into power by Italian conservatives in 1922. Hitler could be considered precisely because he shared some of the values of his sponsors: anti-Bolshevism, anti-socialism, commitment to the restoration of German great-power status and of putatively German values over 'degenerate', libertarian Weimar values. This reminds us that in 1933–4 many western statesmen were not threatened by the prospect of right-wing dictatorship in Germany and Italy, and most saw fascism as less of a peril than the Bolshevism it so vehemently opposed. The Papen administration actually anticipated some of the Nazi measures in 1932 when it purged the Prussian state police force of leftist and liberal elements, and the practice of 'protective custody' that the SA and SS used in 1933 had also been used against communists at Weimar's inception, and so was met with equanimity by many civil servants. The orientation of the established power elite helps to explain how, despite being the greatest perpetrators of violence on the streets between 1930 and 1932, the Nazis actually benefited from fear of a communist coup in the period, and contrived to sell themselves as a force of law and order.[5]

What does the rise of Nazism in Germany tell us about Germany? The fact Nazism happened there has naturally given rise to the search for the origins of Nazism in German culture and history. Such origins there indeed were, but the quest for them can easily lead the seeker to forget that there was no inevitability to Nazi success, and that radical ideas existed in other societies and might have found fertile soil there in circumstances comparable to Germany's in the early 1930s. Because in Germany Hitler carried such strands to power and implementation at a moment of crisis does not mean that Germany was inherently more susceptible to these extremes than other countries in terms of 'national character'.

Nazi Ideology

There was no one Nazi ideology, but a series of related ideas and prescriptions for society that centred on the notion of race and varied in constellation from Hitler through to ideologues like Alfred Rosenberg and the SS chief Heinrich Himmler. These conceptions in turn descended from some of the many German and European ideas in competitive circulation in the later nineteenth century about the origins, destiny, and difference of peoples. Saul Friedländer's influential analysis points to some of the origins of Hitler's beliefs in the Bayreuth circle around the family of the composer Richard Wagner, blending 'German Christianity, neo-romanticism, the mystical cult of sacred Aryan blood, and ultra-conservative nationalism'.[6] *Völkisch* mysticism taken as a roadmap for national development, extreme ethnonationalism, and pseudoscience were combined in a terrifying agenda for unmixing the peoples under German dominion and breeding a race 'worthy' of European mastery.

Because of its peculiar dynamics, Nazi anti-Semitism was not entirely congruent with other exclusionary ideologies. In the Nazi view of Jews, political enmity and biology were coterminous. Conversely, other despised races were intrinsically only inferior (as were sick Germans), and only politically dangerous insofar as they outnumbered Germans, interbred with Germans, or were manipulated by Jews. Jews were actually viewed as an 'anti-race'—a parasitical, polluting people with no authentic culture. Hitler's depiction of their diabolical cunning and inherent, relentless destructiveness would not have looked out of place in medieval associations of the Jew and the Devil. The notion of Jews spreading their influence by blood was in a sense only a modernized version of the old idea of hidden Jewish influence spread through clandestine channels. As Norman Cohn hinted, it was the idea of the Jewish conspiracy, however configured, that marked Jews out among the enemies of Nazism just as among the enemies of medieval Christian culture.[7]

This sort of phobic anti-Semitism, detecting Jewish conspirators everywhere, only gained in strength after the Bolshevik Revolution. If German anti-Semites wished for more evidence of the 'rise of the Jews' to a position of dominance, they only had to look to the Weimar constitution, which gave Jews the fullest social emancipation. Increasingly, among the better educated Nazis that we shall later encounter within the SS, the more emotive anti-Semitism was complemented by a self-styled anti-Semitism of reason, one based on cool, supposedly objective recognition of the battles necessary for German survival, as if the anti-Semites were simply operating according to the competitive laws of nature.[8]

Despite the peculiar quality of anti-Semitism, what connected Jew-hatred with other Nazi obsessions *was* the increasingly pseudoscientific thinking about 'races', heredity, and breeding. The Nazi concern with the health of the German 'race' was graphically manifested within months of taking power in the 'law for the prevention of hereditarily ill progeny'. This was effectively a statutory legitimation for enforced sterilization, and paved the way for some 320,000 such operations over the first six years of Nazi rule, including 5,000 eugenic abortions with subsequent sterilization. Amongst the victims from the very beginning were Romanies, targeted as allegedly feebleminded, black Germans (often the offspring of relationships between German women and French and Belgian African troops from the Rhineland and Ruhr occupations), and 'asocials', including itinerants and some 'hereditary criminals'. There were also a disproportionate number of people who were simply poor and displayed behaviour not considered to be socially appropriate, including prostitutes. Alongside institutional inmates these were the most defenceless groups in society, which is certainly why they were chosen first. From the perspective of some of the newly empowered scientific and political authorities in Germany their fate was only a beginning. From 1933 some authorities were estimating that anywhere from 5–30 per cent of the German population could be targeted for sterilization in future.[9]

Policies against the 'hereditarily ill' reached their apogee in the wartime 'euthanasia' campaign. Even before the war, the combination of Nazi contempt for 'useless eaters' and fashionable scientific doctrine meant that state asylums were systematically underfunded, bringing their patients to near-starvation and thus, in circular fashion, suggesting the 'solution' of outright murder. The line of systematic, life-preventing state-sanctioned violence connecting mass forced sterilization to mass murder on such a scale was straighter and firmer than that connecting prewar anti-Jewish legislation and wartime genocide. One link was provided by the 'child euthanasia' campaign of 1939–44, which was an extension of the logic of the law against hereditarily ill progeny and involved the murder of 5,000 such children born over the previous sixteen years.[10]

Action against the mentally and physically ill was part of a broader set of social policies derived from a vision of the nation as a body whose health could be treated in the same way as an individual. Social problems were increasingly perceived biologically: 'asocial' behaviour, alcoholism, and forms of criminality were supposedly hereditary conditions alongside 'race' and illness. The 'Security Police'—the Gestapo (Geheime Staatspolizei) and the Reich Criminal Police (Kriminalpolizei)—became doctors of the body politic, alongside the whole state scientific, medical, and nursing machinery, which was deeply implicated in Nazism's domestic crimes. And just as the Gestapo developed out of the Prussian secret state police, so too the Kriminalpolizei inherited from the pre-Nazi police both personnel and expertise in tackling 'degenerate' and 'inherited' criminality in radical new ways. For many of these career policemen, the Nazi takeover provided the opportunity to put their ideas into practice untrammelled.[11]

As the remit of the Security Police forces expanded over the Nazi years, they developed wide powers of 'preventive' arrest and incarceration in concentration camps, in what was now openly known as the 'racial-biological fight against crime'.[12] One of the Kriminalpolizei's main victims was Germany's Romany population, with the racialized understanding of 'crime prevention' and social hygiene giving a new slant to centuries-old prejudice.[13] Romanies were not central to Hitler's world-view, and were subject to sometimes contradictory policies until the late 1930s. The main domestic concern about Romany–German relations was miscegenation, a key element in many strands of racist thought, from de Gobineau, the nineteenth-century French 'father of racism' onwards. Thus to suggest, as some have, that Nazi Romany policy was fundamentally different to Jewish policy because Romanies were seen as a social rather than a racial problem is to fail to appreciate the extent to which biological and social concepts coalesced in the period.

In Jewish policy, it is clear in hindsight that Hitler had radical goals to go alongside his rhetoric, but even in hindsight these goals were ill-defined. In their 1920 party programme, the Nazis had asserted that

Jews were not part of the German national community, and therefore could not be citizens of Germany, but what that meant in practice would only be gradually established from the mid-1930s onwards. Genocide was far beyond the horizon in 1933, and while many who voted Nazi were not deterred by Hitler's anti-Semitism, this was not the same as being drawn to it. The Nazis opportunistically contrived to be a catch-all party of social grievance, so it is telling that anti-Semitism was de-emphasized in their programme at the end of the 1920s.[14] That fits with interpretations suggesting that the general level of Jew-hatred in German society had peaked by the mid-1920s, as the first economic crisis and fear of Bolshevik Revolution receded. Even as the Depression of the early 1930s allowed an escalation of anti-Semitic rhetoric—playing on the obscurity to ordinary people of the crisis's origins in order to insinuate the hidden role of 'world finance Jewry'—this was tempered in the Nazi strategy of appearing to be a responsible and trustworthy party. Hitler was wary of pushing Jewish policy too far too fast.

A Third Way: Society and the Nazi Project

While Germany did not have to choose Hitler, Nazism could only have taken hold in a state at Germany's stage of socio-economic development. Nazism was a 'post-liberal' ideology aiming to transcend the fault lines of a society that had already experienced the social impact of modernization. The Nazi dictatorship differed from the right-wing authoritarian regimes of east-central and southeastern Europe in that it grew out of a society with an advanced industrial infrastructure, a civil society, traditions and means of expressing public opinion, growing social mobility, and the experience of parliamentary rule, where the conflicting interests of well-organized social classes were given expression. It was impossible not to take account of these factors and ignore the need for symbols of political legitimacy. While in the dictatorship the relationship between regime and people was unequal, it was not just one way. The Nazi project was partly an expression of tendencies within Germany society, and it would continue to be shaped by mass participation and impulses from below as well as from within.

Social tension had arisen in late-nineteenth-century Germany because of the Catholic question, which fused with the Polish question, and because of the rise of the working class. Political Catholicism represented a rival focus of loyalty in the new German nation-state, albeit that awareness of the potential conflict impelled many Catholics to prove their loyalty ostentatiously. Workers pressed for representation in a state dominated politically by large agricultural interests, the military, and the bureaucracy. If the *Kulturkampf* furthered unity amongst the Protestant majority, it left some Catholics embittered, particularly in Bavaria, which had been equivocal about union in Germany from the start. As to the working class and its political influence, after a period of being outlawed, the SPD was incorporated to a limited degree in the political process, but the constitutional structure meant it had little direct influence on the Crown and the executive. The working class could be substantially mollified by improving their material condition through Bismarck's innovations in social security. For the country as a whole, in the later part of Bismarck's chancellorship and then under the incautious direction of Wilhelm II, unity was increasingly pursued through imperial expansion and the symbols of great power status. But such unity as was achieved was based less on 'positive' political integration by conciliation of differing interests than 'negative integration' against internal 'others' as well as external enemies like Britain.[15]

This is not to subscribe to the *Sonderweg* thesis, the idea Germany had a special, authoritarian path of development leading directly from the Wilhelmine Second Reich, with its 'pre-industrial' social elite and overbearing executive, to the Third Reich. There were, after all, some signs of relative democratization in the years immediately before 1914, if not in the dominant state of Prussia. At the same time, the traditional Right had by that time developed a more populist and modern form of conservatism; indeed, many Europeans of the turn of the century accepted that democratization was neither the only nor the 'natural' destination of modernity.[16] Nor was negative integration at all peculiar to Germany.

The First World War was a watershed in the development of national integration in Germany, as in Britain and France. War meant more than Kaiser Wilhelm's rhetorical aspiration to a '*Volksgemeinschaft*' superseding political and economic divisions. War temporarily broadened German political participation in the interests of maintaining enthusiasm and war production, albeit in limited ways, but expanded participation was conditional on the patriotism of those incorporated. Such commitment was indeed accorded amid the heightened emotion of mobilization, except in Alsace, where the regime's suspicion of an internal enemy would not permit it.[17]

The social 'concertina effect' of the First World War, the increased vertical integration of different social classes with a perceived shared interest that is a common feature of war, was enhanced in the compression stage by use of propaganda.[18] Important in disseminating propaganda in all warring countries were the social elites with traditional social power. These included the clergy and, particularly in the nation-states with their advanced civil societies, members of the liberal professions, known in Germany as *Bildungsbürger*. In political science, these 'intermediary communities' are depicted as potential agents of democratization since they play a supposedly independent role between society and state, and are motivated more by values than material enrichment. For precisely these reasons they were effective in stimulating adherence to 'national values' and exhorting the masses. As war progressed, the more progressive messages of domestic reform preached in some quarters early on were drowned out by exclusivist and retributive pronouncements.[19]

As the concertina of German society decompressed during the final war years and the conjoined experiences of defeat and Versailles, social schisms reopened and became cavernous. Judging by the social friction in Britain in the early 1920s, which, like the German experience, was a result of both the impact of the war and the Bolshevik Revolution, the German path might have been taken elsewhere had the war's outcome been different. Social fragmentation, as expressed through the multitude of political parties and interest groups in Weimar, was a prime Nazi concern. It was the imagined wartime *Volksgemeinschaft* of 1914–16 that Nazism tried to replicate, and did so through the medium of racialized ethnonationalism, using a conception of 'German socialism' based on equality of blood.

The Bolshevik experiment had provided one alternative to liberal democracy but Nazism and Italian Fascism rejected the universalism inherent in communism and liberalism, with the Nazis associating both with international Jewry. German and Italian fascists sought some of the social justice and cohesion promised by socialism for their communities within the ethnopolitical boundaries of the nation-state—minus 'internal enemies', that is. Once again, symbols of national success, from monumental architecture and state-funded civil construction projects to rearmament and conquest, would serve to enthuse people about matters other than their own sectarian interests. Meanwhile the projection of strong leadership would provide reassurance after defeat and depression. The process would be enhanced by more adept use of the tools of mass communication developed in 1914–18.[20]

With the stress still on sentimental unity and negative integration rather than pluralistic political integration in Germany, fascism stressed emotion and instinct rather than reason, and promoted the militarization of society to sustain what had only lasted for a few years in the war. Tangible reward for the 'deserving' in the form of an economic safety net would however remind them of the beneficence of the new order and ensure their loyalty, a lesson learned both from Bismarck's social policy and the desperate years of shortage in 1914–18. Some economic intervention was functionally important given that under both fascist regimes the organized representation of labour was shattered and capitalism perpetuated with only certain modifications.

The Nazi economic recovery provided some of the means for material betterment. Improved welfare provisions compensated for the encroachment on personal freedoms, with mothers, newlyweds, and the young benefiting financially from the stress on 'racial health',[21] just as the brutally successful clampdowns on crime and vagrancy eased any popular misgivings about the inhumanities visited on the 'asocial'.[22] Nevertheless, the government gave priority to investment in armaments and infrastructure, and while the measure expanded employment, spending the resulting income on consumer goods was not encouraged; rather, emphasis was placed upon 'cultural consumption' in the form of, say, tourism and day-trips to the countryside, as organized through the 'Strength through Joy' programme.

Other mass participation exercises served the same function as tourism, which was seen as one way of reducing class divisions because it had formerly been the preserve of the wealthier classes.[23] The Nazis also sought to reconcile confessional divisions with the emphasis in their programme on a non-sectarian 'positive Christianity'. Notwithstanding prominent pagan ideologues such as Rosenberg and Himmler, the Nazis were more anti-clerical than anti-religious. They were suspicious of Catholic institutions because, as before 1914, they provided a potential alternative focus of political loyalty, and one of the characteristic traits of fascism was its extension of 'the political' into every realm of human existence, in principle if not always in practice. The persecution of Jehovah's Witnesses was predicated upon the same rationale, since any Witness prepared to swear loyalty to Hitler could gain release from incarceration.

Beyond a point, the regime could not afford to alienate practising Christians. Moreover, the Nazis shared more of the Christian inheritance than many Christians then and subsequently have been prepared to admit. The Nazified 'German Christian' movement has provided a convenient receptacle in which to cast all of the guilt of German, not to say occidental, Christianity, but the opposition to the regime of such prominent dissidents as Martin Niemöller and his 'Confessing Church' was based more on the regime's threat to the prerogatives of the church than to misgivings about Nazi conceptions of ethnic community. Niemöller was an enthusiastic supporter of the invasion of the USSR and expressed his regret that Jesus had been born a Jew. The protests against 'euthanasia' by the Catholic Bishop of Münster, von Galen, coexisted with his subscription to Nazi Germanization policies and the notion of the 'Jewish-Bolshevik conspiracy'. The clergy, particularly Protestant, proved a bastion of nationalist support for Hitler's foreign policy agenda and the war effort.[24]

It was a sincere concern of the regime to instil an appropriate political consciousness in all 'racially valuable' people. The success of the aim varied along all the predictable demographic cleavages. The longer the party was in power, with its monopoly on the means of communication and its control of education, the more strongly its values permeated, particularly among the young who were socialized under the regime.

Nevertheless, despite the regimentation of public life and widespread though not total mobilization in Nazi organizations, 'ordinary' Germans were not subject to the same disruptions as were, for instance, Soviet citizens under Stalinism.

Terror was more omnipresent in Stalin's USSR, with every citizen a potential suspect for the secret police. In the Third Reich the direct application of terror was more selective, and the political police were keen not to antagonize the majority.[25] Amongst the healthy, law-abiding 'Aryan' population at least, police detention or concentration camp incarceration were more a latent threat. Terror was most publicly deployed at the beginning and the end of the regime, when the party's hold on power was weak or threatened. Around one hundred primitive concentration camps and Nazi prisons were established for 'enemies of the regime' in 1933–4. Many of these were clustered in working class areas, obviously designed to intimidate the constituency of the Left. Thirty to fifty thousand people may have been arbitrarily imprisoned by the SA and SS in 1933 alone. Communist and socialist Jews were treated particularly brutally.[26]

From 1934 almost every camp was closed, and replaced by a small but growing number of large, more organized concentration camps under the authority of the SS's Inspectorate of Concentration Camps. The 'Dachau model' became the one to be emulated, named after the system of disciplined brutality meted out to 'reform' the inmates of the eponymous camp. From around 1937, the major inmate population comprised 'asocials' as well as criminal recidivists and the 'work-shy'. The elasticity of the categories made their application highly arbitrary, giving huge power of discretion to the Security Police. By 1944, some 70,000 people designated in such ways suffered in Germany's concentration camps.[27]

The continuing presence of Dachau and its sister camps and the memory of the early camps and street violence of the SA cannot be ignored in any assessment of the public's interaction with the regime. At the same time, the Nazi party was plainly preoccupied with public attitudes towards its policies. This was not just a concern with outward displays of public support, as in the early plebiscites, but a genuine desire to understand how far policies could be pushed without engendering unease and to learn where further persuasion was required. After all, the support for Nazism that the German people offered increasingly through the 1930s cannot in any straightforward way be translated into a mandate for everything that occurred from 1938. Hitler achieved huge popularity in the mid-1930s as a result of general improvement in the German economy and bloodless foreign policy triumphs, and that was certainly a key factor in increased public acceptance of Nazi domestic programmes, but when continental war became a real possibility the German people evinced considerable anxiety.

The possibilities for 'racial' policy were also unclear. German society before 1933 was full of prejudices, but these were mostly of a similar intensity and chauvinism to other societies of the period. Violence and discrimination against Romanies were more historically consistent in German society, as elsewhere, than against Jews. Romanies were made an object of the Nuremberg 'blood protection law' forbidding marriage and extramarital sexual relations between 'Aryans' and 'non-Aryans', but it was unnecessary for the Nazis to enact a web of legislation de-emancipating and stigmatizing Romanies. They had never experienced emancipation and had always been stigmatized. By the same token, the Nazi persecution of homosexuals could feed off traditions of established legal discrimination and social disapprobation throughout the continent.

Radical anti-Semitism was manifestly present in pre-Nazi Germany, but was mainly the preserve of the Far Right. It filtered somewhat into the mainstream, particularly through student fraternities, which from the early 1920s had excluded Jews on 'racial' not religious grounds. The student body, comprising the future educated middle classes and German political elite, had indeed provided receptive audiences for the influential anti-Semitic lectures of Heinrich von Treitschke in the late nineteenth century. The self-styled avant-garde of European modernity, German nationalist students of the interwar years provided an important Nazi constituency.

Elsewhere, significantly larger parts of the German population probably did feel that Jews needed to be 'put in their place'. The particular strength of that desire at a time of social upheaval may well explain the upsurge in physical attacks on Jews—a relatively uncommon phenomenon in pre-Nazi Germany—at the beginning and end of the

Weimar Republic. Widespread conservative, social anti-Semitism was present in institutions like the German officer corps and political parties of the Centre Right.[28] The role of economic crisis in exacerbating anti-Semitism in Weimar reflected the 1873–96 experience, when members of the German lower middle class resorted to it to explain their misfortune. Easy targets for popular expressions of prejudice were provided by the undeniably high proportions of urban, middle class Jews with higher-than-average incomes, and the large relative numbers of Jews in higher education, banking, and prominent positions in the arts and sciences in Weimar as in late Imperial Germany. That prejudice was certainly deepened by the rhetoric and disinformation propagated around the 1912 'Jewish elections' and the 1916 military 'Jew count', and by the interpretations frequently put on the revolutions in Europe in 1917–18.

A sense among sizeable parts of the population of the difference of a minority, combined with a feeling that the minority enjoyed disproportionate social, economic, and even political influence, provided conditions for a classic reassertion of *ethnic dominance* in Germany. Very different though it was, the Nazi brand of anti-Semitism could build on the limited ground it shared with these more traditional anti-Jewish sentiments that were to degrees embedded in European culture. In post-Anschluss Austria, for instance, periodic, pogrom-like violence (of a significantly higher level than in Germany) was something which the authorities sought to channel into a different and more systematic policy of exclusion.[29] The idea of playing on established anti-Semitic motifs may explain why Nazi propaganda in the 1930s and throughout the war stressed less the question of Jewish biological difference than the ubiquity of Jewish power, which was more comprehensible and more consistent with what many ordinary Germans and ordinary Europeans believed.[30] It is undeniable that for its first five years in power, Nazism pursued measures that could be understood in an idiom of ethnic domination rather than destruction. Exploitation of Jews where Germans had supposedly been exploited by Jews; reversing 'social and cultural hegemony'; reversing emancipation and drawing firmer social lines between Jews and Germans: none of these were in themselves measures of ethnic destruction, even though the German leadership increasingly intended them to facilitate precisely that.

From 1936 at the latest there was an implicit understanding in the state bureaucracy that force might at some point have to be used to render Germany free of Jews, or at least younger Jews who might still reproduce.[31] That does not mean a popular majority apprehended and supported the logic, even while many supported or acquiesced in discrete measures that structurally contributed to its realization. Before 1938 there was no centralized means of enforcing Jewish emigration, only a combination of legal discrimination and harassment by local party members, SA men, and, increasingly, the police and SS. Even those Germans who did indeed support forced emigration, which was the mildest form of ethnic destruction, were less enthusiastic about targeted deportation to eastern Europe, which was at least one step further down the road. And even support of deportation in no way equated to support for mass murder.[32] In other words, from the perspective of the population, there was no necessary link between prewar discrimination and the extremities to which the regime's policy unforeseeably developed during the later war.

From the perspective of the regime, intelligence and propaganda were vital tools as it tested the impact of its policies and pushed the limits of the possible, without itself yet contemplating murder. In waves, the prewar years saw a huge volume of propaganda against Jews, as well as other 'enemies' and 'useless eaters' (meaning the mentally and physically ill). Contrasting images of healthy, hard-working Aryans were simultaneously deployed. The peaks of anti-Semitic propaganda corresponded with the most public peaks of policy against Jews. These peaks included the widespread boycotts of Jewish businesses in 1933; the legal assault in the Nuremberg laws of 1935 and the accompanying campaigns on the issue of 'racial disgrace' through sexual relations; and the cluster of measures in 1938 that included 'Kristallnacht', the beginning of systematic forced emigration, and the full-scale economic assault of centralized 'Aryanization'.

Intelligence reports showed disapprobation, though decreasing over time, of attacks on property and somewhat greater sympathy for sexual segregation, at least judging by the rising, though still statistically relatively small, numbers of private denunciations of transgressors. While some of the opposition to property damage may have been related to concerns with public order and higher future insurance premiums for all, there were also expressions of manifest solidarity early in the regime's life: for instance, continued patronage of Jewish stores amid boycotts. At the other extreme, some members of the public took part in rituals of public humiliation and reprisal for 'race defilers', involving themselves in the parading of 'culpable' Jewish men or the headshaving of 'compromised' Aryan women.[33]

Between the peaks of propaganda and public assaults on Jews came troughs of relative quiet in terms of major policy developments, as around the 1936 Olympics when the Nazi leadership had an eye on external opinion. Official discrimination continued to pick up momentum, however, often via measures conceived at the local level. As the decade progressed, more and more members of the 'intermediary communities' were drawn into the process of discrimination, because even in a dictatorship there was still a public role to be played by intellectuals prepared to embrace the basic tenets of the regime, or simply to express their patriotism.

Academic unemployment in Weimar encouraged many intellectuals into the Nazi camp, especially as they benefited from the systematic removal of Jews from university posts. The number of non-Jewish university lecturers who protested at the dismissal of Jewish colleagues was as small as in the medical, legal, and bureaucratic professions. Willing historians and social scientists were now in the position to make history and remake society. In their attempts—sometimes sincere—to substantiate Germany's claims to empire and to the 'nature of the Jew' they provided the perfect foil to the cruder claims of the Nazi propagandists. Some scientists, who portrayed their work as technocratically beneficial, were attractive to and attracted by a regime that depicted a racially circumscribed national community of equals as a way of overcoming socio-economic divides. Some believed themselves to be performing a valuable function by their eugenic and genetic research, and believed in its potential as 'real science'. Others were tempted by the new sources of state funding and the lure of public recognition and leadership. Those who truly had a 'biomedical' vision of the world, like the non-Nazi proponents of sterilization and euthanasia, could end up being drawn into anti-Jewish policy, where the priorities of the regime made participation particularly professionally attractive.[34] Anthropologists—'scientists of race'—who had been kicked out of the African colonies with the German administrations at the end of the First World War turned their attention to 'race relations' in Germany and eastern Europe.[35] Many universities sought to make Romanies the object of 'racial hygiene' research. The work of one dedicated 'racial hygiene' scientist within the Reich Health Office, Robert Ritter, was hugely influential in shaping official attitudes towards Romanies.

In short, instead of mitigating hard state power with their softer form of social power, these key occupational groups did the opposite. In place of providing intellectual critique and maintaining some form of social bridging to marginalized groups, they helped pull up the drawbridge.

Beyond propaganda and public instruction, there were positive and negative incentives for ordinary people to participate in the new *Volksgemeinschaft*. On one hand, the sense of belonging to a privileged collective—a sense of at least relative well being and superiority—was enhanced by discrimination against others. On the other hand, like the camps, violence against Jews and others by SA men, Hitler Youth members, or party activists represented an implicit threat to all. It was risky to maintain social ties with the victims or lend moral support since this had ramifications for welfare or privileges within the gift of local party representatives, and could bring social stigmatization or even official suspicion.

Helping Jews was increasingly thankless, while doing nothing in the face of their persecution was not only the line of least resistance, it was also potentially rewarding. On the levels of both the ordinary shopkeeper and the big businessman, the removal of economic competition from Jews could be most welcome, irrespective of their attitudes towards Jews.[36] Others might go further down this road and benefit directly from the official theft of Jewish businesses and property. With the legalization of discrimination based on lineage, people who secured the necessary 'heredity certificates' to go about their daily lives were indirectly reinforcing a system in which others were stigmatized by precisely the same official procedure.[37] Denunciations for anything from

Rassenschande ('racial dishonour') to listening to forbidden radio stations need not have had ideological convictions as their primary motive; as anywhere where informing is publicly encouraged, denunciations could stem from personal avarice, score-settling, or conformity.[38] Their aggregate result was, nevertheless, to further the regime's designs and to implicate the denouncers in a national community defined by whom it excluded.

From the state's perspective, there was a functionally important link between general public acquiescence in discrimination and increasing indifference to the Jewish plight in the prewar years and then during the war as genocide unfolded.[39] The earlier period provided conditioning for those who would unforeseeably participate indirectly in mass murder or look on in silence. As the war progressed, even as the Nazi leadership kept the details of the evolving final solution secret, it increasingly used hints and violent if still euphemistic language about solving the 'Jewish question' in order to implicate the German population in its enactment. The spectre of 'Jewish revenge' if Germany lost the war was ever more strongly invoked. Much of the concrete detail of genocide was supplied by soldiers, policemen, and civilians returning from the eastern front with atrocity tales, by news illicitly obtained by Allied broadcasts, and other informal means.

German knowledge about the Holocaust did not bring grief for the victims, yet nor did it bring endorsement of their murder. Insofar as we can tell—and gauging opinion in a dictatorship is difficult, where public displays of conformity were encouraged and 'objective' polling data nonexistent—knowledge induced a closing of ears, combined perhaps with rationalizations that misuse of their own power had brought the Jews to their fate, and with the apologia that would predominate after the war, which reduced the circle of perpetrators and protested individual powerlessness in the face of authority. After all, most of the killing of Jews after 1939 happened outside Germany and away from the eyes of most Germans; most of the victims were not German nationals, meaning there were few residual bonds of connectedness between the groups; genocide happened while Germany was at war, with all of the introspection and bifurcation of the world into 'friends' and 'enemies' that that context brings; and the most extensive information about genocide came when Germany was increasingly on the back foot in the conflict, and thus focusing on its own suffering, from mid-1942 and more particularly from the turn of 1942–3, after the decisive German defeat at Stalingrad.[40]

The German people became complicit in the Nazi project, but not in a straightforward or intentional way. They indirectly encouraged the regime in its extreme experiments by their tacit acceptance of increasingly radical racial policies and their embrace of some of the ensuing benefits, their general failure to resist a host of subtle and more obvious moral compromises, and the momentum they gave the regime by supporting the general thrust of its socio-economic and, up to a point, foreign policies. But direct, political responsibility in driving and facilitating genocide (rather than ethnic domination) lay with the political, economic, administrative, intellectual, and military elite, albeit that significant parts of the elite had become much more open than was traditional by 1939, as the role of the newer intermediary communities showed.

Shaping the German 'Functional' Elites

From the beginning of the regime to its end there was a determined effort to 'Nazify' Germany. This was the expression of an agenda of power and control after the fragmentation of the Weimar years, and a measure in preparation for the implementation of Nazi social goals. It also extended to pro-German organizations working in Austria and to the organized representation of ethnic German communities throughout eastern and southeastern Europe, which was the preserve from 1938 of the SS Ethnic German Liaison Office (*Volksdeutsche Mittelstelle*).[41]

Gleichschaltung, or 'coordination', was an attempt to bring German organizations and institutions under Nazi control. It was complemented by an attempt to inculcate 'national socialist values' in state administrators and shape their views in accordance with a racist, militarist worldview, but also to replace rule-bound proceduralism with initiative and a new, activist ethos (*Menschenführung*). These measures of cooption were not the expression of a masterplan for genocide, nor necessarily a precondition for it. After all, the CUP had contrived to drive through a policy of genocide during the First World War without using the full breadth of the Ottoman state framework, and against the wishes of parts of it. Nevertheless, when combined with the material and professional incentives within the system, Nazi structural and ideological penetration of the state explains why such a multitude of organizations and individuals at many levels of the administrative structure were ultimately prepared not just to participate in increasingly extreme policies, but to seek the policy initiative, and contribute to a radicalizing process that would be vital to the increasingly and peculiarly ambitious reach of Nazi genocide.

Among the first targets of 'coordination' was the German civil service. The bureaucracy would be needed to implement Nazi policy, yet as a matter of simple practicality many pre-Nazi officials would have to remain in post, given the need for trained officials and specialists in the ministries as in the 'Security Police'.[42] Like the equally anti-democratic German military, whose existence also predated the Weimar Republic, the state bureaucracy viewed itself as a guardian of 'real' national interest and values, and had seen Weimar as an imposition. Civil service and military were vigorously opposed to Weimar's democratic regime and accompanying artistic, sexual, and social liberation, which were seen as signs of leftist degeneration (*Kulturbolschewismus*), the very opposite of the order that the conservative Right espoused. Under Weimar, the judiciary, like the police and the public censors, frequently acted with great harshness against left-wing subversives, but with comparative leniency against extreme right-wingers such as Hitler himself after his failed Munich putsch in 1923. Their logic was that while rightists were 'only' anti-regime, leftists were anti-state, and it was the organic state rather than the temporary regime that the civil service identified with.[43]

The idea of their own nationalism as somehow objective or preideological was one of the fatal conceits of the bureaucratic class. It contributed to their sense of natural entitlement in power as representatives of the titular people, and to their acceptance of a Nazi regime whose nationalism was only too evident. Far from being the restraining force on Hitler they portrayed themselves to be after the war, propagating the notion that they stayed in post to curb the worst Nazi excesses, for the most part these were the very people who increased the social reach and effectiveness of the Nazi project.

Very shortly, the belief that the Nazi regime was an entirely legitimate one came to prevail amongst most of Germany's approximately 1.5 million civil servants.[44] The main persuading that had to be done was that the Nazis would not do more harm than good because of concerns about their fundamental competence, and because the established elites viewed them as vulgar and déclassé. Not all bureaucrats fell into line instantly. Some protested at the illegality of the early concentration camps, for instance.[45] From the Nazi perspective, as with the population at large, a carrot-and-stick approach was employed. Pre-Nazi officials became bound to the Nazi project by their acquiescence in the racist restructuring process, notably as the 1933 'Law for the Reestablishment of the Professional Civil Service' and subsequent measures implicated them in their own self-cleansing by targeting leftists, dissenters, and Jews. On one hand, the law served to reassure the bureaucracy that *Gleichschaltung* would be conducted according to legalized, standardized criteria over which it had some control. On the other hand, though the measure only affected a relatively small number of civil servants, it cowed potential dissenters, and gave everyone a clear signpost about the direction in which policy was to head in future, encouraging malleable non-Nazis to prove their loyalty to the new system.

Under the new dispensation, opportunities were opened for rapid career advancement for comparatively young, ideologically committed bureaucrats like Wilhelm Stuckart and Roland Freisler, who became vastly influential state secretaries in the ministries of the interior and justice. At the same time, at the beginning of the Nazi period, both conformism and opportunism swelled the ranks of public officials in the Nazi party. In the judiciary, for instance, there was significant pressure from the party and in internal personnel policy for judges to join and actively support the party.[46]

Discriminatory laws stemmed not just from proposals from the top of the regime downwards but also from the middle ranks of the bureaucracy. Proposals emerged, for instance, from the 'Jewish desks' created in the Foreign Office and Interior Ministry, illustrating the regime's prioritization of Jewish policy and the attempts of these organizations to keep pace. They include measures as petty and bizarre as the proscription on Jewish ownership of pets from February 1942. Official discrimination was also advanced at the local level. Many municipal administrators, by no means all Nazi party members, pressed forward with imaginative new measures of apartheid within their geographical jurisdiction. From as early as 1934 local welfare departments segregated increasingly impoverished Jews in municipal facilities, furthering their social isolation. Some of these local councillors were surely responding opportunistically to the agenda of the party in power and to signals from their superiors, but others took enthusiastically to the Hitlerian call for a more activist expression of their membership of the *Volksgemeinschaft*.[47]

The Nazification of the civil service was exceeded by that of the police forces. In the regular Order Police and the Community Police, preference was immediately given to Nazi party, SA and SS applicants. 'Uncooperative' individuals were removed, as many as 50 per cent of the force in the case of Hesse. Technical training in enforcement and weapons deployment was accompanied by extensive ideological instruction.[48] Unlike the stereotype of 'totalitarian brainwashing', this education, while repetitive, was more interactive and, insofar as it is possible to judge, reasonably effective. In any case, the human material that remained after the early purges was receptive in terms of its macho, authoritarian organizational culture to many of the messages Nazism sought to inculcate.[49] In 1936, the police were merged with the SS.

Like the civil service, the leadership of the *Wehrmacht*, the armed forces, was already a bastion of revisionism, and it shared the civil service's sense of entitlement to social power. One of Hitler's carrots to gain the confidence of the military was the 'night of the long knives', the murder of 150–200 senior SA members in June–July 1934. The massacre illustrated the violent extremes to which Hitler was prepared to go, providing another touchstone to which leading Nazis would later refer as proof of their zeal in fighting 'inner enemies', and it neutered a paramilitary force that threatened the prerogatives of the army. A larger incentive was Hitler's rearmament programme, while his strategic successes in 1938–40 bound the military ever closer to him. By wartime, when the *Waffen-SS* began developing into a formidable, organized fighting force parallel to the army, Hitler's power was firmly entrenched, and the *Wehrmacht* more quiescent.

Ideologically, the *Wehrmacht* leadership was already strongly anti-Bolshevik, conservatively anti-Semitic, and revisionist. A generation of front-line military officers from 1914–18 would enter the Second World War as senior staff officers and field commanders, and they were determined not to allow a repeat of the 'stab in the back' by 'Judeo-Bolshevism'.[50] Having propagated the 'Dolchstoss' myth, the army was prepared to act with massive violence against supposed threats to the rear during wartime. In 1941, the military itself requested a greater SS presence in the conquered Soviet territories to pacify the area. The elements of the military leadership caste from which concerted opposition to Hitler emerged during the war were for the most part not opposed to Nazism on moral grounds, but because they feared Hitler was bringing another defeat onto Germany. Some perpetrators of the final solution were peripherally involved in the famous July 1944 attempt on Hitler's life.

Despite the established elites' accommodation, the Nazi party was not content with simply redirecting the ship of state. The vessel itself required a radical overhaul. Because of the party's philosophy of activism and the desire of its individual members for power, it attacked the bureaucracy as hidebound and inflexible. From the beginning, Hitler established and let grow new organizations whose functions paralleled those of extant state organizations. The most radical elements within the regime were to be found in those organizations created from 1933 to compete with or co-opt existing state organs, and from 1939 to run conquered territories. Pre-eminent in the former category was the SS–Police complex and in the latter category the civil administrations appointed in occupied eastern Europe. To these we can add the new power centres that achieved increasing influence in the wartime economy: Göring's Organization for the Four Year Plan, including the office of Labour Deployment; the Ministry for Armaments and War Production, particularly after Albert Speer took it over in 1942; and, to a lesser extent, the SS economic offices.[51]

The personnel staffing key Nazi institutions represent a microcosm of the most enthusiastic Nazi constituencies. As a simplification, the most aggressive, nationalist elements in interwar Germany can be divided into two groups—the same two groups from which the Freikorps were drawn from 1918. First, those who were deeply influenced by their First World War experience and took this militaristic ethos back into civilian life. Second, those who were too young to join the actual 'front community' but were socialized and educated in the bitter aftermath of defeat, imbibing the mythology of the war, identifying strongly with the embattled German 'ethnic community' shaped by the earlier generation, and seeking their opportunity to avenge Germany's loss.[52]

The first category produced most of the early members of the Nazi party, the so-called 'old fighters', some of the longest standing anti-Semites of conviction. Many had personal ties of loyalty to Hitler, and a disproportionate number had convictions for right-wing political offences and violence. From this category were drawn the class of Nazi regional leaders, or *Gauleiter*, and leaders of smaller territorial subdivisions.[53] These men would be responsible for matters of racial and social policy within their regional spheres, and they also provided the leadership of the German civilian occupation regimes, men like Hinrich Lohse and Erich Koch in the USSR, Artur Greiser in western Poland (the 'Warthegau'), and Artur Seyss-Inquart, governor of the Netherlands. The milieu also produced a high proportion of the Higher SS and Police Leaders (HSSPF) and SS and Police Leaders (SSPF), a select group with ties of loyalty to the SS chief, Heinrich Himmler. The positions of (H)SSPF were established in 1937 to orchestrate joint police operations within their geographical spheres and provide Himmler with direct regional influence over the increasingly complex SS–Police structure of which he feared losing control.[54] These were men like the former Freikorps fighter Hans-Albin Rauter, who as HSSPF in the Netherlands increasingly challenged Seyss-Inquart's authority, or SSPF Odilo Globocnik. Globocnik was a convicted murderer instrumental in Nazi penetration of Austria. He benefited from Himmler's indulgence after being removed for corruption as Gauleiter of Vienna to preside over population policy in the Lublin district of Poland, which became the centre of genocide from late 1942 to late 1943. This sort of relationship of personal indebtedness was one of Himmler's methods of ensuring the fealty of his men.[55]

The second age category provided the kernel of a second wave of Gauleiters as members of the older wave retired or died.[56] It also provided the leadership of the increasingly powerful SS intelligence service, the SD, and, over time, of the leadership corps of the Security Police. As well as being younger than the other elites of the Third Reich, this group, which at the beginning of the war comprised about 400 people, was better educated than the party leaders. In 1939, two-thirds of the top Gestapo and SD leaders were under 36. Almost as many had university degrees, and many of those further degrees, with the largest concentration in the disciplines of law, followed by history and other humanities and social science subjects. These men were predominantly from the middle class, and particularly the lower middle class. Their rise to prominence shows that social mobility was a real possibility in the vanguard organizations, whatever the misleading Nazi propaganda about an ethnic community of equals across society as a whole.[57]

The SD had been established in 1931 under Reinhard Heydrich and rose through the 1930s under his shrewd and ruthless leadership from an unpromising position to one of pre-eminence within the police structure of the Reich. The SD had one important doctrinal advantage. The organization substituted the visceral but distinctly 'unscientific' racism of the party elite and the SA with a more bureaucratic-legalistic but no less ideologically committed approach to the persecution of Germany's 'enemies'. Its approach reflected Hitler's long-standing desire to deal with Germany's 'Jewish problem' not by pogrom and the 'anti-Semitism of emotion', but by systematic pursuit and eructation. Like other SS officers, their training involved them in thinking proactively about how to achieve their ends, with examination questions like 'compile a report for the entire Reich on "Jews in the livestock trade" and propose your own remedies to the evils described'. With the high intellectual calibre of its personnel and their ideological commitment, the SD perceived itself as a 'fighting administration'. It also provided a well of experience for other countries seeking to deal with their Jewish populations in similarly systematic ways.[58]

Heydrich and the SD were further advanced by the general rise of the SS. The SS was the executor of the 'night of the long knives' and its direct beneficiary in the continuing intra-Nazi power play. After decapitating the SA and ensuring its own monopoly control of the concentration camp system, the SS consolidated its position as the Nazi vanguard in the key policy area of the fight against 'inner enemies' when Himmler prevailed in the struggle for control of the German police system by 1936. The continuing 'coordination' of the security police organizations—the Gestapo and Kriminalpolizei—was accelerated from this point. SD men gradually supplanted the established police professionals in leading positions, but this was not just a one-way relationship, because the SD benefited from the infusion of policing expertise.[59] The fusion process was completed in October 1939 when the SD and Security Police were joined under the aegis of Heydrich's newly created Reich Security Head Office (RSHA). The leaders of these police forces were a sort of technocratic vanguard of Nazi 'security' and racial policy, equipped with modern surveillance techniques and under the leadership of one of the most ambitious and ruthless men in the Reich.

As the SD and Security Police were brought together, all of the regular German police agencies were placed under Himmler's jurisdiction as SS head.[60] The incorporation of the regular Order Police furthered the Nazification of the largest force in the land. By the time of the invasion of the USSR, the officer class of the Order Police units deployed there were almost all from the generational and attitudinal milieu of the SD leadership.

Himmler was *de jure* subordinate to Interior Minister Wilhelm Frick, but in the de facto hierarchy he was answerable only to Hitler. Control of the camps and the police, with their increasing powers of pre-emptive and 'protective custody', meant the SS now controlled an entire, enclosed system of extralegal arrest and incarceration. The camps also provided the promise—based on a prisoner workforce—of some independent economic basis for the SS, which helps explain the great expansion of incarcerations of 'asocials' and other 'enemies of the regime' in 1937–8. Independence from state funding meant independence from state intervention, and therefore increased political power.[61] From 1936 new camps like Buchenwald and Flossenbürg were constructed near mineral resources and the traditional purely punitive forms of inmate labour now expanded to incorporate quarrying and brickmaking.

The Contradictions of Prewar Jewish Policy

The rise of new Nazi vanguard organizations like the SS presented an obvious challenge to the established organs of state. Hitler played on this when, at the same party congress in 1935 at which the Nuremberg 'Blood Protection Law' was announced, creating the legal category 'Jew' and forbidding future union between Jews and 'Germans', he declared that 'the fight against the inner enemies of the nation will never fail because of a formal bureaucracy or its inadequacy. . . . What can be solved by the state will be solved by the state. What the state is by its very nature unable to solve will be solved by the movement.'[62] The message was clear: the Nuremberg laws were not an end, as many Germans may have thought and Jews wished to believe. They were a beginning.

The Nuremberg laws created the statutory basis on which more radical action could be taken, but issues of definition were neither easily nor fully resolved. There were many cases of intermarriage in a country where Jews had hitherto been well assimilated, so the proportion of 'German blood' in the individual was an important consideration, as were the non-Jewish Germans who had married Jews. Stopping further mixing was a primary concern of the Nazi policy of segregation, and had been discussed by the SS, party, and government since the accession to power.

The Nuremberg definition emerged from a conflict between two strands of Nazi racial thought. One was the 'contagionist' variety, more popular among party members and particularly the propagandist Julius Streicher. This belief was in the literally infectious quality of Jewishness, such that sexual contact with a Jew would leave a non-Jewish woman forever contaminated. On the other side were the men of the SD, who felt themselves superior in their supposedly 'scientific' racism. They were informed by the strand of eugenic thought that saw all peoples as blends of different 'races', and believed the quality of the German people would be improved by selective interbreeding within the Nordic stock from which the ideal German arose. This belief shared ground with that of the bureaucrats of the Interior Ministry, like Stuckart, who saw that the valuable Germanic blood would, even if mixed, still positively influence the character of any carrier. Certainly for the Interior Ministry, the character of the individual *Mischling*, or 'cross-breed', was important, and many individuals with some proportion of Jewish blood had shown themselves to be committed Germans.[63]

Political considerations were bound up in the interpretative war, not least the sovereign power that always accrues to the arbiter of the exception. There were tens of thousands of people who were useful to the state and did not identify themselves as Jewish who might become alienated, and their families with them, if the category of Jew extended to everyone with any demonstrable Jewish ancestry. Hitler's intercession on the issue ultimately fudged it, which is scarcely surprising since there were no objective scientific standards by which to determine 'Jewishness'.[64] Accordingly, at the margins of the 'second-degree *Mischlinge*' (people with one Jewish grandparent), behavioural and voluntary elements including 'Jew-like' behaviour and religious conviction informed a supposedly biological definition.

Precisely how *Mischlinge* of varying degrees were to be treated was a matter of continuing debate and power struggle throughout the war years, as was the issue of mixed marriages. The SS and the Gauleiters only acted incrementally against the groups concerned. The net result was the survival throughout the war and within Germany of some of the people in these marginal categories. It was also an issue in Nazi-controlled western Europe, where the sensibilities of the racially 'respectable' local population mattered to Germany. It was less a cause for concern in eastern Europe, but nevertheless the SS clashed with Rosenberg's eastern ministry over who constituted a Jew.

Within Germany, the Nuremberg laws symbolized the civic death of the Jews, but contained nothing to promote their physical removal from the German sphere. In the eyes of the outside world these Jews remained a German concern; in the political climate, no other state was desirous of alleviating Germany's Jewish 'burden'. The SD was the most active force in pushing for systematic emigration, as they had done from 1934. They sought to achieve it first by working with Jewish Zionists.

Palestine seemed an ideal place to 'territorialize' the Jews and so render them more visible as well as spatially segregated by national boundaries. It was a place where an increasingly large number of disillusioned Jews wanted to go anyway, while Jews going there could not, by definition, 'spread their influence' in hostile developed states. In practice, though, the Reich authorities were happy to see Jews leave in any direction at all before the war. Hitler actually saw this as a way of increasing anti-Semitism in recipient countries and taunted the liberal democracies for the contrast between their expressed concern for the Jews and their actual asylum policies.[65]

The progress of Jewish policy was impeded by practical obstacles and internal contradictions. The developing consensus from 1934 onwards meant Nazi policy differed from, say, Slovak policy after 1939, which sought to maintain subordinated Jews within the state for the country's economic purposes. Yet too swift and sweeping a removal of the German Jews could have had adverse effects on the economy. Moreover, increasing expropriation and exclusion from trades and professions impoverished the Jews, meaning they lost the means to emigrate even had they wished to, and so they became very unattractive to the already reluctant potential recipient states. Accordingly, German bureaucrats responded with innovations that indeed bore resemblance to events in Slovakia before the idea of deporting Jews dawned on Tiso's regime. From 1938 until their deportation in 1941–2, the increasingly impoverished Jews were used as forced labourers on local work projects, in segregated columns, in accordance with the axiom that 'parasites' should be made to work for their keep. These measures were not conceived of as a prelude to deportation, and were often the result of ad hoc decisions by local and regional authorities.[66]

The SD sought to cut the Gordian knot. But in order to take control of Jewish policy when so many other agencies were involved it had to earn the mandate. This it did by resolving the various contradictions of the emigration policy at a propitious moment, and forcing its advantage in a manner entirely characteristic of the Darwinian intra-Nazi power struggles. The auspicious moment for more extreme population policy arrived, as in other states, in the context of consolidation of new territory for the titular population. The most obvious such point was 1938, with the 'Anschluss' and the dismemberment of Czechoslovakia. But before that came a lesser known opportunity provided by the unique borderland status of Upper Silesia.

Upper Silesia represented virgin soil for Jewish policy. After it had been divided into eastern and western parts between Germany and Poland after the First World War, a bilateral agreement of 1922 protected minorities in both parts. The agreement expired in 1937, which opened a window for what the SD official Adolf Eichmann called addressing the Jewish question 'in its entirety', as the accumulated German anti-Semitic laws suddenly became applicable. Eichmann travelled to Breslau to oversee the immediate registration of all Jews, the arrest of leading Jewish officials in order to control and pressure them, the banning of Jewish communal organizations, and the prevention of the sale of Jewish property to Poland. The initiative confirmed the SD's intellectual leadership on Jewish policy and resulted in it being accorded effective functional and planning leadership too. It would now be given a significantly larger opportunity.

Anschluss and Acceleration

The year 1938 was significant for the Nazi project at many different levels. The Nazi Joachim von Ribbentrop replaced the conservative Konstantin von Neurath as Foreign Minister; Hjalmar Schacht was supplanted in economic and fiscal policy by the 'Office for the Four Year Plan'. Hitler appointed himself commander-in-chief of the armed forces, and created a new umbrella organization for the services, the High Command of the Wehrmacht. This he filled with Nazi sympathizers, with the pliable Wilhelm Keitel at the helm.[67] The year also saw radicalization in Jewish policy leading to a sharp increase in emigration, which was directly related to the major foreign policy developments of the year, especially the 'Anschluss'.[68]

The arrival of German forces in Austria in March triggered a flurry of indigenous anti-Semitic activity in a country with a stronger tradition of violent Jew-hatred than Germany. Eichmann's men, who arrived hot on the heels of the German army, replicated his Upper Silesian procedure, then permitted the release of the chief administrator of the Jewish religious community and the re-formation of a few Jewish organizations for the sole task of facilitating emigration. The operation became partly self-financing as Eichmann extorted funds from the community, and

Figure 7. Entrance to 'eternal Jew' exhibition, Vienna.

richer Jews were taxed to subsidize the emigration of the poor. With the additional stimulus of pogromic anti-Semitism in Austria, the Vienna 'production-line' of 'denaturalization' and expulsion was established. By November 1938, 50,000 Jews had been forced out of Austria.

It was not all a matter of German efficiency versus Austrian brutality. As in Slovakia, Austrians were keen on keeping their hands on the wealth of 'their' Jews, and the arrival of the Germans actually accelerated indigenous measures of legalized theft, or 'Aryanization', that had already been in train. Austrian methods provided something of a model for Germany.[69] Austria also proved a testing ground for the labour projects into which local German authorities would force Jews by the end of the year.[70]

The dubious achievements of the SD in Austria would likely have gained the interest of the central Reich authorities anyway, but the SD's cause was given a great boost by the German 'Kristallnacht' pogrom of 9–10 November 1938. The pogrom directly took the lives of 91 Jews. Around 1,000 synagogues were wholly or partly destroyed and tens of thousands of Jewish shops and businesses vandalized and ransacked. The violence was organized and conducted by party men and the SA, but ordinary Germans were also involved—in fact, in some areas, violence against Jews had preceded the 'official' action. A few non-Jews tried to help the victims, and more opposed the destruction, though often simply because non-Jewish property was destroyed.

The violence was precisely of the crude, non-systematic nature the SD despised, and the aftermath of Kristallnacht provided another opportune moment for Heydrich to purvey his organization's 'solution'. In January 1939 Göring, in his capacity as plentipotentiary for the Four Year Plan (illustrating the continuing significance of the economic aspect of Jewish policy), duly instructed Interior Minister Frick to establish a central office for Jewish emigration from the Reich and to appoint Heydrich director.

The SD once again illustrated its efficiency. By the outbreak of the Second World War, 282,000 Jews had left Germany, and around half of them had left in 1938–9. (About 202,000 remained in Germany and another 57,000 in annexed Austria). The emigration process was given considerable impetus as the political police replicated the terror unleashed in Austria by incarcerating around 30,000 Jews in concentration camps after 'Kristallnacht'.[71] 'Compulsory Aryanization' also began in Germany in December 1938. The pogrom provided the opportunity to launch a concerted economic assault on the Jews on the back of the huge 'fine' levied on the community by Göring for the damage done in November.[72]

The SD method was exported to other territories falling under German rule. Special SD–Security Police offices for Jewish affairs became regular features of the European landscape in the years to come as they were dispatched to advise on and facilitate Jewish deportations, beginning with Eichmann's appointment to the Protectorate of Bohemia and Moravia in summer 1939.[73] The Protectorate was considered to be part of 'Greater Germany' even though it was not directly absorbed into the Reich. Like Austria, it was virgin territory for the avant-garde of German racial policy, which explains why the first outright deportations of Jews from Reich territory occurred from Vienna and the Protectorate to the Lublin district of occupied Poland in October 1939. Control of Poland would only occur through war, however, adding the decisive radicalizing factor in Nazi racial policy.

CHAPTER 5
GENOCIDE IN GERMANY'S EASTERN EMPIRE

Introduction: From *Grenzpolitik* to *Raumpolitik*: German Expansion and Its Goals

Hitler claimed to be a *Raumpolitiker*, a 'geopolitician', concerned with huge imperial spatial goals. He disdained so-called *Grenzpolitiker*, those ordinary politicians concerned with relatively minor border revision.[1] Yet Nazi foreign policy contained both facets. The acquisition of Austria and the Sudetenland (1938), western Poland (1939), Alsace-Lorraine and Luxembourg (1940), and northern Slovenia (1941), all had aspects of a familiar early-twentieth-century ethnonationalist irredentism. So in its own way did the acquisition of the Netherlands in 1940, given that Hitler viewed the Dutch as Aryans to be incorporated into the greater German Reich. Accordingly, the Netherlands was put under a civilian government, like the Protectorate of Bohemia and Moravia and unlike the military rule imposed on Belgium or northern France.

Some of the immediate geopolitical goals of German expansion were similar to those of the First World War, and schemes for bringing ethnic Germans in from eastern Europe to consolidate German demographic control over territory taken from western Poland had also been floated from December 1914. But Nazi racism ensured that attitudes towards non-Germans were much more severe and absolute than they had been either under military rule in the First World War or in the time of forcible Bismarckian assimilation. As Hitler put it in the Reichstag on the conquest of Poland, 'the most important task [is] . . . a new order of ethnographic conditions, meaning a resettlement of the nationalities, so that at the conclusion of developments better boundaries result than is the case today.' He also stated that this would be the context for the solution of the Jewish question.[2] The purified greater Germany would serve as the core of the much larger imperium Hitler envisaged in the shatterzones of the Habsburg and Romanov empires.

Acquisition of new territory had broad ramifications. Intentionally it brought war. War allowed still deeper Nazi penetration of Germany, including, for instance, increased party representation in local and municipal politics.[3] Himmler explicitly recognized that it was during war that the SS had to drive forward its agenda most strongly.[4] War, and the preparation for war, also 'legitimized' more draconian measures against 'inner enemies' in both occupied and German territory, and provided cover and pretext for disposing of the human 'ballast' of the mentally ill.

In October 1939 the 'child euthanasia' programme began in Germany after months of planning. In October, too, Hitler personally approved the 'mercy killing' of adult mental patients in Germany, tellingly backdating his authorization to 1 September, the day of the outbreak of war. By the beginning of 1940 the programme had become systematized and generalized to the extent that gassings of the mentally ill were conducted at select institutions under the auspices of Hitler's personal chancellery. That organization was probably chosen because its low profile in the Nazi machinery made it ideal for such a secret task. To add to the approximately 5,000 child victims of euthanasia, 70,000–80,000 people were murdered under the so-called Aktion T4, the centralized adult euthanasia scheme, until it came to an end in August 1941. Tens of thousands more Germans would still be accorded 'mercy deaths' thereafter.[5]

In the meantime, the first deportations of Jews had occurred from Austria and Moravia. In April 1940, during preparations for the invasion of France and the Benelux countries, the military high command used the old espionage libel to justify asking Himmler to remove Romanies from the western and northwestern border regions. Himmler took the opportunity to do what the Kriminalpolizei had been urging from October 1939 and piggybacked the German Romanies on the transports of Jews from Austria and the Protectorate to Poland: nearly 2,500 were

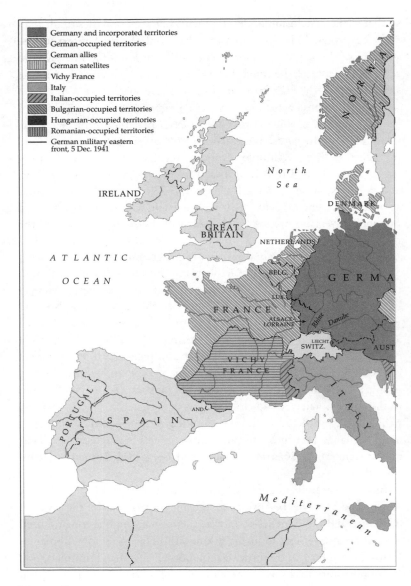

Map 2. Europe

deported to central Poland.[6] The next month, the 'Extraordinary Pacification Operation' was put into action in Poland, allegedly to prevent an uprising. The target was the Polish elite, 30,000 of whom were incarcerated, and at least 6,500 instantly murdered.

The inevitable result of the acquisition of territory, particularly in the east where Hitler's ambitions lay, was that it brought more 'racial inferiors' and Jews with it, undermining the SD's success in evicting the Jews of the Reich. Not only were these lands the heavily ethnically mixed old imperial borderlands, which Hitler had every intention of 'unmixing' in the most radical way, they included the closest thing the Jews had to a territorial home: the Pale of Settlement. Furthermore, these were not like the Jews who had assimilated in Germany over generations. They were predominantly religious 'Ostjuden', in traditional garb, the very 'eastern Jew' of Hitler's memory of *fin-de-siècle* Vienna; the Jew of Nazi stereotype, unmasked, living in lands of foreign customs and tongues.

The relationship between expansion of territory and of Germany's 'racial problems' presented a problem much larger than that resulting from the earlier contradictions between expropriation and emigration. If the question of foreign forced labourers in the Reich could be resolved on paper at least by forbidding sexual relations with the German population on pain of death, the issues of the large eastern Slavic and Jewish populations could never be addressed by legislated segregation. Such problems were not unanticipated. The radicalization in racial policies that followed on successive steps in Germany's expansion stemmed logically from the very decision for expansion, irrespective of specific orders and decisions. By the same token, the recognized radicalizing effects of war were not some purely extrinsic factor, influencing but separate to longer standing perpetrator intent. The very decision to go to war presupposed a radical mindset, particularly in the Nazi regime whose very identity was predicated upon the conflict of nations and races. Everything that happened in war was liable to be interpreted in that light: frustrations were the cause for 'revenge'; successes provided opportunities to create facts on the ground.

Expansion paved the way for new power constellations. As the Austrian case suggested, jurisdiction in the annexed and occupied territories was up for grabs, the more so the greater the degree to which existing elites and structures were obliterated. Obliteration was generally very considerable in eastern locations. The people profiting from the power transfer were drawn from the ranks of the most radical elements. The primary struggle in the new territories was not between representatives of the Nazi party and the pre-Nazi state, but between senior party men and their acolytes on one hand and on the other the growing SS presence, which succeeded in insinuating itself into more and more formal civilian leadership positions during the war. Their battle was not about political disposition, or ruthlessness, though there were differences of nuance about priorities. It was really a power battle for control, with the army and the economic power centres periodically throwing their weight in on either side when the interests of military security and the war economy were at stake.

Beginning in Austria, German forces entering new territories were accompanied by task forces of the Security Police and SD. As part of their security remit, these 'Einsatzgruppen' were responsible for the identification and apprehension of political enemies. They were also an expression of Heydrich's determination to establish the authority of his police forces in new regions. As soon as they had completed their preliminary tasks, they became stationary offices of the Security Police and SD (and thus of the RSHA after its establishment in October 1939). The local commanders of the Security Police became vital in the implementation of population policy and genocide. The Security Police operatives were shortly joined by Himmler's direct representatives, the Higher SS and Police Leaders, who brought authority over the regular German police forces and their local auxiliaries, and whose arrival signalled that the 'Reichsführer-SS' intended to keep ultimate control of security policy.

The SS–Police 'security' role was not simply another of the euphemisms with which the Germans cloaked their increasingly murderous policies. In a world where political and racial enemies were synonymous, 'pacification' was not just a short-term means of gaining stability by the removal of overt political opposition. It was also a matter of identifying threats to the long-term integrity of German control over the newly taken (or retaken) territories, in the form of local identity which might assert itself in future nationalist antagonism, such as had flared at the end of the First World War. Accordingly, security policy was concerned with elite bearers of local cultural or political identity, who became by definition subversive elements.

The territories annexed to Germany were swiftly placed under German civilian rule, in the person of a Gauleiter or lower equivalent. Unlike in Germany, the Gauleiters' authority as regional party representatives was compounded with state authority. Unification of party and state positions also applied in those territories comprising the eastern empire, once they had been pacified and turned over to civilian control.

The Nazi potentates in the east had considerable discretion in moulding or interpreting policy in their colonial experimental chambers. Their often numerically inadequate and poor quality staff frequently consisted of opportunists and adventurers. Some were not considered qualified for service further westward and some, like colonial administrators everywhere, were seeking liberation from the constraints of everyday life at home: a more unbound existence abroad, or an avenue for social climbing. Others wanted to escape military service. The administrations of Poland and the former Soviet lands became the butt of black humour within the Reich bureaucracy owing to the level of corruption there: the Generalgouvernement (GG), the area of central Poland occupied by Germany from 1939 but not annexed to the Reich, came to be known as the 'Gangster-Gau'.[7] Ideology was often a key aspect of recruitment, as shown by the weeding-out of some applicants deemed insufficiently committed. The corporate sense of superiority these unlikely proconsuls shared in the administration of masses of supposedly hostile 'primitives', the oppressive strangeness of their lands of posting, and their unusual executive freedom proved a murderous combination. Let us now consider their demographic policy, working outwards from the German core to the imperial periphery.

In October 1939 Hitler simultaneously set in motion two processes to expedite the 'new order of ethnographic conditions', including the solution of the Jewish question. He gave the German Gauleiters the mandate to Germanize their territories with no questions asked as to the legality of their methods—these remits extended to the territory annexed in the years 1938–41. Swiftly after his Reichstag speech Hitler also conferred on Himmler the responsibility for 'strengthening

Germandom' by eliminating dangerous elements among 'alien parts of the population' and resettling ethnic Germans from the Soviet sphere—Stalin approved since it meant the removal of a distrusted group—into the newly annexed German 'living space'.

Himmler characteristically took maximum advantage of this mandate, now using the additional title of Reich Commissioner for the Strengthening of Ethnic Germandom, and creating a new umbrella organization within the SS with a corresponding title (RKF). In order to reinforce his own control of the project—at least outside German territory, for within it Nazi party organizations still had considerable influence over population policy throughout the war—he made his personal representatives, the HSSPFs and SSPFs, into regional RKF plenipotentiaries. He also made civilian governors into RKF plenipotentiaries where they agreed with his racist philosophy. One such man was Greiser in the 'Reichsgau Posen' or 'Warthegau', the annexed territory of western Poland; Albert Forster of Danzig–West Prussia to the north of the Warthegau was not.[8]

Forster had had prewar disputes with the SS over control of *volksdeutsch* policy and had links with Himmler's rivals in the party hierarchy. While he facilitated the murder of the relatively few Jews in his area, he was a thorn in Himmler's side in his unique interpretation of Hitler's Germanization mandate. Rather than assiduously measuring the Polish population against 'racial' criteria, he simply took at their word Poles claiming German ancestry and declared them citizens of the Reich, thus 'Germanizing' Danzig–West Prussia with minimal effort, but creating a continuing source of conflict with the regional HSSPF because of his ideologically questionable methods.[9]

The RKF coordinated other SS offices. The Race and Settlement Office was responsible for 'racial screening' of conquered peoples; the *Volksdeutsche Mittelstelle* marshalled the settlement of *Volksdeutsche*; and the deportation offices of the newly formed RSHA expelled the unwanted population groups—primarily Jews and Poles in practice. Approximately one million *Volksdeutsche* were resettled during the war, half of these in advance of the invasion of the USSR. The majority were settled on farms in incorporated Polish territory. They came from throughout the German diaspora: the Baltic States, Dobruja, Bukovina,

Bessarabia, Volhynia, and Galicia. Some came enthusiastically, more came reluctantly. Some refused to come in 1939, but did so with considerable relief after persecution at the hands of suspicious Soviet authorities after the German invasion of the USSR in 1941.

The most extensive and enduring population engineering centred on the Warthegau and, to a somewhat lesser extent, Upper Silesia.[10] However, the newly acquired areas in the west also suffered. Luxembourg was subject to linguistic and cultural Germanization and, as everywhere, increasing forced labour and conscription. Alsace was added to the Gau Baden, neighbouring Lorraine to the Saar-Palatinate. Like other contested border areas, these were scheduled for modernization programmes to consolidate them fully within the industrial core of the new Germanic empire. The region was planned to be renamed the Westmark. In both, in the language of the chief of civil administration in Alsace, 'ethnic cleansing'—'völkische Säuberung'—through eviction into the non-annexed areas of France was the fate of tens of thousands of people comprising Jews, 'asocials' of various Nazi classifications, 'inner Frenchmen' (inassimilable on account of their loyalty to France), Romanies, and homosexuals. Some deemed 'Germanisable' were brought into Germany itself. Volksdeutsche were settled in the place of these evictees, as, forcibly, were some unwilling reichsdeutsch colonizers from the neighbouring German territories.[11] Not all the Alsatians were unhappy with the new German dispensation: a combination of military draftees and volunteers provided a Waffen-SS division, appropriately named Charlemagne after the Frankish emperor of the First Reich.

The radicalization of policy involved in consolidating newly acquired regions also provided an opportunity and context for ridding the old Reich of its Jews. In October 1940, 6,504 Jews were deported from Baden, the Saar, and the Palatinate to the internment camp at Gurs in Vichy France. According to Heydrich's report, the operation was 'hardly noticed' by the local population.[12] As we shall see, analogous measures on a much larger scale were more difficult to enact in Poland.

There were borderlands within borderlands. Austria, divided since 1938 into a series of Gaue within the Reich, had regions analogous to Upper Silesia in Germany: places over whose disposition small but vicious unofficial wars had been fought at the close of the First World War, namely the Burgenland, Carinthia, and Styria. The sort of 'borderland consciousness' of an embattled existence propounded in the Palatinate by the West German Borderland Association (*Westdeutsche Grenzlandsmannschaft*) was at least as strong here. These areas, and the Austro-German paramilitaries who had fought for them, provided a cadre of ruthless Nazis and the now-familiar nationalistic paranoia about secessionist threat and racial degeneration. Friedrich Rainer became Gauleiter of his home province of Carinthia in 1941, having been a member of the militia formed to prevent it being incorporated into Yugoslavia. Like Austria as a whole, Carinthia and Styria had increasingly been viewed as bulwarks of Germanic culture against the Slavs in the nineteenth century. Like Eastern Upper Silesia and the Westmark they were now supposed to become models of racial and political consciousness as well as of economic modernity.[13]

The primary enemy in Carinthia and Styria was the Slovene population, in part because of the very small number of Jews in southern Austria. With the invasion of Yugoslavia the annexed parts of northern Slovenia were added to the two Austrian provinces, and policies of Germanization duly intensified. The Slovenes, as a more 'civilized', Catholic and generally conservative former Habsburg group, were considered assimilable. Slovene national consciousness, however, had first to be destroyed, especially given that the territory on which they lived was seen as part of a traditional Germanic sphere of economic and political influence. Cultural and linguistic measures were used, but also increasingly deportation of the intelligentsia, people who had settled since the post-First World War border allocation, and people from the border regions. The programme was a failure in terms of its stated goals of transplanting 260,000 people, but nevertheless more than 50,000 Slovenes were deported to Croatia, Serbia, and Germany. Of those Slovenes deported to Germany, some were deemed Germanisable by the RKF, the others used for forced labour. *Volksdeutsche* from the Italian occupation zone of Yugoslavia were imported to the vacated borderlands.[14]

A different set of racial issues presented itself in the Burgenland on the eastern fringe of Austria, the formerly contested Hungarian-Austrian territory. There, the *Landeshauptmann* placed the relatively large Romany population above the 'Jewish question' as a threat to preserving 'pure German blood in the borderlands'. The extreme pressure emanating from him and from the populace in southern Austria ensured that the RSHA prioritized the removal of the Burgenland Romanies as soon as they were able. In the autumn of 1941, 5,000 were deported to Łódź in the Warthegau.[15]

The scale and ambition of Nazi demographic designs increased in direct relation to the growing scale of the population problems and the socio-economic nature of the regions concerned. While occupied western and northern Europe was primarily administered to exploit its advanced industrial capacity, and planned, in the future, to be a closed market for German goods, eastern Europe had an entirely different function. A glance at *Mein Kampf* shows how much attention Hitler had paid to the Romanov borderlands, particularly the Ukraine with its fertile soil and the mineral-rich Black Sea area. After the consolidation of the German borders, the greater eastern empire was scheduled to be run in the longer term according to the principle of settler colonialism, the most detailed and grim vision of which was laid out from 1940 to 1942 by SS planners in the RKF in various versions of the *Generalplan Ost*.

The *Generalplan Ost* was a design for a utopia of blood and soil. Its designs, to be implemented over the next twenty to thirty years, involved transplanting Reich Germans and members of related 'Nordic' peoples, and deploying some local *Volksdeutsche*, all of whom would live in a neo-feudal system on farms and model villages interspersed with SS outposts along two main communication routes leading from the Reich to Leningrad and the Crimea, respectively. Urban areas would be greatly reduced. With the SS, those on the projected eastern borders of the empire—expanding along with Nazi conquest to the Ural mountains, which were seen as the natural border between Europe and Asia—would fulfil a similar function to the earlier warrior farmers in the Romanov borderlands or Serbs in Krajina: frontier defence against the barbarians (Muslims in those cases, Slavs in this). As much as possible of the colossal cost of this endeavour would be borne by the SS's own expanding economic empire, with its construction and slave labour resources.[16]

The logic, if not always the explicit intent, of modern settler colonialism in Australasia and the Americas had been the systematic removal and mass death of the native population. There was no need for speculation about German intentions. The local populations that could not be incorporated were scheduled for expulsion in the number of scores of millions, except for a minority to be used as helots. It is possible that mass sterilization would have been used to prevent the reproduction of huge parts of the Slavic peoples: such a prospect was certainly brought closer to reality when SS doctors began experimenting with new sterilization techniques in Auschwitz Concentration camp from July 1942.[17] For the Jews there was no place at all, as Hitler stated from September 1939. They would be evicted from areas of German control.

The practice of imperial rule differed from the colonial theory, however. Of the practical problems of Jewish deportation policy we shall learn more soon. Even where the most extensive and enduring Germanization attempts occurred, in the annexed Polish areas, concessions had to be made to the labour needs of the war industry, just as they did in the Protectorate of Bohemia and Moravia. Even in these annexed areas increasing conscription requirements eroded some of the racial restrictions on who was to be allotted German citizenship. Besides, problems analogous to those on the margins of 'defining the Jew' existed for other, much larger population groups. Political and cultural criteria were interspersed with the racial criteria established in the 'German People's List' and other mechanisms used to sift the local population to establish who was to be expelled to make way for German settlers, who allocated second-class citizenship, and who deemed assimilable. If Forster's Danzig–West Prussia was an extremely inclusive case, everywhere there were regional variations and intraregional inconsistencies in German population policy.[18] Indeed, there were frayed edges to Nazi racial *concepts* as well as *practices*, notwithstanding the violence with which boundaries were policed between Germans and Jews and eastern labourers in the Reich. Even in the 'racial state', as with the juxtaposition of interwar Polish nationalists' views of Polish Ukrainians on one hand and Polish Jews on the other, or First World War-era CUP views of Armenians as opposed to Kurds, the Nazis could imagine some 'foreigners' as assimilable, others not, and still others as indeterminate.

Further east, Himmler's more utopian demographic designs were stymied by wartime exigency, resource limitations, not least the number of eligible and willing ethnic Germans, and political opposition from within Rosenberg's eastern ministry. Experiments with German settlements in the Crimea, western Lithuania, the Zhytomyr region of the Ukraine, and the Zamość district of Lublin province in the Generalgouvernement were relatively small-scale affairs. Moreover, in the former Soviet territories the wartime 'settlement pearls' of *Volksdeutsche* and the *reichsdeutsch* mentors sent to improve their cultural consciousness proved inviting targets for partisan attack.

The bulk of the settlement programme was scheduled to take place after a successful conclusion to the war anyway, and the grander schemes were put on ice—permanently, in the event—after the German defeat at Stalingrad when Hitler suspended all further planning. Himmler never realized his aspiration to link the *Generalplan Ost* with the consolidation of the German border regions through a 'General Settlement Plan'.[19] The most significant wartime effect of Himmler's planning for German settlements was arguably that it gave him a channel to press his authority on Jewish matters, as we shall see. The most historically significant aspect of Germany's relations with the ethnic Germans who were not taken into the Reich in 1939–41 was their instrumentalization in genocide: like the Muslims who profited from complicity in the murder of the Armenians of eastern Anatolia, the *Volksdeutsche* of Transnistria or the Ukraine could enrich themselves from participation in genocide. As for the non-Jewish population of the former Soviet lands, they would learn through bitter experience that even if Germany was unsuccessful in the 'constructive' parts of its Germanization endeavours, it could be very effective at the destructive part.

The most important limit on German colonial plans was that the empire was entirely constructed at war. Even many of the plans for *wartime* exploitation of the east remained dead letters, given the primacy of changing wartime security and economic needs. Mercifully, one of the designs put into abeyance was the mooted starvation of many millions of urban Soviet civilians. By some estimates 30 million or even more people would die (if they could not flee over the Urals, as the Nazi documentation put it), in order to remove pressure on resources needed in the short and medium terms for Germany and the occupied areas. Pragmatism militated against the enactment of the 'Hungerplan': logistics, the lack of available manpower for sealing off whole urban areas from their agricultural hinterlands, and the recognition that the policy might lead to mass rebellion anyway. Besides, from around the turn of 1941–2, Soviet civilians were being dragooned in increasingly large numbers for labour in Germany.[20] Fears of arousing rebellion were also behind the postponement of various ideas floated in 1942–3 for the murder of Poles with tuberculosis, or of particular categories of elderly Poles and children.[21]

The context of war made the occupation murderous in a different way. Like Japanese imperialism in southeast Asia, German rule geared itself to short-term hyperexploitation in a conflict against enemies with greater natural resources. This exploitation extended to Germany's western European dominions, with growing ruthlessness as war fortunes were reversed, resistance increased, and Germany started to lose its eastern breadbasket. Nevertheless, as with Japanese views of Chinese and Koreans, the conception of Slavs as inferior legitimated the horrific lengths Germany was prepared to go to in the east. It is in the ideological justification provided by racism for mass death that the abortive Hungerplan, Himmler's settler-colonial utopia, and the actual exploitation and security policy of the war years find their common ground. And it is in the sort of value-laden 'resource calculation' of the Hungerplan that common ground may be found with the actual, rather ad hoc, implementation of starvation policies against discrete captive groups.

The victims of *de jure* or de facto starvation policies included the following: the populations of Athens, Kharkov, and Kiev while under occupation; the population of Leningrad as it was besieged for two and a half years, leading to perhaps a million deaths; Soviet POWs—'useless eaters'—as they were incarcerated and died in their millions from summer 1941; children in Belarussian orphanages; and Jews, as they were isolated from the surrounding populations in closed ghettos in Poland from early 1940, a measure resulting in one in eleven of all Jewish deaths in the Holocaust.[22] For longer term contextualization, it is pertinent to recall that such tacit starvation policies had also been practiced in the run-up phase to the first Nazi genocide, with the inmates of state asylums in the 1930s.

Though the Hungerplan did not materialize, its thrust had broader support among the Reich authorities than did Himmler's agrarian völkisch 'paradise'. Not that the two were remotely mutually exclusive: starvation was a convenient way to reduce populations whose physical removal was ultimately desired. The genesis of the Hungerplan lay not in the SS, but in Göring's Office for the Four Year Plan, his Economic (planning) Staff East, the Reich Ministry for Food and Agriculture, the Quartermaster General's office in the Wehrmacht, and the military economic armament office. However unrealistic, and perhaps wilfully extreme it was—wilful, because reading the documents one senses a determined embrace of its projected death toll, perhaps as a way of proving the 'toughness' of its planners by the cool, 'objective' way they predicted mass famine—the thinking embodied in the Hungerplan was embedded in a real, historical relationship between a more industrialized Europe and its historically less developed east. One might say 'underdeveloped', since the European economic balance in recent centuries had seen the centre and northwest of the continent industrialize while importing grain from an agrarian east that was, until the panicked industrialization of the late Tsarist period and Bolshevik rule, locked into the role of raw-material supplier.

In November 1937, at a secret conference in the Reich Chancellery, Hitler was minuted as declaring that 'it had to be remembered that since the [First] World War, those very countries which had formerly been food exporters had become industrialized'. It was no use trusting in exchange treaties between countries to ensure food supply, he continued.

We were living in an age of economic empires in which the primitive urge to colonization was again manifesting itself. . . . The boom in world economy caused by the economic effects of rearmament could never form the basis of a sound economy over a long period, and the latter was obstructed above all by the economic disturbances resulting from Bolshevism.

Entirely consistently, the 'Guidelines of Economic Policy for the Economic Organization East', provided by its agricultural group on 23 May 1941, stated that

Under the Bolshevik system [of forced-paced industrialisation and economic self-sufficiency] Russia has withdrawn from Europe purely out of considerations of power, and has accordingly disturbed the European balance of work-division. Our task of reintegrating Russia into this balance by definition implies destroying the present economic balance of the USSR . . . . This will necessarily lead to both the industry and a large part of the people in the hitherto food-importing areas dying-off.

Destroying the cities and industries that had expanded in recent decades in western Russia/USSR was a way of destroying the European power basis of the eastern state as it had emerged since the 1890s. These measures were not just anti-Bolshevik, they were part of a grander design for reversing the fragmentation of the European political-economic structure that had occurred with population growth, 'Jewish-driven' modernization, the end of the dynastic empires, and the emergence of the nation-states of east-central Europe.

In one of his monologues to subordinates, Hitler declared in October 1941 that Germany should treat the inhabitants of the east 'like Indians. . . . We eat Canadian wheat and never think of the Indians.' He was expressing the view of the settler-colonial racist. Such remarks have, quite legitimately, been seized upon by scholars seeking to emphasize the colonial nature of the Nazi project and thus its connection with European colonialism outside Europe. But in their allusion to grain supply they also illustrate that Germany's was an imperial project conceived in a very specific spatial and economic setting, one in which eastern and western Europe had once been bound together by raw-material supply and demand. The eastern European colonial territories were seen less as distant possessions and more as an 'organic' extension of what Hitler had, at the 1937 meeting, called Germany's 'tightly packed racial core'.[23]

Imperial Expansion and Jewish Policy

The spatial setting of the imperial project was also important for the coming murder of the Jews, most of whom lived within the eastern realms. While the final solution clearly developed a fully continental dimension, and its architects developed aspirations of corresponding size, the main thrust of murder was against the Jews around the Pale of Settlement, where Nazi rule was direct and the future Nazi empire was to be erected. This was the core of the genocide, and its main object.

It is important to be clear. While Nazi Jewish policy began with a spatial objective—removal of the Jews from German-controlled areas, which over time also entailed mass murder—it also developed a more explicitly universal, 'existential' objective—the physical destruction of the Jewish race to the fullest extent possible everywhere. The transition was not straightforward and 'logical', contrary to the early scholarship on the final solution. In the postwar words of Eichmann's subordinate, Dieter Wisliceny, it 'did not take place from today to tomorrow, but gradually, and it only culminated in spring 1942'.[24] Nor, as this part of the book will argue, did the 'spatial' aspect of the policy ever quite disappear even as the 'existential' aspect gained ground. It is in fact more accurate to talk of different strands within the thinking and policy prioritization of the SS on the Jewish question even at the height of the genocide after spring 1942. We shall see in the following chapter that while particular individuals and agencies had a great deal invested in the most geographically extensive murder, many more were simply pre-occupied with the Jews within Germany's empire—within the territory that it directly controlled and intended to incorporate.

The successes and failures of German military-imperial objectives also shaped the practical parameters within which the developing policy could be pursued. Accordingly, even as Nazi extermination plans were at their most expansive, from spring 1942, the ability to influence other states beyond direct German control to surrender their Jews for murder was dwindling alongside German prospects of victory. And while it is certain that, from some undefined point in early 1942, there was a clear central intention that almost every individual Jew (and certainly every community) under German control would be murdered immediately or after labour exploitation, there were also from around that undefined point European Jews that the Nazis would find it difficult to reach. Some of these Jews dwelled in their tens and hundreds of thousands in the major and minor Axis states, and even in states, like France, in which Germany could claim overlordship. In other words, not a few were actually within grasp *had* the Nazis been prepared (as they were not) to compromise everything else to reach them.

One of the most prominent intellectual historians of the Holocaust writes that Germany made 'the greatest bureaucratic and logistical expenditure, to seek out Jews in the most far-flung reaches of the countries under German control with the sole aim of bringing them to Auschwitz for extermination'. 'Nothing', he continues, 'could make them desist from their deeds. . . . And even the self-interest of the perpetrators, robbery, or the exploitation of labour offered no protection and allowed no exception.' This is also the popular understanding of the Holocaust, the view that the Nazis would have gone literally to the ends of the earth to track down each and every living Jew with no regard for the practical consequences.[25] But the historical record shows it is simply not true. If 'solving the Jewish question' was central to the Nazi world-view, that goal was always intertwined with war-fighting ability, which was the ultimate *raison d'être* of Nazism. The two seemed to go together for much of the war: dealing with the 'internal enemy' was a prerequisite for securing the German war effort, and Jews *internal* to the German empire were by definition irrelevant in alliance policy. The disposition of Jews in other states' jurisdictions was a matter of *strategy rather than tactics*, however, and in this matter, when considerations of war-fighting ability conflicted with Jewish policy, the pressure for genocide was mitigated.

The one place where the fate of European Jewry could be fully controlled by Germany was in the vast cone of direct imperial control from central through eastern Europe, though also including the Netherlands. Beyond the western, northern, and southern boundaries of the cone, the parameters of genocide were variable and even, as we shall see, negotiable. This was partly an outcome of the Nazi imperial structure. In places scheduled for full incorporation into the empire, a heavier and more intrusive German presence was imposed, as distinct from regions like northern France and Belgium which were not to be incorporated, and which proved to be safer places for certain categories of Jews. This interpretation does not detract from the genocidal, obsessive nature of Nazi thinking about Jews. But parameters imposed by space and wartime exigency undermine the notion—a notion feeding into more metaphysical arguments about the unique place of the Holocaust in human history—that the final solution was radically separated from all other considerations.

My interpretation can also be reconciled with the race-biological vision. After the war, Rudolph Höss, commandant of Auschwitz, recalled Himmler commissioning him to 'obliterate the biological basis of Jewry'. Eichmann developed the theme to Höss:

> Eichmann was absolutely convinced that if he could succeed in destroying the biological basis of Jewry *in the East* by complete extermination, then Jewry as a whole would never recover from the blow. The assimilated Jews of the West, including America, would, in his opinion, be in no position (and would have no desire) to make up this enormous loss of blood and there would therefore be no future generation worth mentioning.[26]

This is precisely what Raphael Lemkin, the inventor of the term 'genocide', described as the destruction of a group by its permanent 'crippling', the destruction of its ability to reproduce itself and (thereby) to carry out its supposed collective agenda.[27] The vision of the annihilation of what we might call the 'critical mass' of the victim people at the collective level fits conceptually within the SD's tradition of racism with its concern with balances of blood at the individual level; at the same time, it is also a conception of genocide that has wider applicability than just the Jewish case. The genocide of the Jews had at its heart the assault on their cultural core and most concentrated population centres in and around the old Pale of Settlement. These centres supplied, in the words of one Foreign Office official, 'the regenerative and Talmudic recruits for the militant Jewish intelligentsia': the USSR and Poland.[28]

Twofold Destruction: The Death of Poland and the Jewish Reservation Plans

Lemkin had the Polish experience in mind alongside the Jewish one when he invented the term genocide in 1943–4. For Lemkin, genocide was not simply the physical murder of a people, but the destruction of the 'spirit' of that people by destroying its collective identity. Immediately in advance of the German invasion of Poland, the SS drew up plans for precisely that: more than 60,000 members of the Polish political, administrative, Catholic, and intellectual elites as very broadly conceived were identified as embodiments of Polish national consciousness and (by the Nazi logic) therefore potential leaders of resistance. Thousands were murdered between the invasion and the end of 1939, often as reprisals for resistance provided by the Polish population. Many more were to follow, including during the 'extraordinary pacification operation' the following year. These broad measures of an 'ethnic security policy'[29] formed the first phase of the general attack on Polishness that came with the dismemberment of the state into ethnically gradated strips from east to west and the dislocation and planned 'deracination' of its population.

Thousands of Polish civilians were killed during the invasion itself, possibly more than the soldiers who died. The German army killed many civilians as a result of its established partisan-phobia, stimulated by the prior history of the border regions and by a massacre of local *Volksdeutsche* by retreating Polish troops in the Pomeranian town of Bromberg/Bydgoszcz on 3 September. However, whereas military atrocities dwindled when the lack of real resistance became clear, murders by the SS Einsatzgruppen continued unabated: by the end of the year they had killed approximately 20,000 people, sometimes with the assistance of local *Volksdeutsch* 'self-protection' groups established since Bydgoszcz. Some of this SS violence led the military to a limited protest, less on principle, since the army was complicit in some of the Einsatzgruppen massacres, than because the action challenged military prerogatives and threatened to stain the army's image. The result was a tacit rebuke from Hitler, who pointed out that the tasks of administering Poland would not be the military's concern—news that the army was ultimately relieved to hear, once it had been assured that the demographic reordering process would not affect military operations.[30]

There was a certain inevitability about the violence of the Security Police and SD from September 1939. The Polish campaign was the first time the Einsatzgruppen were deployed during an actual military conflict, and it came after years of mental preparation for Germany's existential battles. All of the leaders had been involved in Freikorps fighting, many over the German–Polish borders after the First World

War. The leaders of the squads did not operate with precise instructions for dealing with enemies amongst the Poles, even with the elites who had already been identified. Rather, in a way that fitted their training in developing their own initiatives, and that was also part of the German military tradition of empowering mid-ranking officers in the field, they were allowed discretion in applying Heydrich's and Himmler's general guidelines on combating resistance movements. 'Ausschaltung' was the injunction, but the precise forms of this 'elimination' were to be decided on the spot.[31]

If there was leeway about the method of dealing with the enemy, there was also deliberate leeway in defining the enemy. As in Germany beforehand, with the increasingly arbitrary powers of the Security Police to define enemies and place them in 'protective custody', so now in Poland the men of the Security Police and SD were presented with 'racial security problems' on a new scale, and with more freedom than before in dealing with them. Much the same went for the related dilemmas of demographic restructuring of the new state. The SD's self-conception as an ideological vanguard meant that it took full advantage of expanding conceptions of the possible and permissible in the experimental chamber of Poland. In the absence of concrete blueprints, policy was shaped by action, and vice versa.[32] The behaviour of these men illustrates the falseness of the dichotomy of ideological intention and structural circumstance—the two poles around which interpretation of the final solution clustered until recently—in the development of genocide.

As significant as the scale of the Einsatzgruppen massacres was the victim profile. Some 7,000 of the 20,000 Poles were Jews, which was a much higher proportion of Jewish victims than those killed by the Wehrmacht. The Order Police also perpetrated significant massacres of Jews.[33] While the Christian Polish victims had generally been members of the elite, the SS–Police's Jewish victims were taken from a wider cross section of Polish society. A basic conviction that Jews were the mortal enemy informed such actions, but there was an important functional quality to them too: the worst individual massacre, of 500–600 Jews, occurred on 20 September at Przemyśl, near the German–Soviet demarcation line. It was part of an attempt by the 'Einsatzgruppe von Woyrsch'—named after its commander, a

Silesian German who had fought there in the Freikorps in 1919—to terrorize Jews into fleeing over the line, a policy pursued until the Soviets closed the border.[34] Jewish policy was still being conducted according to an overall spatial logic: removal. The ultimate displacement of the Polish Jews was inevitable on the invasion. The partition of Poland came into effect early in October 1939, and with it an explicit Hitlerian injunction to cleanse the annexed western territories of 'Jews, Polacks and riff-raff'. The dumping ground would be the Generalgouvernement area of central Poland, where Polish Jews were to be segregated from Christian Poles in an enclosed reservation on the easternmost borders of the current German area of control—the Lublin district up to the Bug River. On 29 September Hitler also told Rosenberg that German Jews would be deported there, indicating a significant policy leap from forced emigration to targeted transplantation. This would affect almost all Jews still in Germany, though the SD did continue pushing some German Jews out to Palestine through 1940.

Not only were the Jews left under German control scheduled to be put in what was effectively a large open-air prison, but the RKF was also working on the basis of removing about 80 per cent of the Poles eastwards. The question was when and how. The first attempt to move Jews from German territory to Lublin, the so-called Nisko-operation, under Eichmann, was designed in typical SD fashion as an experiment to gain experience. It was also a portent of the logistical difficulties to come in 'population transfer'. Inadequate preparations at the reception point meant that the Jews deported on 18–21 October 1939 from Vienna and Moravia, supplemented by others from Upper Silesia, met with starvation and in some cases murder by the SS.[35]

It was axiomatic that before deportation the Jews should contribute to the economy by their wealth and their sweat. Forced labour was swiftly decreed for all Polish Jews, with many German agencies arbitrarily seizing Jews for their own projects. At the end of September Göring was delegated to coordinate economic exploitation in the occupied territories, a mandate including the confiscation of Polish and Jewish property. The accumulated discriminations of years against the German Jews were applied in a few short weeks to the Polish Jews, and much more besides.

On 21 September Heydrich issued a circular to the Einsatzgruppen commanders and the relevant Reich ministries alluding to the 'final aim' of Jewish policy—deportation. It also detailed interim arrangements of dissolving Jewish communities with fewer than 500 people and concentrating the Jews of the incorporated areas in cities and larger towns, near transport links. 'Jewish councils' selected from prominent Jewish community members were to be made responsible for the implementation of future German instructions, which developed Eichmann's 'Vienna process' of forcing Jews to administer their own victimization. In a meeting with the Einsatzgruppen leaders earlier that day he had also specified the deportation of 30,000 Romanies from Reich territory into the Generalgouvernement, forced labour in the Reich for Poles, complemented by resettlement in the Generalgouvernement, and continued elimination or deportation of the elites.[36]

Heydrich announced the plan for the Jews twice because the circular (his infamous *Schnellbrief*) was designed more for the other recipients than the men who would be overseeing the policy. This explains why the circular alluded to the formation of Jewish councils after they had already been established: the circular was simply a way of broadcasting his offices' primacy in Jewish affairs in Poland.[37] Furthermore, the fact that the *Schnellbrief* did not mention Poles and Romanies suggests Heydrich had already recognized Himmler's authority over general population policy in anticipation of Himmler's appointment as RKF.[38] Jewish policy was the vital subset of population policy that Heydrich could exploit and keep as his own, as it had been since the SD's successes in 1938 and his appointment by Göring earlier in 1939 as head of Jewish emigration from the Reich. Under the auspices of the RKF, precisely the same RSHA offices would deal on one hand with the deportation of Jews and Poles together from the annexed territories in 1939–41 and on the other hand with the incoming ethnic Germans. These were the *Einwandererzentralstelle* and the *Umwandererzentralstelle*—the central offices for 'immigrants' and 'emigrants' respectively (names eerily recalling the dual function of the CUP's 'Directorate for the Resettlement of Tribes and Immigrants'). Nevertheless, even as general Nazi population policy—*Volkstumspolitik*—was in its first phase of development, Jewish policy was conceptually being hived off because of the ambitions of a man who knew its special significance for Hitler and, therefore, himself.

The fulfilment of Heydrich's aspirations was not yet within his own gift, however. He had to contend with the logistical problems of deportation, opposition from the new civil authorities in the Generalgouvernement to the use of their territory as a dumping ground, and the protests of Göring about disruptions to the labour supply. The deployment of Jews in the short term for labour would tie them in with war-related projects and put them under the authority of other offices, without and within the SS. For instance in the mineral-rich eastern strip of East Upper Silesia it was actually an SS project (Organisation Schmeldt) initiated for the Reich armaments economy by Himmler himself that would incorporate thousands of Jewish labourers and postpone their deportation until late in the war.

Parenthetically, the intention to Germanize and modernize the eastern strip of East Upper Silesia was boosted early in 1941 as the combine IG Farben decided to build a gigantic rubber-synthesizing plant near the town and concentration camp of Auschwitz/Oświęcim. IG Farben was attracted by the topography and natural resources of the area and by tax breaks offered to companies moving to the incorporated territories. The company's management assumed it could have a large number of incoming *Volksdeutsche* as labourers. It ended up using slaves from the nearby Auschwitz concentration camp, which was itself the hub of a large SS 'interest zone' established to provide services for the German settlers.[39]

German concentration policies for Jews resulted in the reintroduction to European history of the ghetto. This was not the medieval ghetto that functioned as a place of sanctuary as much as segregation. Nor were the new ghettos uniform entities, and nowhere was ghettoization total. Over the war years thousands of ghettos appeared across Nazi-occupied eastern Europe. Some, like the largest Polish ghettos, were sealed from the outside world from spring 1940 onwards: shortly after its sealing, the death penalty was introduced for Jews outside their designated walls in Łódź in the Warthegau. But some were 'open', on the presumption that Jews would find escape or hiding difficult among often anti-Semitic populations, or because there was insufficient manpower and material to seal them. After the invasion of the USSR some were established only briefly as holding points prior to murder; others lasted into 1943 and even 1944. Some provided the workforce for German war-related state and SS concerns and the growing number of private armaments manufacturers establishing themselves in Poland. In other places Jews did not even enter ghettos but from early 1940 were imprisoned in tens of thousands in myriad 'forced labour camps for Jews' run by a range of public and private organizations. Some ghettos developed their own internal economies to sustain themselves prior to the changing 'final goal'.[40]

In every one of these institutions, if to varying degrees, starvation, disease, and the arbitrary brutality of the gaolers and workmasters took a massive toll among millions of inhabitants who were at the bottom of Germany's list of supply priorities. Regional civilian administrations were responsible for the residence, labour, and food supply of most of the Polish Jews, and were thus deeply implicated in what was effectively a course of slow starvation. The Jewish population became increasingly less capable of productive work, while the spread of disease created public health concerns. Jews were also driven onto the black market. So by their treatment of the population, the civil authorities transformed an ideologically constructed 'problem' into a real set of socio-economic problems on a huge scale, given the size of the Jewish population. In the Generalgouvernement in 1939, the Jewish population was around 1,900,000. Its immiseration was also increasingly politically useful to Hans Frank at the head of the Generalgouvernement, because it could be used to justify removing the Jews from the areas under his jurisdiction as soon as possible.[41]

Of course, the SS–Police had their complement to the civil authorities' increasing refrain about Jewish criminality, indolence, and health threats: the idea of the Jewish 'security threat'. Outside of its own forced labour camps, the SS was only responsible for population movement, and for security-related occupation policy. The latter brief created scope for a classic Nazi clash of jurisdictions, because security was such an open-ended concept, with its short- and long-term connotations. The exploitation of the security brief would allow continued SS intervention in Jewish policy on the purported grounds that the Jews were inherently a security threat. Quite how far Himmler and his chief subordinates actually believed in the insidious nature of every last Jew, and how far their depiction as a security threat was a cynical ploy to increase SS power, is unclear, and presumably the proportions varied from person to person. For those who did believe, this was a classic case of an irrational claim that could be used instrumentally and, once internalized, developed its own internal consistencies—its own rationality. For those who did not fully subscribe to the idea, but who nevertheless wished to deploy it to their own advantage, presenting Jews as a security threat chimed conveniently with the depiction of Jews emanating from the very top of the Nazi power structure.

The circumstances of the SS's power play varied from place to place. If relations between the SS and Greiser in the Warthegau were cordial, the battle between Hans Frank and his nominal subordinate HSSPF Friedrich Wilhelm Krüger proved enduring and bitter. In the early months of the occupation, however, the most obvious instance of SS officers trying to expand their prerogatives at the expense of the civil administration is that of SSPF Globocnik in Lublin. It is no accident Globocnik was posted there. Himmler had seized on the Lublin reservation plan not just as a possible 'solution to the Jewish question' but because it provided an excellent way for establishing SS power in the Generalgouvernement. Globocnik set up a local ethnic German self-protection unit that acted as his private militia. He repeatedly, illegally, seized Jews for labour on SS projects. He would become the driving force behind later Germanization settlement projects there, which Himmler not only believed in ideologically, but saw as a way of gaining SS *territorial* control—to go with supremacy in security matters—over the 'outposts', as with Auschwitz and its SS 'interest zone' in Upper Silesia.[42] Germanization and demographic engineering were thus further useful levers in the power play, and accordingly also ramified on Jewish policy, as we shall see later.

The major battle between the Generalgouvernement's rulers and the SS over the first eighteen months was over the influx of Poles and Jews from the annexed territories. The *Volksdeutsche* arriving from eastern Europe required housing. Many of the Baltic Germans were urban, which explains why the major city of Łódź was incorporated into the

Warthegau at the last minute. The majority of the *Volksdeutsche* from further south in the USSR and from Romania were farmers. Accordingly, Polish peasants rather than the predominantly urban Jewish population were deported to make room for them, despite Heydrich's attempts to expel 600,000 Jews from the Warthegau and Eichmann's attempts to expel 70,000–80,000 Jews from East Upper Silesia. Since the ethnic Germans were to be given more space than the indigenes, approximately two Polish families were expelled for every one arrival.

The best indication of the brutality of the process at that point is actually not provided by the experience of deported Poles or Jews. It is provided by the fate of institutionalized mentally ill people caught in the machinery of population transfer. Perhaps 4,000 patients of Polish asylums were slaughtered during and immediately after the invasion and, taking into account not just those in the annexed territories but also Pomerania and West Prussia, the total would reach 10,000–15,000 by the end of winter 1939–40. They were murdered simply to provide temporary accommodation for ethnic Germans because they were seen as worthless, as non-life. By 1941, almost all asylum inmates on Polish territory had been killed. While most were simply shot, in early 1940 hundreds from the Tiegenhof near Gnesen were murdered in special vans engineered in the workshops of Sachsenhausen concentration camp to gas their passengers. The technology was redeployed in May–June 1941 by an SS unit known as 'Sonderkommando Lange' to murder German and Polish patients in East Prussia. These measures were not pursuant to any central order; they were not part of the German 'euthanasia' programme, even though at around the same time Himmler and the euthanasia staff were enacting a joint design to murder the inmates of German concentration camps who were deemed 'unfit for work'. The initiatives in Poland were local initiatives. They were also just a drop in the ocean of Nazi racial plans.[43]

From October 1939 until March 1941, just under 300,000 people were evicted into the Generalgouvernement from the Warthegau in a series of 'short-term' and 'interim' plans, and 408,525 from all of the annexed territories. The first deportations were beset with transport and accommodation difficulties and, while subsequent improvements in efficiency showed the *Umwandererzentralstelle's* adaptability, eviction still did not keep up with the influx of *Volksdeutsche*. By the winter of 1940–1, a quarter of a million ethnic Germans were languishing in improvised resettlement camps in the Reich, and Himmler had met with huge and decisive opposition to more extensive deportation eastwards.[44]

Other developments overtook the troubled eastward movement of Poles and the stymied deportation of Jews. Preparations for invading the USSR acquired logistical priority from spring 1941, but it had already become clear that labour requirements would not allow the continued mass expulsion of Poles, so most who were fit for work became liable for exemption. Some internal forced movement of Poles continued within the Warthegau throughout the war, and in 1940–1 the easternmost part of East Upper Silesia served the same function as a dumping ground that had been scheduled for the Generalgouvernement. But the bulk of the Poles, like the Jews, were now planned to be resettled after the war.

For the Jews, the intervening factor was the successive development of other versions of what has been called the 'territorial solution'. With the conquest of France, and to Hans Frank's excitement, the scheme was briefly but seriously entertained to deport the Jews to the French colony of Madagascar. Originating in the Foreign Office, whose denizens were keen to develop a stake in the fertile land of Jewish policy, the notion had long had purchase in the imaginings of Europe's anti-Semites, and was even entertained by the father of Zionism, Theodor Herzl. The Foreign Office was swiftly joined by the RSHA, which developed its own version of the design in a bid to maintain its own primacy in Jewish policy. According to the scheme, all of the countries involved in a coming peace treaty would be obliged to surrender their Jews for deportation to Madagascar, having first retrained them from their dangerous intellectual pursuits to develop artisanal and agricultural skills.

In reality, no German proponent had much interest in the subsistence of the 4 million or more Jews who would be affected. Tropical Madagascar would have been nothing other than utterly inhospitable for a European population. If not yet quite as extreme as the deportation of the Armenians into the Syrian and Iraqi deserts, this, like the Lublin reservation plan, was a way of slowly and deliberately suffocating the population. An indication of the mindset prevailing while Madagascar still seemed a possibility was the killing of Jews in German asylums, from July 1940, under the 'euthanasia' programme. They were not even permitted the cursory screening granted to their 'Aryan' fellow patients.

The Madagascar plan was discarded in August 1940. The failure to knock Britain out of the war meant that Germany was unable to secure the necessary domination of the seas. It was replaced by a different projected scheme based on the same principles of deporting Europe's Jews to inhospitable regions outside the continent. This time, the notional land boundary between Europe and Asia provided the demarcation line. Hitler decided in November 1940 to invade the USSR. With the beginning of active military preparations for the invasion in March 1941, Göring extended his earlier commissions to Heydrich to prepare for a more comprehensive solution of the Jewish question. The designs now started to coalesce with the developing facets of the *Generalplan Ost*. In March 1941 Hitler indicated that the Generalgouvernement was to be Germanized in the near future. The speculative intention became to force the Jews beyond the northern Ural mountains after the military defeat of the Soviet state, to the lands of the Gulag Archipelago. Jews fit for labour might be exploited, the others left to a 'natural' fate, while the Jewish–Bolshevik intelligentsia would be killed. The major difference between this design and the Madagascar plan was that even more Jews would be involved, since, by definition, the Soviet Jews would also be deported. Moreover, it was a strong possibility that mass sterilization would have been employed to ensure the dying-off of the deportees in one generation.[45]

The Ural deportation scheme, too, came to nought. It was predicated upon a swift victory facilitated by the encirclement and annihilation of the bulk of the Red Army before it could retreat into the interior and regroup, thus also isolating Britain within Europe and concluding the war before the USA might join. None of these ends was achieved. Even so, the idea did not instantly dissolve into the ether. One of its legacies was the euphemism 'deportation to the east', which remained in circulation throughout the war as a way of protecting the secrecy of the killing operations. The very expression 'final solution' also developed during the deportation discussions of 1940–1, and its continued Nazi use when the territorial solution had been largely superseded by the 'existential solution' reminds us that distinctions between particular phases of Jewish policy are more recognizable in hindsight than they would have been to actors at the time.

Wars of Annihilation and Racist Security Policies

Earlier in June 1941, the month that saw the start of Operation Barbarossa, the German invasion of the Soviet Union, the German army had carried out atrocities in southwest Crete in the course of 'pacifying' the island after fierce resistance. The year before, the army had massacred between 1,500 and 3,000 black soldiers on the conquest of France.[46] Prior to the invasion of the USSR, the Wehrmacht occupying authorities in Serbia incarcerated large numbers of Jews and communists identified by the local Einsatzgruppe and used them as a hostage reservoir against partisan activity. Similar 'preventative arrests' occurred in Paris in May. The scene was being set for outright genocide.

In early summer 1941 the resistance activities of Tito's communist partisans and the Četniks in Serbia and the French (communist) resistance spurred intensified 'pacification' measures. Jews and Romanies were disproportionately represented amongst the mushrooming numbers of Serbs murdered in 'reprisal' actions by the SD and Security Police. In France, where the SD and Security Police at the outset had to take seriously the Wehrmacht's (self-interested) desire not to unsettle the population, the Security Police successfully pressured the military into mass arrests of Jews in August.

As resistance grew in Serbia, Hitler delegated the army to crush the partisans. In this it failed, but it succeeded in using Jewish and Romany hostages, as well as communists, to fill 'reprisal' quotas for attacks on troops. In September, the proportions of hostages to German dead were set at 100 to 1. By December, all adult male Jews and Romanies in Serbia had been murdered, primarily by the army. The women and children were incarcerated; their fate would be decided later.[47]

In more 'civilized' France, where there was greater concern for local attitudes, and where reprisals against non-Jewish Frenchmen were increasingly seen as counter-productive, the solution reached in December 1941 was to arrest a number of Jews for future deportation to Poland. The military authorities agreed to the idea as a sop to the Foreign Office and Security Police in pursuit of the larger objective of keeping control of security policy. As it happens, they failed to maintain control: Himmler obtained Hitler's permission to appoint a HSSPF to France in March 1942. Nevertheless, in France as in Serbia, though differing levels of violence were used against non-Jews and Jewish policy was enacted with varying degrees of enthusiasm, Jews were seen as a convenient scapegoat whose murder would meet with approval in Berlin and make the military look harsh while mitigating the effect on the local peoples, who were happier to see ethnic minorities targeted than the majority.[48]

The invasion of the USSR itself brought together the two elements of racism and ruthless, pre-emptive pacification policy.[49] It did so in the context of a much larger theatre of war, and against a demonized political-racial enemy. The invasion also radicalized Nazi security concerns across Europe since it signalled the end of the Nazi–Soviet cooperation that had since 1939 stymied international left-wing cooperation of the sort encouraged from 1934. Furthermore, full cooperation between the army and the SS had been established in advance of the invasion, to prevent any jurisdictional conflicts of the sort that had occurred in Poland and were current in France.[50] The Einsatzgruppen would operate in the rear of the invading armies, which were to provide them with logistical support.

The Einsatzgruppen leaders had attended training courses in advance of the invasion and been issued instructions about whom to execute in the name of the pacification policy. We know their targets included communist functionaries, Jews 'in party and state positions', and 'other radical elements (saboteurs, propagandists, snipers, assassins, agitators, etc)'. They were also to try to stimulate anti-Jewish pogroms. The blend of measures was intended simultaneously to destroy vestiges of armed resistance among the population at large and destroy the personnel through whom the Communist Party had penetrated the state. Jews were obviously depicted as the most successful manifestations of communist *Gleichschaltung*, since they could be targeted if in state or party offices. But there is no reliable evidence of any prewar instructions to murder all Soviet Jews. The terms of the Einsatzgruppen's execution mandate were as open-ended as they had been in Poland, which rendered the personality and sense of duty of individual unit leaders more important than explicit instructions.

The army had orders corresponding to the Einsatzgruppen's radical security brief behind the front. Military license came in the form of the 'Commissar order' and the 'Barbarossa jurisdiction decree'. The former singled out the Bolshevik political 'commissars' attached to Red Army units as the originators of 'barbaric, Asiatic methods of warfare', against whom 'severe measures' must be undertaken 'immediately and without hesitation'. The latter stated that the 'military courts and courts-martial will not be competent for crimes committed by enemy civilians; guerrillas are to be liquidated without mercy by the troops . . .; collective coercive action will be taken immediately against communities from which treacherous or deceitful attacks have been launched'.[51]

The orders were 'justified' by the faulty premise that since the Soviet Union was not a subscriber to the relevant conventions on the laws of war, those laws were not applicable to it. This was subterfuge. One reason the orders were issued was that the USSR was not seen as a legitimate state and its people were seen as savages. The Barbarossa jurisdiction decree was an order straight from the lawless world of colonial warfare.[52] Though debate endures about the relationship between the practice of Nazi rule in eastern Europe and the undoubtedly colonial designs of Hitler and Himmler, there can be no doubting the similarity of ruthless methods and the racist, dehumanized vision of the enemy in colonial 'anti-insurgency' warfare outside Europe and the actions of the Wehrmacht beyond major combat operations against the regular Soviet army. Some commanding field officers ameliorated the terms of the Barbarossa jurisdiction decree, others magnified them and passed on their own exhortations to the troops to exercise the utmost severity towards the 'Judeo-Bolshevik' threat, or some similar formulation. In mid-September Keitel decreed that, as a rule, 'the death penalty for 50–100 Communists' was suitable 'atonement for the life of one German soldier'.[53] There was also a second, structural rationale for the legitimation of severity. The military knew its forces were going to be spread thinly in the eastern territories. Ruthlessness was to compensate for the shortage of manpower.[54]

Because of the racist way pacification was conceived by the SS and the army it was inherently susceptible to expansion within the Jewish population. In the earliest days of the invasion, the Einsatzgruppen killings were generally politically selective, though with highly elastic justifications. They were often shaped by local circumstances, as in a notorious massacre of 201 Jews and suspected communists on the once contested German–Lithuanian border immediately after the invasion began. Putative communists and other resistors were also murdered, as they always would be, while Romanies would continue to be targeted, if not always systematically, as long as the SS–Police roamed the USSR. If in Germany the 'mixed' Romanies were the primary victims on 'race–hygiene' grounds, in the USSR and the Generalgouvernement it was itinerant Romanies who were predominantly targeted as potential spies. Many more were killed in shootings than camps, making the death toll more difficult to calculate.

Over the first weeks of the invasion in July 1941, it soon became clear from the Einsatzgruppen reports, circulated amongst the SS leadership, that Jewish men were being targeted in increasing numbers and increasingly indiscriminately. Over the first six to eight weeks ever more men between the ages of 15 and 60 were shot on the basis that this was the surest way to destroy the Jewish-Bolshevik 'intelligentsia' who might form the kernel of resistance. This supposition explains why over the coming months the developing murder was less extreme in Jewish communities that had been part of Poland rather than the USSR before 1939.

Einsatzgruppe A under Walther Stahlecker proved to be the most expansively murderous of the squads in the opening weeks of the campaign, partly because it incorporated thousands of Baltic auxiliaries. Similar expansion of murder took place later elsewhere, in some places only in September. In September to October complete Jewish communities were murdered across the whole invasion front. The killing extended to Eastern Galicia, the province attached to the Generalgouvernement in July 1941, where mass killing of Jewish men of military age began on the invasion of the USSR. It was given considerable impetus by the local participation that occurred around the discovery in former NKVD prisons in Lvov and elsewhere of bodies of Ukrainian inmates slaughtered by the departing Soviet authorities.[55]

Though techniques varied, the German killings were mainly conducted by firing squads shooting their victims at close range into pre-prepared pits. It was an intimate form of murder, even though the preferred method was to shoot through the back of the neck, thus with the victim facing the other way. The squads quickly learned rudimentary division-of-labour techniques to reduce the time they spent with victims. Increasing systematization and regularization of the practice made it an everyday activity in both senses of the expression. This does not mean all Jews everywhere in the Soviet territories were being killed from autumn 1941: the Einsatzgruppen were simply moving too fast for that, and had too many other responsibilities. Many rural Jews were herded into urban ghettos with the same catastrophic results as in Poland.

As the army pushed deeper into Soviet territory, the 3,000-strong Einsatzgruppen and four Order Police battalions were inadequate for 'policing' the huge area.[56] The 'threat' posed by great, un-policed spaces was highlighted by Stalin's call on 3 July for partisan warfare against the invaders. Hitler's rejoinder was that this was fortunate in providing an opportunity for policies that were in any case necessary: 'in this vast area, peace must be imposed as quickly as possible, and to achieve this it is necessary to shoot anyone who even looks oddly at us.' On 17 July Himmler was given responsibility for all security matters in the USSR, and his remit of orchestrating settlement policy was also expanded to the Soviet territories.[57] He successfully managed to play on the security threat to install HSSPFs alongside the Einsatzgruppen in the areas under military authority.[58]

Given the association of communism and partisan activity with the 'Jewish threat', an acceleration of anti-Jewish measures went hand in hand with the rhetoric of the enhanced 'security concern', as in Serbia and France. In the USSR, the SS presence was much greater and the army more like the Serbian occupying forces than the French in its attitudes. From mid-July, 5,500 Order Policemen were posted to the USSR, alongside a larger build-up in the Generalgouvernement. Added to these were a 25,000-strong series of Waffen–SS regiments and brigades initially acting under the umbrella of Himmler's executive administrative organization, the *Kommandostab Reichsführer-SS*, and a large number of local auxiliaries.[59]

Given the multiplicity of SS–Police forces in the field, the HSSPFs played a key role in leading some of the largest combined shooting massacres and determining the overall expansion of the killing programme from July. In many places their death tolls vastly exceeded those of the Einsatzgruppen. The conglomerate forces of Friedrich Jeckeln, HSSPF for the southern Soviet Union, murdered 44,125 Jews in August 1941 alone. He began to kill all Jews, irrespective of age or gender, even before the Einsatzgruppe (C) in the vicinity.[60] Of the approximately 1,400,000 Jews murdered in the Ukraine, Einsatzgruppe C claimed 118,000, all except 45,000 of whom were killed in conjunction with Jeckeln's forces.[61] Jeckeln's counterpart in the central area of the occupied Soviet Union, HSSPF Erich von dem Bach-Zelewski, was equally important in the development of the final solution. As with Jeckeln, when the murder of Soviet Jewry intensified from mid-July 1941, the turning point from the killings of the initial racist 'security policy' to almost total killing in that sphere, he was accorded regional authority over the vastly increased SS and Police manpower then assigned to the USSR.[62] The Waffen–SS Cavalry Regiments and the First Waffen–SS Infantry Brigade sometimes acted on their own, sometimes with other units under the HSSPFs. These organizations were at the forefront of the transition to general murder in August 1941 as they combed the Pripet marshes of the northern Ukraine and southern Belarus, an inaccessible region regarded as a likely habitat for partisans.[63]

Sometimes the actions of the HSSPFs signalled the direct involvement of Himmler in the development of the final solution. There is substantial evidence, gleaned in part from the discovery of his appointments diary, of Himmler's personal role in driving the murder process, often after meetings with Hitler.[64] He made repeated visits to the eastern killing grounds. On 12 August 1941, for instance, he met with Jeckeln, and at the beginning of October toured the Ukraine, both times to urge an expansion of the circle of victims.[65] Yet acceleration was by no means always driven from the top downwards. Sometimes the interventions of Himmler and other senior SS leaders were in the form of after-the-fact legitimations of the initiative of zealous subordinates. Sometimes they could even intervene to reimpose limits, as they tested what was possible in the field and also sought to maintain some central control over a process that might outrun itself before the leadership had observed the reaction of the military and the outside world.[66] After all, it was in August 1941 that the euthanasia programme had been halted—or, rather, driven underground—by public and clerical opposition.[67] Finally, we should not underestimate the radicalizing effect of competition between different elements of the SS–Police as each sought to show leadership in Jewish policy.

All SS–Police units cooperated with each other in the act of killing, as did the civilian authorities later, but competition for power over Jewish *policy* was more an accelerator than a brake on its development. The circulation of Einsatzgruppen reports highlighted different killing rates and could be used to prompt those squad leaders showing insufficient vigour. Over time, some of the Einsatzgruppen actually exaggerated the numbers of people they had killed in order to give the impression of greater zeal. This practice was also related to the advent of the HSSPFs and the huge number of Order Police on whom they primarily relied for killing operations, which somewhat marginalized the Einsatzgruppen. So influential was HSSPF Jeckeln in the developing murder process, for instance, that in October 1941 a unit of Einsatzgruppe C, Einsatzkommando 4a, anxiously reported back to Berlin that it too had taken part in killings in the area, which were not the achievement of the HSSPF alone.[68]

The circulation of SS–Police reports not only ensured that Himmler and his immediate subordinates were well informed, it also meant that different police branches knew of the others' achievements. Heydrich's irritation at the close relationship between Order Police chief Kurt Daluege, Himmler, and the HSSPFs was exemplified on a 2 July 1941 order when he complained:

> owing to the fact that the Chief of the Order Police invited the Higher SS and Police Leaders to Berlin and commissioned them to take part in Operation Barbarossa without informing me of this in time, I was unfortunately not in a position to provide them with basic instructions about the sphere of jurisdiction of the Security Police and SD.[69]

The diminution of the RSHA's direct jurisdiction would only become more acute over the summer and autumn as large parts of the east were pacified. Despite Heydrich being named Protector of Bohemia and Moravia in late September, giving him personally a large territory in which he was direct ruler, answerable only to Hitler, as civilian regimes were established in Soviet territory his Einsatzgruppen task forces became stationary and formally subordinate to the regional HSSPFs, as in occupied Poland. For leadership on the 'Jewish question', Heydrich and his RSHA would have to look away from the east.

The Wehrmacht partook of the expanding murder. The military provided its agreed logistical support and protection for the Einsatz-gruppen. Rear guard units of the army were also involved in massacres of Jews. The army's conception of 'preventative violence' led it to strike bloodily against any suspect partisans, but also against 'strangers' in rural communities, even if they were simply refugees from the cities or people driven away from their homes by hunger. In the face of unexpec-tedly vigorous Soviet resistance after the initial Blitzkrieg victories, the Wehrmacht's preparedness to commit atrocities was further enhanced by the increasingly large losses it sustained in battle.[70]

One of the legacies of the huge early successes of the invasion, and of further if more limited successes thereafter, was the capture of millions of Soviet soldiers. With their incarceration began one of the major crimes of the war. By the beginning of 1942, 2 million POWs were dead, most through starvation in open-air prison camps in the USSR and the Generalgouvernement. While for the first few months the provisions were woefully inadequate, and resulted in terrible hunger and disease, the real turning point came in autumn 1941 when the military procurement offices and the agricultural authorities determined to provide only for those inmates capable of work. Even for them the rations were insufficient, but for the others there was no chance of survival. The POWs were accepted as 'necessary' mortalities given the need to supply the army and the Reich, and given that other priorities in transport requirements meant most could not be deported westward where there might have been some provision. Aside from the matter of supply, these measures could be enacted simply because of who the POWs were. Not only were they suspected of Bolshevik tendencies, their murder was a strike against the population from which they sprang. In September, the Security Police also began to shoot 'politically suspect'

POWs who had not already been murdered by the army. The army happily opened its POW camps to the SS men. All Jews were included in the measures.[71]

At the same time the POWs seemed an attractive prospect for use in Himmler's economic empire-building further west. He secured an agreement with the army for transfer of POWs and ordered the establishment of his own POW camps. One was Majdanek, in Globocnik's Lublin district. The other was an addition to the Auschwitz concentration camp in Upper Silesia: early in October 1941 the site of Birkenau was selected, and was to have an initial capacity of 50,000 prisoners, expandable to 150,000.[72] And POWs were only a fraction of the potential labour force. In November it was decided that Soviet civilians would also be brought to Germany for labour as the Reich started to exploit its new dominions in earnest.

Administration in the Former Soviet Territories

Civilian regimes were established in the 'pacified' Soviet territories from July through September to take the administrative burden off the military. Soviet resistance meant that not every area could be incorporated, however, so in the eastern marches of the Ukraine, Belarus, and the Crimea, the army remained in control until it was driven back in 1943–4. The two main civilian-ruled areas, both under the jurisdiction of Rosenberg's Eastern Ministry, were the Reichskommissariat Ostland under Hinrich Lohse, incorporating the Baltic states and much of Belarus, and Erich Koch's Reichskommissariat Ukraine, which also incorporated parts of southern Belarus.

The major occupation goals, exploitation and pacification, were shaped by racism and the course of the war. Increased Soviet resistance from late July prompted Hitler to muse about a negotiated peace with Stalin, as long as Germany could keep most of the conquered eastern territory. Some of Hitler's optimism returned in September as the Wehrmacht advanced on Kiev, but the talk now was of winning important battles before winter, not the overall war. The new scenario intensified Germany's self-created economic problems, and pressed the occupiers to more extensive exploitation. Just as military commanders were told to feed their troops from the land, so the administrations erected in the east were given rein to pacify and exploit their lands as best they saw fit. To the manifest ill-will of these new overlords should be added the deficit of any of the experience of imperial administration that benefited the other European colonial powers.[73]

The role of racism was not always even. Collaboration was demanded from the former Soviet peoples in a way it was not in Poland, and they provided not only large numbers of policemen and informers but middle-ranking administrators. Many became apparently willing perpetrators in the murder of the Jews. Conversely, more autonomous cultural activity was sometimes allowed the Poles of the Generalgouvernement than, say, the Ukrainians. Rosenberg himself had ideas of cultivating Ukrainians as an anti-Russian force. Some elements of the military shared this conception, preferring at times to murder Jews (and Russians) rather than Ukrainians in 'reprisal' actions, and sometimes, as in Belarussian territory, using the killing of Jews as a perverse method of appealing to the population. It is certainly true that the Barbarossa jurisdiction decree focused overwhelmingly on the 'Jewish-Bolshevik' threat, leaving more discretion for relative leniency towards other populations. In some areas in 1942 the military attempted constructive engagement, even reducing requisitioning of livestock and grain. But Koch, Lohse, Himmler, and Hitler did not share Rosenberg's vision, and the arrogance and brutality of Nazi rule undermined limited, belated attempts to make some common cause with Ukrainians and Belarussians when the course of the war had turned.[74]

The real resistance that did emerge was not a reaction to the simple fact of Nazi rule, which may at first have seemed preferable to Soviet hegemony. It emerged because of the increasing demands made of the people. The growing role of the SS in occupation politics from 1942 was significant in this reaction, but harsh discipline on work projects, reduced rations, and food confiscations all played their part. Shortage and even outright starvation occurred in Belarus, the Ukraine, the Crimea, and Greece. In the Soviet territories conditions of life for the average non-Jew were certainly worse than in occupied Poland. The fact that the suffering was not of the scale predicted in the Hungerplan made some local military commanders, who were given the responsibility to provide from their areas of control, rather blasé about the ensuing deaths.[75] There is no reason to suggest civilian authorities thought differently. Hermann Göring summed up the mood of the times: when, in November 1941, the Italian foreign minister Count Ciano raised his fears about the situation in Greece resulting from the Italian and German occupation, the Reichsmarschall told him not to worry, just as he himself was unconcerned that Soviet POWs were dying of hunger, as they were indeed at that point at the rate of approximately 6,000 per day.[76]

Labour requisitioning for the Reich was crucial in fostering armed resistance in Ukraine. Working for the Germans was voluntary at first, but from mid-1942 simply achieved by kidnap. One and a half million people from the Reichskommissariat Ukraine and the adjoining military zone to the east were deported into Germany during the Second World War. Resistance to the labour policy brought a reintensification of the anti-partisan war, which, in turn, strengthened the hand of the SS–Police against the civilian administrations in the tussle for power and influence. The goal of exploitation undermined the goal of pacification; economic questions reignited the 'security problem'. As the conflict wore on, it fed in turn into the increasingly violent dynamic between the Ukrainian nationalists and the German occupiers (and Polish nationalists).

Similar factors operated in the territories composing present-day Belarus. They were compounded by more Soviet-organized communist resistance, nationalist Polish resistance part-organized by the Polish government-in-exile, and even resistance from small Jewish bands hiding from the extermination machinery. Partisan activities were particularly intensive in the heavily forested and marshy territories constituting much of the 'Generalkommissariat Weissruthenien' within Lohse's territory, the adjacent, northern part of the 'Reichskommissariat Ukraine', and the military zones to the east of both. This activity helps to explain the especially intense suffering in the Belarussian lands during the war. They lost proportionately more of their non-Jewish population than anywhere under Nazi rule: more than 1.1 million of the 1.7 million who perished, out of a prewar population of 9.2 million people. A further 380,000 were dragged into the Reich as forced labourers. In addition, we should recall that up to 3 million people were left homeless, industrial capacity was reduced virtually to zero, livestock by about 80 per cent. Society was atomized in many places, the people often reduced to a simple desire to survive, which must be taken into account in any generalization about indigenous 'collaboration'.[77]

Perhaps 350,000 people were killed in the anti-partisan war in Belarus. The vast majority were innocent peasants who happened to live near partisan bases or in villages suspected of harbouring partisans. The Wehrmacht, the Waffen-SS, the police, and local auxiliaries were all enlisted in the anti-partisan war. In spring 1943 in the 'Ostland' HSSPF Jeckeln led a campaign to create a 40-km-wide no-man's land along the border between Latvia and the Generalkommissariat Weissruthenien. With 4,000 Latvian, Lithuanian, and Ukrainian helpers he burned down settlements, shot virtually all men between the ages of 16 and 50 as possible partisans, shot anyone incapable of being marched away, sent the women for forced labour in Germany, and divided the children among the wider Latvian population. 'Operation Bamberg' had achieved something similar in southern Belarus and the Pripet marshes the previous year. In this and other actions to create 'dead zones' in the region, thousands of villages were destroyed, resources confiscated, and survivors deported to the Reich.[78]

Economic concerns interacted with pacification policy in a number of ways. The further east the army advanced, the less industry existed, and the less labour power was needed.[79] In the eastern Ukraine, as in eastern Belarus and Lithuania, the need to provide for the military made swathes of the local population not only 'redundant' but a 'burden'.[80] Here, economic considerations entirely dovetailed with summary murder in a policy of extermination *without* labour by the SS–Police forces. In more urbanized areas of the western Ukraine and western Belarus the occupiers realized that removing all the Jews, who formed a high proportion of the skilled labour in the eastern territories, would cripple the local economies. By no means could all Jews be replaced by non-Jews. Even at the height of the killing squad massacres of Jewish communities from autumn 1941, many male Jews were returned to work in what was effectively a policy of extermination *after* labour.[81] Here security concerns—with the SS pressing for almost total murder at the close of the year—were often opposed to the economic concerns of the civil administrations.[82]

A third way presented itself in eastern Galicia, which was attached to the Generalgouvernement from former Soviet-occupied eastern Poland after the invasion, but retained some of the characteristics of Nazi policy in the USSR. There, the SSPF Friedrich Katzmann had access to many potential Jewish labourers because ghettoization had not yet occurred. Under the influence of the Lublin SSPF Globocnik, who had recently been tasked by Himmler with making preparations for the Germanization of the whole Generalgouvernement and the occupied Soviet territories pursuant to the developing Generalplan Ost, Katzmann began the construction of the 'Durchgangstrasse IV'. This was a transport connection corridor into the Ukraine that had military utility but could also be used as a settlement axis for ethnic Germans from Poland into the Crimea. Katzmann literally designated Durchgangstrasse IV as a site of extermination *through* labour. Ultimately, around 20,000 Jews died on the project.[83]

The Jews who were not killed in the 'first sweep' of the Soviet territories by the SS–Police were partially ghettoized from the late summer and early autumn of 1941. They were allocated much lower rations than the non-Jewish populations, who themselves were given less than ethnic Germans. Those considered unfit for labour were massacred in increasingly large numbers from September and October onwards, in parallel to the sharp distinctions being made between POWs on the basis of their labouring ability. Ever-smaller numbers of working Jews would actually survive in the 'eastern territories' until the German withdrawal. They were the residue of another round of massacres across the whole region from spring 1942 onwards. By that time, genocide had become standard practice throughout the Nazi empire.[84]

CHAPTER 6
THE PATTERNS AND LIMITS
OF THE EUROPEAN GENOCIDE

Introduction: The Westward Expansion of Genocide in the German Empire

The acceleration towards total murder in the Soviet territories in the weeks and months following the invasion was not instantly replicated westwards. The exception was eastern Galicia, where shootings continued after the incorporation of the district into the Generalgouvernement.[1] For most of Poland, the idea of the Jewish security threat did not have so much purchase because the country was firmly under civilian control. At the same time, a number of factors swiftly combined to alter the sense of the possible and the necessary for Germany's colonial administrators and the SS. Let us survey the overall situation in Jewish policy within Germany and the other territories under its direct control in autumn and winter 1941.

The first thing to note is that the quest to 'cleanse' the Reich by deportation eastwards was obstructed by overcrowding in the Generalgouvernement and the opposition of Frank's administration. Meanwhile, the Ural deportation scheme was rendered ever less probable because, barring the major twin encirclement victory at Vyasma and Bryansk in October, the war continued along the same disappointing trajectory established in late summer. By early November Hitler was pondering a war of indefinite length. With the failure by December of the army's assault on Moscow (an assault demanded by Hitler against the advice of some of his top generals), the outlook even in some top Nazi circles was bleak.[2] And then the USA entered the war that month. Each of these considerations had ramifications for Jewish policy.

In mid-September, Eichmann rejected a Foreign Office enquiry about deporting the imprisoned Serbian-Jewish women and children to either the Generalgouvernement or the Soviet Union. He recommended shooting them—they were actually murdered in situ in gas vans the following year. Eichmann's suggestion illustrates the rather ad hoc nature of various killing 'solutions' as they developed regionally outside the USSR over the autumn and winter of 1941.[3] Ad hoc does not mean random or fortuitous. The fundamental similarity of these solutions across large tracts of space suggests shared conceptions among the Nazi elite and mid-level leadership about what was appropriate.

If a generalized territorial solution, of the sort conceived before the invasion, was an increasingly distant prospect, Heydrich continued to press for the broadest possible concerted measures. The RSHA chief was seeking to reaffirm his powers in Jewish policy, perhaps spurred on by the increasing eclipse of the Security Police–SD in the acceleration of killing in the USSR. On 31 July 1941 Göring signed a document affirming Heydrich's commission 'to make all the necessary organizational, technical and material preparations for a general solution of the Jewish question throughout the German sphere of influence in Europe'. This document was drawn up by the RSHA, possibly on the same day. Interestingly, on 28 July Göring had stated that 'Jews residing in regions under German rule have no further business there.'[4] Within three days, his aspiration to remove Jews under *German rule* had developed into a concrete instruction to prepare for the removal of Jews living anywhere within the German *sphere of influence*: a significant step that was certainly a result of Heydrich seeking to maximize his authority by enlarging the scope of his responsibilities to incorporate relations with Germany's allies as well as its dominions.

In August, Heydrich instantly joined the Gauleiters who were trying and failing to get Hitler's permission to deport Jews eastwards from the Reich during the war. Hitler was at this stage possibly intent on keeping the bulk of German Jewry as hostages or bargaining tools until deportation at war's end, despite the determination of his regional representatives to rid their spheres of Jews quickly as a matter of principle and pride. He changed his mind in mid-September, and ordered that the Reich and the Protectorate be cleared of Jews, who would first be sent to western Poland and later 'further eastwards'. Furthermore, he assured Seyss-Inquart that around 15,000 German Jews in the Netherlands would soon be deported. Limited deportations of Jews in French detention were also announced around this time. The deportation decisions stemmed from a combination of internal urgings and a suggestion by Rosenberg that the Jews be deported in revenge for Stalin's action against the Volga Germans, who were being deported internally as a Soviet 'security' measure.[5] If the Jews were hostages, this was an 'appropriate' use of them in reprisal.

Owing to limited capacity in the Warthegau, some Jews were dispatched directly to the eastern territories. On 14 October 1941 the first deportation trains rolled eastwards from Germany, Austria, Luxemburg, and the Protectorate to Kaunas in Lithuania, Minsk in Belarus, and Riga in Latvia. Some 20,000 Jews, plus the 5,000 Burgenland Romanies, were dispatched to Łódź in the Warthegau. On 23 October an order prohibiting the emigration of Jews was sent by the RSHA to its representatives in occupied France and Belgium. The order is usually cited as a general instruction to prevent further emigration of any Jews from Germany as well as the territories under German control, but the offices of the order's recipients and the vagueness of the wording shows that was not necessarily so. The order, which was one of a number of related instructions running through into early 1942, refers only to 'Jews', not German Jews in Germany, which leaves open the possibility that it referred only to Jews in Belgium and France.[6] The practical near-impossibility of emigration at this point means that most German Jews could not have left of their own accord anyway, but if the alternative reading of the order is correct one reason for hindering the flight of Jews from Belgium and France may have been to maximize the opportunities for any remaining Jews with the ability to leave German soil. *If* my hypothetical interpretation is correct, it provides but one further illustration of the truth that in Jewish policy, one solution faded into the next in a situation of slowly changing proportions, as forced emigration morphed into projected future expulsion eastwards and in turn into immediate targeted deportation.

There can be no doubt in any case that deportation was a death sentence and it was now the inevitable fate awaiting the vast majority of German Jews. The deportation decision was predicated on the presumption that the deportees would undergo the most extreme hardship and premature death, and it was based on the same logic as the whole 'reservation plan' vision. It was made at a time of transition to total murder of Jewish communities in the USSR. Increasing the aggregate number of Jews in the Soviet territories that had just been pacified and were being increasingly comprehensively 'cleansed' made no ideological sense. Mass murder of local Jews now occurred at destination points to make space for the new arrivals, which was but a continuation of existing practice in Riga, Kaunas, and Minsk. Designs for possible stationary killing centres in Soviet territory developed from around the same time.[7] Mass murder of Jews on the same scale had hitherto not occurred in occupied Poland, however. Moreover, the difference remained between deporting German and other central European Jews to hostile environs and planning to murder them on arrival. The latter did not become general policy until late spring 1942.[8] Indeed, in November 1941, Himmler rebuked Jeckeln, now HSSPF for the northern USSR, for ordering on his own initiative the shooting in Riga of 1,000 Jews arriving from the Reich.[9] The wholesale slaughter of deported German Jews was still too sensitive a matter, because of concerns over the effect on German public opinion and perhaps even in some quarters a residual sense of cultural connectedness.[10]

We have already seen that Polish Jews were further down the list of Nazi priorities than German Jews, and already diminished in terms of ability to work by their living conditions. If the authorities of the Warthegau and the Generalgouvernement did not have the immediate 'security' legitimation, they had their economic and public health legitimations. As early as 16 July 1941 the head of the Posen SD had suggested with breathtaking cynicism that it might be more humane to kill the imprisoned Jews of the Warthegau with some 'fast-acting agent' rather than allowing them to starve to death over the coming winter, as seemed the likely outcome.

Mass murder started to become standard practice in the Warthegau as it had in the occupied eastern territories. As in the USSR, at the outset only native Jews were the victims of direct killing. From the end of September 1941 (shortly after the deportation decisions) the 'Sonderkommando Lange' that had murdered the inmates of the region's asylums had been conducting experimental killings on Jewish communities in the southern Warthegau. The killing technology on which they settled was a newly developed version of the gas van deployed in their earlier killing actions. Mass shootings, after all, may have been acceptable further east, and even in the Generalgouvernement, but for operations on the borders of Germany 'proper' the gas van was more circumspect.

In preparation for the larger tasks ahead, part of the Sonderkommando Lange set about constructing an extermination centre from which multiple gas vans would operate, at Chełmno on the Ner. The other part of the Sonderkommando was temporarily in the USSR, murdering asylum inmates to 'free up bed space'. Gas vans were to be used for that purpose and for the murder of groups of Jews at various locations in the USSR and Serbia from autumn 1941 onwards. Chełmno/Kulmhof began operations at the beginning of December, and in its two periods of existence until mid-1944 it consumed more than 150,000 Jews. All the evidence points to the establishment of the killing centre as an initiative of Greiser and his people and the Warthegau SS, with Himmler's endorsement. If Hitler was involved it was in the capacity of approving the general thrust of measures.[11]

The killings of September and October 1941 in the Warthegau had distinguished between Jews who could work and those who could not. The principle applied for most of the time of the Łódź ghetto's existence. For much of the war, industrial Łódź was an integral part of the war economy as a result of the initiative of the German ghetto administration, which worked in a unique relationship with the Reich Interior Ministry and operated with the cooperation of the ghetto Jewish council under Chaim Rumkowski, the support of the Wehrmacht, and benefited from the greed of the Warthegau civil authorities. The fact that the deported Romanies were outside this arrangement—as well as the fact that their murder would have no impact on public opinion anywhere—explains why they were among the very first victims of Chełmno.

For the Jews of Łódź, the temporary extension of life for those able to work had as its concomitant the murder of the increasing numbers of the 'incapable'. This relationship existed in almost every situation in which Jews would be used as labourers from henceforth. As in the Generalgouvernement and the eastern territories in the months to come, the division of Jews into three classes—important for the war effort; capable of work; incapable of work—effectively bureaucratized and 'rationalized' an increasingly inclusive murder process, and made the arbitrating civilian labour offices into full accomplices to genocide.[12]

It should go without saying that a truly 'rational' approach to the economic problems of conquest (itself an ideological project) would have entailed reversing the concentration process and/or bringing Jews to work in Germany under conditions permitting them to be properly productive. That course, however, would not only have been an unacceptable reversal, however temporary, but it would also presuppose the absence of precisely the ideological imperative driving ghettoization and the deportation plans in the first place. The people dealing with these issues on the ground were not acting in some neutral situation where economically sound suggestions for improving the condition of the Jews would have been given the same dispassionate hearing as suggestions to kill enfeebled Jews. To illustrate this point we need only recall that deliberate starvation was used as one means of murdering the mentally ill in Germany, in a situation where resources *were* available had the authorities chosen to supply them. Even in the Ukraine, according to one historian, economic crises were often 'more apparent than real'.[13]

Only at moments when different discourses within Nazi Jewish policy were opposed can we really test their significance. On the occasions regional economic concerns came into conflict with 'security concerns', the latter generally triumphed, though not always, if the state of the war economy or the balance of power among different German agencies temporarily determined otherwise. The general pattern was certainly related to the onward march of SS power, as Himmler's organization drove home its wartime advantage by expansive manipulation of its security remit. Yet it is also true that the association of Jews with political enmity was the strongest of all anti-minority stereotypes, playing into notions about ethnic fifth columns that had gained in influence in Europe since the late nineteenth century and particularly the First World War era. The allegation had a particular potency when applied to Jews because of the Jewish conspiracy libel. But it was also more unalloyed than other 'legitimations' for mass murder, and so more revealing. It was possible to force Jews into being a health hazard by starving them; it was possible to make them a burden by ghettoizing them and removing them from the fabric of general economic life; it was impossible to force them to act as if they had political or military power, and everything the Nazis did in fact pointed to their lack of such power.

Recognizing the role played by ideology beneath a series of different rationales for killing Jews does not mean that 'material realities' were not relevant to Nazi Jewish policy; their relevance is one of the central arguments of this chapter. The question is how those realities were interpreted through the lens of ideological and political presumptions, and how in turn those realities stimulated increasingly radical measures. At the same time, it is apparent that the absence of external stimuli rarely hindered radicalization, so we may conclude that the relationship between ideology and external circumstance was overwhelmingly unidirectional in its outcomes—and that direction was towards more extreme and inclusive measures. At the heart of the matter within the Nazi empire was the mutually reinforcing relationship between on one hand anti-Semitism, with all its older cultural baggage and more recent ideological inflections, and on the other hand the peculiar Nazi power system as it evolved in the context of war and occupation. In this situation, depending on his own interests, almost everyone could find some corresponding reason for greater radicalism that was legitimate and reasonable by the lights of the Third Reich. Each person forwarded his reason with some combination of racist sincerity, opportunism, and conformism.[14] Outside the German empire, as we shall see, the blend of considerations varied again.

Whatever the balance of factors, in late 1941 the principle of murdering 'useless inferiors' was being developed simultaneously to the south of Łódź, not in Upper Silesia as a whole, but in the microcosm of the Auschwitz concentration camp situated there. From the second half of August, gassing experiments took place with sick Polish prisoners and Soviet POWs who were either exhausted or considered politically dangerous. The disinfection agent prussic acid (Zyklon B) was preferred to the carbon monoxide cylinders used in the 'euthanasia' installations because it was easier to transport and use. From September the bodies were burned in a new crematorium in the camp. Gassings of prisoners continued on a relatively small scale in the crematorium mortuary until December 1942. Around the end of 1941, work also began on converting two farmhouses in nearby Birkenau (Auschwitz II) into gas chambers.

In the Generalgouvernement mid-autumn 1941 was also a seminal period in the development of mass murder, beginning with the Galicia and Lublin districts. The decision-making process was as interactive with Berlin as it was in the Warthegau, though there was also communication across provinces and regions, as between Globocnik in Lublin and Katzmann in Galicia. In Galicia, as it became clear to Hans Frank that the Jews could not be moved eastwards, the creation of ghettos resulted in the Jews being crammed into areas deliberately set too small. Additionally, there was an influx of Jewish refugees returned to Galicia from its unwelcoming neighbour, Hungary, and a typhus epidemic spread from a prison camp where some of the 100,000 Soviet POWs in the Generalgouvernement were dying in agony. The situation was ripe for Katzmann to order the killing of 'superfluous' Jews.

In Lublin, two stationary extermination centres were put under construction, using relatively rudimentary technology to create gas chambers using carbon monoxide. Work started on the Bełżec camp at the end of October 1941, putting the decision to create it somewhere around the beginning of that month: Globocnik had previously secured Himmler's permission for 'radical measures' of a 'security police nature', which was now a standard SS rationale for increased jurisdiction. It completed the circle of Himmler entrusting him with key ideological tasks. The similarity of technology with that used to murder the mentally ill in Germany was not coincidental. Many of the staff who had run the gassing centres of the euthanasia programme were dispatched to Lublin in November, where they helped erect the Bełżec camp and then a further one at Sobibór. (Euthanasia would continue in Germany, just no longer at designated gas chambers. It would be practised by the 'child euthansia' methods, such as lethal injection, and also by simple starvation.)

One important context for the stationing of Bełzec and Sobibór in Lublin was Himmler's commission to Globocnik in mid-summer to extend his Germanization plans from the Lublin district to the whole of the Generalgouvernement and the USSR. Insofar as Germanization could not be furthered by mass population movement under war conditions, the murder of a group already being murdered to the east by some of Globocnik's comrades was a measure in pursuit of the possible during wartime. The German problems with wider population policy in Lublin reminds us once more of the verity that it is easier to destroy than to build. Yet the impulse to murder Jews in increasing numbers had other sources just as significant as attempts at general demographic engineering. One was the ever-tightening squeeze of requisitioning for the German home front: the 'economic' rationale. The other was the competition for power amongst the Nazi hierarchy.

Himmler had long been using Globocnik and the Lublin Germanization schemes as a way of extending his Führer-given authority as RKF in the region, especially as the extent of the SS's 'security' remit was a contested one in all the eastern empire. Rather than Germanization driving murder, might the SS chief and one of his most radical representatives have been using the murder of Jews to further their own powers by exploiting the RKF remit—as well, of course, as pursuing an ideological project that was central in its own right? In any case, Globocnik's Generalgouvernement-wide brief suggests that the establishment of Bełzec and Sobibór had a wider significance than just the Lublin district, even though SS power had yet to be fully extended throughout the Generalgouvernement, and though the balance between labour, immediate killing, and death-by-attrition had yet to work itself out. Certainly by the end of the year Hans Frank had decreed that, one way or another, the Generalgouvernement authorities would get rid of their own Jews without waiting for victory.[15]

In accordance with the injunction to 'liquidate' the Jews of the Generalgouvernement, Bełzec began to function in March 1942, at about the same time as the first of the converted gas chambers in Birkenau. Sobibór was opened in May. Spring 1942 also saw the re-escalation of massacres in the 'eastern territories' after a winter hiatus: winter logistical concerns had affected murder just as they affected war;

it was also a problem for the shooting massacres in the east that the ground became simply too hard to dig the pits into which Jews and others were shot.[16]

Winter had not prevented planning for yet more deportations into the eastern areas where genocide was taking on new dimensions. After the October 1941 deportations from the Reich a second wave had begun in November to Riga and Minsk, and would only be completed in February 1942. Together, they encompassed 58,000 people. A third wave was planned for spring 1942 with the destination of Lublin, the original Polish 'reservation' site, and a place where, as we have just seen, gassing facilities were being developed. Each wave would precipitate the same result that had occurred previously in Łódź and the occupied east: the murder of large numbers of native Jews in order to make space for the new arrivals, and the incarceration of Reich Jews under horrendous conditions where most would have very short life expectancies, even though they were not yet, as a rule, murdered outright.

Towards a European Genocide: Central Decision-Making and Motivation

Most of the scholarship concerned with the minutiae of German decision-making in 1941–2 has addressed the question of the development of *intent* in Jewish policy, as it metamorphosed from 'territorial solutions' to outright, immediate murder. It is now accepted that this was a matter of gradually changing emphases, with more or fewer specific moments of policy acceleration along the way depending on the preferences of the historian in question. The interpretative issues do not concern morality, because mass death was inherent to Nazi designs from before Barbarossa. They are matters of developing imagination, opportunity, and the contexts in which radicalization took place. The question of the projected *extent* of murder is implicit in the examination of intent, but it also had its own dynamics, and these have been less extensively explored than the development of intent. Most historians have simply assumed that once the killing extended westwards beyond Soviet and Polish Jewry, particularly once the German Jews were deported, it would encompass all of Europe's Jews, simply as a 'logical' progression in German policy. The treatment of German Jews has become almost synonymous with the fate of all Jews from outside the German empire, as if the latter were a tactical rather than a strategic concern. Morally speaking, this is a very reasonable projection, since once Germany had effectively consigned its own Jews to death, there was nothing to stop it facilitating the death of the Jews of its allies or enemies. But extent was not just a function of intent. We should think of the development of extent in as complex a fashion as we interpret the development of intent: as a matter of opportunity, context, imagination, and also *priority*. Just as the proportions of intent shifted gradually, the extent of the final solution was a matter of gradual expansion and negotiation, and one contested for much longer than the matter of intent: indeed, it was not settled at all during the war, whatever the words of Germany's leaders.

The words of those leaders are important, but precisely the same phrases could mean different things at different times. In January 1939, after the decision had been made to invade Poland, Hitler made a notorious speech threatening that if 'the Jews' drew Germany into another world war, the result would not be the Bolshevization of the world but the 'annihilation of the Jewish race in Europe'. When he repeatedly alluded to that speech at various points through 1941, how literally he meant 'annihilation' and 'Europe' was a matter of constant development. Both seem to have reached the most literal interpretation by the end of 1941, though even if the crystallization of meaning came somewhat earlier in the year it was already a logical extension of the view Hitler held of Jews from the early 1920s. The question is never about Hitler's extremism, however, it is about the alignment of the people and organizations that would give shape and substance to his violent fantasies, and about the course of events that opened new vistas of possibility.

The development of the war with the USSR was obviously crucial in shaping concrete intent. For a long time the historiography was divided as to how precisely war influenced genocide. One stimulating argument suggested that the victory 'euphoria' of Germany's early military successes and then a renewed Hitlerian confidence upon the major victories of October 1941 prompted twin decisions to seize the day. Others suggested that it was the failure of the German military strategy that was really significant in precipitating complete and immediate genocide either out of a sense of revenge or as a way out of the self-imposed practical problems presented by a large, imprisoned Jewish population.[17] The common denominator is a response to wartime circumstances that entailed a crystallizing determination to solve the Jewish question during rather than after the war. With the American entrance to the conflict it became abundantly clear—though it was already obvious to anyone acquainted with military realities—that the war would be long. The ever more radical messages emanating from the Nazi centre at the close of the year prompted Hans Frank's December pronouncement about the Generalgouvernement dealing with its own Jewish question itself. If murder was clearly the intent, how broad was it to be?

The idea of a final solution extending beyond lands directly conquered by Germany went back to the Madagascar plan. The confluence of events in late summer and autumn 1941 made the abstract idea into a concrete possibility, and we can see the ensuing, gradual expansion of ideas of the possible in terms of the extent of the final solution. On 19 August Hitler told Goebbels that his January 1939 prophecy was coming true, and noted as supporting evidence that Europe was presenting 'an almost united front' ('*eine ziemliche Einheitsfront*') against the Jews. He referred particularly to the Romanian murder of Jews in Bessarabia and Bukovina.[18] Thereafter, the murder of the Serbian Jewish men, the moves towards deporting some categories of Jew from France, and Romania's and Croatia's murder of parts of their own population, all suggested distinctly European-wide possibilities. From the end of October 1941 the Foreign Office approached Romania, Slovakia, and Croatia about the possibility of deporting Jews with their citizenship who happened to be living in Germany. This would help fill German deportation quotas and had the function of setting a precedent for later, more extensive deportations from those states themselves. In this context, on 28 November 1941, Hitler revealed to the Grand Mufti of Jerusalem that 'Germany has resolved, step by step, to ask one European nation after the other to solve its Jewish problem, and at the proper time, direct a similar appeal to non-European nations as well'.[19] (An Einsatzgruppe was scheduled to accompany Rommel's armies into

Palestine in mid-1942, to target the Jews living in the British-controlled area. Owing to British military successes it never left base.[20]) The language here is instructive, talking of a more global 'solution' to the Jewish question as the aggregate of a number of individual 'national solutions', and thereby still maintaining the integrity of the idea of a specifically German solution within the growing whole. Around the same time, Rosenberg made a similar distinction when he proclaimed that 'the Jewish question is solved *for Germany* only when the last Jew has left German territory, and *for Europe* when not a single Jew lives on the European continent up to the Urals.'[21] Even as Nazi genocidal intentions became more fully and ostentatiously European, the solution regarding Jews under direct German rule remained central and also somehow separate.

The most important document of the increasingly far-reaching aims of the final solution is the record of a conference chaired by Reinhard Heydrich on 20 January 1942 at Wannsee, near Berlin.[22] Most of the important offices involved in Jewish policy were represented. Though planned from before the military events of December, proceedings at the conference were obviously affected by those events. Interpreting the document is, however, not as easy as its ostensibly comprehensive agenda suggests.

Above all other documents the Wannsee minutes have served to encapsulate the ambitious scope of genocide. They record Heydrich's intention to 'evacuate' 11 million Jews eastwards, including all the Jewish inhabitants of all European states, neutrals and enemies as well as allies and vanquished. The Jews of England, Spain, and European Turkey were listed alongside those of Croatia and Poland. The minutes refer to the 'practical experience' being gathered at that moment, and the intention to comb Europe from west to east for its Jews, though starting with the Reich territories 'owing to the housing problem and other social and political necessities'. There was a request from the senior civil servant in the Generalgouvernement to begin the final solution on his territory, where there were few transportation or labour concerns, and where the Jews were a source of disease and blackmarketeering. The Foreign Office representative, Martin Luther, saw 'no great difficulties' in securing the deportation of Jews from southeastern and western Europe, presumably on the basis of the success thus far in incorporating some Croatian, Romanian, and Slovakian Jews in the deportation programme.[23]

Early scholarship assumed the meeting must simply have been convened to work out the practical details of a pre-conceived, Europe-wide extermination design, or a more complete coordination of a design already being implemented. Few contested that it was pursuant to a general decision for the outright murder of Europe's Jews, and all references to anything other than instant murder in the document were held to be euphemisms. However, as more recent scholarship has pointed out, a more literal reading of Heydrich's wider scheme is permissible given what we know of the coexistence of economic and security concerns. The minutes referred to the intention to allocate Jews 'for appropriate labor in the East. Able-bodied Jews, separated according to sex, will be taken in large work columns to these areas for work on roads, in the course of which action doubtless a large portion will be eliminated by natural causes.' The remainder 'since it will undoubtedly consist of the most resistant part' would 'have to be treated accordingly, because it is the product of natural selection and would, if released, act as the seed of a new Jewish revival'.

The measures for the deported Jews of western and central Europe were continuations of practices that had developed in the occupied east over previous months, on the 'Durchgangstrasse IV' in eastern Galicia, for instance.[24] One important development is suggested by the preparedness to subject all Jews, irrespective of origin, to the same measures of instant death if they could not work, or slow death if they could. Evidently the SS had overcome any qualms about killing German and other central European Jews directly if they were not 'able-bodied' or if there was insufficient space for them at their destinations. The clearest indication of this development is provided by the shooting of 800–900 Czech Jews on 15 or 16 January 1942. The fact that they were Czech is significant, because Heydrich, as Protector of Bohemia and Moravia, would have had to approve the killing. Moreover, the responsible SD-Security Police officer was not only close to Heydrich, and attended the Wannsee conference a few days later, but had been involved in the unauthorized shooting of Reich Jews in November for which Himmler had rebuked Jeckeln. Given the sensitivity of the earlier matter, renewed killing of central Europan Jews must have had central authorization. Later in January and early in February, around 3,500 Jews from Germany and Austria were killed on arrival in Riga, some by gas van.[25]

Nevertheless, in connection with Jews from the Reich, the Wannsee minutes contain the proviso that the Führer needed to 'give the appropriate approval in advance'. This probably refers to Hitler's continuing qualms about the effect deportations and news of general slaughter might have on German opinion, even as trains were already rolling eastwards with his permission. It explains why Jews from central and western Europe who arrived in Poland and the USSR even in March 1942 were not at first deported directly to extermination camps nor generally murdered en masse.

In the intention to work Jews in a closely confined environment until they died or were killed there were still aspects of the attritional features of the territorial design. So it is perfectly consistent that only five days after Wannsee, Himmler instructed the Inspectorate of Concentration Camps to prepare for the reception in the concentration camps of 150,000 German Jews (an unrealistic number) for 'major economic tasks'.[26] In March 1942 Himmler again ordered the incorporation of Jews alongside POWs and criminals in SS construction brigades for large projects in the Reich, the Generalgouvernement, and the Eastern Territories.[27] The numbers of inmates in the German concentration camps and in Auschwitz, Majdanek, and Gross-Rosen, all of which were under the control of the Inspectorate of Concentration Camps, increased vastly from 1942. The accompanying attempt at rationalization of labour usage was given institutional form in March 1942 as the Inspectorate was subsumed within the newly formed SS Business-Administrative Head Office (WVHA).[28]

These labour-related developments did not hinder the development of mass murder. Jews were only a small part of the SS's growing slave-labour empire, and the fact Soviet POWs and non-Jewish concentration camp inmates were to be deployed for labour in increasingly large numbers (as well as the millions of forced foreign workers) meant at this point that the final solution could proceed without much regard for Jewish labour.[29] The temporary influx of Jewish labourers actually simultaneously increased the economic power and political relevance of the SS, and prevented potential workers from falling into the hands of civilian or military industrial concerns, meaning they could be killed more easily when the SS so desired.[30]

While the aspects of Heydrich's plan concerning intent were more evolutionary than revolutionary, those concerning extent were more ambitious, and it is on the complex relationship between intent and extent that my interpretation of the Wannsee conference differs from others. The number of 11 million Jews had been suggested by Eichmann to Himmler before Barbarossa in reference to the now defunct 'Ural plan', but the state of the war also meant that a genuinely continental solution incorporating so many Jews was beyond Heydrich's control. The deportation of Jews of neutral and Allied states could only have occurred after a German victory, and, probably, only an unconditional victory. Putting aside the questionable likelihood of such a victory by early 1942, and taking it seriously in its own claims, Heydrich's design must have been in part for the postwar period. In the circumstances, 'aspiration' is a better word than 'plan', and it was an aspiration dependent upon the fortunes of a rather larger German organization: the Wehrmacht.

The evidence the Wannsee minutes presents of the all-encompassing breadth of genocidal intent is less analytically significant than what they tell us about the Nazi power structure. The extent of genuine possibility was of less concern to Heydrich than the claim to authority over continent-wide deportation *if* it ever became a possibility. He was staking the earliest claim to a more genuinely 'European solution' than was currently the case, because, whatever the reference in the minutes to the geographical extent of his authority—'without regard to borders'—his personal control over Jewish policy in the German eastern empire was already compromised.

The majority of the people professionally concerned with Jewish policy were concerned with it from a territorial perspective and had a finger in the pie within the boundaries of their jurisdiction. The German Gauleiters were concerned with their districts. The Interior Ministry was concerned with the Reich territories. The leaders and administrations of each of the territorial divisions of the German empire and the corresponding (H)SSPFs were concerned with making their spheres 'Jew-free'. The RKF and its subordinate organizations were concerned with the larger but still finite territory directly governed by Germany. Moreover, in Poland and the USSR, the HSSPFs and other police agencies had eaten away at the authority Heydrich had tried to establish in Jewish affairs, and the civil authorities and military had incorporated many surviving Jews into work projects. This was an unsatisfactory state of affairs for a man of whom it was said by one of his most important erstwhile collaborators that 'in the acceptance of the notorious commission for the "final solution of the Jewish question", he barely spared a hateful thought for the Jews, but only focused on the scale of his supranational task and the necessity of demonstrating his energy and his destiny'.[31]

The RSHA, more specifically the chain running from Heydrich through to Eichmann's Jewish desk, was one of the few German entities with a direct concern with the 'Jewish question' in countries beyond German control. The other significant organization was the Foreign Office's Jewish desk, which eagerly promised its cooperation to the RSHA at Wannsee. For both organizations, seizing on the international dimension to the Jewish question had been their main route to gaining (or perpetuating) influence in Jewish policy in the changing circumstances of 1939–41, as with the Madagascar plan. Both continued to push the international, rather than intraimperial dimension as hard as they could from 1942 to 1944. Both had to do so in the interests of their own relevance. Institutional and professional interest is very important here, because while the RSHA was disproportionately manned by ideologues, the same was not at all the case for the Foreign Office Jewish desk. If the leader, Martin Luther, was an ultra-opportunistic 'amoral technician of power', who had jumped on the bandwagon of Jewish policy in 1941, Christopher Browning's seminal study has shown that three of his four underlings were simple careerists. They acted, however, with as much vigour as Eichmann's office in their pursuit of Europe's Jews, even doing all they could to prevent the flight of Balkan Jewish children to Palestine in 1943, because that is what they perceived was expected of them by way of doing a good job.[32]

It is convenient today to believe that the Nazis were driven by a self-fuelling anti-Semitic hatred so strong it overpowered everything else. This would put them into the realms of people who no longer exist in 'rational western civilization', and may explain why some western observers are keen today to equate fundamentalist-informed Muslim terrorists with Nazis. The really terrifying thing about the regime is that some of its most destructive agents contrived to commit the most far-reaching genocide in history while still obeying some of the laws of 'normal' political behaviour. Such a blend was only to be expected, given that essentially their agenda concerned the very real matter of *organizing* mass killing in the form of war and genocide. That the scope of the killing aspired to be as wide as it did was in significant part the result of the actions of people who were acting within the anti-Semitic 'rules' of the Third Reich as established by its highest leaders, but who were stimulated at least as much by established tenets of organizational and professional behaviour: competition and self-advancement. Such was the 'strength' of the post-liberal Nazi system with its open elite. In that system lay the massive destructive potential of Nazism, at least as much as it did in the 'logic of ideas'.

In terms of what could actually be planned and acted-upon during the war from the time of the Wannsee conference, a better guide is a document submitted to Heydrich from the Foreign Office in preparation for the meeting. It suggested deporting all Reich Jews 'to the east', plus the Serbian Jews (the bereaved women and children), and pressure on the southeastern European states to take similar measures.[33] The design was an anticipation of Heydrich's intentions, an attempt by the Foreign Office to ingratiate itself with the RSHA in this vital policy field. With the exception of parts of German-influenced northern and western Europe, which it did not mention, it was also a good elucidation of Göring's 31 July 1941 commission of Heydrich for a 'general solution' within the *'German sphere of influence in Europe'* — the commission that Heydrich had appended to the conference invitations. But Heydrich had gone one step further, as he had when the RSHA developed a competing design to the Foreign Office's Madagascar plan. Capitalising on the mood of the times, Heydrich claimed at the meeting the authority for the 'final solution of the Jewish question in *Europe*'.

This was possibly his second success in expanding his own authority if we consider that before signing the 31 July commission Göring may have been thinking only of areas under *German rule in Europe*. The fact that the other representatives at Wannsee bowed to Heydrich's authority was a source of his jubilation after the meeting; success in unilaterally extending his remit must have doubled his satisfaction.

Heydrich's representatives were swift to brandish their new credentials. The RSHA developed a deportation plan for six countries. It enjoyed most success where the groundwork had already been prepared as a result of local factors, as with the imprisoned, mostly foreign, Jews who had been scheduled for deportation to France from December 1941, or the Slovakian Jews the Tiso regime was increasingly happy to surrender. Deportations of both groups began in March 1942. They too, were predominantly used as slave labourers, even the ones sent to Auschwitz—indeed the Foreign Office stipulated that the Slovak Jews be young, strong men.[34] Despite the superficial certainty of Heydrich and Luther at the Wannsee conference, however, the attempted 'Europeanization' of the 'final solution' in the early months of 1942 was exploratory and sometimes frustrated.[35]

The main energies of the German killing machine would be taken up at that time and for a long while beyond in completing murder in the USSR and attacking the great Jewish communities of Poland. The RSHA would be involved in genocide, as with the deportation of Jews from Germany, Austria, and the Protectorate, but it would not be involved as much as Heydrich desired.

With the opening of Belżec in March 1942 the facilities existed for mass murder of local Jews in the Generalgouvernement. Following the pattern established the previous autumn and winter in the USSR and the Warthegau, Lublin Jews were murdered to make space for the incoming central European transports. Polish Jews were also deported to Belżec from eastern Galicia, the other centre of mass murder in the Generalgouvernement at that time. This process expanded over the month of May, as Sobibór opened, to encompass Jews from all of the districts of the Generalgouvernement. The executioners were learning by doing, and the limits of the possible obviously expanded around the same time, albeit with periodic prompts from Himmler, to include the outright murder of central Europeans too. Many German Jews were murdered on arrival from May onwards in Łódź. Those arriving in the Generalgouvernement or the Soviet territories were either shot in forests or directed straight to killing centres. Around the same time, a larger extermination camp, Treblinka, was put under construction in Lublin.[36]

Florent Brayard has suggested that the final stage in the evolution towards total and immediate murder of all Jews within German reach was triggered by Heydrich's assassination by Czech partisans. Speaking on the day of Heydrich's funeral, 9 June 1942, Himmler declared, in the context of a broader discussion of forced population movement, that the extermination of the European Jews would be completed within the year.[37] The final solution was accelerated in various directions thereafter, but it is unlikely that the assassination itself provided significant impetus beyond further strengthening the security rationde.[38] One thing Heydrich's death did provide was a name for the continuing murder of the Jews of the Generalgouvernement: it was dubbed 'Aktion Reinhard' in his honour. More important than Heydrich's death in terms of genocide in Poland was the SS's increasing authority within the Generalgouvernement as it gained the upper hand in the battle against Hans Frank. In May, HSSPF Krüger was made state secretary for security, and in early June he was given authority for all Jewish affairs; through him, Himmler now had huge authority in the Generalgouvernement.[39] And as of July he had the use of Treblinka, and refurbished gas chambers with larger capacities at Bełżec and Sobibór. He also tried to accelerate Germanization programmes in Lublin from this point, which does not prove the ongoing functional interdependency of Germanization and genocide (though there was clearly an elective affinity between the two things), but does show Himmler's awareness of how to increase his power in several jurisdictions simultaneously.[40]

Heydrich's death also gave Himmler another administrative hat to wear. Himmler's combined 'security' and Germanization powers in Poland and the USSR were formidable, but Heydrich's demise, while mourned because it meant the loss of the SS's best administrator, allowed Himmler to take over the RSHA as he cast around for a suitable successor. In this capacity, Himmler was in closer control of the RSHA's deportation machinery and personnel, and was stepping into the shoes of the man with the remit to solve Europe's Jewish question without regard to borders. Himmler would ultimately hand the reins over to Ernst Kaltenbrunner at the end of 1942, but before he did so he tried to accelerate the murder of the Jews not just in Germany's eastern empire but beyond it, swiftly increasing the pressure for deportations from France, Belgium, and the Netherlands.[41]

The year from mid-March 1942 was the most murderous of the whole genocide. More than half of the victims of the Holocaust were killed in that time, and the vast majority were Polish. Indeed, the most murderous *weeks* were the seven from late July to mid-September 1942, as daily death tolls were in the tens of thousands.[42] On 19 July 1942, after meetings with Hitler and at the end of a tour of Polish killing centres, Himmler ordered Krüger to complete the murder of the region's Jews by the end of the year (the date that was to mark the end of his tenure at the RSHA helm). The only exceptions were Jews in SS-controlled labour camps. He said:

These measures are necessary for the ethnic division of races and peoples for the New Order in Europe, as well as the security and cleanliness of the German Reich and its spheres of interest [*Interessengebiete*]. Any infringement of this ruling provides an endangerment of the peace and order of the entire German sphere of interest, a focal point for the resistance movement and a moral and physical centre of contagion.[43]

Three days later, deportations began to Treblinka from the largest ghetto, Warsaw. By September, 310,000 of the 380,000 ghetto inhabitants had been murdered. By the end of 1942, most Generalgouvernement Jews were dead.

Even in the Generalgouvernement it is wrong to think of a genocide simply kept alive by its own momentum. Himmler's formulation of 19 July to justify murdering the remaining Jews covered all bases. It contained the SS's RKF Germanization and security rationales, and the public health rationale which the civil authorities had long invoked. For the most part the civil authorities collaborated fulsomely, even accelerating the genocide in harmony with their labour selection and rationing policies.[44] There was some military opposition to the murder of Jewish labourers, however.[45] Moreover, even while many non-SS forced labour camps were indeed closed, some were enlarged, and a few large ones founded (for instance Płaszów near Cracow). They survived for longer than Himmler desired because of their particular importance for the war effort.[46] Some of the SS and Police leaders also compromised their function of reinforcing Himmler's authority by pursuing their own empire-building on the back of Jewish labour, including SSPF Globocnik in Lublin and SSPF Katzmann in Galicia.[47] The minority of Generalgouvernement Jews who avoided deportation to the Aktion Reinhard camps in 1942 and 1943 were either in hiding or working as slave labourers. These Jews were in turn only a small residue of the workers who had been employed chiefly in textile and woodwork in the Cracow district, and in armaments production in Radom.[48] By June 1943, the labour camps contained around 120,000 Polish Jews, a tiny fragment of the prewar population.[49]

The authorities of the Eastern Ministry were better at defending their sovereign prerogatives than Hans Frank's regime. On 26 July 1942, Himmler told one of his senior colleagues that 'the occupied territories are to be made free of Jews. The Führer has laid the implementation of this very difficult order on my shoulders,'[50] but there is no evidence to suggest a blanket extension of his existing authority in the Soviet territories. He failed to match Krüger's appointment as Generalgouvernement state secretary for security with an equivalent in the Eastern Ministry. The Eastern Ministry was also openly critical of and resistant to some of the RKF's Germanization schemes, presumably at least in part because Himmler was using his RKF remit to try to expand his authority there; in May 1942 the third and final version of the abortive *Generalplan Ost* was issued.[51] In most of the former Soviet territories a basic confluence of interest in getting rid of Jews, radicalized further in some areas by the 'security rationale' of the anti-partisan war, brought much the same results as in the Generalgouvernement. Interestingly, however, in places like Riga where security reasons could not be plausibly invoked owing to the absence of partisan activity, the civil authorities did contrive to hold Jews back from extermination until 1944.[52]

Himmler also spent the second half of 1942 creating a more central- ized policy towards the Romanies of the greater Reich and the military zones of France and Belgium. On 16 December he ordered the deportation to a concentration camp of all 'racially impure' Romanies: the RSHA chose Auschwitz-Birkenau. The deportations were drawn out over more than a year, and in the course of them many policemen and local officials used the opportunity to deport all Romanies, not just those from the specified category. Around 22,600 were deported to Auschwitz, of whom more than 5,600 were gassed. Most of the rest perished from the conditions of the camp.

The Patterns and Limits of Genocide Outside the Imperial Cone

The occupied Soviet territories were the epicentre of genocide for approximately a year from June 1941. The Generalgouvernement, and particularly Lublin, took their place for the next year. By the time it closed in November 1943, the death toll of Jews at Treblinka was possibly in excess of 900,000. Sobibór had consumed at least 167,000 people, and Bełżec at least 434,500 and possibly 600,000. To their numbers need to be added hundreds of thousands more shot by Order Police and other units under the instructions of local Security Police leaders and SSPFs. One especially infamous place had yet to come into its own, however. By March 1943, the Auschwitz-Birkenau complex had received no more than 280,000 Jews, and still had only the two relatively low-capacity gas chambers in the converted farmhouses. Most of the arriving Jews—probably three-quarters—were murdered instantly, while the remainder lived brief and horrific lives in the dystopia of the concentration camp universe, subject to backbreaking work and the arbitrary violence of the guards and inmate functionaries.

Despite the image we now have of Auschwitz as the centre of genocide on a continental scale, barely 150,000 of the first 280,000 Jews deported there were actually from outside the cone of direct German control. The proportion of such Jews received actually fell in the first three months of 1943, even as the overall numbers of Jewish arrivals increased relatively. (The majority came from the Reich, the Białystok district, and the Generalgouvernement.) This was not how the RSHA had intended it. With its strategic rail location, Auschwitz was ideally situated for a far-reaching murder programme. From July 1942 four new, large crematoria and associated gas chambers had been scheduled for construction at Birkenau in anticipation of the arrival of the western, northern, and southeastern European Jews that Himmler had been pressing for since June. Slow progress was made on the facilities, because of uncertainty about when and how frequently the transports would arrive. All the gas chambers were operational by June 1943, but never operated at anything like full capacity until well into 1944. From the beginning of April 1943 until the end of March 1944, 'only' 160,000 more Jews arrived at Auschwitz. Other than the remaining sliver of Polish Jewry, including relatively large numbers from the formerly part-exempted Upper Silesia, these comprised Croatian Jews, the dwindling continuations of transportations of particular categories of Jews from France and Belgium, and Jews seized from Italy and formerly Italian-controlled Greece. During this period, insufficient deportees arrived for what the SS considered the real labour requirements of the camp.[53]

Though Auschwitz has come to symbolize the Holocaust, and with it the image of railway lines running from the most distant corners of Europe to a fully industrialized killing centre, the deportation programme for Jews outside of the German empire was by no means always successful. Despite the undoubted geographical breadth of the deportations by the turn of 1943–4, there were close limits to the 'depth' of the deportations from within sovereign and semi-sovereign national communities. As Wisliceny put it, 'up to spring 1944 deportations had taken place from almost every country under German influence. Everywhere, however, the operations were incomplete or unequally carried-through.'[54]

Those Jews killed by the Third Reich before spring 1944 were mostly from two categories. Overwhelmingly largest were Jews within the German empire—its expanded 'Germanic core' and its eastern dominions—where most of the European Jews lived and where German power was unchallenged and the former rulers and citizenship status of the Jews were irrelevant. The second category comprised Jews from third-party de facto and *de jure* sovereign states, including part-occupied France, Jews given up because they were not considered citizens of those states in the fullest sense. In this category were not a few de-nationalized former German citizens.

The administrations of the third-party states had a sliding scale of concern for Jews of different politico-legal status. As we saw in the first part of the book, the greater concern for Jews with full citizenship was partly related to concerns about sovereignty and-or economics (France, Italy, Bulgaria, Romania), partly to some enduring sense of connection with Jews in the absence of an extreme domestic anti-Semitism (Belgium, France, Denmark, Norway, Italy, Hungary, the former Ottoman states), and, increasingly, to the way the likely victors in the Second World War would regard them as collaborators in the final solution (France and all the Axis states). Equally, the German authorities, as allies or occupiers, were concerned that variations in other national attitudes towards the Jews could affect the prosecution of the war. The German concern on this count was analogous to the concern evinced by the gauging of German public opinion on the deportation of the German Jews. It was a concern for unity and stability in war.[55]

As the war progressed, and Germany's fortunes were reversed, it became more and more important for the Nazi leadership to bind its allied and subordinate states in the same 'community of fate' that it decreed for its own citizens. Increasing diplomatic pressure was exerted upon the other Axis states to deport their Jews, lest the Allies have a wedge to drive between them. Yet, contrary to the strand of opinion suggesting the extermination drive overrode all else in its 'planned total murder of an entire people' anywhere,[56] Jewish policy could not be a matter for overbearing pressure or military intervention in reluctant states, precisely because that measure would further the splintering of the alliance Germany was so concerned to maintain by the means of—amongst other things—its Jewish policy.

The most radical Jew-hunters acting outside the imperial cone, the RSHA's Jewish desk, were not mindless zealots, though zealots many were. Their training had led them to see themselves as the shapers of a new order, and enabled them to imaginatively overcome all manner of administrative barriers, but it was precisely this consideration of the practical implementation of radical design, intrinsic to their self-image as 'heroic realists', that meant they had to recognize obstacles. Pushing the limits of the possible involved an acknowledgement that limits did exist. Pride in efficiency was one of their hallmarks, which explains

Eichmann's petulant threat, as he encountered difficulties in fulfilling deportation quotas in France in 1942, to 'drop France entirely as a deportation country'.[57] Every state into which the RSHA's 'Jewish advisors' were inserted presented different challenges. Responding to these challenges was not a question of reshaping the mechanics by which policy was realized, but of modifying policy itself in accordance with the situation on the ground.

The heart of the matter was the organization of local collaboration in identifying, collecting, and deporting Jews. Even in some states under direct German influence this could be difficult. The situation in, say, the Netherlands, a small country under full civilian occupation and scheduled for full incorporation in the Reich, was very different to that in, for instance, France, a large country with a large and dispersed Jewish population and a relatively small German presence. In the Netherlands, the local police were under SS control and the administration was ever more heavily directed by German personnel. The French bureaucracy and police forces had considerable independence. The German occupiers relied on the French to maintain order, public security, and war production. In later 1942 and 1943 mass incarceration and deportation of Jews with full French citizenship could ultimately not be forced through because of the fear of non-cooperation then and in future by French bureaucrats and police who were still concerned with their own sovereign prerogatives and with French public opinion.

Himmler himself ultimately decreed that 'fully French' Jews should not be deported until further notice, given the importance of the French economy to the war, and many regional SD-Security Police adopted relatively moderate lines on all aspects of 'security policy' out of pragmatism. It was impossible in France during 1942–3 to reconcile exploitation and pacification with extermination.[58] This was by no means the only time Himmler accepted practicality over the anti-Semitic imperative outside the German empire. His stance can partly be explained by his focus on securing absolute dominance over all questions of population policy and 'security' *within* the Nazi empire, within what he referred to as the German 'sphere of interest' on 19 July 1942. Himmler's attitude is particularly important since, however involved Hitler was at earlier key points in the development of the final solution, it was in the reactive capacity we encountered in the Warthegau of approving suggestions forwarded by his lieutenants. With the passing of Heydrich, Himmler was the most important conduit for such suggestions. Kaltenbrunner would prove no 'worthy' successor to Heydrich in this regard; from his takeover of the RSHA at the beginning of 1943, the organization's influence dwindled somewhat in the intra-SS power play, with the rise of the more economically minded Business-Administration Head Office, the WVHA.[59]

In the independent states of the Axis alliance, the organization of collaboration was even further out of German hands than in France. Early in the war, German success and hegemony contributed to the radicalization of anti-Semitism in the Balkan states, and even in France as that country sought a scapegoat for its defeat.[60] Competition was stimulated between states for German favour, with a view to a German-arbitrated postwar settlement, which helps explain the escalation of anti-Jewish policy in Hungary and Romania in 1941.[61] I have suggested that the 'multiplier' effect even encouraged Nazi Germany in turn to take its own policies further still at propitious moments: as when the Lithuanian Activists' Front, many ordinary Lithuanians and Latvians, and Romanian forces eagerly murdered Jews in summer 1941, or when Croatia, Romania, and Slovakia seemed happy to deport their Jews in autumn 1941. But if Nazi Jewish policy was not purely self-driven, and could be accelerated by external influences, it could on occasion be forcibly decelerated by the same means. The Holocaust was not just a product of German history but in some way a product of European history: of its socio-economic and political discontents from the late nineteenth century onwards, and the ever-shifting geopolitical relations of greater and lesser powers. The changing constellations of those forces in European history could also limit the extent of the Holocaust.

As the war developed and turned, the 'multiplier effect' was indeed reversed. Other states became more aware of their increased leverage over Germany, and the USA, the USSR, and Britain looked the likely arbiters of the peace. The failure of the German summer offensive of 1942 to defeat the USSR contributed to a sharp decline in the frequency of deportation trains from western and southeastern Europe, even as the RSHA was drawing up its June 1942 deportation programme from western Europe that was supposed to be carried through by September 1942.[62] After mid-1942, and particularly after the German loss at Stalingrad at the close of 1942, such competition as existed between Germany's major and lesser allies was not to mimic Nazi racial laws or to supply the murder machine, but to justify their own diminishing collaboration with reference to the diminishing collaboration of others. Jews without full citizenship status were sometimes used as sacrificial lambs in this changing dynamic, both to rid the states concerned of a 'foreigner problem' and to placate Germany. Increasingly, though, as in France, full citizens were not surrendered, while neutral countries like Sweden became more willing to accept Jewish refugees.

Romania was happy to consign the Jews of Bessarabia and Bukovina to their deaths in Transnistria, but the Jews of 'old Romania' were not surrendered to German custody. By December 1942, the Foreign Office recognized the Romanian deportations had 'come to a standstill' — in fact they had never started. At that point Germany increased pressure on Hungary for its own sake but also to pressure Romania indirectly. It failed on both counts. The Hungarian government invoked alliance parity with Italy in support of its protection of most Hungarian Jews in German-controlled territory, demanding that in every facet of the Jewish question it be treated according to the established diplomatic most-favoured-nation principle.[63] This was an important objection, because the earlier surrender of the Balkan states' nationals living abroad had been used by the German Foreign Office and the RSHA as a precedent for full deportations from those countries which agreed to it. Germany got no further at this stage on the question of 'Magyarized Jews'.[64] Bulgaria was not dissimilar. Happy to deport the Jews of newly acquired Macedonia and Thrace to their deaths in March 1943, it surrendered no Jew from 'old Bulgaria'.

Italy was a particular obstacle to German designs, since it had a supranational jurisdiction and was Germany's chief ally in Europe. Italian refusal to hand Greek Jews over to Germany, and the protection of Jews in Italian-controlled Croatia, was extended to the French Jews coming under Italian control as Italy and Germany moved into southern France in November 1942 upon the Allied landing in north Africa. Even

Croatia, which happily handed its Jews over from late autumn 1942, used the German extermination drive to play Germany off against Italy. Resentful of Italian imperialism in the former Yugoslav lands, the Croatian government suggested that Germany begin its deportation of Croatian Jews by rounding them up in the Italian occupation zone.[65]

There was nothing even Hitler could do about the reluctant states, despite his exhortations to Hungary's Regent Horthy and Bulgaria's King Boris in April 1943. Germany even had to stand by in spring 1943 and watch as Romania, Hungary, and Bulgaria permitted some of their own Jewish nationals to be evacuated to British-controlled Palestine. In Poland, however, genocide was still proceeding apace: on 11 June Himmler ordered the liquidation of all ghettos in Poland. This occurred over the ensuing months, with the exception of Łódź in the Warthegau, because of its special status as administered by the Ministry of the Interior. As the remnants of the great Białystok, Minsk, Vilna, and Riga ghettos disappeared over the summer and autumn in shooting massacres and in the gas chambers of the Aktion Reinhard camps, with them went most of the last forced labour camps where Jews were working for anyone other than the SS.

Outside the imperial cone, the only thing that could alter the deportation situation was the progress of the war. The Allied invasion of Italy did precisely that. But the developments in the Mediterranean war, in terms of the sheer numbers of additional Jewish victims ensuing from them, were nowhere near as significant as the unforeseen events attendant upon the collapse of the Axis in the Balkans in 1944. The Italian armistice with the Allies in September 1943 triggered the German occupation of northern Italy and the Italian zones of occupation. It also resulted in a spate of massacres of surrendered Italian troops and, thereafter, of suspected Italian partisans and their supporters. Deportations of Jews swiftly began, too, from the new puppet republic in northern Italy and from the former Italian zones of Greece and Yugoslavia. The Jews of Salonika, so dear to the now-defunct Italian imperial vision, were the most numerous victims of the German takeover. France's much larger Jewish population remained relatively safe since Himmler was still privileging French stability and war production.

Stability was also a significant concern in autumn 1943 in one of the more bizarre episodes of the war and the Holocaust, the net result of which was that a small but almost complete national community of Jews evaded Nazi clutches altogether. At the end of September and the beginning of October, most of the 5,000-strong Jewish community of Copenhagen, which comprised the great bulk of Danish Jewry, escaped a Security Police round-up. They sailed to nearby neutral Sweden in a flotilla of fishing boats manned by non-Jewish Danes. The undoubted courage of many of the rescuers fits happily into a tradition of Danish assimilation and toleration, but structural factors conditioned the escape and the relative restraint shown by the German police and their Danish SS assistants in pursuit of the Jews.

As a country of 'racial equals' that had surrendered without a fight, and was positioned in a vital strategic location, Denmark occupied a uniquely favourable position in the Nazi sphere. The German civilian and military presence was opposed to any radical action against the Jewish community because it would affect future collaboration from the Danish side, which possessed considerable internal autonomy. The German Foreign Office had, hitherto, not pressed the Danish government for precisely that reason, and because the Jewish community was small enough not to be a priority. The deportation order came during a state of emergency declared after the Danish government had fallen at the end of August 1943 in the face of a national uprising. The precise chain of events thereafter is unclear. The German civilian plenipotentiary and SS officer Werner Best ordered the round-up but this may have been because he anticipated a central order to that effect anyway, given Berlin's tendency to take advantage of opportunities like the state of emergency. Best may have then been involved in alerting representatives of the Jewish community to the coming deportation as a way of squaring the need to appear tough with the need to maintain future good relations with the Danes for the time when the state of emergency ended. In any case, the news of the looming round-up got out on 28 September, and the growing stream of Jews leaving Copenhagen became a flood up to and including the night of the scheduled round-up on 1 October. Contrary to normal practice, the police were not permitted forcibly to enter the homes of the Jews they were seeking.

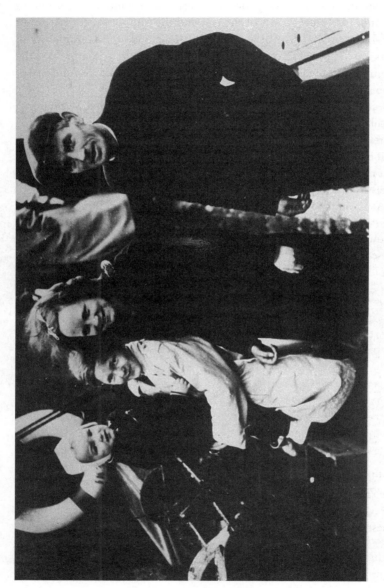

Figure 8. Jewish refugees ferried out of Denmark.

On the escape, Eichmann demanded an explanation, angry that the RSHA had not been able to fulfil its designated task. Himmler's response was much milder, however. He did transfer control of the police to a new HSSPF with enhanced authority, but Best was neither removed nor otherwise punished; indeed, when the state of emergency was ended on 6 October he recovered all his other political powers. Best himself justified the situation as effectively a successful measure of ethnic cleansing, claiming that 'the Jewish Aktion' had been 'conducted without incident' and 'Denmark can from today be declared de-jewified.'[66]

The Danish affair made no difference to the overall state of the 'Jewish question', and it is apparent from its aftermath that not everyone shared Eichmann's disappointment with the outcome. On 4 October, only two days after Best's self-justification, Himmler made one of his most notorious speeches to a group of SS leaders in Posen. It was delivered in the past tense:

> I also want to talk to you quite frankly about a very grave matter. . . . I am referring to the Jewish evacuation programme, the extermination of the Jewish people. . . . This is a glorious page in our history and one that has never been written and can never be written. For we know how difficult we would have made it for ourselves, if, on top of the bombing raids, the burdens and the deprivations of war, we still had Jews today in every town as secret saboteurs, agitators and troublemakers. We would now probably have reached the 1916–17 stage when the Jews were still part of the body of the German nation. . . . We had the moral right, we had the duty to our people, to destroy this people which wanted to destroy us. All in all, we can say that we have fulfilled this most difficult duty for the love of our people.[67]

Himmler then moved on from a seeming fait accompli to address the tasks that next awaited the SS: his ill-fated colonization programme for the occupied east. He repeated the message about the Jewish question two days later at another speech in Posen. After discussing the necessity of murdering Jewish women and children, he observed that the task of removing the Jewish people from the face of the earth *had been accomplished* ('*Er ist durchgeführt worden*'), with no reference to restricted geographical location. Shortly afterwards, he declared that all that remained was to mop up individual Jews with particular special statuses, and to 'cleanse' the remaining armament works of Jewish labourers. With that, 'the Jewish question will be settled by the end of this year *in the countries under our occupation.*' The reference to the direct German sphere of control as opposed to the whole of Europe was not in any way an admission of failure, nor a qualification of his claim to general success.[68] The same equation of 'all Europe' with 'German-occupied Europe' was evident in Goebbels' diary entry about this 6 October speech, in which he wrote of Himmler's conviction that the Jewish question in 'ganz Europa'—'the whole of Europe'—would be solved by the end of 1943.[69] The failure of two senior Nazis to attribute importance to such an obvious difference in geographical scope, while talking openly about the achievement of a fundamental Nazi goal, indicates that the initial aim of the final solution—the removal by increasingly radical means of all Jews within the German controlled territory—retained its central significance throughout the most intensive period of the Holocaust and, indeed, throughout the war. Despite Himmler's conflation of German-occupied Europe and the continent as a whole, Hitler's and Rosenberg's distinctions of late autumn 1941 between Germany's Jewish problem within its (expanded) borders and other states' Jewish problems had not been rendered irrelevant by the policy escalations of the following two years. Indeed, it was the over-riding importance of the completed 'cleansing' of the German empire that allowed Himmler to pronounce general success in solving the Jewish question even as he contradicted himself about the genuine geographical extent of that 'solution'.

Early the following month, the final act of Aktion Reinhard took place. 'Operation Harvest Festival' involved the murder over 2–3 November of 42,000 Jews in and around the Majdanek concentration camp in Lublin, including many who had previously been exempted as important for the war economy. The massacre was centrally ordered by Himmler in response to the 'security threat' posed by recent Jewish uprisings in Sobibór and Treblinka. The situation may also have provided the opportunity for a wider SS clampdown in places of contested jurisdiction in the eastern territories, because simultaneously non-working family members of labourers in the Riga ghetto were murdered.[70] The next day, 4 November, the anti-Semitic newspaper *Der Stürmer* reiterated the relevant part of Himmler's Posen speeches. The editor, Julius Streicher, was close to Hitler and well informed about Jewish policy. He quoted an article from the Swiss *Israelitisches Wochenblatt* of 27 August to the effect that the Jews had vanished from eastern Europe, meaning there was no longer a counterbalance to the assimilatory impact of the West. 'It is really true', he continued, that the Jews have, "so to speak", disappeared from Europe and that the Jewish "Reservoir of the East", from which the Jewish pestilence has for centuries beset the peoples of Europe, has ceased to exist.'[71] Though Streicher went on to play on the ongoing hostility of Jews in the Allied countries in order to stiffen German backs in the war effort, his language was reminiscent of that which Höss had recalled Eichmann having used earlier in the war about 'destroying the biological basis of Jewry *in the East*'. Most importantly, from the perspective of Himmler, its key administrator, the final solution had achieved its central object by the end of 1943. World Jewry had been dealt what Lemkin would have called a 'crippling' strike in its heartland.

To anyone acquainted with the outlines of the Holocaust, the idea that Himmler and others may have perceived the final solution to be over in autumn 1943 may cause puzzlement. After all, the occupations of Hungary and Slovakia had still to occur, and with them the final killing frenzy that befell the Jews. But the decisive victory for Himmler was that the Jews had been removed from Germany and its empire, which was also the centre of gravity of the world's Jewish population. The two really significant entities with a prevailing concern with a fully European genocide, the Foreign Office and Eichmann's Jewish desk, were still dependent upon wartime contingency for their 'success'.

It has been contended that any European Jews exempted from genocide during the war would have been murdered had the Nazis won.[72] Barring perhaps the small Jewish communities of the Iberian peninsula and in other neutral countries this is a sensible contention, though, depending on the absolute or conditional nature of victory British Jewry may also have escaped. The only problem with the argument is that it is an extrapolation based on a constant trajectory rather than the changing trajectory that actually existed. One might equally posit that, had the USSR been defeated as swiftly as Hitler intended, the policy of immediate killing of the majority of Jews would not have occurred, and the destruction of the Jews would have been a matter of more drawn-out attrition, as some of the unrealized Nazi deportation plans suggested.

Alternatively, had German victory transpired, the death of European Jewry would have been only one part of a much larger programme of direct and indirect genocide. The swift defeat of the USSR would have permitted the enactment of the *Generalplan Ost* with all the horrors that that implied for tens of millions of Slavs. To their numbers could probably be added increasingly large sections of the ethnic German population itself, and many other groups besides, for, as Tim Mason put it, the regime thrived 'upon the supposed threat from the enemies which it persecuted so implacably.'[73] An ongoing supply of enemies was needed for the self-justification of Nazism as an ideology of constant struggle and ever-greater racial fitness.

An equally plausible counterfactual is to ask what our conception of the Holocaust would be had not the last great episode of the final solution taken place. The murder of Hungarian Jewry in 1944 has done most to entrench the notion of a fully continental genocide. It was also the part of the genocide that hinged most on wartime contingency. In other words, it might well not have happened.

The German invasion of Hungary in March 1944 opened up a hitherto closed field for the RSHA men. The prospect of deporting Jews was not, however, a significant factor in the military's decision. The Wehrmacht had been planning for the eventuality of invasion since the Allied push into Italy the previous autumn and during the continuing Soviet advance through the Ukraine. Both developments pushed the Hungarian leadership into considering Allied peace overtures. Not only would the departure of Hungary from the alliance have meant the loss of an important strategic ally, but also of important Hungarian raw materials. Labour, too, was becoming an ever more pressing concern given the German retreat in the east.

The horrors following the German invasion are well known. From April the Hungarian Jews were gathered together in ghettos. In six weeks from mid-May 1944, 438,000 Jews were deported, the vast majority to Auschwitz-Birkenau. About three-quarters were killed instantly on arrival. The speed of the murder exceeded even German plans, and killing rates at Auschwitz reached 20,000 per day.

Explaining these events from the German side is easy: it was inevitable that the SS would try to murder the Hungarian Jews when the opportunity presented itself. The most high-powered team ever assembled from the RSHA's Jewish desk was sent to Hungary, led by Eichmann himself. The real question is why the Hungarian administration cooperated as it did. Without Hungarian assistance, Eichmann's 150–200 men, plus some Order Police units and some swiftly installed regional Security Police offices, were nowhere near sufficient to pursue hundreds of thousands of Jews.

The question opens up a classic historiographical debate about the relative role of external and internal forces in Hungary. As in most such debates, like the top-down versus bottom-up interpretations of the evolution of Nazi Jewish policy, the dichotomy is false. Let us examine the German side first. The German invasion and the consequent presence of military and police units and a German civilian plenipotentiary (Edmund Veesenmayer from the Foreign Office) provided the decisive context for the deportations, which would not otherwise have occurred. The German attitude towards Hungary and its Jewish question was different to that regarding the French and Danish Jewish questions. In those cases, the Jewish issue had never been associated with defection to the other side, merely greater non-compliance among the French and Danish people. Hungary had already wobbled, and now Germany was in a position to pressure the Hungarian government into action to prove its allegiance to Germany. This explains Hitler's later indirect threat of military action as the head of state Horthy called a stop to the deportations on 9 July. (With one eye still on an Allied victory, Horthy had been swayed by the outside world's vigorous reactions against the deportations of the previous weeks, by Allied aerial bombardment, and by increasing pressure from the Hungarian churches and the Papacy; the stop order primarily affected the Jews of Budapest, the major remaining community untouched by deportations, and the most visible to the outside world.) Hitler never made a similar threat against the French or the Danes.[74]

The most obvious way in which the German influence was channelled into the Hungarian administration was through the enforced changes of personnel at the head of the government. The new Prime Minister and Foreign Secretary, Döme Sztójay, was a pro-German and an anti-Semite. As Hungarian Ambassador to Germany up to 1944 he had urged the Hungarian government to surrender to German pressure to deport the Jews in the interests of the alliance. Now, with the much-changed alliance dynamics, he was in a position to carry out his own advice. He increased the number of extreme right-wingers in his cabinet and legalized the fascistic Arrow Cross party. The anti-Semites László Baky and László Endre were appointed as state secretaries in the interior ministry, where they keenly embraced their new remit for ghettoization and, ultimately, deportation. They were also in charge of the 20,000 or so Hungarian gendarmes who would provide the essential manpower for the destruction process. As Sztójay took office, changes of Hungarian personnel were made at the heads of regional administrations. Germany also made it clear that the SD-Security Police would not leave Hungary until the Jewish question had been resolved to its satisfaction. Accordingly, the earlier tendency to reject the surrender of Hungarian Jews because it represented an infringement of Hungarian sovereignty was strongly tempered by the fact that deporting Jews had now become a method of *restoring* an aspect of sovereignty.

Beyond the keenest anti-Semites in the new regime, the Hungarian administration was drawn into the deportation programme step-by-step, because it played on established priorities about categories of people and citizens. As part of persuading the Slovakian regime to begin deporting its Jews in 1942, the SS had stipulated the provision of a large contingent of able-bodied male labourers. This provided the Slovaks with the rationalization for taking the first step down a slippery slope. The same happened in Hungary early in April 1944 (and, as we shall see, many of these Jews were indeed used for labour). Further, the country was divided into different deportation zones. The first and largest deportations to take place were from the Carpatho-Ruthenian region ('Subcarpathen Rus') taken from Czechoslovakia in 1938 and northern Transylvania, taken from Romania in 1940. The Jews there were not considered 'Magyarized', and their removal would elicit less of an outcry. Hungary's leaders could also play on the advance of the Red Army as a legitimation for 'security measures'. Nearly 290,000 of the 438,000 deportees came from those regions. The remainder came from the provinces. Of the 255,000 Jews who fortuitously survived the Holocaust in Hungary as a result of the developments enumerated below, some 190,000 had been citizens of Hungary within its 1920 borders.

German pressure and 'advice' was obviously significant in the radicalization of Hungarian Jewish policy, in the same way but to a greater extent than had been true in Slovakia. But, in the introduction of ghettos and restrictions on the freedoms and rations of Jews, independent, local Hungarian initiative was frequently manifest. The distinction between Hungarian policy and German policy is less over the sharpening of anti-Jewish measures than over the perceived ends. A good case can be made that even ghettoization measures were not in the earliest days conceived by the Hungarians as a prelude to deportation, but as an end in themselves, a means of dislocating, segregating, and dispossessing a Jewish community that had been increasingly perceived in the interwar period as foreign and overly influential. Ghettoization and other simultaneous Hungarian policies were classic measures of ethnic dominance rather than destruction, before the SS revealed that the gathering of Jews was only a prelude to their deportation. When, around the end of May 1944, the Hungarian leadership agreed to the deportation of all Hungarian Jews, that was not an expression of a uniform desire across the administration to see the Jews murdered. Among the newly empowered extremists within the government it was a welcome means of ridding Hungary of its Jews, but for many others it was an expression of simple collaboration—the line of least resistance.

The limits of collaboration were shown by Horthy's stop order. It was not relayed out of concern for the Jews but for the sake of Hungary's image. The politics of that order and the war situation led to turmoil in the Hungarian government. Veesenmayer and Eichmann continued to push for deportations, with Eichmann in particular showing how committed he was to doing as complete a job as possible by the orchestration of the deportation of more than 3,000 Jews at the end of July against Horthy's express wishes. Hitler himself sought to trap Horthy by suggesting he would permit Hungary to deliver 40,000 Jews to neutral countries as a sop to external opinion, but only on condition that Horthy carry the rest of the deportation programme through as planned.

The delicate balance of alliance politics was about to shift again, with Romania's defection to the Allied side on 23 August. Not only did the consequent German troop redeployments remove the railway capacity for further deportation of Jews, Germany could not push the Jewish question for fear that Hungary might follow Romania's example. As it was, Hungary actually took the opportunity to re-emphasize its alliance commitment to Germany because it now saw the opportunity to gain territory at Romania's expense during the war. On 25 August, in tune with the mood in Budapest, and now that Hungary had seemingly bound itself to Germany once again, Himmler strictly forbade further deportations. The gas chambers of Auschwitz found employment in August, however: all of the remaining 2,900 inhabitants of the Romany enclosure were murdered there.

The final chapter of Hungary's Holocaust story occurred after Horthy finally did attempt to withdraw from the Axis on 15 October. He himself was incarcerated by Germany and an Arrow Cross government was established under its leader Ferenc Szálasi. Despite the rather unsystematic murder of thousands of Jews within Hungary by the anti-Semites of this radical faction, and the enlistment of many other Jews for forced labour, deportations of Jews to German control were not resumed because of Allied pressure. The exception was about 76,000 Jews who were marched directly to the Reich (not to Auschwitz) for labour purposes.

Our understanding of the Holocaust has been greatly shaped by the murder of Hungarian Jewry. Auschwitz would probably not have achieved its notoriety had it not been the destination for this huge, most public, and arguably most avoidable national killing operation of the final solution. Out of approximately 960,000 Jews killed at the Auschwitz complex overall, more than 320,000 were Hungarian.[75] The numbers of murdered Poles, Romanies, and Soviet POWs bring the total death toll of Auschwitz to around 1.1 million, approximately 865,000 of whom were murdered immediately on arrival. The image of Auschwitz in full swing, fed by a bureaucratic machine and by Eichmann's transcontinental transports, conceals a lot about the Hungarian Aktion.

It ended up being one of the fastest mass murders in history, but to get to that point required frantic improvisation at Auschwitz, not least the digging of huge pits to burn the bodies that the crematoria could not handle. Summer 1944 was the first time that the large new gas chambers and crematoria had been pushed to full capacity for any length of time. The emblematic image of the camp is of deportation trains passing into Birkenau through the main guard tower at the front, to deposit their victims adjacent to the gas chambers; but the rail extension through the tower was only completed in spring 1944, long after the vast majority of Holocaust victims had met their deaths.

The murder of the Hungarian Jews was not representative of the murder of most of the Holocaust's victims. Most had not been deported halfway across Europe; for most of their deaths Eichmann's Jewish desk had had little direct responsibility, whatever his and Heydrich's aspirations. Most of the victims of the Holocaust died in the lands of their birth, in and around the old Pale of Settlement. They died from disease or starvation in the ghettos, or in the relatively primitive but deadly gas chambers of Aktion Reinhard, or by the bullets of SS–Police killing squads, whose shooting massacres continued throughout the war. Contrary to popular conception, extermination camps complemented rather than replaced the more intimate method of murder.

Slave Labour and Mass Murder in the Final Months of the War[76]

The focus upon the extermination machinery of Auschwitz can also obscure the complex's function as a slave reservoir and, particularly from the end of 1943, the hub of an obscene labour exchange. The Auschwitz inmates were not only liable to be used by the SS for internal construction and resource-extraction projects, but increasingly to be hired out to private industry. The most famous case of industrial slave deployment is that of IG Farben, whose plant at 'Monowitz' in eastern Upper Silesia took advantage of the labour pool in the nearby Auschwitz camp. Around 30,000 people died under IG Farben's watch or when they were returned, exhausted, to Auschwitz to be murdered. And IG Farben was only one company amongst hundreds that exploited Jewish labour and that of other concentration camp inmates. The brutal treatment meted out to the labourers notwithstanding (many companies were no more merciful than the SS), the actual decision to apply to the SS for slaves had a rational basis given the limited alternatives later in the war.

The rational aspect of slave-labour deployment further qualifies the popular depiction of the deportation of the Hungarian Jews as one of the final acts of a regime in its death throes seeking to destroy European Jewry irrespective of logistical and economic ramifications. The terrifying truth is that Germany contrived to murder so many people so swiftly and still gain some economic benefit. For most of the war, Jewish labour was quantitatively not very significant relative to the overall numbers of forced labourers. *Some* Jews were *always* being used for work, however, and in parts of Poland and the Soviet territories skilled Jewish labour was *qualitatively* significant. And at the moment Jewish labour did achieve a real *quantitative* importance, in 1944, the general German policy of destruction proved itself to be sufficiently flexible to exempt unusually large proportions of Jews from immediate murder. The one quarter of the deported Hungarian Jews selected for labour at Auschwitz or deported straight from Hungary to Germany was indeed a relatively large proportion. Added to those temporarily exempted should also be the approximately 80,000 Jews of the Hungarian labour service, who were left at the service of the Hungarian war effort, having been excluded early on from the SS's plans to deport the whole of Hungarian Jewry.

The availability of Jews and other concentration camp labourers developed real significance for the war economy and private and public industry after Stalingrad and subsequent conscription campaigns. The ruthless desperation for labour from that point can be seen in Rosenberg's decision in mid-1944 to kidnap 40,000 Polish children between the ages of 10 and 14 for slave labour in the Reich. Though the SS had gained increasing control over where and how concentration camp inmates could be used as labourers, the overall war situation compromised the 'security' rationale. Increasing pressure for camp labour was forthcoming from Minister of Armaments and War Production Albert Speer, who had acquired the vital support of Hitler in this matter over the preceding year. Speer's demands were reinforced by some of the members of the WVHA with whom he had developed a good relationship. From the turn of 1943–4 the number of concentration camp labourers in the armaments industry increased from around 30,000 to around 500,000, and the total number of camp inmates to over 700,000. WVHA chief Oswald Pohl estimated that in the second half of 1944 230,000 to 250,000 slaves worked for private industry, with another 170,000 working in the construction of underground factories and 15,000 in above-ground construction and clearing rubble after bombing raids.[77] The moves for increased camp inmate deployment in the armament industry also affected Jews, and particularly the Hungarian Jews. Many of these were deployed in the Reich, even after it had officially been rendered 'free of Jews'.

Construction workers were in particularly great demand in 1944 because of the massive Allied aerial bombardment of German industry. In an effort to safeguard the production of important war machinery a plan developed in the air ministry, Speer's armaments ministry, and the WVHA for the creation of vast subterranean factories. The planners cast jealous eyes over the Hungarian Jews. The most notorious underground project was that which used 60,000 Buchenwald inmates to create space for a factory producing the secret 'V' weapons. The accommodation section for the complex of facilities in the Harz Mountains consisted of sleeping-bays cut into the walls of the tunnels. The inmates incarcerated there worked up to eighteen hours daily, only surfacing from their underground hell for the further torture of the roll call. Some 20,000 of the 60,000 labourers died, including many thousands of Jews who arrived in the course of 1944. At the extreme, the average life expectancy of the workers was reduced to a matter of weeks.

It is a fair generalization that Jews were used for the most arduous and dangerous tasks. Nevertheless, in these labour programmes in the final war months the fate of Jews fused with other groups to an extent that had not been the case since early on in the war. Jews and non-Jewish concentration camp inmates were often used in the same production processes in the same complexes, and though according to the SS conditions on Jewish labour usage they were generally supposed to be quartered separately, and Jews were always to be kept in closed facilities, exigency sometimes prevented this.[78] Moreover, thousands of

Wehrmacht soldiers as well as the employees of private industry were used to guard the greatly increased number of camp inmates, and in some instances this improved the lot of the prisoners relative to the treatment they had received at the hands of the men of the Inspectorate of Concentration Camps.[79]

Both Jews and non-Jews were hired out to state and private industry, and at similar rates. Each group was involved in both production and construction. Death rates in construction work were on average between five and ten times as high as in production, and allocation of particular people to either task was often a matter of pure chance.[80] In the final five months of the war, by some estimates 350,000 concentration camp prisoners of all types died or were killed as a result of brutal labour, food shortages amid German logistical failure, and the intensified disciplinary measures and executions characterizing the retreat. Overall, around 1.2 million inmates had died or been killed in the history of the German concentration camp system beyond those Jews murdered immediately on arrival at the extermination centres.[81]

A certain collapsing of the distinctions between categories of inmate also occurred in the semi-organized chaos of the death marches that marked the final phase of Nazi brutality against racial and political enemies. The westward exodus of tens of thousands of concentration camp inmates with the retreating frontiers of the Nazi empire began in the second half of 1944 as Auschwitz and Gross-Rosen were partly emptied. From around the turn of the year the process became much more frantic and murderous. Operating under contradictory impulses from Himmler, who vacillated between keeping the remaining prisoners alive with an eye to the postwar period and murdering inmates who would otherwise fall into enemy hands, and with a good measure of local initiative thrown into the mix from the side of the camp commandants, the guards of these forced marches killed huge numbers of people, irrespective of the original reason for their incarceration.[82] Others perished simply from the conditions of the marches. The Security Police often also systematically murdered the inhabitants of their own prisons in the retreat, as the NKVD had done in 1941.

The extreme military and paramilitary violence that had been employed on the eastern front, in Yugoslavia, and Greece, was brought nearer to home, after the Wehrmacht's and the SS's scorched earth retreat in 1943–4. In only the most obvious example, the Polish 'Home Army's' rising from August to October 1944 resulted in up to 200,000 deaths, most civilian. The German military operation was primarily conducted by the Waffen-SS, under the command of Erich von dem Bach-Zelewski, who had distinguished himself as a murderer while a HSSPF and commander of Himmler's anti-partisan forces in the USSR. And it was not just in the east that this sort of behaviour was now permitted. In February 1944 the military commander in France condoned shooting non-Jewish hostages in large numbers. The mindset legitimating this sort of utterly ruthless 'preventive' and punitive destruction was also introduced into the Reich in the final months of the war.

The Endphase in Germany and Visions of the Nazi Future

Himmler's 6 October 1943 speech in Posen did not just address the final solution. Like his 4 October speech, it tackled the coming Germanic battles with Slavs and 'Asiatics' with an eye to the enactment of something like the *Generalplan Ost* in the future. It also looked inwards to Germany, because Himmler had recently (on 25 August) replaced Wilhelm Frick as Minister of the Interior. The appointment represented a significant expansion of Himmler's personal authority and that of the SS over the German population. As he said, he had every intention of bringing the values of the SS into his new post as he strengthened the central power of the Reich authorities. This was the mandate Hitler had given him after his achievements in other policy spheres, in the quest to stiffen the resolve of the home front.[83]

Himmler used his position to drive through one of the final acts of the final solution. The Łódź ghetto had remained in rump form until 1944 owing to a combination of its economic usefulness and its unique status under the jurisdiction of the Interior Ministry. As minister, Himmler could now close what remained of the ghetto. In August he dispatched its last workers to the gas chambers of Auschwitz.[84] In general, his gaze was now more firmly upon the German people itself, however, and as Interior Minister, he was in a position to further the SS's penetration of the state. He had automatic authority over citizenship questions,

Figure 9. Two SS survivors of the Hadamar 'euthanasia' Institute sitting on a bed.

which he delegated to the RSHA. The RSHA also took control of the ministry's ethnicity department (Abteilung Volkstum), matching its new domestic role to that it had played in the annexed territories under the RKF's umbrella.[85] This was an ominous portent of what would have transpired for German citizens who did not meet the SS's standards of racial purity.

The SS had already made further wartime inroads into the prerogatives of other ministries of state. Its quasi-judicial powers had further expanded in September 1942 when the Justice Ministry agreed to hand over particular categories of prisoners to be worked to death in the concentration camps. The Justice Ministry retained more than enough power to terrorize the population, however, as it did with the summary 'justice' handed down in the form of frequent death sentences for hints of defeatism, or anti-Hitler sentiment. The Gauleiters were also significant powerbrokers in the closing stages. In their capacity as Reich defence commissars, they had the absolute power to mobilize all men between the ages of 16 and 60 in their districts for often suicidal struggle against trained enemy troops. The punishment for reluctant fighters was predictably lethal. Military justice also intensified. It had already been extremely harsh: 30,000 German soldiers were executed during the war for cowardice, desertion, and undermining morale, compared to just 48 executed on all grounds in the First World War.

For many non-Germans within Germany the last phases of the war became even more murderous than the preceding years. On 6 September 1944 the Interior Ministry ordered the collection into designated hospitals of eastern European forced labourers unable to work owing to 'mental illness'. They were, of course, to be murdered, as so many Germans had been at the same hospitals. Many did not have mental illnesses and were in no way 'handicapped', but were suffering from physical illnesses such as tuberculosis.

The circle of victims subject to a 'mercy death' was also expanding among the German population as Allied bomb damage destroyed hundreds of thousands of homes and injured as many people. Great significance was accorded as a result to the office of the Reich Plenipotentiary for State Hospitals and Nursing Homes, which was affiliated to the Interior Ministry. The Plenipotentiary since July 1942 had been one Dr Karl Brandt, Hitler's personal physician. Brandt had been key to the establishment of the original 'euthanasia' programme and its extension, even after Hitler's 1941 'stop order', to include victims from a range of 'asocial' groups. From 1943, and with greater intensity through 1944, he and his euthanasia staff selected additional victims for murder in order to free up beds. Even more than before, the criteria was the ability or otherwise of the people to work. The killing even extended to elderly people who had developed illnesses or senile dementia, or had simply been bombed-out of their homes and threatened to put a burden on resources 'better' deployed elsewhere.[86]

Hitler's 'political testament', recorded just before his suicide, records his exhortation to 'the government and the people to uphold the race laws to the limit and to resist mercilessly the poisoner of all nations, international Jewry'. It says all that needs to be said of his racist and more specifically anti-Semitic obsession. But the executors of his apocalyptic desires were not all walking embodiments of his consuming passion. The fact that so many murderers of Jews were also murderers of non-Jews, even of fellow Germans, is only the first complicating factor. No one sociological, political, or psychological profile can do justice to the multitude of perpetrators of the genocides of the Third Reich, as it cannot for the perpetrators of any other case of state-sponsored mass murder. It is to the comparative analysis of perpetrators both within and between systems, therefore, that we now turn, in order to try to explain why so many people followed the Nazi leadership into mass murder and did so without much in the way of obvious compulsion.

PART III PERPETRATORS AND THEIR ENVIRONMENT

❝ It is not of the man, prince or legislator, that we ask about the sense of his acts; it is of the acts themselves. **❞**

Joseph-Pierre Proudhon

CHAPTER 7
WHY DID THEY KILL?

Introduction: The Individual in the System; the System in the Individual

When Himmler took over the Interior Ministry, he left personnel policy in the hands of Wilhelm Stuckart, the Nazi lawyer who had risen to great influence as state secretary and had represented the Ministry at the Wannsee conference. Stuckart claimed he wanted administrators who appreciated 'the grand political, legal, economic, cultural and social contexts' of their work. For him, the state needed people who combined in their person the 'promoter of culture, coloniser and economic organiser'.[1] In other words, he wanted people who could look beyond the confines of their office and its daily routine, people who could drive the Nazi project because they understood all of its ramifications and interconnections. Stuckart's ideal Nazi bureaucrat was the very antithesis of the desk-bound time-server who got by doing what he was told and no more. He was a master of his own destiny.

Stuckart perhaps had in mind the RSHA's brand of professionally efficient yet zealous activism, its 'fighting administration'. In the RSHA, which was something of a Nazi organizational ideal, traditional social and professional hierarchies and formal qualifications were de-emphasized, and greater priority given to ability and concrete achievement—the *Leistungsprinzip*. This encouraged both initiative and organizational fluidity. Vertical and horizontal integration across the SS could also be furthered by 'ideological education'.[2] Generally enthusiastic endorsement of the organization's ideological goals meant that the RSHA staff correspondingly identified with each other and the collective vision, providing each with more than just a pecuniary motivation for his labours.[3] The result was a very modern managerial vision, at least for the higher and middle ranks of the organization.[4]

Manifestly, Stuckart would not have settled for the vision of the world encapsulated in Proudhon's statement, quoted at the head of this part of the book. What the anarchist philosopher meant by studying the acts of men for their significance rather than the men themselves was that within the context of any given socio-political system, acts themselves embody logic consistent with the overall direction of the system, irrespective of whether the actor in question has a deep or long-range understanding of where her/his acts ultimately lead. For example, large numbers of people who would not have considered themselves Nazis benefited financially and professionally from 'Aryanization' in the 1930s. At war, the ethnic Germans who were the dubious beneficiaries of Germany's coming eastern empire would be clothed from the plunder of Jews murdered in the Polish extermination camps. The economy as a whole benefited somewhat from the theft of Jewish property throughout Germany and occupied Europe, since this wealth was generally nationalized before it was privatized. National wealth obtained in this manner meant wartime subsidies for the German economy as a whole, in the form of lower taxes. 'Euthanasia' freed resources for the majority. When we add the burgeoning concentration camp population of the war years, incarcerated and labouring in proximity to German settlements, often under guard not by SS men but by employees of German industrial firms, and the forced labourers working on German farms and in factories, we get a sense not just of how much better off Germans became because of the suffering of others, but also that *some* of that suffering was before the eyes and ears of its beneficiaries.

Some, but not all, and herein is the danger of generalization and easy condemnation. The breadth of vision and understanding on the part of any given German is intimately related to the moral judgements that can be made. 'Innocent' is not the word for indirect beneficiaries of genocide, but for many their responsibility stems not from personal intent. It is entwined with the complexity of the German state-system and the concomitant difficulty for any individual of, first, recognizing it for what it was and, second, breaking out of it (if he or she indeed wanted to). That complexity is on a continuum with other complex structures and would include every Briton who benefited indirectly from the Atlantic slave trade or the Chinese opium trade, every European who benefited from the imperial extraction of mineral wealth from Africa, and every person today whose standard of living has risen on the back of unequal trade relations with the undeveloped world. Studying the acts of such ordinary beneficiaries is indeed a better way of understanding how Nazism worked than is asking how 'Nazified' any given German was, because even while many were demonstrably not Nazis, their acts were rationally self-interested within a system that related self-interest to racism and exploitation. Balancing an understanding of the more and less subtle incorporative capacities of 'the system' with different levels of participation in it is the heart of the matter in establishing levels and qualities of responsibility, but also in understanding why the system became quite so radical.

The Sources of Human Behaviour

The abundant source material bequeathed by Nazi Germany is not always helpful in establishing motive. The racist 'bottom line' of the regime influenced the way all actors expressed themselves, which is why expanding murder could be justified on all manner of secondary or tactical, 'practical' grounds. If a hypothetical German official had sought amelioration of the conditions of Jews and others, he would have had little success pleading for it on humanitarian grounds, and would not have wished to appear an obstacle, since outright obstruction was one offence not tolerated, unlike simple non-participation. He would have had to use the same idiom as the proponents of killing, or perhaps even the appeal to German honour. If a policeman objected to shooting people, the evidence shows he would rarely have protested on ethical grounds lest this seem like an accusation of his colleagues. He might have claimed personal weakness as an excuse. In any case that was how it would be depicted by superiors and peers: killing for the SS–Police was officially a matter of necessity, of *raison d'état*, no more and no less.

'Acceptable' justifications for action and inaction were inverted in the postwar world. Even if the homicidal *intent* of German soldiers, policemen, and officials was evident by the very nature of their actions, the matter of *motive* was hotly contested. For the German actors, denying racist motivation or venality was paramount because of the German legal system within which they could be tried. The German penal code stipulated that first degree murder must be a product of the killer's 'base motives' (hatred, bloodlust, greed, etc.), of which routine participation in state-sponsored mass murder was not considered one. Participation in genocide out of simple obedience to orders was a lesser offence with a smaller penalty. Accordingly, the plea 'I was only obeying orders' formed the basis for one of the most enduring stereotypes of German behaviour in the Nazi era, but also of perpetrators of war crimes and crimes against humanity everywhere. Versions of it were embraced across the spectrum of perpetrators, from Military High Command chief Wilhelm Keitel at Nuremberg, through the lowliest Order Policemen in German courts, to the most famous bureaucratic perpetrator, Adolf Eichmann. Eichmann consciously propagated an impression of a humble functionary in a top-down dictatorial system in his 'memoirs', written while in captivity in Jerusalem.[5] Immediately from the end of the war—from even before then, in fact[6]—legal and moral self-defence strategies contributed to an image of the 'final solution' that was literally 'ordered' from the top-down. Initiative or improvisation in killing was the last thing to be admitted, and as that disappeared from view, so too did the national and local variations in the Holocaust, to be replaced with an impression of a much more uniform genocide. Instead of a fluid, evolving genocidal structure, the very internal dynamics and mid-level personnel of which shaped the development and contours of genocide, the image was of a static machine operated from above, its human components merely cogs in the machine. This image, in which the agency of subordinate perpetrators was stripped away almost as much as that of their victims, achieved a fleeting popularity in Holocaust scholarship.[7] It endures today in conceptions of bureaucracy. As one anthropologist has observed, 'the most commonly invoked stereotype of all is perhaps that of bureaucracy itself, and it is often bureaucrats themselves who invoke it. A feature of the symbolic world that bureaucrats share with . . . other people is the ethical alibi of the heartless "system." '[8]

A great deal of scholarly endeavour has recently gone into exposing the enthusiastic engagement in their task not just of the likes of Eichmann, but of a much broader cohort of German administrators. This historiographical development has been labelled the 'voluntarist turn', and, for its historians, finding the 'real' motive generally means cutting through the courtroom apologia.[9] Yet we have already noted that such wartime evidence as has been bequeathed by the perpetrators can distort in different directions to the postwar legal evidence. A good illustration of the way even apparently enthusiastic killing can stem from motives other than a priori enthusiasm for killing comes from a case where killers had already been tried and so had nothing to fear from talking openly about motivation. They had also been tried in a legal system in which, unlike Germany's, the emphases on intent and motivation were different.

The case is drawn from the 1994 Rwandan genocide, and a rich set of interviews conducted by the journalist Jean Hatzfeld with a group of ten Hutu men from the Nyamata region, each convicted of multiple murders. None confessed to deep-seated hatred of the Tutsis they had killed, though some admitted to levels of mundane prior prejudice or suspicion. A few of the men shed light on precisely how they then moved to kill, and the claim was that they instrumentalized hatred as the easiest way to do the job. One said that 'the hatred came with the moment of killing. I adopted it by imitation and convenience.' Another said that 'to kill so many human beings without thinking, it is necessary to hate without indecision.'[10] To simplify considerably, hatred was *in this instance* an *effect* of participation rather than its *cause*. As one criminologist has put it in a different connection, 'the motions of battle sometimes call up the emotions that would sustain them.'[11]

There are two basic categories of motivation for participation in murder, as in other acts. They conform to the two options in a long-standing sociological dilemma: is human behaviour determined by 'values', belief that the action is right according to some abstract standard, or is it based in the pursuit of narrower self-interest? Each category can be subdivided. Interests can be related to positive or negative incentives. Positive incentives might be economic gain, professional advancement, or social capital ('kudos', fame, or peer recognition). Negative incentives are the prospect of loss in those fields, or outright physical punishment. A crosscutting but perhaps clearer distinction of incentives is between material rewards on one hand and physical or psychological pressures on the other. For present purposes, no better categorization of particular types of value exists than the sociologist Max Weber's distinction between an ethic of conviction and an ethic of responsibility.

Weber's ethic of conviction means an inner imperative that an individual feels it necessary to follow whatever the cost and countervailing pressures. His ethic of responsibility is 'consequentialist', meaning the actor is aware of the cost of pursuing one among many potentially legitimate ends. The difference, as far as this chapter is concerned, is between an individual's unswerving loyalty to his beliefs or his loyalty to a larger entity which he understands as having the legitimacy to represent the community of which he is a part. In Weber's tradition that entity was the state. The ethic of conviction might be associated with the charismatic leader, the 'conviction politician'. The ethic of responsibility might be associated with 'consensus politicians', though Weber particularly associated it with bureaucrats. Bureaucrats had to consciously repress their personal preferences in order for them to do their jobs, which meant implementing impartially policies with which they might not agree. The same could apply to other arms of state, such as the military. A 'legitimate' instruction or policy was simply one which the recipient understood the issuer had the legitimacy to issue.

Each ethic expressed itself through a particular form of rationality. 'Value rationality' meant a rationality oriented to *ends*, always keeping in mind the ultimate value embodied in the political conviction. 'Instrumental rationality' meant a rationality restricted on moral principle to *means*, the process of administering whatever policy was the order of the day, without moral assessment of the policy. Theoretically, this blend of ethics and rationalities could facilitate genocide, just as it could facilitate democratic harmony. All that is needed is an appropriately directed ethic of conviction and for the leader in question to wield sufficient legitimacy to be followed by those working according to an ethic of responsibility.

Weber himself was aware of the coexistence and tension between his two ethics and rationalities.[12] He would also have been first to recognize that neither existed in the 'ideal type' in which he elucidated them. Boiling down human motivation to simple, single causes is to ignore what it is to be human: acculturation, socialization, and the interplay of interests, pressures, and values shape everyone. Acts of 'pure evil' are as rare as acts of 'pure good', if by this we mean acts of good solely for good's sake or evil solely for evil's sake. This is even true for 'extremists'. Heydrich was anti-Semitic but his ambition, which we might call 'amoral', was as strong a motivation. Stahlecker, leader of the first Einsatzgruppe to systematically murder women and children, may have been partly driven to impress Heydrich after earlier disagreements. Like Otto Ohlendorf, leader of Einsatzgruppe D, he was a bureaucrat sent to prove himself in the field. Eichmann's men were anti-Semites, but their dedication derived partly from the debt they owed the SS for career opportunities and renewed self-esteem after earlier social marginalization as failed small businessmen.[13]

If the question remains to be asked of even proven racists as to how much they had to believe—or to hate—before no additional motivation to involvement in killing was needed, so much more does it need to be asked of people drawn from the full breadth of German society. Perhaps the most we can do as historians is try to identify the most significant driving force in any historical actor. This chapter is concerned not with the most obvious racists. The significance of Himmler's HSSPFs and the RSHA men in driving the process has been established. The following pages are only concerned with such people in relation to the rest of the system of destruction, as they helped realign values and incentives in that system.

State Bureaucracies: Competition, Material Interest, Anticipatory Obedience

We have seen that organizations disproportionately staffed by committed Nazis were at the forefront of the policies of genocide. Here I distinguish killing policies from policies of domestic discrimination, in which the regular offices of state played a proportionately great part. It was consistent with the premium put by Hitler on full ideological identification with Nazism that, alongside the SS, the impetus for mass murder and hyperexploitation came from new organizations like the labour administrations, the office for the Four Year Plan, and the party-run civil administrations appointed in occupied eastern Europe. Most of the Order Police battalions deployed for killing purposes were led and manned by professionals who, like their Waffen-SS and Einsatzgruppen counterparts, had imbibed the SS spirit. *Relatively* few were reserve units like the famous battalion 101 whose deeds were so superbly elucidated by Christopher Browning, as he showed precisely how ordinary men could become mass murderers.[14] In other words, in the Nazi state, those Germans acting most clearly according to an ethic of conviction about Nazi goals were disproportionately represented in the vanguard of genocide.

A decided impact of new organizations like the SS was to encourage others along new paths or further down existing paths. The pattern can also be seen graphically in Stalin's USSR, where purges of the state and party by the OGPU-NKVD security apparatus sowed the seeds of further radicalization. Like the party *apparat* itself, the NKVD, heir of the civil war-era 'Cheka', did not deploy specialists from the Tsarist days in responsible positions: it was predominantly manned by the ideologically committed. The purges, however, introduced into central and local administrations not only individuals keen to show loyalty and ruthless rigour, but also a stream of opportunists. Both contributed to further radicalization, which was nowhere better illustrated than in quotas for execution or imprisonment. As one scholar writes about later parts of the 'dekulakization' campaign and the 1937–8 purges, 'planned orders from the centre plus bureaucratic reflexes naturally spurred local officials, many of whom had just recently been promoted, to anticipate and surpass the desires of superiors further up the hierarchy and the directives that arrived from Moscow.' So extreme did this process become that by 1938 'the local authorities, who had generally been purged several times in the previous year and whose new staff were eager to show their zeal, demanded a further increase of [punishment] quotas.' This pressure vastly increased numbers in the labour camps, creating a problem of supply and accommodation: 'in this situation, the obvious solution, for the NKVD, was to have a certain number of people in prisons or camps shot.'[15]

If fear was a lesser factor for German bureaucrats than for their counterparts in the USSR, opportunism and other elements were common to the two states. Vanguard organizations provided vehicles for individual advancement, personal power bases of the sort Heydrich exploited with the SD and Stalin exploited with the Organizational Bureau of the Central Committee of the Communist Party, before becoming party General Secretary. Like Nazi party membership, SS membership could be a good method of professional advancement and social climbing. The organizations attracted talented people and were shaped by them as well as shaping them with their own ethos. The new vanguard agencies also modified the nature of bureaucracy by introducing competition to areas of administration that had hitherto been state monopolies. This injected an entrepreneurial spirit into the bureaucratic sphere.

The duplication and overlapping of functions between organizations is not in itself unusual, contrary to what is often written of the Third Reich, though the phenomenon was particularly marked in the Nazi state, a sort of administrative manifestation of social Darwinism. To varying degrees, conflict between state agencies with similar remits transpires in all complex states, authoritarian and democratic. Alongside the USSR, examples include Imperial Japan, Wilhelmine Germany,[16] the USA in the later twentieth century,[17] and the Latin American dictatorships of the 1970s–80s. The competitive environments thus engendered have led one commentator on bureaucracy to write that 'the most basic goal of any bureaucrat or bureaucracy is not rational efficiency, but individual and organizational survival.'[18]

The response of the German bureaucracies outside the vanguard Nazi agencies was entirely consistent with this competitive vision. They started to show initiative in matters of the regime's ideological priority in which they had a jurisdictional stake. Though levels of individual commitment to Nazism varied within the state ministries,[19] the Interior and Foreign Ministries were responsible respectively for innovations in 'racial' segregation, and for advancing, in the Madagascar deportation plan, a new conduit for Jewish policy at the continental level.[20] A similar logic influenced the Justice Ministry (whatever the individual political persuasions of its members) to respond to the arbitrary powers of incarceration of 'enemies of the state' arrogated to the political police by increasing the harshness of its sentences, and by advising judges to put more people in 'preventive detention' themselves, to avoid being outdone, to preserve some formal jurisdiction.[21]

Conflict was not omnipresent within the Nazi empire, nor was it necessarily a hindrance or waste of resources.[22] Conflict stemmed from power struggles between major figures with independent power bases. It could, if resolved, lead to clarification of policy lines.[23] Hitler's occasional personal interventions also determined jurisdictions—though sometimes they simply recognized faits accomplis by successful subordinates—as well as signalling policy preference, as with his tacit rebuke of the army after its battles with the SS over policy in Poland.[24] His personal authority could also be vested in his direct representatives, as at the heads of the Reich or Party Chancelleries, and a stream of 'commissars' with personalized remits to bring together different agencies with overlapping competencies in specific policy areas. Himmler's position as RKF was precisely such a thing, as was the creation of the HSSPFs, which brings us to the personal level.[25]

For many ordinary German bureaucrats—meaning conservative non-Nazis—working in the established ministries of states and in the municipalities there was a direct personal adaptation parallel to the overall response of their organization. Many German bureaucrats worked effectively in their posts from Weimar through the Third Reich to the later Federal Republic—from democracy to genocidal dictatorship back to democracy.[26] In some cases this adaptability may have been the expression of an ethic of service responsibility, but in other cases it was undoubtedly just the line of least resistance. The same went for Dutch bureaucrats or the bureaucrats of the Channel Islands. These people were not crying out for a campaign of racial persecution before the imposition of German rule, and could scarcely have attributed legitimacy to their conquerors, but they nevertheless did what they were asked to do in locating and deporting Jews on their conquerors' behalf. Insofar as we have evidence, it seems that they were not acting as unthinking automata, they simply felt the moral responsibility to lie with those who had instructed them.[27]

More committed or opportunistic individuals were better placed to rise to prominence than before because of the general emphasis on the *Leistungsprinzip*, the principal of rewarding achievement. Even the ultimate vanguard organization, the RSHA, contained racists of different levels of obsession who nevertheless worked together to produce the output of the most extreme anti-Semitic policy,[28] while at least some of the WVHA men were apolitical careerists.[29] Nevertheless, all followed the practice, elucidated by Ian Kershaw, of 'working towards the Führer', in the sense of using their instincts and initiative, adapting to regime norms often without explicit orders.[30] 'Anticipatory obedience', *vorauseilender Gehorsam*, was another contemporary term for the same process, and the concept was employed in SS–Police killing units amongst other organizations.[31]

Any notion that 'anticipatory obedience' of this sort is particularly Germanic or particularly Nazi-like results from a want of comparative study. It appears simply to be what humans do in political systems and, terrifyingly, the incentives seem to be more important than the direction of the policy. As one Iraqi said during the Saddam Hussein regime in the 1990s, 'You have to understand: this was a system where everyone knew what was expected of them. Most of the time, we didn't even have to be told what to do.'[32] Precisely the expression 'anticipatory obedience' has also been used in entirely 'ordinary' circumstances in the constitutional affairs of liberal democracies.[33] In the Soviet system, interpretative leeway accelerated policy under conditions of a general sense of 'appropriate' policy direction. The NKVD operatives and local authorities were responsible for radicalizing policy in the field. Like Nazi operatives in the early weeks of the invasion of the USSR, they were often acting with enormous licence in accordance with only vague guidelines on the 'struggle with the enemy',[34] as had the *Cheka* in 1917–22.[35]

A key difference between the Nazi and Soviet systems was that episodes like the 'great terror' and dekulakization were initiated and terminated with explicit instructions from the very top.[36] Likewise, when the world war was won, and when Stalin died (and de-Stalinization began), there was a decided de-radicalization and even reverse of the policies against the deported nationalities. The contrast is clear with Nazism, where Hitler set the general tone and indicated preferences, but rarely made concrete decisions, and almost never reversed radical policies except tactically. Insofar as we can tell, German victory in the Second World War would have resulted in extensions of genocide in a number of directions indefinitely. The contrast indicates that however murderous Stalinism was as a political *system*, communism as an *ideology* was not inherently eliminationist. Nazism was both inherently eliminationist as an *ideology* and inherently, ceaselessly dynamic as a political *system*. If the former quality rendered it different from communism, the latter quality rendered it different from the authoritarian dictatorships elsewhere in Europe at the time and in Iraq and Latin America later, since those dictatorships prized control and stability where Nazism sought ever deeper penetration of the state and society.

Regime, State, and Society: A Comparison of Genocides

The Nazi state became a genocidal state, but this does not mean Germany was a genocidal society. Genocidal societies there have been in specific historical situations. One might be the colonial context, as, say, in early-nineteenth-century British Australia.[37] When, predictably, indigenous resistance emerged to the theft of land by white settlers, those settlers had a sufficient combination of racist contempt and greed—and sometimes fear—to do 'what they needed to do' to secure their future in the colonies. In cases like these, where the state was remote from the killing fields, though providing tacit endorsement by the very logic of colonialism itself, we can talk meaningfully of a genocidal society at work, albeit amongst a partly self-selecting perpetrator population and in a situation where a disproportionately large number of that population were on the 'front line' in terms of perceived threat from their victims.

In the modern period, structurally the most similar state undertaking to genocide is war.[38] The two are not identical in their aims and conditions—war is classically not directed at non-combatants, while genocide requires of the killers less sacrifice than war—yet they share large, blurred margins. Both entail large-scale killing of people that the state has designated as enemies, irrespective of the disposition of individual killers. To incite killing, the state may deploy propaganda to denigrate or even dehumanize the enemy, but it relies upon the obedience of its own population at a crisis moment. Hatred may be cultivated in training and during the conflict itself, but this only reinforces the fact that in war brutalization and the will to kill happen more because of war than the other way around.

When popular obedience is forthcoming in conscription for war, it generally stems from one of two sources, loyalty or incentive, rather than hatred of the enemy. Loyalty is an ethic of responsibility and is predicated upon the perceived legitimacy of the regime taking the state to war. Where legitimacy and thus loyalty are lacking, incentive can operate instead, generally in the form of some level of coercion. The regime will succeed in coercing the disloyal only in so far as the threat of punishment is real and substantial enough to be more significant than whatever objections they may have. The alternative for the regime doubtful of the loyalty of its population is to look elsewhere, either to mercenaries or to paramilitaries who may also be motivated by material incentives or by identification with the values of the regime—by an ethic of conviction. The situation is somewhat different in civil wars, which tend to be more overtly ideological in their demand that citizens choose one or other version of the state identities on offer, thus demanding an active choice based on an ethic of conviction rather than soliciting acquiescence based on an ethic of responsibility. Yet even in civil war, participants in no way need to subscribe to the central ideological cleavage motivating their leadership, and frequently act out of localized incentives instead.[39]

Many of these considerations also apply to genocide, and we can see their relevance as we examine relations between governing regime on one hand and state and society on the other. Genocide is indeed a form of ideological war, but, as in the instance of civil war, that does not mean it needs every fighter to be an ideological warrior. In illustration, let us consider the Rwandan genocide, when direct participation in killing was about ten times as high per capita as it was in Nazi Germany.[40]

Only if we accept the racist caricature of 'savage African tribes' does the staggering level of popular participation in the Rwandan genocide become easy to explain. The truth is that while many

Hutu perpetrators perceived Tutsis as somehow different before the genocide—unsurprisingly, given a background of Belgian colonial divide-and-rule—the idea of difference did not necessarily translate into enmity. Intermingling in local communities was common. In the days immediately after the precipitant event of the genocide, the shooting-down of the aeroplane of President Juvenal Habyarimana on 6 April 1994, in some prefectures local militia forces dispatched to keep the peace had mixed Hutu and Tutsi membership. The Hutu members of these militias would shortly afterwards be prominent amongst the killers in a way that simply cannot be ascribed to long-standing interethnic antagonism.

In Rwanda, genocide occurred as a section of the pre-existing political, administrative, commercial, military, social, and religious elite sought to maintain what it saw as the appropriate level of Hutu domination in Rwandan society.[41] Between 1990 and 1994 it recast a set of complicated challenges to the political order as a simplified matter of intra-Rwandan ethnic struggle. The most significant challenge was war with the Rwandan Patriotic Front (RPF), a predominantly Tutsi army composed largely of Rwandan exiles, whose military successes resulted in it occupying large tracts of northeastern Rwanda and gaining an internationally mandated power-sharing agreement. The RPF's actions allowed members of the ruling MRNDD party and the extremist CDR to depict Rwanda's entire Tutsi minority as a fifth column at a time of national instability. In addition to the perhaps 800,000 murdered Tutsis, tens of thousands of Hutus were also killed, notably political oppositionists and moderates who had supported some form of power-sharing, but also many who were simply mistaken for Tutsis by overzealous killers.

The preparedness of the *génocidaires* to murder actual and would-be opponents cowed administrators and ordinary citizens alike into cooperation. Apart from the political parties, the leaders of the killing were drawn from the defence ministry, the army, particularly its Presidential Guard, created in 1992, and key figures from the world of business and finance, as well as social elites at the regional and local level. At the rock face, genocide was led by military units, the national and communal police, civil defence units,[42] and party-run militias, notably the MRNDD's Interahamwe and the CDR's Impuzamugambi.

The militias illustrate the significance of organizations from beyond the state framework, as does the phenomenon of youth gangs lending power to local bigwigs who did not necessarily wield formal authority before the genocide.[43] This confederation of extremists and opportunists within and beyond the state asserted themselves violently to drive the killing in places. Some local officials sought to use symbols of legitimate authority to organize killing, as when they ordered ordinary Hutus to gather for communal labour projects, as was traditional, with the intention of using them as murder squads. However, the threat of violence was omnipresent, as the *génocidaires* deliberately broadened the circle of complicity throughout Hutu society. This policy replicated itself as many ordinary men then pressed others to kill as they had, in order to mitigate their own sense of exceptionalism and, thus, guilt.[44] In the process of destroying the Tutsi population there was a parallel process of restratifying Hutu society and the power structure in a form of 'nation-building' by violence.

Using the analogy with a state at war, in Rwanda there was massive and violent conscription of the population by a coalition of forces that by no means enjoyed legitimacy across the breadth of the society it was seeking to mould. A variation on the theme is provided by the Armenian genocide, where, rather than coercing the population at large, the leaders opted proportionately more for mercenaries and paramilitaries to do the killing.

Enough of the Ottoman organs of state *were* involved in the destruction and expropriation process, and enough of its interests vested in the removal of the Armenians by some means, for the genocide to be seen as a state project. The Interior Ministry under Committee of Union and Progress triumvir Talât housed the two bodies most closely involved in the ordering and administration of the major Armenian deportations in 1915: the Directorate for the Settlement of Tribes and Immigrants (IAMM) and the Directorate for General Security. The Ottoman army, ultimately under Minister of War and CUP triumvir Enver, is implicated, though not uniformly, in the killing of Armenians in Eastern Anatolia in situ and during deportations. The murderous 'Special Organization', if we can use what may be a rather catch-all and imprecise term, was an irregular formation within the armed forces, though partly directed in its killing actions by the CUP through members of the party's vastly influential central committee. Looking to the pre-history of the genocide, some state officials had been at least complicit by omission in the 1894–6 Armenian massacres, and in further killings in 1909. We have seen that the successive regimes of Abdülhamid II and the CUP shared an increasing suspicion of non-Muslim populations and a preparedness to use massacre as a means of combating putative secessionist threats. By the close of the Balkan wars inter-religious pluralism was all but extinguished in the Ottoman Empire. Yet it is doubtful that the CUP was committed to outright extermination at the beginning of the First World War, and still more so that ideas in that direction were endorsed in 1914 by the state infrastructure as a whole.

The layer of central administration involved in issuing the major deportation orders in 1915 was comparatively thin. It involved the higher echelons of the Ministry of the Interior, and the two Directorates. Interior Minister Talât was a micromanager of the deportation process, regularly checking on the execution of his instructions and acquiring feedback on the process of expulsion of deportees and settlement of Muslims in their stead. He was aided by the IAMM's chief, who frequently oversaw the enactment of the deportations in the provinces. The IAMM, as we know, was established by the CUP in 1913 and as such was more closely identified with the ruling faction than were other state organs.[45] Meanwhile, in Anatolia, party men, notably the central committee member Bahaettin Şakir, also policed the actions of irregular forces on the ground, exhorting their men to keep up the tempo of killing.[46]

The murderous assaults on Armenian deportation convoys were administratively light, and the perpetration machinery as a whole 'bottom-heavy', in comparison with the other cases studied here. This was functionally useful. Talât's exploitation of the telegraph system was a time-tested means of keeping the paper trail to a minimum, and of supplementing or supplanting paper orders. As the postwar trials of some of the perpetrators revealed, Talât issued oral and coded orders countermanding 'official' orders for the protection of the deportees, and in this 'second track' of orders the emphasis was very definitely on murder.[47] Meanwhile, the contracting-out of irregulars for 'dirty work' was a time-honoured tradition in the Ottoman domains and in parts of the Balkans: their actions provided governments with plausible deniability for the atrocities.[48]

The manpower of the Ottoman irregulars was partly drawn from Muslim refugees from Russian rule in the Caucasus and former Ottoman territories in the Balkans, and their descendents. These men would aid in ethnic warfare and help foment Muslim insurgency in Tsarist territories; many were strongly anti-Christian. But common criminals released from jail for the purpose figured very heavily, just as such people would be deployed in large numbers in ethnic cleansing and massacre in the 1990s in Serbian paramilitary forces. In both 1915 and the 1990s, such men were attracted to killing by the possibilities of enriching themselves from their victims, not to mention the opportunities for sexual and sadistic gratification. Historically, these bands of irregulars had in fact been expected to live off plunder. Similar pecuniary motives influenced the various Kurdish tribes that also attacked Armenian deportation caravans once the tacit message had been transmitted from the CUP that the Armenians were fair game by the very fact of their removal.[49] Individual motives of common criminality—'base motives', as the German criminal code would put it—were at least as prominent as any ideological commitment among the criminal elements.

The cost to the CUP in shaping the genocidal system thus was that they did not enjoy the same level of control of the destruction process as (say) their Nazi counterparts, who could call on the disciplinary norms of the traditional state infrastructure. On one hand, some of the local auxiliaries had to be exhorted to kill as well as simply plundering.[50] On the other hand, with an eye to the opinion of the outside world, the CUP centre was worried by some of the massacres conducted at particularly visible points along the deportation routes rather than at the desert destinations, since these killings compromised the secrecy of the real, murderous nature of the ethnic cleansing.[51]

Compared to the late Ottoman state, a broader cross section of the German state and society participated and did so much less from motives of criminality, family connection, or the possibility of loot. The grand theft that was Aryanization is to be differentiated because, while certainly theft in a moral sense, it was legalized and subject to official procedures which delineated it from other forms of strictly illegal theft. Corruption there certainly was in the Third Reich, particularly in the eastern administrations and among the auxiliaries, but it remained officially a criminal offence. Despite containing many corrupt individuals, the SS–Police and Wehrmacht forbade plunder as a point of honour and discipline. Discipline and detachment in killing was central to the idea that this was a military-type exercise.

Compared to Rwanda, Nazi Germany was not physically coercive in bringing ordinary people to kill. The fact so many Germans participated in genocide without the threat of serious punishment could tell us that most Germans were vehement racists, or that Germans are particularly prone to doing whatever they are told. Or, as in the analogy to war, it could simply confirm what we already know: that Nazism had had a long time to insinuate itself into the German state and that large numbers of Germans attributed legitimacy to the regime in general because it came to power legally (unlike the other regimes just mentioned) and pursued many other goals congruent with popular belief in the 'national interest'. A majority, led by traditional social elites such as the churches, the military, and the bureaucracy, also believed the conflict with the USSR—the over-riding context for genocide—to be a just one when it was in progress, even though few wished the war in advance. Given that broader perspective, it is consistent that the 'functional elites' and 'hands-on' perpetrators involved in genocide within this war context worked overwhelmingly within organizations tasked to 'safeguard, defend, and pacify'—goals intimately associated with notions of national interest and national security.

Certainly the greater levels of coercion in the other genocides mentioned here do not indicate a more prevalent intrinsic humanitarianism among their administrators, so much as illustrating in those cases the core *génocidaires'* fear of opposition of a general political nature. (The fear of potential opposition to genocide was subsumed within this broader concern.) It would be comforting to believe that there were large numbers of officials protesting against any and every genocide, but the evidence of this diverse selection of historical cases suggests that the default position is at 'best' quiet acquiescence. The honourable few who resisted involvement in each case, and the fewer who actively opposed genocide, require more explanation than the many who fell into line.

Part of the explanation for the limited input from the regular state bureaucracy in the Armenian genocide was that the process was clandestinely driven by the CUP and its regional agents, to the extent that some cabinet ministers were kept in the dark about the reality of Armenian policy.[52] When general deportation had become policy in 1915, it was rigidly enforced by party agents, with many provincial and district governors shadowed by watchful 'responsible secretaries' of the CUP, who distributed Talât's coded orders and ensured execution of them.[53] The most enthusiastic killers in the provinces, men like Mehmed Reşid in Diyarbakır, who set the pace for mass murder even before the fully fledged policy of genocide was in place, were recent appointments combining party and state posts, as were many of the Gauleiter corps sent to govern parts of Nazi-occupied eastern Europe.[54] Reluctant Ottoman officials, who tended to be state rather than party appointments, were replaced by more enthusiastic ones, and a few obstructers were killed.[55]

In Rwanda, the genocidal ringleaders dealt with the utmost ruthlessness with opposition from within the state. The level of intra-Hutu violence was much greater than the level of intra-Muslim violence in the Ottoman state, and reflects the greater speed with which genocide was implemented and the greater political power struggle between different Hutu political factions. While genocide served to 'coordinate' the Rwandan state *and* reshape Hutu society, the CUP was somewhat less ambitious in 1915, using genocide to take the first step of penetrating the Ottoman state. Concluding that project, and building the 'Turkish' nation, was the achievement of Kemal 'Atatürk'.[56]

By the Second World War, the Nazi movement and the German state had already pulled closely towards each other. When ordinary citizens were called upon to participate in genocide the response was generally positive, but for most Germans this participation was mediated through the state. No German was asked outside of a recognized institutional structure to hack his neighbour to death with a machete. Quite how far German society itself was Nazified by 1939 is, as we have seen, difficult to judge, but there was no doubt in the popular mind about the regime's attitudes to Jews and others, and no doubt about the commitment and sacrifice it sought from its people, as well as the potential rewards it could provide. There was clearly an expectation that Germans chosen at random, as in reserve Order Police battalions or the military, would do 'their duty', but for the population as a whole the regime sought to keep mass murder a qualified secret. The vaguely approximate parallel to the Rwandan process of forcing complicity amongst the people was in the Nazi use of wartime propaganda about the fate of the Jews, where coded language was calculated to tie the people to the regime by implication.[57] This is obviously a much lower level of coimplication, though it is not insignificant.

It is a basic truth that state administrations anywhere will, over time, increasingly imbibe and reflect regime values, for no bureaucracy exists independently of its surrounding culture. Weber observed as much, as did Ernst Fraenkel, the earliest theorist of the relationship between Nazism and the German state.[58] The Nazi party forced the pace of change with its drive to control the state machinery, but the adaptation of that machinery in the Third Reich was not different in principle from changes over time in the character of other bureaucracies in more moderate states. For example, the SS, to continue with the analogy to the war machine, was a paramilitary organization (of the ideological rather than mercenary sort) that increasingly fused with existing state organizations, first the police but then, through the Waffen-SS, the army, and even the civilian administrations of the Reich.

The absence of physical coercion for Reich Germans does not, however, mean there was no coercion at all. Psychologically the presence of the concentration camps, the SS, and the militaristic imagery that pervaded the Third Reich were important. In the German power hierarchies, the competition even between different vanguard organizations could also send stark warnings about whose lead to follow. One of the victims of Himmler's jurisdictional conflict with the civil authorities in the Generalgouvernement was the governor of eastern Galicia, Karl Lasch. Lasch's involvement in corruption was seized upon by Himmler as a way of increasing SS power in the region and attacking Lasch's friend and superior, Hans Frank. Lasch was investigated and executed.

On a more subtle plane, the civil service laws of the 1930s had served to 'discipline' state employees—those who needed disciplining, which very many did not. The very continuance of their tenure implied at least acquiescence in Nazi projects, and the more so when they came under increasing direction from active Nazis. In the case of Stuckart's interior ministry, for instance, the state secretary never had his wish fulfilled for an organization full of ideological soldiers. Indeed, he kept a large number of old hands in post so long as they proved competent. It takes little imagination to see that civil servants who owed their position to his indulgence would be particularly keen to do his bidding. Some of the not inconsiderable number of Gestapo operatives who had been in the SPD before 1933 ended up performing all of the nefarious functions with which the Gestapo would be associated after its penetration by the SD and co-option for the Nazi project.[59] The changing ethos of the organization itself helped condition these men. There is a sliding scale where more subtle forms of manipulation increase in importance as explicit coercion decreases.

Much less subtle were the power relations between Reich Germans and collaborators in eastern Europe. Further to the analogy with the structure of war, Germany did use outright coercion, as well as unofficially providing 'base' material (mercenary) incentives in the form of plundered possessions, for some of the foot soldiers of genocide involved in some of the dirtiest work. This includes the auxiliaries from the occupied Soviet lands. Most of the guards of Bełżec, Sobibór, and Treblinka were Ukrainians drawn from POW camps. Had they chosen to stay in those camps rather than act as so-called volunteers, they would have died. The *Volksdeutsche* who were used for killing in Poland and the USSR and for liaising between the SS–Police and local auxiliaries were often also treated as second-class Germans and subjected to correspondingly harsher discipline. 'Inappropriate' behaviour could lead to them being categorized as non-Germans, with all the accompanying connotations.[60]

Once we move out into the killing fields where these auxiliaries operated, the contextual balance shifts. On one hand, the further we

Figure 10. Group portrait of ethnic German guards at Bełżec concentration camp.

go towards the periphery of the German empire in eastern Europe, the further we get from the competition characterizing the Nazi power centre. Here, where manpower was often in short supply, murderous collaboration between organizations was often the order of the day. On the other hand, a different and more important set of radicalizing factors came into play: war and the control of foreign territory were the conditions for the most extreme Nazi tendencies to be unleashed.

Lands of Exception, Zones of Exception[61]

Almost all the Third Reich's killing took place beyond Germany's pre-1939 borders, and more specifically in the east and southeast of Europe. This was partly to do with the desire for secrecy in Germany and the west, but it also pertained to some enduring institutional arrangements in Germany. In Poland and the USSR, conversely, the destruction of native administrations and the establishment of new German administrations happened with reference purely to German needs and goals as defined by the most radical Nazi actors, with no intervening constitutional rationale.

An argument illustrating the significance of the different 'constitutional' and administrative status of different territories can to degrees be applied to every land earmarked for settlement by colonial states of all sorts, whether internally democratic or authoritarian. Before those lands were properly incorporated and brought under the full administrative control of the colonial power, they remained frontier zones or wildernesses, approximations to warzones in which laws simply did not apply as they did at home. They became the preserve of military martial law, or of militias from the settler community. As the colonial comparison suggests, cultural considerations were inextricable from the constitutional-administrative considerations. The justification for appropriating land in Africa, Australasia, or the Nazi eastern empire was that the native population had no civilization worthy of consideration, and that to put the land and its resources to proper use would entail the obliteration of native culture and its replacement by the cultural and economic patterns of the settlers.

In the case of the Nazi empire, the significance of different statuses becomes clear when contrasting the ease with which Polish Jews could be murdered with the wrangles in Germany over defining German part-Jews or Jews in mixed marriages in order to deport them for murder, probably in Poland. As we move further eastward, to the Soviet lands where German control was more tenuous and contested, and where there was already some interethnic ferment to exacerbate the situation, so the general violence became still greater. Not even the summary justice of the German civil courts that condemned so many ethnic Poles to death was needed to murder Soviet citizens under large swathes of German military jurisdiction. But it is telling that the German leadership still felt obliged to find a *legal* justification for the sort of arbitrary violence legitimated by the Barbarossa jurisdiction decree: the Soviet failure to ratify the Hague and Geneva conventions.

It is true, of course, that in some sense Germany itself had been ruled under a sort of state of emergency since the Enabling Act of March 1933 and the passing of arbitrary laws by decree. This did make Germany into a 'land of exception', but not of quite the same sort as the lands to the east. Again, there is an obvious cultural reason for the distinction: German *Kultur* was at the centre of the Nazi world-view, and destroying its expressions made no sense. There is a strong contrast here with the USSR at the time, where Russian culture was as much a target of the regime as was the traditional economic dispensation; the USSR is unique among the empires in the egalitarianism with which it visited destruction across all of its component peoples, as well as in the egalitarianism with which it theoretically regarded all peoples. In Germany, the Nazis could not go as far or as fast as they wished in removing pre-Nazi constitutional arrangements because of the desire to maintain legitimacy, if also because the efficient running of the state was at stake. (Germany of course already had the advanced economic and administrative infrastructure that the Soviet leadership was seeking to acquire in such a desperate, violent way.) This is not an argument for the inherent good of the German people or the pre-Nazi state, merely a comment on the complex web of rules and customs that a *Rechtsstaat*—a state based on the rule of law—throws up over time and which it is impossible to undo summarily. No matter the Nazi desires to revolutionize German society, Nazism found its most unbridled expression outside Germany.

If continuity as well as change was the order of the day for the German state, Nazism created enclaves across its territory that had a similarly exceptional legal status to that imposed on Poland and the USSR. Within Germany itself, certain places already had a special position before 1933, as they did in other countries: prisons and asylums were always areas where the hand of unmediated state power lay heavily; where the 'rights' of inmates were diminished according to their inability or unwillingness to discharge their social responsibilities; and where abuses took place away from the public gaze. Both became nodal points of Nazi political and racial persecution.

The Nazis themselves built a huge edifice of legal 'zones of exception' on the modest precedent of the 'protective custody' incarcerations of communists in the aftermath of the First World War. Concentration camps, company-run labour camps, Gestapo-run 'work-education' camps, special facilities to murder the 'handicapped'; all these places created closed universes of unbridled, unaccountable power, not only places where human beings could be abused in the extreme, but where their victimizers could discover something new about themselves. Every sovereign state ultimately reserves the right to create such zones in order to protect what it regards as its sovereign prerogatives: the US prison camp in Guantánamo Bay is a twenty-first-century example. The Nazis were unusual only in their level of violence. If it is meaningful to talk of anywhere where morality was inverted, it may be in some of these institutions. The most murderous of all were those 'zones of exception' within the 'lands of exception': ghettos, forest shooting sites, military combat theatres, anti-partisan 'free-fire zones', and extermination centres.

The places of exception conditioned behaviour at least as much as did attitudes to specific victim groups. This is true of any environment in which the rules are just different, and it helps explains why, when soldiers and policemen returned from the places of exception to a land of 'normality' (Germany) at war's end they reintegrated relatively easily. License dovetailed with overall ideological imperative, and killers often acted in these environments according to a general *Feindbild*, a vision of Germany's collective enemies, rather than a specific anti-Semitism.

It was in the Dachau system that the personnel of the Inspectorate of Concentration Camps (IKL) developed their own brutal ethos and *esprit de corps*. This began with violent initiation rituals and continued through the normalization of harsh physical 'punishment' of the inmates. Most of their victims in the early years of the regime were leftists, then 'asocials', before Jews were incarcerated in large numbers—though it is significant that the politically active Jews who were imprisoned earlier were subject to particular brutality. Several of the concentration camp guards took the spirit with them to the eastern front when they were put on combat duty in the Waffen-SS, and distinguished themselves by their extreme violence against Soviet POWs and civilians. To be sure, the early concentration camp SS were a self-selecting group in terms of their politics and personality, and it is noteworthy that when Wehrmacht soldiers were drafted as guards with the great expansion of the camp network late in the war, they tended to be more lenient towards inmates. Nevertheless, the camp environment itself was a radicalizing factor, as was shown by the difficulty the WVHA had in curbing the arbitrary violence of the IKL men when Himmler decided to increase the productive capacity of the prisoner population from 1942.[62] In the camps, the complete disparity of power between guards and victims was reinforced by the depersonalization of the victims through their pitiful uniforms and shaved heads. As they also became exhausted and emaciated, they started to conform to the regime's image of them as subhuman. There were parallels with the way that the squalor of the Polish ghettos was filmed for German public consumption and euthanasia propagandists deployed special lighting techniques to make asylum inmates appear grotesque.

The concentration camp SS moved between camps in Germany and Poland. Other links between eastern and western zones were provided by the T-4 killers, who shifted frictionlessly from murdering the handicapped in special German institutions to the Reinhard camps of Poland where they murdered Jews. Within the 'east', Wehrmacht troops, SS divisions, and police battalions alike were deployed interchangeably in anti-partisan actions and 'Jew-hunts' in the USSR, and there is little evidence that they behaved differently in either capacity. The Sonderkommando Lange likewise moved easily between victim groups in Russia and the Warthegau.

As the war drew on and German control over more territory was threatened, the distinction between the lands of exception and the more rule-bound world beyond became blurred. Learned behaviour in the east was imported to the west, in Waffen-SS massacres of western POWs, such as that of Americans at Malmédy during the Battle of the Bulge in December 1944, and in massacres of civilians, such as that at Oradour-sur-Glane in June 1944. But this does not just indicate a predictable German response to changed circumstances; habituated differences in behaviour were displayed even among the changing RSHA representation in occupied France. Those commanders of the SD–Security Police who had been stationed in France from early in the war had imbibed the relative moderation that characterized the occupation there. As resistance increased, other commanders arrived from Poland and the USSR, and their behaviour was markedly more radical simply as a result of their prior experiences in murder.[63]

Figure 11. Female SS auxiliaries on a fence being passed blueberries.

The Killing Act: Duty, Conformity, Brutalization, and Culture

Let us dwell on the east, however, the epicentre of genocide, where tens of thousands of Germans killed millions of human beings, men, women, and children, often at close range. The search for the relative roles played by different motivations takes us to two organizations involved directly in mass killing that issued murderous orders and conducted murderous policies but also drew on the German population irrespective of political affiliation, personal disposition, or professional ambition. One was the reserve Order Police, the other was the military.

Up to eighteen million people served in the Wehrmacht during the war, most in the army. In absolute terms, though not relative to its overall size, military participation was great in the final solution, the murder of Romanies, and 'pacification' campaigns in the USSR and the Balkans, as well as innumerable war crimes on the frontline. At the highest levels the army was 'coordinated' with Nazism by the time of the Second World War. But even without that factor the military was already a bastion of anti-bolshevism and revisionism. In war with the USSR, the army's geopolitical goals and commitment to ruthless 'security' measures were not dissimilar to Hitler's. Nevertheless, the debate over Wehrmacht complicity remains heated in German academic and public life because of the size and breadth of the military constituency, and the fact that it was a pre-Nazi institution with its own traditions and conceptions of honour.

The police forces' leaderships were also all Nazified by 1939, yet the manpower for the reserve Order Police was unremarkable in physical and ideological terms. The force comprised men who were either too old or unfit for military service, and were generally used for policing duties in occupied territory, including shooting massacres, ghetto round-ups, and guarding trains to extermination centres. The many who were too old were accordingly also politically socialized before the Nazi years, while, as draftees, they had not been exposed for as long as regular policemen to the Nazified-militarized ethos of the German police.

One key difference between army and Order Police was that the army was engaged in major military actions. Yet the army needs to be divided between frontline troops and rear guard units. The frontline troops were predominantly younger and had been socialized under Nazism and had thus disproportionately been in organizations like the Hitler Youth. These young men at the sharp end of war were the most obvious candidates for a sort of *interactive brutalization*, a reduced sensitivity to the infliction and suffering of violence because of exposure to both. Such was the situation from the late summer of 1941 as the war on the eastern front swiftly started to look less like a victory parade and more like the drawn-out conflict associated with the lost First World War. Soldiers who realized they were going to be in a foreign field for some time to come, and who were losing comrades with whom they had trained and bonded, started to develop a siege mentality. They increasingly lost inhibitions about acting at the moral level at which they perceived the enemy. The group transgression of norms even became a new bonding activity, often led by more experienced soldiers who had the wherewithal to survive longer than others, and who came to be a focus of identity in the unit, inducting new arrivals into extreme violence as a fact of life on the eastern front. Leadership in the sense of the attitude of the commanding officer was also clearly important in determining the murderousness of the men, who tended to coalesce around the example set to them and to develop similar reflexes.[64]

Rear army units and reserve troops were somewhat older. Though not identical in demographic profile to the reserve Order Police, they were nonetheless similar enough to be discussed together, particularly as their security functions mirrored the tasks of the Order Police more closely than the fighting functions of the frontliners. These troops were directly involved in genocide and 'pacification' functions outside major military operations on a significantly larger scale than the frontline troops. Clearly brutalization in these roles was not of the same sort as at the front, since these men did not generally experience anywhere near the same levels of loss and threat. If brutalization came, it was from the infliction of violence rather than its receipt. But to get to that level of *unilateral brutalization* they had first to perpetrate extreme violence in a pre-brutalized state.

Let us construct a hypothetical situation for the first killing experience of a reserve Order Policeman in order to identify key factors on the journey to becoming a seasoned killer. Let us select the most obviously morally indefensible act that policemen were asked to perform, the murder of an infant. Say that before enrolment our man was an 'average' 40 year old living in Hannover in 1939. It is highly unlikely that he would then, on the suggestion of his wife, have picked up his own shotgun, dragged a Jewish child off the streets, and shot his prisoner in his own backyard. Yet move on two years, during which time the man was enrolled in the police; substitute a forest clearing in the occupied USSR for the backyard, and a service rifle for the shotgun; enrol third parties to present the victim ready for execution; put the man in the company of other men doing the same thing as him; exchange the wife for a commanding officer, perhaps one leading by example; and history shows that in the vast majority of cases the result would be the creation of a killer.

Some of the differences between the two scenarios are obvious: the environment of an officially ordered task, with the trappings of state authority obviously present, and the job reduced to simple and impersonal basics. Other differences require more reflection: the conceptual time and space between the two scenarios would include the induction and training of the man in his police unit, the donning of a uniform of a state organization, some ideological education, growing acquaintance and bonding with the others who would participate in the unforeseen task. Then there would be lengthy travel to a foreign country, a 'state of exception' with an alien landscape and language, amongst peoples whom he probably considered culturally inferior and who profoundly resented their occupiers. Then there would be the specific, microcontext of travel to a killing place, a 'zone of exception', accompanied by short-term mental preparation and the physical manifestations of nervous anticipation. And all this while Germany was involved in the greatest war in its history; a time when feeble reservists were particularly keen to prove they could play their part. Who was *he* to question what his fellows and his state were doing? Who was he to leave his comrades with more people to kill than was their share because he failed to pull his weight? A sense of duty, obligation to his peers, reluctance to stand out from the crowd, shame, and adrenaline all combined to produce a situation in which the choice 'to do good or do evil' would have been an absurd simplification. The point is perhaps accentuated if we reflect that many killers started with shooting men of fighting age, who could plausibly be presented as potential threats, before 'graduating' onto women and children. Nevertheless, the most important aspect of the policeman's 'dilemma' here is that his victim is not in the centre of the picture but rather he himself (and in a much more pointed way than the more abstract dilemma confronting the officials of the Reichsbahn, organizing railway transports to the death camps): his fears, doubts, ambitions, and sense of self. This would certainly explain the abiding sense of self-pity that many killers exhibited when investigated after the war as they bemoaned having been put in that position.

Social psychological factors are very important. Simple peer pressure was sometimes at play, sometimes the factor technically known as 'pluralistic ignorance'. This is the phenomenon whereby the seeming acceptance of a situation as 'normal' by a group, caused by a general reluctance to speak up, causes every individual within the group to convince himself that it is indeed normal, even though he and one or more of his fellows may well not regard it as normal. The classic illustration would be where one man is more likely to stop to aid a stricken person in an otherwise empty street than if the street were full of people all indifferently walking by. Peer-group relations were also influenced by the presence of an authority figure.

Over time the relative significance of the psychological factors varied. Repeated participation in killing operations 'normalized' the act, such that pluralistic ignorance became entrenched, and the initial 'push' provided by more overt considerations of deference to authority and peer pressure diminished. Peer pressure became transformed into shared, exclusive experience, the basis of bonding. The initial moral barrier—assuming there was one—and the barrier of sensibility to killing had been overcome, or at least significantly diminished. The result was the 'cold-bloodedness' (or the appearance of it), or the situation known as brutalization, which might obtain over time in a minority of killers enjoying or seeming to enjoy their acts within their communities of violence. Indeed, part of the habituation process is to begin seeing the victims as less than human (or as real or potential threats), fitting targets for abuse and murder, as a sort of rationalization for the killer's acts present and past, in a way similar to the Hutus in Hatzfeld's study who instrumentalized hatred. In social psychology this phenomenon is known as cognitive dissonance. By this, one of its most important theorists means the internal conflict that appears when someone's actions contradict their self-image. In order to maintain the self-image, the action itself is justified. As the human distance between abusers and abused was artificially increased in this way we see the fulfilment of a parallel process, identified by Emmanuel Levinas, in which human vulnerability can in certain circumstances lead to sympathy, while in others it can promote victimization.[65] In turn, that psychological process explains why some of the greatest horrors at the killing sites were reserved for the most obviously vulnerable victims: children.

In other genocides, ostensible acts of sadism have been dissected with anthropological or social-psychological explanations that render them explicable without recourse to the language of ideology or deviance.[66] Indeed, each of the behavioural phenomena considered in these paragraphs has been traced in many other cultures and situations besides the Holocaust.[67] We may argue over precisely what weight to attribute social-psychological factors in situations of 'real-life' extremity which are impossible to replicate fully in experiments, but only if we assume that mid-twentieth-century Germans were uniquely unsusceptible to patterns affecting the rest of humankind can we ignore them. In order to prove ordinary Germans killed primarily because of their values, one would have to do the impossible and remove them from their places of exception, and from human power and social structures, thus hiving them off from the psychological processes that together are colloquially known as 'coping mechanisms'.

The implication is not, however, that values are unimportant, for just as it is impossible to isolate the human from the immediate social context, it is impossible to isolate 'him' from the values inculcated in 'him' over the longer term. Values were obviously central for those relatively few extreme characters who may be found in any society—those for whom the ethic of conviction over-rides all other considerations. Real sadists also need little explanation. But even for the remaining majority, it is simplistic to posit the question as 'situation *versus* belief', or the answer as 'context trumps character'. The immediate context of the killing did not just act upon reserve Order Policemen or rear-guard soldiers like some extraneous force, it played on cultural norms and tendencies prevalent in the society of which the men were a part and which was a part of them. One tendency concerned their relationship to their task as a responsibility; the other concerned the depiction of their victims.

The first cultural tendency involved the normative value of obedience—the idea of militaristic discipline, to whatever end, as an expression of an ethic of responsibility.[68] This is complicated since the laws of war, even as they were inscribed in the pocketbook of the German soldier, prescribed disobedience for orders that were clearly criminal: they set limits to the soldier's instrumental rationality by pointing to the illegitimacy of the order. Yet the waters had been muddied so much in legal terms by the claims about the USSR's outlaw status and by the emphasis in Germany about working to a new quasi-legal norm, the 'will of the Führer' (to whom the soldiers had personally sworn oaths), that it is scarcely surprising that enlisted German privates did not quote international legal standards back at their superiors. Moreover it is questionable in any case to what extent any soldiers anywhere would have protested during the crisis of war, because that was the very moment when their ethic of responsibility was most needed by the state.

In the Vietnam War, soldiers from the democratic USA, operating under localized orders that had not clearly emanated from the power centre, committed widespread atrocities. Those seeking to escape the task rarely refused outright; some injured themselves with their own weapons as a way out, illustrating the lengths to which soldiers are prepared to go to avoid being seen to evade their responsibilities.[69] Whatever the oddities of the Federal Republic of Germany's penal code, which led to derisory sentences, its leniency towards acts committed under orders reflected a cultural presumption about obedience. Even the Nuremberg courts, while not allowing obedience to orders as an outright defence, did allow it as an argument in mitigation of punishment. That was still insufficient for opponents of trial in Germany and among the Allies who, Churchill included, fulminated against prosecutions of senior soldiers who had endorsed the Wehrmacht's criminal orders. For such critics, the acts of dedicated servants within traditional state organizations were different to the acts of the SS.[70]

As to the second tendency, we have already seen that the notion of eastern Europe as a 'land of exception' was *culturally* determined, and so determined in much broader swathes of German society (and of other western societies[71]) than the Nazi or Wehrmacht leaderships. For German killers working within the eastern milieu, the concept that Jews and Slavs were somehow more legitimate targets than, say, the civilians of the Channel Islands, need not have resulted from a personally vehement anti-Slavism or anti-Semitism, but from an internalized understanding that Jews and Slavs were precisely the people the regime was likely to target and were by definition beyond the obligations of the killer as a German acting in an official capacity. I can put this no better than Moishe Postone, who concurs with the conclusion that conflating anti-Semitism as state policy with anti-Semitism as individual motivation is wrong, but adds that the same mistaken conflation 'also underlies the contrary argument—namely, the claim that anti-Semitism was *not* of central importance because Nazi anti-Jewish policies were not implemented in a linear fashion, and many individual Germans appear not to have been motivated by a particularly powerful hatred of the Jews.' The latter position, he explains, fails 'to distinguish ideology—as a general cultural framework, a horizon of meaning—from individual affect and motivation'.[72] In other words, the regime's racism and anti-Semitism, layered upon varying thicknesses of such prejudices in central Europe—and, for Germany's auxiliary killers, eastern Europe—had done some of the groundwork in preparing these men for the idea that Jews, Romanies, and Slavs might 'have' to be killed. After all, in every one of the instances of intergroup violence mentioned in these pages, the violence was committed against a backdrop of social cleavage and stereotype, and whether or not any given individual subscribed to the stereotypes, he or she was inevitably aware of the social significance of them.

To put these reflections in concrete terms, let us consider the arguments of Christian Gerlach, whose deep empirical work has done as much as anyone's to develop our understanding of the complex, multicausal nature of Nazi policy in eastern Europe. In his studies of the administration of Belarus, he has laid great stress on the 'cold' economic rationality which led labour administrators to condemn to death Jews who were 'useless eaters' incapable of work, and to reduce rations for Slavs and particularly Jews in a way that guaranteed they would die in the short or the medium terms. Now, we have already encountered the slipperiness of the term 'rationality': does Gerlach have in mind here Weberian instrumental or value rationality? If Gerlach's administrators were simply acting mechanically, like the bureaucratic automata of stereotype, then they contrived to divorce their allotted job completely from the circumstances under which they were asked to perform it: they ignored their immediate milieu, the land of exception, in which they were colonial overlords; they were blind to the murderous results of their policies, results which were occurring under their noses; and they belied their reputations, which Gerlach has himself been important in establishing, as proactive and voluntaristic perpetrators. So to be consistent Gerlach must mean his men were acting according to a value rationality based on enthusiastic awareness of Nazism's goals. That awareness in turn clearly entailed knowledge of the regime's assumptions about Jews and Slavs, and why it was 'legitimate' that they should die to provide for Germany; otherwise, there was no basis for the rationality in the 'cold economic rationality', no means of deciding who starved and who did not. Accordingly, whether or not these men would self-identify as racists, they were acting as racists because they had imbibed the regime's goals. To return to Proudhon's words at the head of this chapter: look not to the actors for the meaning of their acts, but 'to the acts themselves'.[73]

Conclusions

This discussion does not provide an exhaustive picture of the motivations of the perpetrators. Its intention has been to provide an alternative to the accounts of too many historians who have sought to identify the essence of the *génocidaire*, as if there were only one. It has sought to do this by breaking down the overly rigid divides between 'material interest', 'circumstantial pressure', an 'ethic of conviction', and an 'ethic of responsibility' in the explanation of perpetrator behaviour. Rather than putting individuals in one of four boxes, it is more helpful to imagine the four factors as stakes demarking a space of variable permutations over the surface of a field called culture. Other than for a few people, perpetration rarely sprang from a single, decisive prioritization of one factor over the others, but from a series of incremental and not always conscious movements across the space to a point where it could be more easily self-justified.

The fact that people of such demonstrably different characters and values as the RSHA leaders and some of the men of the reserve Order Police participated in genocide should give pause for anyone propounding a simple voluntaristic explanation for participation based on ideology. Personal disposition and conviction assuredly influences the zeal the perpetrator brings to the task and the status he or she enjoys within the perpetrator hierarchy; but the evidence of widespread participation in genocide across time and space could equally lend itself to the conclusion that it is difficult for anyone to resist involvement in certain socio-political contexts. The question then is not why individuals participated but how extensively and enthusiastically they participated.

A closer study of the Rwandan genocide, now a benchmark case in terms of popular participation, reveals vital sociological factors. The overall profile of Rwandan perpetrators corresponded approximately to the profile of adult Hutu males in the country as a whole,[74] but this conceals important distinctions. The enlistment of large numbers of demonstrably ordinary Hutus was key to the reach of the killing; yet, as in other genocides, there was scope for purely mechanical, 'minimal' contributions alongside creative or 'maximal' contributions. Examining perpetrators in that light sheds important light on the complexity of participation. Some Hutus volunteered out of greed or prejudice, though hatred was partly dependent upon the state of existing interethnic relations on the ground and the state of party political allegiance; most participated owing to some level of implicit or explicit coercion. In terms of the most enthusiastic killers, the core of non-military perpetrators was drawn from disaffected youths and youth militias—angry, unemployed young men killed proportionately more than others—and special 'self-defence' cells, established and militarized in every commune and village during the prior civil war.[75]

In every case mentioned earlier, state-sponsored mass killing was spearheaded by an ideologized core with strong party-political affiliations. This core fashioned new, militaristic vanguard organizations

bolted onto the pre-existing state structure and new, ideologically dedicated or opportunistic sub-elites to provide greater functional and
geographical integration. The penetration of key administrative positions and the creation of violent, activist organizations with relatively
high proportions of ideologically committed members deployed in areas
transcending traditional political-administrative boundaries, accelerated
the realignment of the rest of the state structure. These measures
indicated to all surviving functional and social elites where lay the
future—and thus material advantage ranging from financial enrichment to career advancement to security of life and limb. This schema
does not preclude complementary 'bottom-up' interpretations: while
each new regime succeeded in its penetration, the fact each had to
deploy differing levels of coercion was related not just to its time in
power, but also to the varying levels of legitimacy accorded to it by
popular and professional identification with its basic agenda. Only in
the Nazi case did the regime come to power constitutionally, and while
the Soviet regime exceeded Nazism in longevity, it only acquired a comparable legitimacy after the 'great fatherland war' (the Second World
War), during which it played increasingly on popular patriotism rather
than the people's questionable loyalty to the communist project.[76]

In all of the cases, vanguard organizations had to rely on other
perpetrators with different balances of commitment and motivation. In
the final solution, by the same token that SS and party offices would
not have needed to provide the policy lead if a general murderous
consensus existed, the genocide would not have been what it was
without the participation of pre-Nazi organs of the German state or
the bureaucracies in allied or satellite countries. A range of positive and
negative incentives were on offer to increase the capacity of the overall
organization by motivating agencies and individuals in both of what
today we would call the public and private sectors.

In every case, different agents worked towards the new governing
norm, whether out of shared values, fear, licence, careerism, greed,
sadism, weakness, or, more realistically, a combination of more than
one of these. Concluding on the precise significance of any given one
is difficult because of the basic heterogeneity of human motivation.
Instrumental rationality in its 'purest' form is nothing but a modern

conceit, for it implies untenably that actions can be divorced from the 'person' of the actor—his environment and sensibility.[77] Nevertheless 'just doing the job' had different connotations for different actors by definition of the different jobs they were required to do, from the Reich railway authorities scheduling trains at a distance in Berlin to the SS and police units in the killing fields of Ukraine.

In the killing fields, leaving aside the committed *génocidaires*, the question of whether a given German had followed orders out of an ethic of responsibility or duress became almost impossible to answer. Duress—or even 'putative duress', meaning fear of punishment even if not objectively justified—was tainted as an explanation by its use as a defence in postwar courts. There is a third possibility between the two. While it was legally more advantageous after the act for some killers to claim obedience to orders than to confess person-al enthusiasm for shooting Jews, it may also have been true during the act for killers such as our hypothetical policeman that, given the cultural emphasis on discipline, the very fact of 'higher orders' provided a welcome opportunity for abrogation of personal respons-ibility, at least in initial killing actions, before murderous socialization was complete.[78] This initial surrender was perhaps eased by the per-ception that it would be understood by others as justifiable in the circumstances.[79] I can conceive of no more tragic example of what the existentialist philosopher Søren Kierkegaard called man's fear of being free.[80]

The equivalent psychological escape route for bureaucrats working in large administrative structures distant from the killing fields was to persuade themselves—as they certainly would portray themselves if ever put on trial—that they were simply small, interchangeable cogs in a large, unstoppable machine, or that by remaining at their desks they prevented someone worse taking their place, or even that their continued tenure could mitigate the worst excesses of the machine. Self-serving and misleading though such arguments generally are, this should not obscure their real appeal during the act, *in lieu* of admitting moral cowardice or over-riding self-interest, for administrators uncommitted to genocide but equally unprepared to make personal sacrifices by resignation or meaningful protest.

In different ways, organizational power structures everywhere shaped, amplified, and inhibited agency. This is why they continue to exist. Yet the organizations were themselves composed of humans acting in accordance with values, beliefs, and interests, each of which varied according to time and place. 'Structure', agency, and the acculturated person were brought together within these microcosmic communities.

PART IV CIVILIZATION AND THE HOLOCAUST

CHAPTER 8
LOCATING GENOCIDE IN THE HUMAN PAST

Confronting the Holocaust as we now understand it was not on the agenda of Europe in 1945. In liberated, defeated, and victorious states alike the emphasis was on the reinforcement of national identities and the creation of convenient narratives of the war. The primary legal reckoning with Nazism did not really redress the balance towards examination of the Holocaust. In some ways, the Nuremberg trials reinforced the nation-state view of minorities and the strategic priorities of the managers of the international system. The major goal of Nuremberg was to outlaw the grand destabilizing factor in international relations—aggressive war, at least as it was pursued by enemies of the hegemonic powers in their new postwar constellation. The prosecution of Japanese politicians and diplomats for aggressive warfare in southeast Asia against a backdrop of long-standing and violent Western imperialism there, and at a time when Europe was busily re-establishing its regional influence, revealed either hypocrisy or a distinct lack of self-awareness. The prosecution of crimes against humanity was a subordinate concern. Sovereign states were left much latitude in dealing with 'troublesome' minorities; indeed, at precisely that time, the most obviously troublesome minorities—the ethnic Germans of east-central Europe—were being bodily removed as another plank in the strategy of reducing the risk of future destabilization.

The struggle of each European society to reconcile the experience of war or subjection or collaboration or perpetration with the needs of cohesive identity for the future was swiftly complicated by the Cold War redivision of the continent. The role of the new ideological conflict does not support generalizations about Eastern bloc distortion of memory versus more 'authentic' Western confrontation with the past. The record of genocide perpetrated by Nazi Germany and its accomplices was a wild card in the (re)formation of identity and the re-establishment of stability and sovereignty. It was played selectively, if at all, by everyone. Crimes against diaspora communities like Jews and Romanies were especially vulnerable to elision when the emphasis was on the restoration of state boundaries and monolithic national or class-based identities. Nevertheless, and paradoxical as it sounds, the building blocks were in place for most interpretations of Nazism and even of the Holocaust that would govern historiographical debate until the present.

Sometimes the building blocks were created almost accidentally, by default, as ways of avoiding responsibility. One of Germany's foremost historians, Friedrich Meinecke, wrote in 1947 that Nazism was one of the products of a quintessentially modern 'utilitarian spirit'.[1] With this analysis, which was really a means of alleviating Germany's guilt by reference to a more universal phenomenon, he touched on an idea—the dark potentiality of Europe's post-Enlightenment modernity—being developed from the other side of the political spectrum, by the members of the Frankfurt School of Social Theory and the philosopher Hannah Arendt.[2] Still more radical critiques were in incubation, because the war and its horrors were a formative experience for a group of cultural theorists and philosophers who would come to be known as postmodernists, including Levinas and Jacques Derrida.[3] It is perhaps no accident that some of these critics were Jewish as well as leftist, since their status as potential victims of Nazism meant they had nothing to hide in seeking to explain it.

The Left–Right political divide would become more important in the reckoning with the past from the 1960s, in the atmosphere of student revolution and campaigns for openness by a generation that was not personally involved in the war. Conversely, the small number of Germans dedicated to genuine self-examination in the immediate postwar years were heterogeneous in philosophy. The journal *Frankfurter Hefte*, edited by Catholic conservatives, stands out alongside Karl Jaspers' *The Guilt Question* as a representative of the few intellectually frank engagements with the different qualities and sources of German responsibility. Further to the left, in the early years of the Federal Republic of Germany, only a number of committed socialist activists and communist party supporters—a very small minority of the West German public—were opposed to the prevailing doctrine of 'drawing a line under the past', or at least the harm Germany had inflicted, if not that it had suffered. Even the Social Democrats accepted the line as the route to electoral success but also because many came from a milieu which had spent the war years trying to persuade the Allied powers of the existence of 'the other Germany' and in so doing had both played up the extent of Nazi persecution of other Germans vis-à-vis that of Jews, and played down the complicity of the German army in Nazi crimes.[4]

Later in the century, conservative historians also stressed the non-Nazi element in German society, though rarely the left-wing opposition to Nazism. Once they overcame an early belief that the plotters were traitors, they focused particularly on the July 1944 bomb plot on Hitler's life, and the military and clerical opposition, as an extension of the 'other Germany', however unrepresentative it was of the accommodation of Nazism by most of the German elites.[5] The 'other Germany' argument did not have the same content as Meinecke's 'modernity' argument but it did have the same goal: to depict Nazism as inauthentically German. Here the culprit was something like the 'totalitarian' system.

An important early scholarly foray into the history of the Holocaust itself was made by the British Jewish art historian Gerald Reitlinger, a man driven by the impact the murder of European Jewry had on his sensibilities.[6] Elsewhere, a large series of testimonies of the Holocaust were being gathered at what was to become the major Israeli documentation centre: Yad Vashem. There was also more engagement with the Holocaust than has generally been acknowledged at the level of popular culture, in novels and televisual productions.[7] The most sophisticated early history of the Holocaust was that by Léon Poliakov. His book's title, *Bréviaire de la Haine—Harvest of Hatred*—confirmed his enduring concern with the history of anti-Semitism. Unlike Reitlinger and some of his successors, however, Poliakov was concerned with the other forms of exclusionary thought that developed in the nineteenth century and provided a context for the development of Nazi anti-Semitism as well as the murder of other victim groups.[8] Moreover, he did not see genocide as a simple, logical outcome of 'hatred'. In his broader under-standing of context and in his divergence from what would become known as the 'intentionalist' vision of the Holocaust—one grounded in the assumption of a consistent Hitlerian desire for genocide well before the killing began—Poliakov established a series of contexts that would sometimes be overlooked in the decades to come.

If it was not a matter of no one *talking* about the Holocaust in the postwar years, it certainly was a matter of few *listening*, and certainly few 'mainstream' historians, whether because of other priorities or a closing of ears. The first surveys of the war paid barely any attention to the final solution, as a glance at Basil Liddell-Hart's *The Other Side of the Hill* shows; nor did the self-serving memoirs of German military commanders. David Thomson's *Europe since Napoleon*, the most popular general history for a British audience in the 1960s, does not mention the Holocaust at all.[9] Raul Hilberg's massive, seminal study of the final solution, *The Destruction of the European Jews,* struggled to get into print. It eventually appeared, in 1961, with a small publisher, Quadrangle. Even Jaspers and the *Frankfurter Hefte* shared with Meinecke the focus on 'the German catastrophe': in their overwhelming concern with German guilt, they rarely examined what Germany had actually done in terms of concrete crimes. Any substantial discussion of mass murder of non-Germans is absent from their pages.[10] It is only in the past two decades that the scholarship on the Holocaust has merged on a large scale with the scholarship on Nazi Germany and on the course of the war. That is part cause, more effect, of a more general interest in the Holocaust and genocide in the mainstream of historical research and in the wider public sphere in the western world.

In this concluding chapter, the scholarship is dealt with in general terms. Every book or article is more nuanced than will appear here, for it is in the nature of an exercise in historiographical writing to simplify.[11] Each of the traditions I address has competing accounts within it, some of which are written in the best faith, some of which may be characterized as apologetic. Some of the finest analyses of Nazism and the Holocaust appear only in footnotes, alongside more flimsy and tendentious explanations. The only way to experience the richness of the former and to confirm or undermine my criticism of the latter is to read the works themselves.

The Focus on the German State

Owing to the documentation that they gathered and ordered, the Nuremberg trials were a great help to what we might call 'institutionalist' students of the Third Reich: those compiling deep empirical accounts of it, its institutions, and its policies. The Nuremberg documentation also substantiated the theories with which the American-led Nuremberg prosecution tried to expose the workings of the Nazi state. Telford Taylor, chief-of-counsel at the Nuremberg subsequent proceedings—the twelve successor trials to the first and best-known Nuremberg trial—once attributed the blame for the catastrophe of the Second World War to 'the unholy trinity of Nazism, militarism and economic imperialism'.[12] More clearly than was the case for the first Nuremberg trial, with its unavoidable concentration on individuals and organizations, Taylor intended to focus upon structures that long predated 1933, as well as the ideology that drove the Hitler regime.

The Nuremberg prosecutors themselves had extant interpretations of German state criminality to refer to. The German-Jewish émigré Franz Neumann had written *Behemoth* during the war for the US Office of Strategic Services. It was a remarkable study considering the limited source materials on which it had to be based. It analysed the regime as based on four pillars: the Nazi party and its arms such as the SS, the army, German bureaucracy, and industry.[13] Neumann's ideas influenced Hilberg and the classification of the mass of Nuremberg documentation. Indeed, Taylor's triumvirate of Nazism, militarism, and economic imperialism illustrates the shared conception, allowing that the German state bureaucracy was complicit in both militarism and economic imperialism.

While Taylor meant the villains in his triptych to be examined together, it was more convenient for many politicians and intellectuals to pick on one and absolve the other two. His targets boil down to 'the traditions of the German state', 'Nazism', and 'big business'. The final villain looks the least likely culprit from a contemporary Western perspective. This is because blaming big business increasingly became the preserve of the communist bloc during the Cold War, and the subject of often highly ideologized polemics in the vein of Marxist–Leninist orthodoxy. The idea had been established well before the war about the role of monopoly capitalism in forcing imperial expansion as the capitalist system came under increasing pressure because of its internal contradictions. More often than not in this Marxist conception, Jews as victims were subsumed under the general category of citizens of the country in which they lived.

More solid, thoughtful, and nuanced scholarship was sometimes concealed between introductions and conclusions paying tribute to the party line—the 'sandwich principle'—and some war crimes trials in eastern Europe did address Nazi Jewish policy in some detail. Moreover, scholars from behind the Iron Curtain shed important early light on the context for the final solution of wider Nazi population policy, particularly the *Generalplan Ost*, as was only to be expected given the vast scale of wartime losses among the Soviet population as a whole.[14] Nevertheless, the thought that analysis from the Eastern bloc might be able to cast any light on the European crisis was lost amid the political battle in which East German authorities suggested that their state had done away with Nazism when they did away with capitalism, and pointed the finger at the capitalist West as the true heir to Nazism. In the early Cold War environment, Taylor's staff came under pressure—which they resisted—not to put industrialists on trial. The difficulties of establishing 'structural responsibility' in the legal forum meant that this was the least successful part of the subsequent Nuremberg programme. We still await an analysis that fully integrates the role of deep, pre-Nazi economic structures with the political history of the Nazi drive for expansion and exploitation, though Adam Tooze's *The Wages of Destruction* admirably relates economics to politics and genocide during the Nazi period itself, with some debts along the way to the work of Christian Gerlach.[15]

Taylor's other two suspects are more familiar. 'German traditions' and 'Nazism' meant either a culpable national culture or a type of political system that was theoretically transferable. Respectively, these interpretations fed into the differing theories of Germany's *Sonderweg* (or 'special path') and of 'totalitarianism'.

The idea that Germany was victim of a 'totalitarian' system imposed upon it had an obvious attraction for the German people and its new political leaders. Playing on the supposedly intrinsic connection between Christianity and 'occidental' culture was not just a gambit to gain the approval of the Anglo-Americans.[16] Like the other side of the coin, anti-Sovietism, it provided some common ground for former Nazi supporters and many opponents of the Hitler regime within and also beyond Germany because it simultaneously, if ambiguously, conflated 'anti-Christian', 'totalitarian' but aberrant Nazism with despiritualized Bolshevism, portraying Germany's 'Christian essence' as the real victim while retrospectively part-justifying Nazi anti-communism. Meinecke again, mentioning no victim group, averred that 'in the gas chambers of the concentration camps the last breath of Christian-occidental civilization and humanity finally expired'.[17] Anti-communism itself remained laden with degrees of anti-Slav racism: even concentration camp survivor Ernst Wiechert invoked 'the Asiatic methods' of the Gestapo, which had 'poured more blood and tears over the German people than a century of occidental history could have induced'.[18]

The notion that Germany's virtue could be restored simply by removing the parasite of Nazism increasingly appealed to the Western Allies as they sought to reintegrate West Germany into the Western alliance. Yet it also fed a need to believe that a fellow Western culture had not been completely debased. It was embraced by the Church of England, not as a Cold War convenience, but out of the conviction established since 1933 that a fundamental antipathy to Christianity was the primary characteristic of Nazism, like that of Nazism's twin totalitarian brother to the east.[19]

The totalitarianism thesis enjoyed its heyday in the 1950s and 1960s but has had periodic resurgences that correspond roughly with the varying political utility of the idea.[20] Its early Cold War use was mirrored during the re-escalation of East–West tensions during the 1980s, notably when Ronald Reagan gave a speech at the Bitburg cemetery and described those buried in it, including soldiers and Waffen-SS men, as victims of the totalitarian regime just as much as the concentration camp inmates. By this time, as a result of an increased scholarly focus (see below) and perhaps particularly because of the 1978 television miniseries *Holocaust*, which attracted huge American and German audiences, it was no longer possible not to talk about the Holocaust. Nevertheless, some of the techniques honed during and immediately after the Nazi period were deployed by the right-wingers in what became known as the 'historians' debate' (*Historikerstreit*) of 1985–8. The leading conservative protagonist, Ernst Nolte, contended that Nazism was a sort of cultural reaction to Bolshevism, and Auschwitz a Western response to the Gulag. The idea that Nazism and its most notorious product were effectively mirror images of pre-existing political forms and crimes was self-evidently designed to undermine the notion that either were 'unprecedented', thereby removing the special historical burden of guilt on its people. Given the traditional reluctance of scholars to look outside Europe in debates such as these, it is a good indicator of the extent of Nolte's determination that he also reached for the example of the Cambodian genocide as another incident of murderous terror inflicted on its people by a 'totalitarian' regime.[21]

Adherents of the totalitarianism thesis were given encouragement even as the Cold War ended. Encouragement came with the rise of a new political enemy completing the unholy trinity of mortal historical enemies of 'Western values' alongside fascism and communism—those strands of fundamentalist Islam willing to embrace terrorism. The new totalitarianism scholarship suffers from similar flaws to the earlier totalitarianism thinking in its failure to emphasize the very significant differences as well as the commonalities between its targets. In fact the exclusive comparative focus on radical Islam is even more misplaced, because the most obvious factor binding Nazi Germany and Soviet Russia, for instance, was what looked from the outside like extreme statism. The sort of Islam on which the new totalitarian theorists focus is notable for being an idea without a state framework through which to express itself, notwithstanding the anti-Semitism of Iran's president Ahmadinejad.[22]

Like the 'totalitarian' explanation, the idea of Germany's 'special path' predated the Second World War. *Sonderweg* explanations do not primarily or even directly address the Nazi period, but their relevance to it is clear. They have their origins in explanations of German political behaviour since unification. The argument concerns the alleged peculiarity of German development as an industrial country that had not developed a liberal political culture, where the progressive role of the middle classes had been restricted to the economic sphere as part of a tacit agreement with traditional landowner elites, including the influential military whose officer class was drawn from landowning circles. Arriviste industrialists within the system sided with the aristocracy against the working classes to restrict the power of organized labour. Aggressive nationalism and economic and territorial imperialism were used not only to expand the market and resource base of the industrial system but to redirect the energies of the classes whose interests were not fully represented in parliament. The picture, then, was of an economically modern but politically retrograde system that sought deliberately to live in the past.

For non-Germans, the sort of thinking behind the *Sonderweg* theory was politically convenient. The idea that a German phenomenon —Nazism—can provide a useful counterpoint to Anglo-Saxon liberalism, especially bearing in mind that the Anglo-Americans fought Germany in war (twice in a generation), helps explain the contemporary eagerness of Britain and the USA to embrace the Holocaust in its memorial culture.[23] Historically, too, the picture had been a convenient one for Germany's competitor states to paint while imperial competition was still in progress. While Britain or post-revolutionary France could link their empire with their own liberal domestic traditions, which was the logic of the 'civilizing mission', Germany's quest for empire and influence was rendered illegitimate. The whole notion of a special path was implicitly comparative, or, rather, contrastive: the very idea of a German *Sonderweg* relied upon some spurious normative standard. Seizing, as some scholars have done, on the supposed contradiction between Nazi Germany's technical modernity and its reference to a mythologized past fails to comprehend what was outlined in the first chapter of this book: that romantic nationalisms looking 'backwards' to some imagined community, as all nationalisms do to some degree, are themselves a product of modernity and legitimations for the modern nation-state in the present and the future.[24]

The best *Sonderweg* scholarship, like the best scholarship in any interpretative tradition, certainly throws important light on aspects of modern German history. The most sophisticated accounts of Germany's special path emerged from the 1960s onwards from the German Left.[25] This is related to the belated determination of the German Left not to be seen to excuse national responsibility for Nazism by suggesting it was an alien imposition—an admonition for Germany to take responsibility for its actions in the way it did not in the late 1940s and 1950s. It also explains why the leftists in the Historikerstreit were the ones to endorse the idea of the uniqueness of the Holocaust, creating an interesting mirror image with the rest of the world, wherein it tends to be conservatives who stress the uniqueness of the Holocaust (and Nazism) and leftists who seek to draw parallels. Leftist philosophers and social scientists like Jürgen Habermas and Ralf Dahrendorf suggested that Germany needed to make its political culture more Western, ignoring the many crimes of which the more 'civilized' countries were guilty in more obscure parts of the world than eastern Europe.[26] Indeed, much historical debate from the 1960s to the 1980s on Europe's earlier catastrophe was conducted seemingly oblivious to the human cost that European 'decolonization' and its legacies were then exacting in Africa and southeast Asia.

Most striking about so much of the scholarship for and against the *Sonderweg* was the absence of the crimes in which it culminated. In this sense the scholarship mirrored the perspectives of Jaspers and the *Frankfurter Hefte* in the immediate postwar period. Even the closest cognate area to the Holocaust, the study of Nazi Germany itself, flourished from the 1960s onwards with precious little reference to Nazi genocide.[27] The most sustained scholarly examination in any major German book of the 1960s was the large section on Nazi Jewish policy by Helmut Krausnick in the *Anatomy of the SS State*. That volume only came into being and prominence because the four authors were asked to write their expert opinions for the court that tried a number of Auschwitz staff in 1963–5.[28] But the title of that book itself suggested the preoccupation, which would only gather in strength into the 1970s, with the structures of Nazi rule and the German state. Administration, governance, socio-economic change, foreign policy, the penetration of the established hierarchies, and Nazi friction and accommodation with existing social elites and other social classes: these were the order of the day for most scholars of the period.

A tendency has developed to suggest that this trend was a deliberate, politically motivated avoidance of what we now know as the Holocaust.[29] Certainly the self-exculpatory responses of the German people to the Auschwitz trial (as to the Nuremberg trial), and the significant number of former Nazis in the judiciary, show that there were enduring social and bureaucratic pressures against a full reckoning with the Nazi past.[30] And yet the fact that so many intellectuals, including some who were not of the age of majority in the Nazi period, were focusing on similar issues suggests an integrity in the desire to work out simply what had gone wrong with Germany as the best way of explaining what it had then done. Moreover, at a time when the Holocaust was not at the centre of attention anywhere outside Israel, even the conception of what Germany had done centred as much on war and imperial expansion (the continuous themes of Germany's twentieth century) as genocide. This was actually the introspective agenda that the Nuremberg trials and de-Nazification had set. Besides, the same scholarly trajectory was being followed not just by German scholars but by American and British scholars who clearly had no investment in obfuscation of genocide, and who were interested in many of the same 'institutionalist'-type questions as their German colleagues, if also with an abiding obsession about who voted for Hitler in the first place.[31] Even Hilberg's masterpiece was concerned with 'the storm that caused the wreckage' of genocide rather than 'the wreckage' itself.[32]

The Return to Ideas and to the Phenomenon Itself

Though the 'intentionalist–functionalist' debate was only given its name at the end of the 1970s, it began around a decade earlier. From the inception of the limited German scholarly engagement with the final solution in the late 1960s a classic argument was in process about the role of social structure versus human intention and agency in history, analogous on a larger scale to the later debate over the relationship between social pressures and individual conviction among the killers facilitating the final solution. The main German protagonists were Helmut Krausnick and Andreas Hillgruber on the side of a more Hitler-centric, determinist analysis, and Karl Schleunes, Uwe Adam, Martin Broszat, and later Hans Mommsen on the other side. As much as anything, the scholarship of the latter group was a rejection of a tendency towards intellectual history in Western historiography, and a continued emphasis on social forces rather than ideas in shaping state policy. Though Mommsen and Broszat have particularly, and sometimes unfairly, been criticized for downplaying the significance of anti-Semitism as a motivating factor in the Holocaust, the ramifications of their work were in some ways even more disturbing because they pointed the way to what has now become a commonplace in the historiography—the important role of 'non-Nazi' elites, and a simultaneous de-emphasis on terror and coercion and re-emphasis on cooperation and interests.[33]

The functionalists' response to the early German intentionalists in turn met with a reassertion of the intentionalists' case. Historians such as Lucy Dawidowicz, Gerald Fleming, Eberhard Jäckel, and Yehuda Bauer, all writing between the mid-1970s and mid-1980s, placed the explanatory emphasis firmly on anti-Semitic ideology and the role of Hitler and his chief lieutenants.[34] Of these scholars, Bauer and Dawidowicz at least were also keen to put Jews back into the picture as well as the Nazi decision-makers, in a way that fitted Israeli and diaspora historiographical tradition. They thereby paved the way for Saul Friedländer, who later wrote the most persuasive account in the anti-Semitism-centric tradition, embedded in deep institutionalist knowledge of the Nazi state as well as of the sources bequeathed by the victims.[35]

Also new to historical scholarship with the intentionalist wave of the 1970s–80s, and inherited by the most simplistic of all such accounts, Daniel Goldhagen's *Hitler's Willing Executioners* (1996), was the idea that the Holocaust was 'unique'. With a stress on the exceptional nature of Hitler's Jew-hatred, and because of their downplaying of broader, cross-cutting contexts, the intentionalists were reluctant to examine the Holocaust on a continuum of other genocides, even other Nazi genocides. Dawidowicz stated the case plainly in 1981 in an article entitled 'The Holocaust was Unique in Intent, Scope and Effect'.[36]

Bauer's earlier writings reached similar conclusions, as did the finest historiographer of the Holocaust, Michael Marrus.[37]

The rhetoric of uniqueness stemmed partly from a determination to draw attention to a subject that had remained marginal in the postwar decades, but the examination of the Holocaust as lived experience shaped perspectives too. Beyond doubting the explanatory value of their opponents' arguments, the intentionalists' position was based on a sense that structuralist interpretations simply did not do justice to the magnitude of what is known in Hebrew as the *Shoah*, the catastrophe. To the extent that this sense was only an underdeveloped assumption in many of their writings, we may call it a moral sense only. It was also clearly shaped by identity politics, meaning the need to give a special significance to the past suffering of Jews in the name of present communal identity.[38]

One of the roots of the uniqueness claim lay in Jewish theology. From the 1960s, Richard Rubinstein, followed by the likes of Emil Fackenheim, claimed that the magnitude of the Holocaust made it a uniquely difficult challenge to traditional justifications of god and his special relationship to the Jews.[39] The claim, it should be noted, was contested: theologians had long had to square centuries of discrimination, interspersed with murderous pogroms, with the supposed status of the Jews as chosen people. Besides, whether or not the Holocaust actually was a qualitatively different challenge, it could not be denied that pre-Holocaust intellectuals had used the language of uniqueness to address their own periods and crises.[40]

Other scholars have developed the uniqueness claim into a philosophical proposition. Steven Katz adopted a case-by-case study of other instances of mass killing in history to establish that the Holocaust 'is phenomenologically unique'. Katz seized upon the 'Nazi racial imperative that *all* Jews must die, and that they must die here and now'.[41] Moishe Postone and Dan Diner effectively adopted the same approach, though without Katz's extensive comparative analysis. Their approach entailed viewing the final solution from the perspective of the completed event, which meant examining it partly outside the surrounding contexts within which it developed, and contrasting it at its most expansive with other genocides. Postone wrote that 'the Jews were not murdered for any "extrinsic" goal. Their extermination was not only to have been total, but apparently was its own goal—extermination for the sake of extermination—a goal that acquired absolute priority.' Functionalist interpretations and interpretations emphasizing aspects of Nazi ideology other than anti-Semitism 'cannot really explain the attempted extermination of *all* Jews *everywhere* (from Norway to Rhodes)'. He also stated that such interpretations 'take for granted what has to be explained—that a program of extermination could even become thinkable'. Those interpretations 'help illuminate how that program was and could have been executed, but do not explain the program itself'.[42]

The 'uniqueness' claim is thus based on (1) the absence of any real German-Jewish dynamic that can from our perspective be seen as the remotest justification—the sense that genocide was the product of a pure, ideological utopianism; and (2) the unusual totality of the Nazis' murderous intentions towards Jews and the 'absolute prioritization' of the relentlessness pursuit of their victims. The propositions are related because the abstract 'Jew' was by definition a ubiquitous enemy who by the logic of the ideology had to be pursued everywhere.

Let us first consider proposition (2). While the scale, determination, and intensity of the Nazi pursuit of Jews across Europe is exceptional even within the annals of genocide, we have seen earlier in this book that the murder was not perpetrated mindless of the economic, political, or logistical cost, and that up to the last stage, it was paralleled by less destructive forms of ethnopolitics against other groups. We have also seen that the idea that Hitler (and Himmler) actively sought to murder every last Jew everywhere is open to question. It is far from clear that even Hitler himself was overly concerned with the fate of the Jews of Norway or Rhodes. As to Postone's related differentiation of the idea (what he calls a 'program') of genocide from its implementation, if this book has sought to show anything, it is the impossibility of making such a distinction. The dynamics and personnel of the administrative machinery of the Third Reich were intrinsic to the ongoing development of Jewish policy. The idea evolved with the policy. Indeed, the very extremity of policy—the pursuit of Europe's Jews even outside the Nazi empire—that Postone adduces as evidence of the all-encompassing nature of the idea was at least as much as anything else a result of the organizational and power structure of the Reich, and more specifically the SS. The agenda of the RSHA illustrates this point clearly. While Postone insightfully and correctly brings the functionalists' attention to the significance of anti-Semitism as 'a general cultural framework, a horizon of meaning', this does not mean that everything that happened to Europe's Jews was a logical expression of that anti-Semitic framework. There was a contingent element to the expansion of genocide all through the war, just as there was to its frustration in places like Denmark and Bulgaria. Murderous intent was not embodied in one 'will' so much as in a system. The system gave the pursuit of murder its vigour and potency but also—without one single, unitary drive—its protean nature.

Regarding proposition (1) it is true that, say, the Pakistani state had a political problem in East Pakistan in 1971, whereas the Jewish problem existed only in Hitler's head (and the heads of many non-Germans too). Yet the distinction between 'real' and 'imagined' political dynamics as motives is unsatisfactory, because in both cases genocide could only be conceived in response to the 'problem' on the presumption that the victim groups as a whole were a danger on the grounds of their identity, rather than anything they had actually done. In both cases, the victim group—men, women, and children—could be killed precisely because of the great gulf in power separating them from their murderers in actuality.

Ultimately, uniqueness is not susceptible to proof by agreed means of testing. As A. Dirk Moses puts it, 'whether the similarities [between the Holocaust and other genocides] are more significant than the differences is ultimately a political and philosophical, rather than a historical question. . . . Uniqueness is not a category for historical research; it is a religious or metaphysical category.'[43] But it is possible to go further still. The claim of uniqueness must mean 'unique from any perspective', European, modern, 'eastern', past or future. Yet since some of these perspectives have not been sought out (all of the arguments to uniqueness stem from Western intellectual traditions) and some are impossible to know (who can tell what future scholars will think about the Holocaust?), the only claim could be that 'the Holocaust is unique from our perspective', which is a relativist argument that undermines itself: 'relatively unique' is not what the theorists of uniqueness mean.

The truth is that most other genocides have been of insufficient interest to Western intellectuals for them to ponder their metaphysical dimensions in the way the Holocaust has been pondered. This tells us a lot about why the Holocaust is held to be such a challenge for Western traditions of thought. Let me be clear: something of the dimensions of the final solution *should* prompt huge and sustained philosophical self-reflection, but it is the 'surprise' that registers in so much of the scholarship that is telling, since Europe had not only witnessed other genocides, it had inflicted them on its colonial peripheries well before the continent erupted at its own core in the twentieth century. Zygmunt Bauman's *Modernity and the Holocaust*, for instance, raises important questions about the exclusionary potential of 'rationalized' modern societies.[44] His conclusion that genocide (in this case a genocide of the dimensions of the Holocaust) is a 'legitimate resident in the house of modernity' is correct, but the fact remains that it took the Holocaust to give force to this truth for him as for many others, when, had 'the West' displayed any self-reflection about its capacity for rationalized destruction, this was already plain to see. Thus, even in this attempt at contextualizing the Holocaust within broader patterns of human development, it is still, paradoxically, de facto attributed a special position. We can thus see that, while the claim to uniqueness can be related to Jewish identity politics, it can also be another instance of Western-centrism. It fits into a long tradition of the West's attempts to universalize its own values—and uniqueness in the totalistic sense it is meant must be a demand for universal significance. Those very claims to universalism have themselves been at the heart of Europe's violent interaction with the rest of the world.[45]

When the uniqueness debate has entered the scholarship of comparative genocide, it has done so at the same level of identity politics from which the uniqueness claims first emerged, in the sense of claiming that other genocides were 'like' the Holocaust, or of fitting the Holocaust completely into one or other general paradigm of genocide. This is partly due to the universalistic implications of uniqueness outlined in the previous paragraph. Indeed, the relationship of the study of genocide outside the West (particularly in the European colonies) to the study of the Holocaust can sometimes be analogous to the relationship between the study of non-Western history and Western history more generally, with students of the former being particularly sensitive to claims to universality and primacy made by some of the students of the latter, precisely because of the historical association of such claims with imperialistic tendencies. It should go without saying that neither the end of establishing complete co-identification of cases nor the uniqueness position is the point of comparative history as generally understood, which is concerned equally with similarities and differences. The study of the Holocaust should be no different to the study of any given genocide in terms of understanding the balance between general and specific features.

As far as the strictly historical scholarship is concerned, the uniqueness 'debate' has lost most of its steam. Yet the idea of uniqueness, and thereby universal significance, is important to the establishment of various Holocaust memorial days and museum exhibitions across the Western world. If there is a 'Holocaust industry', these areas of didactics and commemoration are its workshops and uniqueness one of its most important raw materials. It is no accident that assailants of that 'industry' have directed much of their energy at the uniqueness claim.[46]

Moreover, other disciplines have clung to the significance of the uniqueness idea. A range of artists and scholars in fields such as literature, film, theology, and cultural studies, which together with history and the social sciences contribute to the subdiscipline known as 'Holocaust studies', predicate their work on the *contention* of uniqueness as established in the 1980s as if it were an empirical or logical *given*. To take but one example of how the uniqueness claim has become internalized, a volume of essays from various disciplines titles itself *Problems Unique to the Holocaust*, yet contains very few such problems not equally applicable to any genocide.[47]

From the assumption of uniqueness about the event comes the claim of uniqueness about the difficulties of representing it. Here is Claude Lanzmann, director of the seminal documentary *Shoah*:

> In a way, I am incapable of substantiating my claims. Either one under-
> stands them or one does not. It is a bit like the Cartesian ego: at the
> end one gets stuck, that is the ultimate knot, you cannot go further. The

holocaust is unique in that, with a circle of fire, it builds a border around itself, which one cannot transgress, because a certain absolute kind of horror cannot be conveyed.[48]

However, as Dan Stone points out, the problems of representing the Holocaust are 'theoretically the same as for other events: it is just that the effects of doing so are of greater concern where the Holocaust [and any other genocide] is concerned'.[49]

New Institutionalist Approaches

Whatever the philosophical issues, the historical branch of the uniqueness-anti-Semitism school is generally wanting in its explanatory ability. It shares with the *Sonderweg* school a de-contextualization from the history of all but the immediate protagonists: Germans in one case, Jews in the other. But while the strictly historical areas of disagreement between intentionalists and functionalists have not been entirely resolved, they have become significantly less pointed as the field has converged on something like a middle path. A key moderating factor was the intervention at the height of the debate of Christopher Browning, who became the pre-eminent institutionalist scholar of the final solution after Hilberg. His 'moderate functionalism' kept the elements of central direction and the centrality of anti-Semitism, but wove this into a narrative of expansion, thus explaining how the increasing demographic 'problems' facing the Reich, including the politics of reshaping Poland's population, plus the opportunities presented by military victory, precipitated key Hitlerian decisions for outright genocide.[50]

Browning's lead has latterly been followed by a cohort of predominantly German institutionalist historians who have furthered the integration of the history of the Nazi state with that of genocide. These historians do not share a common position on the deeper origins of the Holocaust, but operate on the presumption of Nazi racism. They focus upon the way it was internalized by functionaries, and how it interacted with the circumstances of war, the complexities of occupation policy, and indigenous peoples (in eastern Europe) and non-German administrative structures (in western Europe). Their main contribution has been to add nuance to our understanding, to remove the focus further from Hitler and to place it instead on regional SS leaders and members of regional German civil and military administrations.[51]

Instead of one or two outright, seminal decisions, the state-of-the-art institutionalist scholarship has revealed a more gradually evolving 'consensus politics' that did not fully crystallize into total murder until spring 1942. Even in that finding, however, one can detect the tendency, explicit in the philosophical writing, of viewing the event from the perspective of posterity—of viewing with hindsight the final solution in its most expansive form, say in later 1942, treating that form as its real essence, and then finding the time by which it attained this real, essential quality. In that sense, even in Peter Longerich's monumental 1998 study *Politik der Vernichtung*, which was seminal in elongating conceptions of Nazi decision-making in both directions from 1941, we have still not got away from a fascination with 'moments' and 'decisions', but simply created more of them. The unending evolution of Nazi policy—its ongoing *processual* quality for the *full* duration of the Nazi period—is thereby elided.

In so far as they show the breadth of participation in the Nazi project, these newer institutionalist scholars are the heirs of Mommsen and Broszat. Bridging the two generations of German institutionalists is the work of Götz Aly, whose early work on Nazism was impelled by a concern about the endurance of structures and technologies of domination into the Federal Republic. He has consistently stressed the technocratic, modernizing quality of Nazism in his continuing contributions to the field, which has had the effect of downplaying the motive significance of anti-Semitism for large swathes of the Nazi-German state and society. Though the extent of each of his claims can be contested, he has illustrated variously the discriminatory economic visions of the eastern empire developed by mid-level German planners; the interrelation of the final solution with other Nazi demographic designs (building on the work of Browning and others); and the economic incentives the state provided to ordinary Germans as a result of wartime occupation and Aryanization.[52]

Another bridge between generations has been provided by Ulrich Herbert, though he points in a slightly different direction to Aly.

His important earlier work concerned the huge role played by foreign labourers in Germany during the war, and certain continuities between German foreign labour policies in and beyond the Third Reich. His key contribution to the discussion of Nazi racial policies is his biography of the architect of the SD, Werner Best. Along with Michael Wildt's massive study of the wider 'unbound generation' to which Best and much of the SD and then RSHA leadership belonged, Herbert's work illustrates the key role of a specific social cohort, delimited partly by age and partly by socio-economic background and advanced education, in providing a dynamic, professional driving force in one of the central SS agencies. With their focus on the impact of the First World War experience in fostering revisionism, a desire for those who had not fought to prove themselves in future combat, concern for ethnic Germans beyond German borders, and perceptions of 'inner' as well as external enemies, Herbert and Wildt also make concrete links between the scholarship on the general cultural impact of 1914–18 and the genocide committed by Nazi Germany during the next war.[53]

As to the act of murder itself, the focus of the younger institutionalist generation has tended to be on the killing fields of Poland and the USSR, which has drawn them to emphasize the 'hands-on' nature of genocide, moving away from a more 'clinical' Auschwitz-centred view of industrialized mass murder to a world of blood-soaked shooting massacres, ghetto 'clearances', and labour camps. The same cohort has also exposed the extent to which the home front benefited from genocide, and non-Nazi Germans contributed to persecution. Their emphasis on active ideological engagement in the east and the mobilization of the *Volksgemeinschaft* at home is an important corrective to the early postwar vision of a 'top-down' system of ordered destruction and the alternative vision of a genocide run predominantly by detached, dispassionate 'desk murderers'.[54]

As the previous chapter's discussion of situational factors in creating killers showed, however, we should be careful not to replace the earlier totalizing models of perpetrator behaviour with a new one with different flaws. As all historical scholarship is coloured by the broader political and intellectual trends of the day in which it is written, the 'new' perpetrator literature, with its emphasis on voluntaristic engagement, seems coloured by the perspective of seeming contemporary freedoms of expression and the post-Cold War triumph of individualism. There is a delicate balance to be established. If we ignore factors like obedience, conformity, coercion, and diverse forms of psychological rationalization beneath the levels of ideology and conscious interest-maximization, then we are in danger of misrepresenting the range of perpetrators as much as if we accepted those factors as the only explanations for perpetratorhood.

Modernization and 'Modernity'

One of the many ways in which contemporary history and politics has shaped approaches to the Holocaust is in the greater concern to relate it to other genocides. Comparative genocide scholarship began with Lemkin himself and was continued by a small group of scholars through the later Cold War period, but proliferated in the 1990s, as the Rwandan slaughter hammered home the truth that genocide was not a thing of the past, while the implosion of Yugoslavia showed Europe could still host the crime. The decidedly 'hands-on' nature of the new wave of violence was echoed in the way the new institutionalists decentred Auschwitz in their depiction of Nazi criminality.

Much of the early comparative scholarship was conducted by social and political scientists and had the strengths and weaknesses of those methodologies. Either it tended to focus on a few ostensibly similar cases to try to establish general similarities or patterns or it sought to categorize cases according to broad typologies, with the result that at the same time as being insufficiently nuanced and overly schematic in its approach, it was also too exclusive in its frame of reference. It created a conceptual trap for itself because of a preoccupation with the definition and applicability of the term genocide. This approach provided an interesting replication of the uniqueness battle in Holocaust scholarship, and has ramifications for historical understanding, with instances of outright genocide being accorded more attention than other related phenomena, and, more importantly, being extracted from historical contexts in which other forms of collective violence are intrinsic to the picture.

If there was one term that captured the political and, therefore, historical imagination after the end of the bipolar Cold War, it was 'globalization'. The idea of an ever more interconnected world centred on a Western political-economic core sent scholars scurrying to find historical precursors and antecedents in the expansion of the West before the twentieth century. The notion of tying discrete events and national histories to transnational and international processes was replicated in genocide scholarship, whose gaze gradually shifted from comparison of discrete events to a more contextual attempt to place those events in relation to one another.[55] A contemporary interest in the connections between genocide in the European colonies and the Holocaust at Europe's core should be understood within this framework.

Those studies that have gone furthest in putting Nazism into colonial perspective have shed very important light on both Nazi and non-Nazi colonialism, and confirmed that colonial is an appropriate word for Nazi attitudes towards eastern Europe.[56] Nevertheless, we saw in Part II of this book that German colonial designs and the final solution were often not interdependent, and the final solution did spread for complex reasons beyond the space designated for the future German empire. Moreover, as Alison Palmer, one of the first comparative historians of colonial genocide showed, the differences between instances of colonial genocide can be at least as important as the similarities, rendering the term itself of limited general value, just as other categorizations like 'industrial genocide' or 'bureaucratic genocide' may conceal as much as they reveal.[57] The idiom of colonialism can be used to describe any genocide that involves either territorial expansion bringing rule over different groups, or internal 'consolidation' through the destruction of heterogeneous and thus threatening domestic populations ('internal colonization').[58] Since these two categories encompass most of the recorded instances of genocide, the explanatory power of the term colonialism is perforce limited. The more it claims to account for, the less it can explain beyond a general, sometimes even metaphorical level.

The scholarship of Jürgen Zimmerer suggests how this problem of weak generalization might in future be circumvented. Zimmerer's work on Imperial German rule in Southwest Africa in the early twentieth century has, firstly, elucidated the origins, context, and dynamics of the genocide of the Herero and Nama peoples. Secondly, with an eye to the

Third Reich and Nazi rule in eastern Europe, it has gone beyond important generalities about what Zimmerer dubs 'Rasse und Raum' mentalities ('race and space': the two preoccupations of colonialists everywhere), and illustrated connections between the Imperial German and Nazi cases in the intrusive bureaucratic regulation and surveillance of victim populations, and the rigorous imposition of laws of racial segregation.[59]

Hannah Arendt's 1951 study *The Origins of Totalitarianism* is ubiquitous in the footnotes of the scholars who have established links between 'colonial genocide' and the Holocaust, and there are distinct traces of her approach in Zimmerer's work. Not primarily interested in the Holocaust, Arendt was concerned with Nazism, Stalinism, and the sorts of environments created in settler-colonial environments as a result of the drive for exploitation and control. For her, the colonies provided Europe's colonial rulers and settlers with what I earlier called a land of exception: an experimental chamber where they could operate without reference to norms established in the more constitutional, tradition-bound domestic political sphere. According to Arendt, the Nazi dictatorship recreated some of these exceptional conditions and took them to a new level of systemization, thus spawning a cohort of people like Adolf Eichmann. Her analysis of the 'banality of evil', elaborated in her account of Eichmann's Jerusalem trial, depicted him as someone who never made a political-ethical 'choice' about his participation in genocide. He simply adapted to the politically uncontested norms of the Nazi system (uncontested within Germany after 1933, that is). To deploy Weber's terms used in the past chapter, she saw Eichmann adopting value-rationality in his enthusiastic and innovative participation in the final solution without evincing the ethic of conviction that Weber saw as accompanying value-rationality.[60]

If Arendt described particular regime sorts in a specific developmental context, from her contemporaries Theodor Adorno and Max Horkheimer onwards, other theorists looked more to the climate of modernity itself. Modernity refers to an economic order following upon the Industrial Revolution, a political order growing out of the French Revolution, and particularly a post-Enlightenment cultural order embodied in growing secularism and a spirit of scientistic investigation and 'rational' governance and society. Zygmunt Bauman's *Modernity and the Holocaust* fits into the tradition of Adorno and Horkheimer: the title of the German translation of his book is *Dialektik der Ordnung* (*Dialectic of Order*) which clearly alluded to their 1947 study *Dialectic of Enlightenment*. It is the most extensive examination of the Holocaust as an outgrowth of modernity—not inevitable, but not aberrant either. For Bauman, as for Michel Foucault, modernity is characterized by man's belief that he can reshape humankind in an image of perfectibility that in a more religious age was regarded as the sole preserve of God. Modern genocide is the radical application of this doctrine of perfectibility by one particular section of mankind against debilitating or imperfectible elements within and outside its collective body. Once the target group—the cause of heterogeneity, the enemy of uniformity—is selected, genocide is perpetrated according to the technical-rational spirit of amoral problem-solving. Drawing heavily on Weberian language, Bauman portrays the archetypal perpetrator as a blinkered bureaucrat, one following the rules of instrumental rationality. Unlike Arendt's Eichmann, Bauman's bureaucrats are not acting with vision and enthusiasm (value rationality), but, like him, they are acting in a manner divorced from any original ethical 'choice'—in this case, the ethic of responsibility.

Notwithstanding the inaccuracy of his portrayal of German bureaucrats, Bauman's analysis of modernity is challenging and has inspired many followers.[61] In many ways Aly's work also fits into the tradition in which Bauman writes, given Aly's concern with state surveillance and demographic ordering processes. The chief shortcoming of both interpretations in the case of the final solution, and one shared by the 'modernization/developmentalism' school as a whole, is the inability to account for the specific choice of victim groups, and the peculiar intensity and supranational scope of the pursuit of Jews. The best known recent attempt to consider genocide in a comparative developmental framework, Michael Mann's huge *The Dark Side of Democracy*, is very successful in many respects. By its own admission, however, it meets with less success when trying to fit the Holocaust into its depiction of the violent potential of ethnically plural societies as they pass through key developmental phases when the ethnopolitical identity and territorial integrity of the state is contested.[62]

The focus on modernity in all its guises brings the historian a great deal. Modern concepts certainly fostered new and more impenetrable barriers between peoples, most obviously with the notion of race. Secular modernity removed religious precepts that prohibited certain forms of killing (i.e. of particular, 'tolerated' religious minorities and the 'disabled'), and introduced the notion of the 'constructive' death. The Enlightenment's bequest of liberalism helped pave the way for nationalism. The capitalist system, which gained such a boost from Enlightenment rationalization, was amply capable of enslaving men. The ideas and technologies bequeathed by the Enlightenment enshrined a desire and a capacity to order and control the natural world and, by extension, the world of human nature. Yet reducing the Holocaust to the (modern) preoccupation with 'suppressing difference', which is what some of the critiques of modernity boil down to,[63] can tell us nothing about why Jews in particular were targeted so extensively *and* intensively.

The historian of medieval anti-Semitism Gavin Langmuir observed that anti-Semitism, medieval or Nazi, is 'the hostility aroused by irrational thinking about "Jews" '. Whether based on pseudo-biological theories, belief in spurious political conspiracies, or accusations of poisoning wells, the end result was similar: the attribution to Jews of malign collective characteristics and agendas that could be disproved by empirical investigation. Langmuir distinguished anti-Semitism from theological thinking about Jews—often referred to, though not by him, as theological anti-Judaism, and based on the biblical critique that Jews had rejected Christ's covenant. He illuminated the way that ideas about the intrinsic nature of Jews as people (rather than Judaism as a religion) gained currency in medieval Europe. Those medieval ideas are best described as anti-Semitic, despite the fact that the word only came into existence in the nineteenth century.[64] The accusations, which were a product of Christian *cultures* rather than the Christian *religion* per se, included profanation of the host, ritual murder, usury, theft, and the desire to overthrow Christian authorities. They also included allegations that Jews were in league with the devil and 'the Turk'—Muslims. Christopher Probst has shown that Martin Luther's influential diatribes against Jews combined theological elements with culturally informed anti-Semitic accusations.[65] This mixed rhetorical attack reflected and reinforced a set of stereotypes that would endure within Christian civilization up to and through the Nazi period. While a 'synchronic' approach to European violence in the decades leading up to the final solution indeed reveals the crisis of a Europe reshaping itself according to modern ideas that legitimated violence of unprecedented intensity, a diachronic approach (across time) shows that it was no surprise that proportionately the greatest victims of ethnic murder in greater Europe in the past hundred and fifty years have been Muslims in Christian states, Christians in a Muslim empire, and Jews in a Christian continent.

It would be wrong, however, to finish a chapter on historiography appearing to stress one historical factor—deep, cultural anti-Semitism—more than others. After all, this book has gone to pains to create a multicausal explanation and to examine the murder and expulsion of other groups besides Jews. The problems of each of the interpretative strands I have examined in this chapter stem not from their irrelevance, but only from their claim to too great an explanatory ability. While proponents of any given explanation may proclaim that other explanations have simply 'got it wrong', they are generally just answering different questions.

Hans Mommsen, for example, takes Hitler's anti-Semitism for granted, yet recognizes it to be insufficient to result in genocide, and so focuses upon the structure of the Nazi state. The scholars who have expended so much time on the issue of when a 'decision' was made for genocide do likewise concerning the course of the war. They act on a tendency, identified by John Stuart Mill, to identify causation in the variable that 'came last into existence', focusing on the 'proximate, antecedent' factor rather than longer standing states of affairs, of which Hitler's anti-Semitism, or modern German history, are examples.[66]

At the opposite end of the spectrum, the likes of Bauman broaden the investigation to the 'nature' of Western modernity. In warning that the specialist historian misses the bigger picture, they assume their subject of enquiry is really the essential one, because it is the *condition* for all of the other more purely contingent, proximate *causes*.[67] But Mill also pointed out that there is no philosophical difference between a cause and a condition, only different levels of enquiry that focus upon explaining different aspects of a historical question and accordingly treat some things as causes and some as conditions. What for Mommsen was a condition for genocide—Hitler's anti-Semitism—was a proximate cause for Bauman. Yet Western modernity was not a given state of affairs imposed from on high onto the world, supplanting all that went before it and creating 'objective conditions' (as Karl Marx called them) for future, more contingent historical development, though many scholars of 'the modern' treat it as such in their desire to work from a point of origin, a concrete base on which they can build claims for the historical particularity of their epoch. 'The Enlightenment' itself (with its many facets and phases) was contingent on causes, just as there were causes for the inflection of Enlightenment ideas by statesmen and thinkers. So if we accept an explanation for the Holocaust that incorporates mindsets derived from the Enlightenment, a 'full' explanation of 'why the Holocaust?' must be followed by 'why the Enlightenment?', which leads to an 'infinite regression of explanation'.[68] And when we have disposed of the notions of Enlightenment as basic condition, and the 'last' factor as key cause, we must accept that factors intruding before the Enlightenment, after it, and up to the 'last factor' need full explanation in their own terms.

If history is 'argument without end', as Pieter Geyl put it, one of the reasons is that even when different historians approach the same subject matter they rarely do so from the same angle. The most intelligent ponderings on modernity and modernization (stressing the belief systems and crises of the modern world); the 'special path' (with its emphasis on national historical particularity); anti-Semitism (stressing the essence of ideology); totalitarianism (which is but a variant of an explanatory tendency emphasizing the centrality of political systems); the cultural impact of the First World War; and the events of the Second World War and the circumstances of Nazi invasion and occupation (of which more below) can each only shed light on part of the common problem of 'why?' in the Holocaust. The same goes for all other approaches, including those professing to have no particular approach. Exactly the same applies to the present book. There is no such thing as the 'total history' of any event.

What, then, is new about what I have tried to accomplish? As ever in a historical account, the novelty stems from the selection and connection of component themes, which in turn dictates periodization. This book has sought to retain the historical specificity of the Holocaust—a process that happened on one continent at one time and with the ultimate sanction of one figure—while insisting that respect for its peculiar features is not at odds with an approach situating it in relationship to other genocides, and to a Europe in the flux of borders and identities. It has tried to show that an explanation rooted in Nazism and anti-Semitism is necessarily inadequate when set against one prepared both to give due weight to immediate contingent circumstances and to situate them within the broader patterns of human behaviour in the late-modern world. That series of undertakings comprised three areas of enquiry. One entailed matters specific to the causation of the final solution; a second concerned issues general to the continent and the time in which the final solution emerged; and the third addressed questions applicable to instances of genocidal violence occurring in other times and places. Approximately speaking, the three areas of enquiry correspond respectively to parts II, I, and III of the book.

As much as anything else this book has been an experiment in combining different methodologies. Its aim was to maximize the light thrown onto the final solution not only by studying its development in detail but by studying prior European ethnopolitics and genocides elsewhere in the world—and to reflect light back onto those other episodes in turn. Chapters 1 to 3 were concerned with *correlating* the incidence of exclusion and violent ethnopolitics in modern Europe and thereby *connecting* ostensibly separate episodes in a pattern. The pattern formed a broad context for Nazism and the final solution. Chapters 4 to 6 were concerned with the immediate *causation* and pattern of the final solution in the context of the Nazi project as a whole and the spatial and cultural crucible established in the first chapters. Chapter 7 was concerned with direct *comparative* history.

In the matter of Nazi policy—the heart of the book and the subject of part II—I follow E. P. Thompson's description of history as 'a discipline of context and of process'.[69] To recognize the dynamic interaction of the two elements is to jettison the idea that there is any one 'essence' to a complex series of events like the one we now call the Holocaust, and to acknowledge that any one conceptualization of the entirety will be based on a generalization from only part of it. This conclusion is directly related to the above point about an irreducible plurality of causes. It is not an anti-conceptual point; analysing process *becomes* the dominant conceptual matter. To process are subordinated mid-range abstractions or paradigms, which in turn can be broken down, depending on the empirical precision of the analysis. In practice these paradigms always need to be combined with others, but for the sake of clarity I shall isolate them in a few examples. A demographic engineering paradigm helps explain the final solution in the Warthegau; an economic paradigm is important at times for Belarus, Lithuania, or parts of the Generalgouvernement; a colonial paradigm is useful for events in parts of Lublin or the Ukraine; a security paradigm is important in analysing the warzones and rear army areas at key points of Nazi expansion and contraction; a focus on geopolitics and diplomatic history is important for explaining the genuinely European dimensions of the Holocaust and the limits of its Europeanization; an institutionalist analysis is necessary, though insufficient on its own, for properly comprehending each of these areas of enquiry. For the historian, whose discipline involves balancing general trends with specific features, a multifaceted, multicausal account of process can deploy a variety of paradigms as helpful shorthands, while also recognizing their explanatory limits.

Each paradigm or mode of analysis can be adapted to parts of many other genocides, or deployed in comparative study. (Though, just like the Holocaust, and as we can infer from Palmer's critique of the concept of 'colonial genocide', no genocide can simply be reduced to one or other paradigm.) However, the book's part I primarily restricted its analysis to Europe from the late nineteenth century, more specifically the area from the continent's centre to the Eurasian rimlands in the east and southeast. It did so because there were some particularly European qualities and patterns to the crisis culminating in the Second World War and the Holocaust. The cradle of modernity, which gave the world its state system, and had until the early twentieth century been a net exporter of violence, exploded at its heart, and brought its advanced capacity for military and administrative violence to bear upon itself. A series of social, cultural, and economic developments found their most violent expression in geopolitical shifts. Increasing incidents of violence in the European colonies and on the Ottoman periphery of Europe were the first indicators, and they raised the pressure within the centre of the continent. Geopolitics and economics were central to the general violence of the period, but civilians were increasingly targeted as new conceptions of difference were layered onto existing cultural cleavages and were ever more closely associated with new state identities and, thus, with new forms of domination. The obverse side of equating certain peoples with certain states was the idea of minorities within their borders as undesirable and potentially disloyal by their very identities.

The European Jews had had to deal with the stigma of difference and disloyalty for longer than any other minority because of religious cleavage and the cultural associations accreting to it. Their pariah status was changed, but not removed, by the modernity that had promised to revoke it. One reason is that even with—in fact partly because of—the proliferation of nation-states within Europe, the role of supranational forces in influencing national affairs became more pronounced. Borderless high finance, international minority 'protection', and the great powers' arbitration of borders provided the grounds for new stereotypes of invisible, rootless influence, and of the fifth column: the link between 'inner and outer enemies'.

The observation that the greater Europe of approximately 1875–1949 was a particularly fertile place for specific patterns of ethnic violence is not intended to convey any complacency about the happier situation in which today's Europe temporarily finds itself. Nor is it to deny that many aspects of the European crisis have been mirrored elsewhere and at other times. Indeed, Europe bears a share of the responsibility for many of the violent explosions that have occurred elsewhere across the modern world, because it exported its state system and economic order to the rest of the globe. If anything, the detailed focus on Europe's recent past should draw our attention to the strong correlation between on one hand border shifts, competition over commerce and natural resources, sovereignty debates, rapid modernization processes, and warfare, and on the other hand the intergroup violence that can culminate in genocide. Further to the European case study, the dynamics of any given 'zone of violence'[70] across the world can be greatly agitated—and, on occasion, ameliorated—by the actions of regional or external great powers.

Inevitably there will be significant local inflections to mass political violence across the world, depending on culture, but also on the relative strengths and institutional arrangements of state and sub-state actors in the region in question. These variations help determine the identity of victim groups on one hand, and the breadth and forms of complicity in perpetration on the other hand. As part III's comparative discussion implied, however, human societies across the world seem to be eminently capable of creating the contexts in which many of their members will kill.

ENDNOTES

Introduction

1. See Chapter 6.
2. Berel Lang, 'The Evil in Genocide', in John K. Roth (ed.), *Genocide and Human Rights: A Philosophical Guide* (New York: Palgrave Macmillan, 2005), 5–17, here 12. On Cambodia, see Ben Kiernan, *The Pol Pot Regime: Race, Power, and Genocide in Cambodia under the Khmer Rouge, 1975–79* (New Haven, CT: Yale University Press, 1996); on Latin America, see Daniel Feierstein, *El genocidio como práctica social* (Buenos Aires: Fondo de Cultura Económica, 2007).
3. Mark Levene, *Genocide in the Age of the Nation State*, vols. i and ii (London: I. B. Tauris, 2005), is the best attempt at a comprehensive history of the subject for the modern period.
4. Daniel J. Goldhagen, *Hitler's Willing Executioners: Ordinary Germans and the Holocaust* (New York: Knopf, 1996).
5. See Chapter 8.
6. Michael Marrus, *The Holocaust in History* (Harmondsworth: Penguin, 1989), and Dan Stone (ed.), *The Historiography of the Holocaust* (Basingstoke: Palgrave, 2004) cover many of the historiographical issues splendidly.
7. e.g. Saul Friedländer's superb two-volume *Nazi Germany and the Jews* (New York: Harper Collins, 1997, 2007).

Documentary Traces

1. Federation of the Romanian Jewish Communities, neg. 11561, courtesy of United States Holocaust Memorial Museum (USHMM) photograph archives, W/S 58558.
2. Ibid. W/S 58559.
3. Aimé Césaire, *Discourse on Colonialism* (New York: Monthly Review Press, 1972), 14.

4. Nuremberg Document PS-1919. The translation here is culled mostly from the excellent rendering in Jeremy Noakes and Geoffrey Pridham (eds), *Nazism 1919–1945*, vol. 3: *Foreign Policy, War and Racial Extermination* (Exeter: University of Exeter Press, 1988), 919–21 and 1199–1200.

5. Bradley F. Smith and Agnes F. Peterson (eds), *Heinrich Himmler. Geheimreden 1933 bis 1945* (Frankfurt Am Main: Propyläen, 1974), 169, 201–3.

6. Richard Kalfus, 'Euphemisms of Death: Interpreting a Primary Source Document on the Holocaust', *The History Teacher*, 23:2 (1990), 87–93, here 87–8.

7. Zygmunt Bauman, *Modernity and the Holocaust* (Ithaca, NY: Cornell University Press, 1989), 197.

8. From J. B. Jackson, American consul, Aleppo in the Ottoman Empire, to Henry Morgenthau, American ambassador to the Ottoman Empire in Istanbul.

9. US National Archives and Records Administration, College Park, Maryland, Record Group 59, 867.4016/219.

10. Peter Balakian, *The Burning Tigris: The Armenian Genocide and America's Response* (New York: HarperCollins, 2003), 182–6, 190–95 and ch. 14 as a whole.

Chapter 1—Europe on the Brink

1. Susanna Burrows, *Distorting Mirrors: Visions of the Crowd in Late Nineteenth-Century France* (New Haven, CT: Yale University Press, 1981); Clive Ponting, *Progress and Barbarism: The World in the Twentieth Century* (London: Chatto & Windus 1998), part 1.

2. Cited in Ponting, *Progress and Barbarism*, 33.

3. David Vital *A People Apart: The Jews in Europe, 1789–1939* (Oxford: Oxford University Press, 1999), p. vii, also cites Lenin in this context concerning Christian–Jewish relations. My analysis concurs with his as far as his goes, but applies it to many other dynamics than simply the Jewish–Christian one. Indeed, it is a development and generalization of my arguments about ethno-religious polarization in the late Ottoman Empire, as detailed in the first chapter of my *The Great Game of Genocide: Imperialism, Nationalism, and the Destruction of the Ottoman Armenians* (Oxford: Oxford University Press, 2005). Related analyses of other group conflicts from social-scientific perspectives are Susan Olzak, *The Dynamics of Ethnic Competition and Conflict* (Stanford, CA: Stanford University Press, 1992); Roger D. Petersen, *Understanding Ethnic Violence: Fear,*

Hatred, and Resentment in Twentieth-Century Eastern Europe (Cambridge: Cambridge University Press, 2002).

4. As does Niall Ferguson in *War of the World: Twentieth-Century Conflict and the Descent of the West* (New York: Penguin, 2007).

5. Albert Lindemann, *Esau's Tears: Modern Antisemitism and the Rise of the Jews* (Cambridge: Cambridge University Press, 1997).

6. Eugen Weber, *Peasants into Frenchmen: The Modernization of Rural France 1870–1914* (Stanford, CA: Stanford University Press, 1976). This interpretation has distinct echoes of Mark Levene, *Genocide in the Age of the Nation-State* (London: I. B. Tauris, 2005), vol. i.

7. R. Po-chia Hsia, *The Myth of Ritual Murder: Jews and Magic in Reformation Germany* (New Haven, CT: Yale University Press, 1988); Andrew Colin Gow, *The Red Jews: Antisemitism in an Apocalyptic Age, 1200–1600*, ed. Heiko Oberman (Leiden: Brill, 1995).

8. Léon Poliakov, *The History of Anti-Semitism*, vol. i (London: Routledge, 1974), 73 ff.

9. Yuri Slezkine, *The Jewish Century* (Princeton, NJ: Princeton University Press, 2006).

10. On the philosophical side, Adam Sutcliffe, *Judaism and Enlightenment* (Cambridge: Cambridge University Press, 2003). On politics, Shulamit Volkov, *Germans, Jews, and Antisemites: Trials in Emancipation* (Cambridge: Cambridge University Press, 2006); Heinz-Dietrich Löwe, *Antisemitismus und reaktionäre Utopie: Russische Konservatismus in Kampf gegen den Wandel von Staat und Gesellschaft* (Hamburg: Hoffman und Campe, 1978); John W. Boyer, *Political Radicalism in Late Imperial Vienna: Origins of the Christian Social Movement, 1848-1897* (Chicago: University of Chicago Press, 1981).

11. Isaac Deutscher, *The Non-Jewish Jew and Other Essays* (Oxford: Oxford University Press, 1968), 27.

12. Norman Stone, *Europe Transformed 1878–1919* (London: Fontana, 1983), 410–11; Werner Sombart, *Die Juden und das Wirtschaftsleben* (Leipzig: Duncker, 1911).

13. Karl Polanyi, *The Great Transformation: The Political and Economic Origins of Our Time* (Boston: Beacon, 2001), 11.

14. The word 'race' had traditionally been used in reference to cultural superiority: Paul Gilroy, *The Black Atlantic: Modernity and Double Consciousness* (London: Verso, 1993), 8.

15. Richard Wiekart, *From Darwin to Hitler: Evolutionary Ethics, Eugenics, and Racism in Germany* (New York: Palgrave, 2004).

16. Stefan Kühl, *The Nazi Connection: Eugenics, American racism, and German National Socialism* (New York: Oxford University Press, 1994); Paul Addison, *Churchill on the Home Front 1900–55* (Oxford: Oxford University Press, 1992), 124–6.

17. Sophie Bessis, *Western Supremacy: The Triumph of an Idea?* (London: Zed Books, 2003); Gilroy, *The Black Atlantic*, 190.

18. R. I. Moore, *The Formation of a Persecuting Society: Power and Deviance in Medieval Europe 950–1250* (Oxford: Oxford University Press, 1987).

19. Rolf Fischer, *Entwicklungsstufen des Antisemitismus in Ungarn, 1867–1939: Die Zerstörung der magyarischen-jüdischen Symbiose* (Munich: Oldenbourg, 1988).

20. Lisa Moses Leff, *Sacred Bonds of Solidarity: The Rise of Jewish Internationalism in Nineteenth-Century France* (Stanford, CA: Stanford University Press, 2006).

21. Cited in Merryn Williams (ed.), *Revolutions 1775–1830* (Harmondsworth: Penguin, 1971), 30–2.

22. David A. Bell, *The First Total War: Napoleon's Europe and the Birth of Warfare as We Know It* (New York: Houghton Mifflin, 2007); the significance of the matter is central to Levene, *Genocide*.

23. Anthony Marx, *Faith in Nation: The Exclusionary Origins of Nationalism* (Oxford: Oxford University Press, 2003); Heather Rae, *State Identities and the Homogenisation of Peoples* (Cambridge: Cambridge University Press, 2002). On modern Britain, Tony Kushner, *The Persistence of Prejudice: Antisemitism in British Society during World War II* (Manchester: Manchester University Press, 1989).

24. Cited in Hans Rosenberg, 'Political and Social Consequences of the Great Depression of 1873–1896 in Central Europe', in James Sheehan (ed.), *Imperial Germany* (New York: New Viewpoints, 1976), 44–5.

25. Ronald Beiner (ed.), *Theorizing Nationalism* (Albany: SUNY Press, 1999).

26. R. A. Kann, B. K. Kiraly, and P. S. Fichtner (eds), *The Hapsburg Empire in World War I* (New York: Columbia University Press, 1977).

27. For a Russian example Peter Holquist, 'To Count, to Extract, and to Exterminate: Population Statistics and Population Politics in Late Imperial and Soviet Russia', in Ronald Grigor Suny and Terry Martin (eds), *A State of Nations: Empire and Nation-Making in the Age of Lenin and Stalin* (Oxford: Oxford University Press, 2001), 111–44. On the importance of communication networks, Karl W. Deutsch, *Nationalism and Social Communication* (New York: Wiley, 1953).

28. Readers will note my various debts to Ernst Gellner, *Nations and Nationalism* (Oxford: Blackwell, 1993) and Benedict Anderson, *Imagined Communities* (London: Verso, 1991).

29. E.g. Eugen Weber, *Peasants into Frenchmen: The Modernization of Rural France* (Stanford, CA: Stanford University Press, 1976).

30. On the general 'racialization' of European nationalism from the later nineteenth century: Eric Weitz, *A Century of Genocide: Utopias of Race and Nation* (Princeton, NJ: Princeton University Press, 2003).

31. The Austro-Marxism of Karl Renner and the belated federalism of Kaiser Karl.

32. At the outset of WWI Habsburg forces deported some 10 per cent of the Serb population for labour purposes, and massacred sporadically. The Serbs would emerge from the war with the highest per capita death toll of any combatant state.

33. Erich Haberer, *Jews and Revolution in Nineteenth-Century Russia* (New York: Cambridge University Press, 1995).

34. Bloxham, *Great Game*, Ch. 1.

35. L. L. Farrar, Jr., 'Realpolitik versus Nationalpolitik: Rethinking Nationalism during the Eastern Crisis, 1875–1878', *Eastern European Quarterly* 30 (1996).

36. Kemal Karpat, 'The Transformation of the Ottoman State, 1789–1908', *International Journal of Middle East Studies* 3 (1972), 243–81, at 272.

37. Rogers Brubaker, *Nationalism Reframed: Nationhood and the National Question in the New Europe* (Cambridge: Cambridge University Press, 1996).

38. Bascom Barry Hayes, *Bismarck and Mitteleuropa* (Madison, NJ: Fairleigh Dickinson University Press, 1994), Ch. 8; George F. Kennan, *The Decline of Bismarck's European Order: Franco-Russian Relations, 1875–1890* (Princeton, NJ: Princeton University Press, 1979).

39. Bloxham, *Great Game*, Ch. 2.

40. Jelle Verheij, 'Die armenischen Massaker von 1894–1896: Anatomie und Hintergründe einer Krise', in Hans-Lukas Kieser (ed.), *Die armenische Frage und die Schweiz (1896–1923)* (Zurich: Chronos, 1999), 69–129.

41. Marx, *Faith in Nation*, ix, 19; on Hamidian policies, Bayram Kodaman, *Şark Meselesi Işiği Altinda Sultan II Abdülhamid'in Doğu Anadolu Politikası* (Istanbul: Orkun Yayınevi, 1983).

42. Ronald Grigor Suny, 'Nationalities in the Russian Empire', *The Russian Review*, 59 (2000), 487–92.

43. N. M. Gelber, 'The Intervention of German Jews at the Berlin Congress 1878, *Leo Baeck Institute Year Book* 5 (1960), 221–47, here 243; Carole Fink, *Defending the Rights of Others: The Great Powers, the Jews, and International Minority Protection, 1878–1938* (New York: Cambridge University Press, 2004).

44. Hayes, *Bismarck*, 336–7.

45. R. T. Shannon, *Gladstone and the Bulgarian Agitation 1876* (Hassocks: Harvester, 1975), 16–19.

46. Brubaker, *Nationalism Reframed*, 154. On Muslim suffering in and around this era, Justin McCarthy, *Death and Exile: The Ethnic Cleansing of Ottoman Muslims, 1821–1922* (Princeton, NJ: Darwin Press, 1995).

47. L. L. Farrar, Jr., 'Aggression versus Apathy: The Limits of Nationalism during the Balkan Wars, 1912–1913', *East European Quarterly* 37 (2003), 257–280.

48. Feroz Ahmad, *The Young Turks: The Committee of Union and Progress in Turkish Politics 1908–1914* (Oxford: Oxford University Press, 1969).

49. See Chapters 2 and 7.

50. Stephen P. Ladas, *The Exchange of Minorities: Bulgaria, Greece and Turkey* (New York: Macmillan, 1932), 18–20.

51. A process elucidated, and perhaps slightly overstated, by Eric Lohr, *Nationalising the Russian Empire: The Campaign against Enemy Aliens during World War One* (Cambridge, MA: Harvard University Press, 2003).

52. Wolfgang Wippermann, 'Das Slawenbild der Deutschen im 19. und 20. Jahrhundert', in Geraldine Saherwala and Felix Escher (eds), *Slawen und Deutsche zwischen Elbe und Oder vor 1000 Jahren: Der Slawenaufstand vom 983* (Berlin, 1983), 15–29.

53. Michael Mann, 'The Darkside of Democracy: The Modern Tradition of Ethnic and Political Cleansing', *New Left Review* 235 (1999), 18–45, at 30.

54. Norman Cohn, *Warrant for Genocide: The Jewish World Conspiracy and the Protocols of the Elders of Zion* (London: Serif, 1996).

55. Mariana Hausleitner, *Deutsche und Juden in Bessarabien 1814–1941. Zur Minderheitenpolitik Russlands und Großrumäniens* (Munich: IKGS Verlag, 2005), 40–2; Petersen, *Understanding*, 87–93; Robert Weinberg, 'Workers, Pogroms, and the 1905 Revolutions in Odessa', *The Russian Review* 46 (1987), 53–75; James E. Casteel, 'The Russian Germans in the Interwar German National Imaginery', *Central European History* 40 (2007), 429–66.

Chapter 2—The First World War Era

1. Imannuel Geiss, *Der polnische Grenzstreifen 1914–1918. Ein Beitrag zur deutschen Kriegszielpolitik im Ersten Weltkrieg* (Hamburg, 1960).

2. Devin Pendas, ' "The Magical Scent of the Savage": Colonial Violence, the Crisis of Civilization and the Origins of the Legalist Paradigm of War', *Boston College International and Comparative Law Review* 30 (Winter 2007), 29–53.

3. Though the following books sometimes reach different conclusions, all are Western-centric: Modris Eksteins, *Rites of Spring: The Great War and the Birth of the Modern Age* (London: Houghton Mifflin, 1990); Stéphane Audoin-Rouzeau and Annette Becker, *1914–1918 Understanding the Great War* (London: Profile Books, 2002); Omer Bartov, *Mirrors of Destruction: War, Genocide, and Modern Identity* (Oxford: Oxford University Press, 2000). Jay Winter, *Sites of Memory, Sites of Mourning: The Great War in European Cultural History* (Cambridge: Cambridge University Press, 1995).

4. Fritz Fischer, *Germany's Aims in the First World War* (London: Chatto & Windus, 1967), 141–3.

5. Mark Levene, 'The Balfour Declaration: A Case of Mistaken Identity', *English Historical Review* 107 (1992), 54–77.

6. D. Gaunt, *Massacres, Resistance, Protectors: Muslim-Christian Relations in Eastern Anatolia during World War I* (Piscataway, NJ: Gorgias Press, 2006).

7. Eric Lohr, *Nationalising the Russian Empire: The Campaign against Enemy Aliens during World War One* (Cambridge, MA: Harvard University Press, 2003); Donald Bloxham, *The Great Game of Genocide: Imperialism, Nationalism, and the Destruction of the Ottoman Armenians* (Oxford: Oxford University Press, 2005), Ch. 2.

8. Peter Holquist, 'The Politics and Practice of the Russian Occupation of Armenia, 1915–Feb. 1917', in Ronald Grigor Suny, Fatma Müge Göçek, and Norman Naimark (eds), *A Question of Genocide, 1915: Armenians and Turks at the End of the Ottoman Empire* (Oxford: Oxford University Press, forthcoming). More generally on resettlement and deportation in this period, see Peter Holquist, 'To Count, to Extract, and to Exterminate: Population Statistics and Population Politics in Late Imperial and Soviet Russia', in Ronald Grigor Suny and Terry Martin (eds), *A State of Nations. Empire and Nation-Making in the Age of Lenin and Stalin* (Oxford: Oxford University Press, 2001), 111–44.

9. Bloxham, *Great Game*.

10. Cited in Taner Timur, *Türkler ve Ermeniler* (Ankara: Imge, 2000), 33.

11. Fuat Dündar, *Ittihat ve Terakki'nin Müslümanları Iskân Politikası (1913–1918)* (Istanbul: Isis, 2001).

12. Holger Herwig, *The First World War: Germany and Austria–Hungary* (London: Arnold, 1997), 127–8; E. F. Benson, *The White Eagle of Poland* (New York: George H. Doran, 1919), part II; Geiss, *Der polnische Grenzstreifen*.

13. Vejas Liulevicius, *War Land on the Eastern Front: Culture, National Identity, and German Occupation in World War I* (New York: Cambridge University Press, 2001); Jürgen Matthäus, 'Vorboten des Holocaust? Deutschland und die litauischen Juden während des Ersten Weltkrieges', in Wolfgang Benz and Marion Neiss (eds), *Judenmord in Litauen: Studien und Dokumente* (Berlin: Metropol, 1999), 35–50.

14. Troy Paddock, 'Historiker als Politiker', in Mechthild Keller (ed.), *Russen und Rußland aus deutscher Sicht. 19./20. Jahrhundert: Von der Bismarckzeit bis zum Ersten Weltkrieg* (Munich: Wilhelm Fink Verlag, 2000), 298–348.

15. John D. Klier, 'Russian Jewry as the "Little Nation" of the Russian Revolution', in Yaacov Ro'i (ed.), *Jews and Jewish Life in Russia and the Soviet Union* (London: Routledge, 1995), 146–56.

16. Norman Cohn, *Warrant for Genocide: The Jewish World Conspiracy and the Protocols of the Elders of Zion* (London: Serif, 1996).

17. Holger Herwig, 'Tunes of Glory at the Twilight Stage: The Bad-Homburg Crown Council and the Evolution of German Statecraft 1917/1918', *German Studies Review* 6 (1983), 475–94, here 478.

18. Joseph W. Bendersky, *'The Jewish Threat': Anti-Semitic Politics of the US Army* (New York: Basic Books, 2000), Chs. 2–3.

19. Michael Makovsky, *Churchill's Promised Land: Zionism and Statecraft* (New Haven, CT: Yale University Press, 2007), Ch. 3.

20. Michael Kellogg, *The Russian Roots of Nazism: White Russians and the Making of National Socialism, 1917–1945* (New York: Cambridge University Press, 2005).

21. Robert Gerwarth, 'The Central European Counter-revolution: Paramilitary Violence in Germany, Austria, and Hungary after the Great War', *Past and Present* 200 (2008), 175–209.

22. Bernhard Sauer, 'Vom "Mythos des ewigen Soldatentums". Der Feldzug deutscher Freikorps im Baltikum im Jahre 1919', *Zeitschrift für Geschichtswissenschaft* 10 (1995), 869–902; Boris Barth, *Dolchstoßlegenden und*

politische Desintegration. Das Trauma der deutschen Niederlage im ersten Weltkrieg 1914–1933 (Düsseldorf: Droste, 2003).

23. Henry Abrahamson, *A Prayer for the Government: Ukrainians and Jews in Revolutionary Times, 1917–1920* (Cambridge, MA: Harvard University Press, 1999); David Vital, *A People Apart: The Jews in Europe, 1789–1939* (Oxford: Oxford University Press, 1999), 724–6.

24. Stephane Courtois, Nicolas Werth, Jean-Louis Panne, Andrzej Paczkowski, Karel Bartosec, and Jean-Louis Margolin, *The Black Book of Communism* (Cambridge, MA: Harvard University Press, 1999), 138–40.

25. Bloxham, *Great Game*, Ch. 4.

26. René Hirschon (ed.), *Crossing the Aegean: An Appraisal of the 1923 Compulsory Population Exchange between Greece and Turkey* (New York: Berghahn Books, 2003); on the ethnic Germans later, Philipp Ther and Ana Siljak (eds), *Redrawing Nations: Ethnic Cleansing in East-Central Europe, 1944–1948* (Lanham, MD: Rowman & Littlefield, 2001), parts I and II; Detlef Brandes, *Der Weg zur Vertreibung 1938–1945* (Munich: Oldenbourg, 2002).

27. Marc David Baer, 'Globalization, Cosmopolitanism, and the Dönme in Ottoman Salonica and Turkish Istanbul', *Journal of World History* 18 (2007), 141–70.

28. Eberhard Jäckel and Axel Kuhn (eds), *Hitler. Sämtliche Aufzeichnungen 1905–1924* (Stuttgart, 1980), 775; Dominik J. Schaller, 'Die Rezeption des Völkermordes an den Armeniern in Deutschland, 1915–1945', in Hans-Lukas Kieser and Dominik Schaller (eds), *Der Völkermord an den Armeniern und die Shoah* (Zurich: Chronos, 2002), 517–55.

29. MacGregor Knox, 'Das faschistische Italien und die "Endlösung" 1942/3', *Vierteljahrshefte für Zeitgeschichte*, 1 Sonderdruck (2007), 53–92; Götz Aly and Suzanne Heim, *Vordenker der Vernichtung: Auschwitz und die deutschen Pläne für eine neue europäischen Ordnung* (Frankfurt am Main, 1993), Ch. 13; Mark Levene, 'The Limits of Tolerance: Nation-State Building and What it Means for Minority Groups', *Patterns of Prejudice* 34:2 (2000), 19–40.

30. Aristotle A. Kallis, 'The Jewish Community of Salonica under Siege: The Antisemitic Violence of the Summer of 1931', *Holocaust and Genocide Studies* 20 (2006), 34–56.

31. Marsha L. Rozenblit, *Reconstructing a National Identity: The Jews of Habsburg Austria during World War I* (Oxford: Oxford University Press, 2001).

32. Rolf Fischer, *Entwicklungsstufen des Antisemitismus in Ungarn, 1867–1939: Die Zerstörung der magyarischen-jüdischen Symbiose* (Munich: Oldenbourg, 1988).
33. Rozenblit, *Reconstructing*, epilogue.

Chapter 3—Ethnopolitics, Geopolitics, and the Return to War

1. As adopted from Alan Palmer's *The Lands Between: A History of East-Central Europe since the Congress of Vienna* (London: Macmillan, 1970).
2. Margaret Ball, *Post-War German-Austrian Relations: The Anschluss Movement, 1916–36* (Stanford, CA: Stanford University Press, 1937).
3. On Czechoslovakia, Roger D. Petersen, *Understanding Ethnic Violence: Fear, Hatred, and Resentment in Twentieth-Century Eastern Europe* (Cambridge: Cambridge University Press, 2002), 197.
4. Tony Kushner, *The Holocaust and the Liberal Imagination* (Oxford: Blackwell, 1994).
5. Mark Levene, 'The Limits of Tolerance: Nation-State Building and What it Means for Minority Groups', *Patterns of Prejudice* 34:2 (2000), 28–30; Patrick Finney, '"An Evil for All Concerned": Great Britain and Minority Protection after 1919', *Journal of Contemporary History* 30 (1995), 533–51; cf. Jacob Robinson, *Were the Minorities Treaties a Failure?* (New York: Institute of Jewish Affairs, 1943), 244.
6. Finney, '"An Evil for All Concerned"'. On Iraq, Robinson, *Minorities Treaties*, 238.
7. Bloxham, *Great Game*, second interlude.
8. Cornelia Schenke, *Nationalstaat und nationale Frage: Polen und die Ukrainer 1921–1939* (Hamburg: Dölling und Galitz, 2004).
9. Jean Ancel, 'German–Romanian Relationship and the Final Solution', *Holocaust and Genocide Studies* 19 (2005), 252–275', here 268–9.
10. Alexander Victor Prusin, *Nationalizing a Borderland: War, Ethnicity, and Anti-Jewish Violence in East Galicia, 1914–1920* (Tuscaloosa: University of Alabama Press, 2005), conclusion.
11. Zygmunt Bauman, 'Allosemitism: Premodern, Modern, Postmodern', in Bryan Cheyette and Laura Marcus (eds), *Modernity, Culture and 'the Jew'* (Stanford, CA: Stanford University Press, 1998).
12. Hans Lemberg, 'Das Konzept der ethnischen Säuberung im 20. Jahrhundert', in Dittmar Dahlmann and Gerhard Hirschfeld (eds), *Lager, Zwangsarbeit, Vertreibung und Deportation* (Essen: Klartext, 1999), 485–92, here 486–7.

13. Joanna Michlic, *Poland's Threatening Other: The Image of the Jew from 1880 to the Present* (Lincoln: University of Nebraska Press, 2006), Chs. 1–3; Emanuel Melzer, 'Relations between Poland and Germany and Their Impact on the Jewish Problem in Poland (1935–1938)', *Yad Vashem Studies* 12 (1977), 193–229.

14. Magnus Brechtken, *'Madagaskar für die Juden': antisemitische Idee und politische Praxis 1885–1945* (Munich: Oldenbourg, 1997), 81–91; Christian Gerlach and Götz Aly, *Das letzte Kapitel: Der Mord an den ungarischen Juden* (Stuttgart, 2002), 422 on Rumania.

15. Marsha L. Rozenblit, *Reconstructing a National Identity: The Jews of Habsburg Austria during World War I* (Oxford: Oxford University Press, 2001), 164.

16. Erwin Oberländer (ed.), *Autoritäre Regime in Ostmittel- und Südosteuropa 1919–1944* (Paderborn: Schöningh, 2001).

17. Maria Bucur, *Eugenics and Modernization in Interwar Romania* (Pittsburgh, PA: University of Pittsburgh Press, 2002) on the centrality of Moldovan to Romanian eugenics. Note, though, that Moldovan's views had some idiosyncracies even among other such thinkers. Michel Foucault later popularized the notion of biopolitics.

18. Patrick Wagner, *Volksgemeinschaft ohne Verbrecher. Konzeptionen und Praxis der Kriminalpolizei in der Zeit der Weimarer Republik und des Nationalsozialismus* (Hamburg: Christians, 1996).

19. Hans Raupach, 'The Impact of the Great Depression on Eastern Europe', *Journal of Contemporary History* 4:4 (1969), 75–86; Rawi Abdelal, 'Purpose and Privation: Nation and Economy in Post-Habsburg Eastern Europe and Post-Soviet Eurasia', *East European Politics and Societies*, 16 (2003), 898–933.

20. Gerlach and Aly, *Das letzte Kapitel*, Chs. 2 and 4; Tatyana Tönsmeyer, 'The Robbery of Jewish Property in Eastern European States Allied with Nazi Germany', in Martin Dean, Constantin Goschler, and Philipp Ther (eds), *Robbery and Restitution: The Conflict over Jewish Property in Europe* (Oxford: Berghahn, 2006), 116–139.

21. Zafer Toprak, *Türkey'de 'Milli Iktisat' (1908–1918)* (Ankara Yurt Yayinlari, 1982); Edward C. Clark, 'The Turkish Varlık Vergisi Reconsidered', *Middle Eastern Studies* 8 (1972), 205–16.

22. Dean, Goschler, and Ther (eds), *Robbery*.

23. Mariana Hausleitner, *Deutsche und Juden in Bessarabien 1814–1941. Zur Minderheitenpolitik Russlands und Großrumäniens* (Munich: IKGS Verlag, 2005), 164.

24. Carole Fink, ' "Defender of Minorities": Germany in the League of Nations, 1926–1933', *Central European History*, 5 (1972), 330–57.
25. Lemberg, 'Das Konzept', 487–8.
26. Detlef Brandes, *Der Weg zur Vertreibung 1938–1945* (Munich: Oldenbourg, 2002).
27. Rüdiger Overmans, *Deutsche militärische Verluste im Zweiten Weltkrieg* (Munich: Oldenbourg, 2000).
28. Gerlach and Aly, *Das letzte Kapitel*, 425–33.
29. Richard Blanke, *Orphans of Versailles: The Germans in Western Poland, 1918–1939* (Lexington, KY: University Press of Kentucky, 1993); T. David Curp, *A Clean Sweep? The Politics of Ethnic Cleansing in Western Poland, 1945–1960* (Rochester, NY: University of Rochester Press, 2006), 14–17.
30. Curp, *A Clean Sweep*; Tadeusz Piotrowski (ed.), *Genocide and Rescue in Wolyn: Recollections of the Ukrainian Nationalist Ethnic Cleansing Campaign against the Poles during World War II* (London: McFarland, 2000); *idem, Poland's Holocaust* (London: McFarland, 1998).
31. Part I of Philipp Ther and Ana Siljak (eds), *Redrawing Nations: Ethnic Cleansing in East-Central Europe, 1944–1948* (Lanham, MD: Rowman & Littlefield, 2001); Timothy Snyder, ' "To Resolve the Ukrainian Problem Once and for All": The Ethnic Cleansing of Ukrainians in Poland, 1943–1947', *Journal of Cold War Studies* 1 (1999) 86–120.
32. Bill Nicholov, 'Aegean Macedonia since 1946', *Macedonia for the Macedonians* [online]. Accessed 12 December 2007. Available at URL:http://www.makedonija.info/aegean3.html
33. Terry Martin, 'The Origins of Soviet Ethnic Cleansing', *Journal of Modern History* 70 (1998), 813–61; Nicolas Werth, 'Repenser la Grande Terreur', *Le Débat*, 122 (Nov.–Dec. 2002), 118–39; Michael Gelb, 'The Western Finnic Minorities and the Origins of the Stalinist Nationalities Deportations', *Nationalities Papers*, 24:2 (1996), 237–68.
34. Terry Martin, *The Affirmative Action Empire. Nations and Nationalism in the Soviet Union, 1923–1939* (Ithaca, NY: Cornell University Press, 2001), 273–4; Andrea Graziosi, 'Les famines soviétiques de 1931–1933 et le *Holodomor* ukrainien. Une nouvelle interprétation est-elle possible et quelles en seraient les conséquences?', *Cahiers du monde russe* 46:3 (2005), 453–72.
35. Martin, 'Origins'; Pavel Polian, *Against Their Will: The History and Geography of Forced Migrations in the USSR* (Budapest: Central European University Press, 2004).
36. Melzer, 'Relations'.

37. Martin Dean, *Collaboration in the Holocaust* (New York: St. Martin's Press, 2000), 4–6. More generally Jan T. Gross, *Revolution from Abroad: The Soviet Conquest of Poland's Western Ukraine and Western Byelorussia* (Princeton, NJ: Princeton University Press, 1988).

38. On Poland, Günther Häufele, 'Zwangsumsiedlungen in Polen 1939–1941', in Dahlmann and Hirschfeld (eds), *Lager*, 515–33.

39. In this and subsequent sections, endnotes are limited because many of the subjects are revisited, with references, in Chapter 2.

40. Vladimir Solonari, 'An Important New Document on the Romanian Policy of Ethnic Cleansing during World War II', *Holocaust and Genocide Studies* 21 (2007), 268–97.

41. Hans Werner Neulen, *Eurofaschismus und der Zweite Weltkrieg. Europas verratene Söhne* (Munich: Universitas, 1980). Generally on collaboration, Christoph Dieckmann, Christian Gerlach, and Wolf Gruner (eds), *Kooperation und Verbrechen: Formen der Kollaboration im östlichen Europa 1939–1945* (Göttingen: Wallstein, 2003).

42. Frederick B. Chary, *The Bulgarian Jews and the Final Solution, 1940–1944* (Pittsburgh: University of Pittsburgh Press, 1972); Tzvetan Todorov, *The Fragility of Goodness: Why Bulgaria's Jews Survived the Holocaust: A Collection of Texts*, trans. Arthur Denner (Princeton, NJ: Princeton University Press, 2001); Gerlach and Aly, *Das letzte Kapitel*, 430.

43. Solonari, 'Document'.

44. Tönsmeyer, 'The Robbery'.

45. Radu Ioanid, *The Sword of the Archangel* (New York: Columbia University Press, 1990), Ch. 6.

46. Radu Ioanid, *The Holocaust in Romania: The Destruction of Jews and Gypsies under the Antonescu Regime, 1940–1944* (New York: Ivan R. Dee, 2000); Andrej Angrick, *Besatzungspolitik und Massenmord. Die Einsatzgruppe D in der südlichen Sowjetunion 1941–1943* (Hamburg: Hamburger Edition 2003); Ancel, 'German-Romanian'; Ingeborg Fleischhauer, *Das Dritte Reich und die Deutschen in der Sowjetunion* (Stuttgart: DVA, 1983). Generally on Hungarian–Romanian relations, see Holly Case, *Between States: The Transylvanian Question and the European Idea during WWII* (Stanford, CA: Stanford University Press, 2009).

47. MacGregor Knox, 'Das faschistische Italien und die "Endlösung" 1942/3', *Vierteljahrshefte für Zeitgeschichte*, 1 Sonderdruck (2007), 53–92; Lidia Santarelli, 'La violenza taciuta. I crimini degli italiani nella Grecia occupata', in Luca Baldissara and Paolo Pezzino (eds), *Criminie Memorie di Guerra. Violenze Contro le populazione e politiche del ricardo* (Naples: Ancora

del Mediterraneo, 2004), 271–91; *idem*, 'The Righteous Enemy? Fascist Italy and the Holocaust in Axis Occupied Greece', Fellows Meeting, US Holocaust Memorial Museum, 28 November 2007; H. James Burgwyn, *Empire on the Adriatic. Mussolini's Conquest of Yugoslavia, 1941–1943* (New York: Enigma Books, 2005); Davide Rodogno, *Fascism's European Empire: Italian Occupation during the Second World War* (Cambridge: Cambridge University Press, 2006); Mark Mazower, *Inside Hitler's Greece: The Experience of Occupation* (London: Yale University Press, 1993).

48. Burgwyn, *Empire*; Stevan Pavlowitch, *Hitler's New Disorder: The Second World War in Yugoslavia* (New York: Columbia University Press, 2008); Alexander Korb, 'Understanding Ustaša Violence', *Journal of Genocide Research*, forthcoming.

49. Tatjana Tönsmeyer, *Das Dritte Reich und die Slowakei 1939–1945* (Paderborn: Schöningh, 2003), 137–62; Wolfgang Benz (ed.), *Jahrbuch für Antisemitismusforschung* 7 (Frankfurt am Main: Campus, 1992), especially the essays by Eduard Nižňanský, 'Die Deportation der Juden in der Zeit der autonomen Slowakei im November 1938', 20–45; Livia Rothkirchen, 'The Situation of Jews in Slovakia between 1939 and 1945', 46–70; and Konrad Kwiet, 'Der Mord an Juden, Zigeunern und Partisanen. Zum Einsatz des Einsatzkommandos 14 der Sicherheitspolizei und des SD in der Slowakei 1944/1945', 71–81.

50. Robert Paxton, *Vichy France: Old Guard and New Order, 1940–44* (New York: Columbia University Press, 1982).

51. Susan Zuccotti, *The Holocaust, the French and the Jews* (New York: Basic Books, 1993).

52. Pim Griffioen and Ron Zeller, 'Anti-Jewish Policy and Organization of the Deportations in France and the Netherlands, 1940–1944: A Comparative Study', *Holocaust and Genocide Studies* 20 (2006), 437–73.

53. Christoph Dieckmann and Saulius Sužiedelis, *The Persecution and Mass Murder of Lithuanian Jews during Summer and Fall of 1944* (Vilnius: Margi Raštai, 2006), 176.

54. Jan T. Gross, *Neighbors: The Destruction of the Jewish Community in Jedwabne, Poland* (Princeton, NJ: Princeton University Press, 2001).

55. Hans-Heinrich Wilhelm, 'Antisemitismus im Baltikum', in Helge Gräbitz, Klaus Bästlein and Johannes Tuchel (eds), *Die Normalität des Verbrechens* (Berlin: Edition Hentrich, 1994), 85–102; Bogdan Musial, *'Konterrevolutionäre Elemente sind zu erschießen'. Die Brutalisierung des deutsch-sowjetischen Krieges im Sommer 1941* (Berlin: Propyläen, 2000), 71.

56. Dieter Pohl, 'Schauplatz Ukraine', in Norbert Frei, Sybille Steinbacher, and Bernd Wagner (eds), *Ausbeutung, Vernichtung, Öffentlichkeit* (Munich: Saur, 2000), 135–73, here 138; *idem, Nationalsozialistische Judenverfolgung in Ostgalizien 1941–1944: Organisation und Durchführung eines staatlichen Massenverbrechens* (Munich: Oldenbourg, 1997), 54–7, 64–5.

57. On the interethnic situation, Michael MacQueen, 'Polen, Litauer, Juden und Deutsche in Wilna 1939–1944', in Wolfgang Benz and Marion Neiss (eds), *Judenmord in Litauen: Studien und Dokumente* (Berlin: Metropol, 1999), 51–68.

58. Timothy Snyder, *The Reconstruction of Nations: Poland, Ukraine, Belarus, 1569–1999* (London: Yale University Press, 2004), Chs. 3, 4, 8, 9; Pohl, *Judenverfolgung in Ostgalizien*, 43–67; Karel C. Berkhoff, *Harvest of Despair: Life and Death in Ukraine under Nazi Rule* (Cambridge, MA: Harvard University Press, 2004), Chs. 1–3.

59. Dieckmann and Sužiedelis, *Persecution*, 95–177; Joseph Goebbels, *Die Tagebücher von Joseph Goebbels*, ed. Elke Fröhlich (Munich: K. G. Saur, 1996), part II: 1941–1945, vol. I, 269.

Chapter 4—Nazism and Germany

1. Martin Cüppers, *Wegbereiter der Shoah: Die Waffen-SS, der Kommandostab Reichsführer-SS und die Judenvernichtung 1939–1945* (Darmstadt: Wissenschaftliche Buchgesellschaft, 2005).

2. A concept developed by John Horne.

3. Richard Bessel, *Germany after the First World War* (Oxford: Oxford University Press, 1993).

4. Tim Mason, 'The Legacy of 1918 for National Socialism', Ch. 1 of his *Social Policy in the Third Reich: The Working Class and the 'National Community'* (Oxford: Berghahn, 1993). My arguments here also owe something to Fritz Fischer.

5. Dirk Blasius, *Weimars Ende: Bürgerkrieg und Politik 1930–1933* (Göttingen: Vandenhoeck and Ruprecht, 2005); Jane Caplan, 'Political Detention and the Origin of the Concentration Camps in Nazi Germany, 1933–1935/6', in Neil Gregor (ed.), *Nazism, War and Genocide: Essays in Honour of Jeremy Noakes* (Exeter: University of Exeter Press, 2005), 22–41, here 30.

6. Saul Friedländer, *Nazi Germany and the Jews*, 2 vols (New York: Harper Collins, 1997, 2007), i, 86–90.

7. Norman Cohn, *Warrant for Genocide: The Jewish World Conspiracy and the Protocols of the Elders of Zion* (London: Serif, 1996).

8. Lutz Hachmeister, *Der Gegnerforscher: Die Karrier des SS-Führers Franz Alfred Six* (Munich: Beck, 1998), 184.

9. Statistics from Gisela Bock, 'Racism and Sexism in Nazi Germany: Motherhood, Compulsory Sterilization, and the State', *Signs* 8 (1983), 400–21, here 412–13. Henry Friedlander, *The Origins of Nazi Genocide* (Chapel Hill: University of North Carolina Press, 1995).

10. Bock, 'Racism and Sexism', 415.

11. On the Gestapo, Shlomo Aronson, *Reinhard Heydrich und die Frühgeschichte von Gestapo und SD* (Stuttgart: Deutsche Verlags-Anstalt, 1971); on the Kriminalpolizei, Patrick Wagner, *Volksgemeinschaft ohne Verbrecher: Konzeption und Praxis der Kriminalpolizei in der Zeit der Weimarer Republik und des Nationalsozialismus* (Hamburg: Christians, 1996).

12. Ulrich Herbert, *Best: Biographische Studien über Radikalismus, Weltanschauung und Vernunft 1903–1989* (Bonn: Dietz, 1996), 170–7; Michael Wildt, *Generation des Unbedingten: Das Führungskorps des Reichssicherheitshauptamtes* (Hamburg, Hamburger Edition, 2003), 314–21.

13. e.g. Michael Zimmermann, *Rassenutopie und Genozid: Die nationalsozialistische 'Lösung der Zigeunerfrage'* (Hamburg: Christians, 1996), from whose volume stems most of the detail on Romanies in the following chapters.

14. Ian Kershaw, 'The Persecution of the Jews and German Public Opinion in the Third Reich', *Leo Baeck Institute Yearbook* 26 (1981), 261–89, covering both the pre- and post-1933 periods.

15. Hans-Ulrich Wehler, *The German Empire, 1871–1918*, trans. K. Traynor (Oxford: Berg, 1985), 93.

16. Geoff Eley, *Reshaping the German Right: Radical Nationalism and Political Change after Bismarck* (Ann Arbor: University of Michigan Press, 1990).

17. Alan Kramer, 'Wackes at War: Alsace-Lorraine and the Failure of German National Mobilization, 1914–1918', in John Horne (ed.), *State, Society and Mobilization in Europe during the First World War* (New York: Cambridge University Press, 1997), 105–21.

18. The term is Arthur Marwick's.

19. Steffan Bruendel, *Volksgemeinschaft oder Volksstaat: Die 'Ideen von 1914' und die Neuordnung Deutschlands im Ersten Weltkrieg* (Berlin: Akademie Verlag, 2003).

20. Here and elsewhere, my analysis is indebted to William Sheridan Allen, 'The Appeal of Fascism and the Problem of National Disintegration', in Henry A. Turner (ed.), *Reappraisals of Fascism* (New York: New Viewpoints, 1975), 44–68.

21. Michael Burleigh and Wolfgang Wippermann, *The Racial State: Germany 1933–1945* (Cambridge: Cambridge University Press, 1991).

22. Robert Gellately, *Backing Hitler: Consent and Coercion in Nazi Germany* (Oxford: Oxford University Press, 2001), synthesizes a large German literature on the subject.

23. Shelley Baranowski, *Strength through Joy: Consumerism and Mass Tourism in the Third Reich* (Cambridge: Cambridge University Press, 2004).

24. Richard Steigman-Gall, *The Holy Reich: Nazi Conceptions of Christianity, 1919–1945* (Cambridge: Cambridge University Press, 2004); Thomas Lawson, *The Church of England and the Holocaust: Christianity, Memory and Nazism* (London: Boydell and Brewer, 2006); Beth A. Griech-Polelle, *Bishop von Galen: German Catholicism and National Socialism* (New Haven, CT: Yale University Press, 2002).

25. Eric Johnson, *Nazi Terror: The Gestapo, Jews and Ordinary Germans* (London: John Murray, 2000).

26. Joseph Robert White, 'Introduction to the Early Camps', in Geoffrey P. Megargee (ed.), *The United States Holocaust Memorial Museum Encyclopedia of Camps and Ghettos*, vol. I (Bloomington: Indiana University Press; Published in Association with USHMM, 2009), 3–16; Caplan, 'Political Detention', 30.

27. Wagner, *Volksgemeinschaft ohne Verbrecher*.

28. On the complex situation in Weimar, see Nicola Wenge, *Integration und Ausgrenzung in der städtischen Gesellschaft. Eine jüdisch-nicht jüdische Beziehungsgeschichte Kölns 1918–1933* (Mainz: Philipp von Zabern, 2005). On party-political anti-Semitism, Peter Pulzer, *The Rise of Political Antisemitism in Germany and Austria* (London: Halban, 1988). On violence against Jews, see Frank Bajohr's essay in his and Dieter Pohl's *Der Holocaust als offenes Geheimnis: Die Deutschen, die NS-Führung und die Alliierten* (München: C. H. Beck, 2006).

29. Hans Witek and Hans Safrian, *Und keiner war dabei. Dokumente des alltäglichen Antisemitismus in Wien 1938* (Vienna: Picus, 1988); Gerhard Botz, *Wohnungspolitik und Judendeportation in Wien 1938 bis 1945* (Vienna: Geyer-Edition, 1975);

30. Jeffery Herf, *The Jewish Enemy: Nazi Propaganda during World War II and the Holocaust* (Cambridge, MA: Harvard University Press, 2008); Bernward Dörner, *Die Deutschen und der Holocaust. Was niemand wissen wollte, aber jeder wissen konnte* (Berlin: Propyläen, 2007).

31. 'Staatssekretärsbesprechung im Reichsinnenministerium', 29 September 1936, rprt in Wolf Gruner (ed.), *Die Verfolgung und Ermordung der*

europäischen Juden durch das nationalsozialistische Deutschland 1933–1945 (Munich: Oldenbourg, 2008), 603.

32. Bajohr and Pohl, *offenes Geheimnis*.

33. Ibid.; Peter Longerich, *'Davon haben wir nichts gewusst!' Die Deutschen und die Judenverfolgung 1933–1945* (Munich: Siedler, 2006); Michael Wildt, *Volksgemeinschaft als Selbstermächtigung. Gewalt gegen Juden in der deutschen Provinz 1919 bis 1939* (Hamburg: Hamburger Edition, 2007).

34. Claudia Koonz, *The Nazi Conscience* (Cambridge, MA: Harvard Belknap, 2003); Alan Steinweis, *Studying the Jew: Scholarly Antisemitism in Nazi Germany* (Cambridge, MA: Harvard University Press, 2006); Paul Weindling, *Health, Race, and German Politics between National Unification and Nazism 1870–1945* (Cambridge: Cambridge University Press, 1989).

35. Gretchen E. Schafft, *From Racism to Genocide: Anthropology in the Third Reich* (Urbana: University of Illinois Press, 2004); Alexandra Przyrembel, *'Rassenschande': Reinheitsmythos und Vernichtungslegitimation im Nationalsozialismus* (Göttingen: Vandenhoeck und Ruprecht, 2003).

36. Frank Bajohr, *'Arisierung' in Hamburg: Die Verdrängung der jüdischer Unternehmer 1933–1945* (Hamburg: Christians, 1997).

37. Eric Ehrenreich, *The Nazi Ancestral Proof: Genealogy, Racial Science, and the Final Solution* (Bloomington: Indiana University Press, 2007).

38. Stephanie Abke, *Sichtbare Zeichen unsichtbarer Kräfte: Denunziationsmuster und Denunziationsverhalten 1933–1945* (Tübingen: edition discord, 2003).

39. David Bankier, *The Germans and the Final Solution: Public Opinion under Nazism* (Oxford, Blackwell, 1992), 72, 84, on the increasing indifference of the majority of the population to the Jewish plight.

40. Dörner, *Die Deutschen*; Longerich, *Davon*.

41. Johann Böhm, *Die Gleichschaltung der Deutschen Volksgruppe in Rumänien und das 'Dritte Reich' 1941–1944* (Frankfurt am Main: Peter Lang, 2003).

42. Hans Mommsen, *Beamtentum in Dritten Reich* (Stuttgart: Oldenbourg, 1966).

43. Devin Pendas, 'Retroactive Law and Proactive Justice: Debating Crimes against Humanity in the British Occupation Zone, 1945–1950', forthcoming in *Central European History*; Donald Bloxham, 'Organized Mass Murder: Structure, Participation, and Motivation in Comparative Perspective', *Holocaust and Genocide Studies* 22 (2008), 203–45, here 215–16.

44. Mommsen, *Beamtentum*.

45. White, 'Introduction'.

46. On the civil service law, Horst Matzerath, 'Bürokratie und Judenverfolgung', in Ursula Büttner (ed.), *Die Deutschen und die Judenverfolgung im Dritten Reich* (Hamburg: Christians, 1992), 105–29, here 107–10. On the judiciary, Diemut Majer, *'Non-Germans' under the Third Reich* (Baltimore: Johns Hopkins University Press, 2003), 29, 32–3.

47. Wolf Gruner, *Öffentliche Wohlfahrt und Judenverfolgung: Wechselwirkung lokaler und zentraler Politik im NS-Staat (1933–1942)* (Munich: Oldenbourg, 2002).

48. Edward B. Westermann, *Hitler's Police Battalions: Enforcing Racial War in the* East (Lawrence: University Press of Kansas, 2005); Stephan Linck, *Der Ordnung verpflichtet: Deutsche Polizei 1933–1949: Der Fall Flensburg* (Paderborn: Schöningh, 2000), 27.

49. Jürgen Matthäus, 'Ausbildung zum Judenmord? Zum Stellenwert der "weltanschaulichen Erziehung" von SS und Polizei im Rahmen der "Endlösung"', *Zeitschrift für Geschichtswissenschaft* 47 (1999), 677–99.

50. Manfred Messerschmidt, '"Harte Sühne am Judentum". Befehlswege und Wissen in der deutschen Wehrmacht', in Jörg Wollenberg (ed.), *'Niemand war dabei und keiner hat's gewußt': Die deutsche Öffentlichkeit und die Judenverfolgung 1933–1945* (Munich: Piper, 1989), 113–28.

51. Walter Naasner, *Neue Machtzentren in der deutschen Kriegswirtschaft 1942–45* (Boppard am Rhein: Harald Boldt, 1994).

52. For a synthesis of the large literature on this subject, see Omer Bartov, *Mirrors of Destruction: War, Genocide, and Modern Identity* (Oxford: Oxford University Press, 2000), Ch. 1.

53. Peter Hüttenberger, *Die Gauleiter: Studie zum Wandel des Machtgefüges in der NSDAP* (Stuttgart: Deutsche Verlags-Anstalt, 1969), 173–4.

54. Bernd Wegner, *The Waffen SS: Organization, Ideology and Function* (Oxford: Blackwell, 1990), p. ix.

55. Ruth Bettina Birn, *Die Höheren SS-und Polizeiführer* (Düsseldorf: Droste, 1986), 350–62.

56. Maurice Williams, *Gau, Volk, and Reich: Friedrich Rainer and the Paradox of Austrian National Socialism* (Klagenfurt: Verlag des Geschichtsvereins für Kärnten, 2005); Hüttenberger, *Die Gauleiter*.

57. Herbert, *Best*, 13 and part III, Ch. 4; Wildt, *Generation*; Hachmeister, *Der Gegnerforscher*, Ch. 2 on the social background of key RSHA men.

58. Michael Wildt, *Die Judenpolitik des SD 1935–1938* (Munich: Oldenbourg, 1995); *idem, Generation*; Götz Aly, '"Judenumsiedlung": Überlegungen zur politischen Vorgeschichte des Holocaust', in Ulrich Herbert (ed.), *Nationalsozialistische Vernichtungspolitik 1939–1945: Neue Forschungen und*

Kontroversen (Frankfurt am Main: Fischer, 1998), 67–97; Andrej Angrick, *Besatzungspolitik und Massenmord: Die Einsatzgruppe D in der südlichen Sowjetunion 1941–1943* (Hamburg: Hamburger Edition, 2003), 121.

59. Herbert, *Best*, 170–77; Wildt, *Generation des Unbedingten*.
60. Hüttenberger, *Die Gauleiter*, 172–3.
61. Hermann Kaienburg, 'Vernichtung durch Arbeit': *der Fall Neuengamme* (Bonn: J. H. W. Dietz, 1990), 35–7, 452–3; Enno Georg, *Die wirtschaftlichen Unternehmungen der SS* (Stuttgart: Deutsche Verlags-Anstalt, 1963), 72.
62. Max Domarus (ed.), *Hitler. Reden und Proklamationen 1932–1945*, 2 vols. (Neustadt: Schmidt, 1962), vol. i, 10 September 1935, p. 525.
63. Cornelia Essner, *Die 'Nürnberger Gesetze' oder Die Verwaltung des Rassenwahns 1933–1945* (Paderborn: Schöningh, 2002).
64. Schafft, *From Racism to Genocide*, 32.
65. Domarus (ed.), *Hitler. Reden*, vol. ii, 30 January 1939, pp. 1055–6.
66. Wolf Gruner, *Der geschlossene Arbeitseinsatz deutscher Juden: Zur Zwangsarbeit als Element der Verfolgung 1938–1943* (Berlin: Metropol, 1997).
67. Martin Broszat, *The Hitler State: The Foundation and Development of the Internal Structure of the Third Reich* (London: Longman, 1981), 294 and Ch. 9 *passim*.
68. Marion A. Kaplan, *Between Dignity and Despair: Jewish life in Nazi Germany* (New York: Oxford University Press, 1998).
69. Hans Safrian, 'Expediting Expropriation and Expulsion: The Impact of the "Vienna Model" on Anti-Jewish Policies in Nazi Germany, 1938', *Holocaust and Genocide Studies*, 14 (2000), 390–414.
70. Gruner, *Der geschlossene Arbeitseinsatz*.
71. Aly, ' "Judenumsiedlung" ', 69–73; Wildt, *Generation*. On the security police, Herbert, *Best*, 221–4.
72. Hilberg, *Destruction*, i., 95 on 'voluntary' and 'compulsory' Aryanization.
73. Wolf Gruner, 'Das Protektorat Böhmen/Mähren und die antijüdische Politik 1939–1941. Lokale Initiativen, regionale Maßnahmen und zentrale Entscheidungen im "Großdeutschen Reich" ', in *Theresienstädter Studien und Dokumente*, 12 (2006), 27–62.

Chapter 5—Genocide in Germany's Eastern Empire

1. Gerhard L. Weinberg, *Germany, Hitler, and World War II: Essays in Modern German and World History* (New York: Cambridge University Press, 1995), 2.

2. Max Domarus (ed.), *Hitler. Reden und Proklamationen 1932–1945*, 2 vols (Neustadt: Schmidt, 1962), vol. ii, 6 October 1939, p. 1383. On the First World War, Fritz Fischer, *Germany's Aims in the First World War* (New York: Norton, 1961), 278–9.

3. Ralf Blank, 'Albert Hoffmann als Reichsverteidigungskommissar im Gau Westfalen-Süd. Eine biografische Skizze', in Wolf Gruner and Armin Nolzen (eds), *'Bürokratien'. Initiative und Effizienz* (Berlin: Assoziation A, 2001), 189–212.

4. Diemut Majer, 'Führerunmittelbare Sondergewalten in den besetzten Ost- gebieten', in Dieter Rebentisch and Karl Teppe (eds), *Verwaltung contra Menschenführung im Staat Hitlers. Studien zum politisch-administrativen System* (Göttingen: Vandenhoeck und Ruprecht, 1986), 374–94.

5. Henry Friedlander, *The Origins of Nazi Genocide* (Chapel Hill: University of North Carolina Press, 1995); Ernst Klee, *'Euthanasie' im NS-Staat: Die 'Vernichtung lebensunwerten Lebens'* (Frankfurt am Main: Fischer, 1983); Götz Aly (ed.), *Aussonderung und Tod. Die klinische Hinrichtung des Unbrauchbaren* (Berlin: Rotbuch 1985).

6. Michael Zimmermann, *Rassenutopie und Genozid: Die nationalsozialistische 'Lösung der Zigeunerfrage'* (Hamburg: Christians, 1996), 168–73.

7. Dieter Pohl, *Nationalsozialistische Judenverfolgung in Ostgalizien 1941–1944: Organisation und Durchführung eines staatlichen Massenverbrechens* (Munich: Oldenbourg, 1997), 403–4; idem, *Von der 'Judenpolitik' zum Judenmord: Der Distrikt Lublin des Generalgouvernements 1939–1944* (Frank- furt am Main: Lang, 1993), 37–41. On Belarus, Christian Gerlach, *Kalkulierte Morde: Die deutsche Wirtschafts- und Vernichtungspolitik im Weißrußland* (Hamburg: Hamburger Edition, 1999), 177, 1151–4; Bogdan Musial, *Deutsche Zivilverwaltung und Judenverfolgung im Gen- eralgouvernement: Eine Fallstudie zum Distrikt Lublin 1939–1944* (Leipzig: Harrassowitz, 1999), 23–64. David Furber, 'Going East: Colonialism and German Life in Nazi-Occupied Poland', PhD dissertation, State University of New York, 2003.

8. Alexa Stiller, 'Reichskommissar für die Festigung deutschen Volkstums', in Ingo Haar and Michael Fahlbusch (eds), *Handbuch der völkischen Wissenschaften* (Munich: KG Saur, 2008), 531–40.

9. Herbert S. Levine, 'Local Authority and the SS State: The Conflict over Population Policy in Danzig-West Prussia, 1939–1945', *Central European History* 2 (1969), 531–55.

10. Michael Alberti, *Die Verfolgung und Vernichtung der Juden im Reichsgau Wartheland 1939–1945* (Wiesbaden: Harrassowitz, 2006), 517.

11. 'Mitteilung einer Bilanz der "völkischen Säuberung" im Elsaß', 22 April 41, Akten der Partei-Kanzlei der NSDAP, rprt. in *Deutsche Geschichte im 20. Jahrhundert Online. Nationalsozialismus, Holocaust, Widerstand und Exil 1933–1945. Online-Datenbank*, ed. K. G. Saur Verlag. On the 'Westmark', Celia Applegate, *A Nation of Provincials: The German Idea of Heimat* (Berkeley: University of California Press, 1990), 222–5.

12. Heydrich to Luther, 24 October 1940, in *Die drei verantwortlichen SS-Führer für die Durchführung der Endlösung der Judenfrage in Europa waren: Heydrich—Eichmann—Müller : eine dokumentarische Sammlung von SS- und Gestapo-Dokumenten über die Vernichtung der Juden Europas 1939–1945*, ed. Tuviah Friedman (Haifa: Institute of Documentation in Israel, 1993), part II; on the context, Jacob Toury, 'Die Entstehungsgeschichte des Austreibungsbefehls gegen die Juden der Saarpfalz und Badens (22/23 Oktober 1940—Camp de Gurs)', *Jahrbuch des Instituts für Deutsche Geschichte* 15 (1986), 431–64.

13. Maurice Williams, *Gau, Volk, and Reich: Friedrich Rainer and the Paradox of Austrian National Socialism* (Klagenfurt: Verlag des Geschichtsvereins für Kärnten, 2005); Stefan Karner, ' ". . . Des Reiches Südmark". Kärnten und Steiermark im "Dritten Reich" 1938–1945', in *NS-Herrschaft in Österreich: Ein Handbuch* (Vienna: öbv & hpt, 2001), 292–324. On Upper Silesia, see below.

14. Heydrich to Finance Ministry, 21 April 1941, in *Die drei verantwort-lichen*, ed. Friedman, part. II; Hans-Ulrich Wehler, ' "Reichsfestung Belgrad"—Nationalsozialistische "Raumordnung" in Südosteuropa', *Vierteljahreshefte für Zeitgeschichte* 1 (1963), 74–86; Valentin Sima, 'Die Kärntner Slowenen unter nationalsozialistischer Herrschaft. Verfolgung, Widerstand und Repression', in *NS-Herrschaft in Österreich*, 744–66; Stiller 'Reichskommissar'.

15. Michael Zimmermann, 'Die nationalsozialistische "Lösung der Zigeuner-frage" ', in Ulrich Herbert (ed.), *Nationalsozialistische Vernichtungspolitik 1939–1945: Neue Forschungen und Kontroversen* (Frankfurt am Main: Fischer, 1998), 235–62, here 249.

16. Mechthild Rössler and Sabine Schleiermacher (eds), *Der 'Generalplan Ost': Hauptlinien der nationalsozialistischen Planungs und Vernichtungspolitik* (Berlin: Akademie Verlag, 1993).

17. Götz Aly and Suzanne Heim, *Vordenker der Vernichtung: Auschwitz und die deutschen Pläne für eine neue europäischen Ordnung* (Frankfurt am Main, 1993), Ch. 13.

18. Chad Bryant, 'Either German or Czech: Fixing Nationality in Bohemia and Moravia, 1939–1946', *Slavic Review* 61 (2002), 683–706; Hans Safrian, *Eichmann und seine Gehilfen* (Frankfurt am Main: Fischer, 1995), 105–6. Isabel Heinemann, *'Rasse, Siedlung, deutsches Blut': Das Rasse- und Siedlungshauptamt der SS und die rassenpolitische Neuordnung Europas* (Göttingen: Wallstein Verlag, 2003).

19. Czesław Madajczyk, 'General Plan East: Hitler's Master Plan for Expansion', *Polish Western Affairs*, 3:2 (1962), 391–442; Norbert Kunz, *Die Krim unter deutscher Herrschaft (1941–1944). Germanisierungsutopie und Besatzungsrealität* (Darmstadt: Wissenschaftliche Buchgesellschaft, 2005); Wendy Lower, *Nazi Empire-Building and the Holocaust in Ukraine* (Chapel Hill: University of North Carolina Press, 2005).

20. Nuremberg Document NOKW-1535; Christian Gerlach, *Krieg, Ernährung, Völkermord: Forschungen zur deutschen Vernichtungspolitik im Zweiten Weltkrieg* (Hamburg: Hamburger Edition, 1998), 29–56; William Carr, *Poland to Pearl Harbor: The Making of the Second World War* (London: Arnold, 1985); 123.

21. Musial, *Deutsche Zivilverwaltung*, 345–6.

22. Ibid. 210; Safrian, *Eichmann und seine Gehilfen*, 141; Gerlach, *Krieg, Ernährung, Völkermord*, Ch. 1.

23. Werner Jochmann (ed.), *Adolf Hitler: Monologe im Führerhauptquartier, 1941–1945. Die Aufzeichnungen Heinrich Heims* (Hamburg: Albrecht Knaus, 1980), 90. For the 1937 and 1941 quotations, see Nuremberg Documents PS-386 and EC-126 respectively.

24. Testimony of 18 November 1946, repr. in *Das Dritte Reich und die Juden: Dokumente und Aufsätze*, eds. Leon Poliakov and Joseph Wulf (Berlin: Fourier Verlag 1989), 87–98, here 90.

25. Steven T. Katz, 'The "Unique" Intentionality of the Holocaust', *Modern Judaism* 1:2 (1981), 161–83. See, e.g., p. 162: 'Hitler... sought to make the world Judenrein by the elimination of all "racial" Jews, i.e. all Jews as concrete individual human beings.' See also Dan Diner, 'Epistemics of the Holocaust Considering the Question of "Why?" and of "How?"', *Zeitschrift für deutsch-jüdische Literatur und Kulturgeschichte* 1 (2008), 195–213, here 197.

26. Rudolf Hoess, *Commandant of Auschwitz: The Autobiography of Rudolf Hoss* (London: Phoenix Press, 1961), 206–8; 214–15. Emphasis added.

27. Raphael Lemkin, 'Genocide as a Crime under International Law', *American Journal of International Law* 41:1 (1947), 145–51, here 147.

28. Christopher R. Browning, *The Final Solution and the German Foreign Office: A Study of Referat D III of Abteilung Deutschland, 1940–43* (New York: Holmes and Meier, 1978), 36. My concern with the central status of the destruction of the Jews of Poland and the USSR stems from my earlier interest in the prosecution of Holocaust perpetrators and the representation of the Holocaust in the Nuremberg trials, where the obliteration of Polish Jewry was accorded little attention relative to the wider continental aspects of the genocide. See Donald Bloxham, *Genocide on Trial: War Crimes Trials and the Formation of Holocaust History and Memory* (Oxford: Oxford University Press, 2001), 109–28.

29. I have adapted this expression from my own 'ethnic reprisal policy', which I elucidate as the first phase in the Armenian genocide. See Donald Bloxham, *The Great Game of Genocide: Imperialism, Nationalism, and the Destruction of the Ottoman Armenians* (Oxford: Oxford University Press, 2005), Ch. 2.

30. Helmut Krausnick and Hans-Heinrich Wilhelm, *Die Truppe des Weltanschauungskrieges. Die Einsatzgruppen der Sicherheitspolizei und des SD 1938–1942* (Stuttgart: Deutsche Verlags-Anstalt, 1981); Safrian, *Eichmann und seine Gehilfen*, 137.

31. Klaus-Michael Mallmann, Jochen Böhler, and Jürgen Matthäus (eds), *Einsatzgruppen in Polen. Darstellung und Dokumentation* (Darmstadt: Wissenschaftliche Buchgesellschaft, 2008), 19–46, 55–6.

32. Michael Wildt (ed.), *Nachrichtendienst, politische Elite und Mordeinheit: Der Sicherheitsdienst des Reichsführers SS* (Hamburg: Hamburger Edition, 2003), 24–5, 33–7.

33. For slightly different estimates of the level of Wehrmacht involvement in anti-Semitic murder, see Klaus-Michael Mallmann and Bogdan Musial (eds), *Genesis des Genozids: Polen 1939–1941* (Darmstadt: Wissenschaftliche Buchgesellschaft, 2004), 43–7, cf. 112.

34. Alexander B. Rossino, 'Nazi Anti-Jewish Policy during the Polish campaign: The Case of the Einsatzgruppe von Woyrsch', *German Studies Review* 24 (2001), 35–53; Mallmann et al. (eds) *Einsatzgruppen*, 85–8.

35. Christopher Browning and Jürgen Matthäus, *The Origin of the Final Solution: The Evolution of Nazi Jewish Policy, September 1939–March 1942* (Lincoln: University of Nebraska Press, 2004), 36–43.

36. Mallmann et al. (eds), *Einsatzgruppen*, 144–6.

37. Dan Michman, 'Why did Heydrich Write the Schnellbrief? A Remark on the Reason and on Its Significance', *Yad Vashem Studies* 32 (2004), 433–47.

38. The protocols, reproduced in Mallmann et al. (eds), *Einsatzgruppen*, 144–5, stated: Himmler is to be 'settlement commissioner for the east'. See also Zimmermann, *Rassenutopie*, 167, on the 'Himmler getragene Ziele'.

39. Sybille Steinbacher, *'Musterstadt' Auschwitz: Germanisierungspolitik und Judenmord in Ostoberschlesien* (Munich: K. G. Saur Verlag, 1999); Deborah Dwork and Robert Jan Van Pelt, *Auschwitz: 1270 to the Present* (New York: Norton, 1996).

40. Christopher Browning, *The Path to Genocide: Essays on Launching the Final Solution* (Cambridge: Cambridge University Press, 1992), 28–56; Peter Klein, 'Die "Ghettoverwaltung Litzmannstadt" als städtische Behörde', *Fritz Bauer Institut Newsletter* 32 (2008), 7–9.

41. Musial, *Deutsche Zivilverwaltung*, 343. Thomas Sandkühler, *'Endlösung' in Galizien: Der Judenmord in Ostpolen und die Rettungsinitiativen von Berthold Beitz 1941–1944* (Bonn: J. H. W. Dietz, 1996), 110; on the Warthegau, Ian Kershaw, 'Improvised Genocide? The Emergence of the 'Final Solution' in the "Warthegau"', *Transactions of the Royal Historical Society*, 6th ser., 2 (1992), 51–78, here 58.

42. Browning and Matthäus, *The Origin*, 145–9; Bruno Wasser, 'Die "Germanisierung" im Distrikt Lublin als Generalprobe und erste Realisierungsphase des "Generalplans Ost"', in Rössler and Schleiermacher (eds), *Der 'Generalplan Ost'*, 271–93.

43. Götz Aly, '"Judenumsiedlung": Überlegungen zur politischen Vorgeschichte des Holocaust', in Herbert (ed.), *Nationalsozialistische Vernichtungspolitik*, 86; Friedlander, *Origins*, 142–50.

44. Phillip T. Rutherford, *Prelude to the Final Solution: The Nazi Program for Deporting Ethnic Poles, 1939–1941* (Lawrence, KS: University Press of Kansas, 2007).

45. Aly, 'Vorgeschichte', 91; Bogdan Musial, 'The Origins of "Operation Reinhard": The Decision-Making Process for the Mass Murder of the Jews in the Generalgouvernement', *Yad Vashem Studies* 28 (2000), 113–53, here 123.

46. Raffael Scheck, *Hitler's African Victims: The German Army Massacres of Black French Soldiers in 1940* (Cambridge: Cambridge University Press, 2006).

47. On Tito's partisans and Serbia, W. Manoschek, *'Serbien ist Judenfrei': Militärische Besatzungspolitik und Judenvernichtung in Serbien 1941/42* (Munich: Oldenbourg, 1993), 12, 122–3.

48. Ibid.; Ulrich Herbert, 'Die deutsche Militärverwaltung in Paris und die Deportation der französischen Juden', in *idem* (ed.), *Nationalsozialistische Vernichtungspolitik*, 170–208.

49. Donald Bloxham and Tony Kushner, *The Holocaust: Critical Historical Approaches* (Manchester: Manchester University Press, 2005), 73, 78, 131, 142–3.

50. On France, see Ch. 6.

51. Nuremberg Documents NOKW-484 and C-50.

52. Bloxham and Kushner, *The Holocaust*, 142–3. A. Dirk Moses (ed.) *Empire, Colony, Genocide* (New York: Berghahn, 2008), especially the editor's introductory essay.

53. Nuremberg Document PS-829. On variations in the severity of the jurisdiction decree as it was passed on, see Felix Römer, '"Im alten Deutschland wäre solcher Befehl nicht möglich gewesen". Rezeption, Adaption und Umsetzung des Kriegsgerichtsbarkeits-erlasses im Ostheer 1941/42', *Vierteljahrshefte für Zeitgeschichte* 56 (2008), 53–99.

54. Ben Shepherd, *War in the Wild East: The German Army and the Soviet Partisans* (Cambridge, MA: Harvard University Press, 2004), 73–4, 103–6.

55. On the Einsatzgruppen, Peter Klein (ed.), *Die Einsatzgruppen in der besetzten Sowjetunion 1941/42. Die Tätigkeits- und Lageberichte des Chefs der Sicherheitspolizei und des SD* (Berlin: Wannsee-Haus, 1997); Andrej Angrick, *Besatzungspolitik und Massenmord: Die Einsatzgruppe D in der südlichen Sowjetunion 1941–1943* (Hamburg: Hamburger Edition, 2003); Ralf Oggoreck, *Die Einsatzgruppen und die 'Genesis der Endlösung'* (Berlin: Metropol, 1996); Krausnick and Wilhelm, *Die Truppe*.

56. The 3,000 number is an approximate figure for the number in the field at any one time. Approximately 6,000 men served in total in the Einsatzgruppen.

57. Richard Breitman, *The Architect of Genocide: Himmler and the Final Solution* (New York: Knopf, 1991), 181–4. Cf. Peter Witte et al. (eds), *Der Dienstkalendar Heinrich Himmlers 1941/1942* (Hamburg: Christians, 1999), 58–62.

58. Hans Umbreit, 'Zur Organisation der Besatzungsherrschaft', in Johannes Houwink ten Cate and Gerhard Otto (eds), *Das organisierte Chaos* (Berlin: Metropol, 1999), 35–54, here 54.

59. Martin Cüppers, *Wegbereiter der Shoah: Die Waffen-SS, der Kommandostab Reichsführer-SS und die Judenvernichtung 1939–1945* (Darmstadt: Wissenschaftliche Buchgesellschaft, 2005); Yehoshua Büchler, 'Kommandostab

Reichsführer-SS: Himmler's Personal Murder Brigades in 1941', *Holocaust and Genocide Studies* 1 (1986), 11–25, here 13–14.

60. H. Höhne, *The Order of the Death's Head* (London: Pan, 1972), 333; Browning, *The Path to Genocide*, 108–9.

61. Dieter Pohl, 'Die Einsatzgruppe C', in Peter Klein (ed.), *Die Einsatzgruppen in der besetzten Sowjetunion 1941/42: Die Tätigkeits- und Lageberichte des Chefs der Sicherheitspolizei und des SD* (Berlin: Edition Hentrich, 1997), 71–110.

62. Christopher R. Browning, *Ordinary Men: Reserve Police Battalion 101 and the Final Solution in Poland* (New York: HarperCollins, 1993), 10–11.

63. Cüppers, *Wegbereiter*.

64. Witte et al. (eds), *Dienstkalendar*. For examples of Hitler's input, Peter Witte, 'Two Decisions Concerning the "Final Solution of the Jewish Question": Deportations to Lodz and Mass Murder in Chelmno', *Holocaust and Genocide Studies* 9 (1995), 293–317.

65. Dieter Pohl, 'Schauplatz Ukraine', in Norbert Frei, Sybille Steinbacher, and Bernd Wagner (eds), *Ausbeutung, Vernichtung, Öffentlichkeit* (Munich: Saur, 2000), 135–73, here 143; Wendy Lower, ' "Anticipatory Obedience" and the Nazi Implementation of the Holocaust in the Ukraine: A Case Study of Central and Peripheral Forces in the Generalbezirk Zhytomyr, 1941–1944', *Holocaust and Genocide Studies* 16 (2002), 1–22.

66. Jürgen Matthäus, 'Controlled Escalation: Himmler's Men in the Summer of 1941 and the Holocaust in the Occupied Soviet Territories', *Holocaust and Genocide Studies* 21 (2007), 218–42.

67. Hans Mommsen, 'What Did the Germans Know about the Genocide of the Jews?', in Walter H. Pehle (ed.), *November 1938: From 'Reichskristallnacht' to Genocide* (New York: St. Martin's Press, 1991), 187–221.

68. Ruth Bettina Birn, *Die Höheren SS-und Polizeiführer* (Düsseldorf: Droste, 1986), 171–2; Pohl, 'Schauplatz Ukraine', 140.

69. Guidelines by Heydrich for Higher SS and Police Leaders in the Occupied Territories of the Soviet Union, July 2, 1941, from Yitzhak Arad et al. (eds), *Documents on the Holocaust* (Lincoln: University of Nebraska Press, 1999), part III. On relations between Heydrich and Daluege, Richard Breitman, *Official Secrets: What the Nazi Planned, What the British and Americans Knew* (New York: Hill and Wang, 1998), 73–4.

70. Gerlach, *Kalkulierte Mord*; Omer Bartov, *Hitler's Army: Soldiers, Nazis and War in the Third Reich* (Oxford: Oxford University Press, 1992).

71. Christian Streit, *Keine Kameraden: Die Wehrmacht und die sowjetischen Kriegsgefangenen 1941–1945* (Bonn: J. H. W. Dietz, 1991); Karel

C. Berkhoff, *Harvest of Despair: Life and Death in Ukraine under Nazi Rule* (Cambridge, MA: Harvard University Press, 2004); Gerlach, *Krieg, Ernährung, Völkermord.*

72. Steinbacher, *'Musterstadt' Auschwitz*, 211, 238–9.

73. For military assessments in mid-July that the critical operation objectives had not been achieved, see Horst Boog et al., *Germany and the Second World War*, vol. iv: *The Attack on the Soviet Union* (Oxford: Oxford University Press, 1998), 1251; on Hitler's fluctuating perceptions, Goebbels' diaries cited in Musial, 'Generalgouvernement', 125–6. On the remit of the administrations, Wolfgang Benz, Konrad Kwiet, and Jürgen Matthäus (eds), *Einsatz im 'Reichskommissariat Ostland': Dokumente zum Völkermord im Baltikum und in Weissrussland* (Berlin: Metropol, 1998), 13–17.

74. Benz et al. (eds.), *Einsatz*, 13–17; Bernhard Chiari, *Alltag hinter der Front: Besatzung, Kollaboration und Widerstand in Weissrussland 1941–1944* (Düsseldorf: Droste, 1998); Berkhoff, *Harvest*; Truman Anderson, 'Incident at Baranivka: German Reprisals and the Soviet Partisan Movement in Ukraine, October-December 1941', *Journal of Modern History* 71 (1999), 585–623; Shepherd, *War*, 132–4, 157–62.

75. e.g. Kunz, *Die Krim.*

76. Madajczyk, 'General Plan East'.

77. Chiari, *Alltag*, 4–5 on 'collaboration'; on devastation in Belarus, Gerlach, *Kalkulierte Morde.*

78. Benz et al. (eds), *Einsatz*, 9–10; Gerlach, *Kalkulierte Mord*; Hannes Heer and Klaus Namann (eds), *War of Extermination: The German Military in World War II 1941–1944* (New York: Berghahn Books, 2000).

79. Pohl, 'Schauplatz Ukraine', 144.

80. Gerlach, *Kalkulierte Mord*; Christoph Dieckmann, 'Der Krieg und die Ermordung der litauischen Juden', in Herbert (ed.), *Nationalsozialistische Vernichtungspolitik*, 292–329.

81. Dieckmann, 'Der Krieg', 293, 321; and *idem*, 'Das Ghetto und das Konzentrationslager in Kaunas 1941–1944', in Ulrich Herbert et al. (eds), *Die nationalsozialistischen Konzentrationslager. Entwicklung und Struktur*, 2 vols (Göttingen: Wallstein, 1998), i, 439–71. Christian Gerlach, 'The Wannsee Conference, the Fate of German Jews, and Hitler's Decision in Principle to Exterminate All European Jews', *Journal of Modern History* 70 (1998), 759–812, here 763.

82. 'Burkhardt-Bericht' of Einsatzgruppe A, repr. in Benz et al. (eds.), *Einsatz*, 111–15.

83. Sandkühler, 'Endlösung', 146–59; Hermann Kaienburg, 'Jüdischer Arbeit an der "Strasse der SS"', 1999. Zeitschrift für Sozialgeschichte des 20. und 21. Jahrhunderts 11 (1996), 13–39.

84. Benz et al. (eds), Einsatz, section III, 115 ff; Jürgen Matthäus, '"Reibungslos und planmäßig": Die zweite Welle der Judenvernichtung im Generalkommissariat Weißruthenien (1942–1944)', Jahrbuch für Antisemitismusforschung 4 (1995), 254–74.

Chapter 6—The Patterns and Limits of the European Genocide

1. Dieter Pohl, Nationalsozialistische Judenverfolgung in Ostgalizien 1941–1944: Organisation und Durchführung eines staatlichen Massenverbrechens (Munich: Oldenbourg, 1997), 67–71, 139–51.

2. Peter Witte, 'Two Decisions Concerning the "Final Solution of the Jewish Question": Deportations to Lodz and Mass Murder in Chelmno', Holocaust and Genocide Studies 9 (1995), 293–317; Hannes Heer, 'Killing Fields: The Wehrmacht and the Holocaust in Belorussia, 1941–1942', Holocaust and Genocide Studies 11 (1997), 79–101. See also Uwe Dietrich Adam, Judenpolitik im dritten Reich (Düsseldorf: Athenaum Verlag, 1979), 303–12, 355–61.

3. On the local quality of these decisions, Peter Longerich, Politik der Vernichtung: Eine Gesamtdarstellung der nationalsozialistischen Judenverfolgung (Munich: Piper Verlag, 1998), 440.

4. Christian Gerlach, 'The Wannsee Conference, the Fate of German Jews, and Hitler's Decision in Principle to Exterminate All European Jews', Journal of Modern History 70 (1998), 759–812, here, 777.

5. Witte, 'Two Decisions'; Pim Griffioen and Ron Zeller, 'Anti-Jewish Policy and Organization of the Deportations in France and the Netherlands, 1940–1944: A Comparative Study', Holocaust and Genocide Studies 20 (2006), 437–73, here 448.

6. I thank Jürgen Matthäus for drawing my attention to the order's restricted list of recipients, though stress that he bears no responsibility for my potentially erroneous interpretation. For the order, see Joseph Walk (ed.), Das Sonderrecht für die Juden im NS-Staat Eine Sammlung der gesetzlichen Maßnahmen und Richtlinien—Inhalt und Bedeutung (Heidelberg: Uni-Taschenbücher Verlag, 1996), 353. For other related orders before and afterwards, see also 341, 361, and 363.

7. Christian Gerlach, 'Failure of Plans for an SS Extermination Camp in Mogilev, Belorussia', Holocaust and Genocide Studies 11 (1997), 60–78.

8. See below, and Peter Klein, 'Die Rolle der Vernichtungslager Kulmhof (Chełmno), Belzec (Bełżec) und Auschwitz-Birkenau in den frühen Deportationsvorbereitungen', in Dittmar Dahlmann and Gerhard Hirschfeld (eds), *Lager, Zwangsarbeit, Vertreibung und Deportation* (Essen: Klartext Verlag, 1999), 459–81, here 481.

9. Michael Wildt, *Generation des Unbedingten: Das Führungskorps des Reichssicherheitshauptamtes* (Hamburg: Hamburger Edition, 2003), 628.

10. Christopher R. Browning and Jürgen Matthäus, The *Origin of the Final Solution: The Evolution of Nazi Jewish Policy, September 1939–March 1942* (Lincoln: University of Nebraska Press, 2004), 388–90, 394–8.

11. Michael Alberti, *Die Verfolgung und Vernichtung der Juden im Reichsgau Wartheland 1939–1945* (Wiesbaden: Harrassowitz, 2006); Ian Kershaw, 'Improvised Genocide? The Emergence of the "final solution" in the "Warthegau"', *Transactions of the Royal Historical Society*, 6th ser., 2 (1992), 51–78; on the killing of the mentally ill in the USSR, Angelika Ebbinghaus and Gerd Preissler, 'Die Ermordung psychisch kranker Menschen in der Sowjetunion. Dokumentation', in Götz Aly (ed.), *Aussonderung und Tod. Die klinische Hinrichtung des Unbrauchbaren* (Berlin: Rotbuch, 1985), 75–107.

12. Alberti, *Wartheland*, Ch. 5; Peter Klein, 'Die "Ghettoverwaltung Litzmannstadt" als städtische Behörde', *Fritz Bauer Institut Newsletter* 32 (2008), 7–9.

13. Karel C. Berkhoff, *Harvest of Despair: Life and Death in Ukraine under Nazi Rule* (Cambridge, MA: Harvard University Press, 2004), 44.

14. For an expansion on this point, see below, and Chapter 7.

15. On 16 December 1941 Hans Frank had spoken openly about the implicit but clear message from Berlin: 'liquidate them yourselves': doc. 15, in *Tagesordnung, Judenmord: Die Wannsee-Konferenz am 20. Januar 1942: eine Dokumentation zur Organisation der 'Endlösung' (Reihe Dokumente, Texte, Materialien)*, ed. Kurt Pätzold and Erika Schwarz (Berlin: Metropol, 1992).

16. Browning and Matthäus, *Origin*, 394.

17. The 'euphoria' position is Christopher R. Browning's, from his *Fateful Months: Essays on the Emergence of the Final Solution* (New York: Holmes and Meier, 1985). Browning's position has been updated, but maintained in its essentials, in Browning and Matthäus, *Origin*. For references to the contrary positions, which have been dubbed 'functionalist', in contrast to Browning's 'moderate functionalism', see Ch. 8 of this book.

18. Joseph Goebbels, *Die Tagebücher von Joseph Goebbels*, ed. Elke Fröhlich (Munich: K. G. Saur, 1996), part II: 1941–5, i, 269.

19. Browning and Matthäus, *Origin*, 379, 406.

20. Klaus-Michael Mallmann and Martin Cüppers, *Halbmond und Haken-kreuz: Das dritte Reich, die Araber und Palästina* (Darmstadt: Wissenschaft-liche Buchgesellschaft, 2006); Browning and Matthäus, *Origin*, 406. The leader of the Einsatzgruppe went on to murder 2,500 Tunisian Jews in 1942–3, mostly through labour.

21. Browning and Matthäus, *Origin*, 404. At that point of course, he, like his leader and the SS leadership, were pushing for the fully 'European' solution.

22. Reproduced in *Tagesordnung: Judenmord*.

23. *Tagesordnung: Judenmord*, doc. 24.

24. See previous chapter. For recent interpretations of the conference and minutes, stressing a re-reading in light of the evolution of Jewish policy on the ground, see Peter Longerich, *Die Wannsee-Konferenz vom 20. Januar 1942* (Berlin: Edition Hentrich, 1998); Mark Roseman, *The Villa, the Lake, the Meeting: Wannsee and the Final Solution* (London: Penguin, 2003).

25. Andrej Angrick and Peter Klein, *Die 'Endlösung' in Riga: Ausbeutung und Vernichtung 1941–1944* (Darmstadt: Wissenschaftliche Buchgesellschaft, 2005), Ch. 9 and Exkurs I; Browning and Matthäus, *Origin*, 396–7.

26. Nuremberg document NO–500, Himmler to Glücks, 25 January 1942; Walter Naasner, *Neue Machtzentren in der deutschen Kriegswirtschaft 1942–45* (Boppard am Rhein: Harald Boldt, 1994), 366. See also Christoph Dieckmann, 'Das Ghetto und das Konzentrationslager in Kaunas 1941–1944', in Ulrich Herbert et al. (eds), *Die nationalsozialistischen Konzentrationslager. Entwicklung und Struktur*, 2 vols (Göttingen: Wall-stein, 1998), i, 439–71, here 460 and passim.

27. Nuremberg Document NO–1292, Kammler to Glücks, 10 March 1942.

28. Helmut Krausnick et al., *Anatomie des SS-Staates*, 2 vols (Freiburg im Bresgau: Walker, 1965), ii, 132.

29. Ulrich Herbert, 'Labour and Extermination: Economic Interests and the Primacy of "Weltanschauung" in National Socialism', *Past and Present* 138 (1993), 144–95.

30. *Faschismus—Ghetto—Massenmord: Dokumentation über Austrottung und Widerstand der Juden in Polen während des zweiten Weltkrieges*, ed. Tatiana Berenstein et al. (Berlin: Rütten and Loening, 1960), 446–7.

31. *Dänemark in Hitlers Hand. Der Bericht des Reichsbevollmächtigten Werner Best über seine Besatzungspolitik in Dänemark*, ed. Siegfried Matlok (Husum: Husum Verlag, 1988), 170.

32. Christpher Browning, *The Final Solution and the German Foreign Office: A Study of Referat D III of Abteilung Deutschland, 1940–43* (New York: Holmes and Meier, 1978), 170–4, and *passim*.

33. *Tagesordnung: Judenmord*, doc. 14.

34. Ibid. doc. 27.

35. Browning, *Foreign Office*, 90 ff, and the following section of this chapter.

36. Witte, 'Two Decisions', 333–4; Alberti, *Wartheland*, 508; Pohl, *Ostgalizien*, 208 ff.

37. Florent Brayard, *La 'Solution Finale de la question juive': La technique, le temps et les catégories de la décision* (Paris: Fayard, 2004); *Heinrich Himmler. Geheimreden 1933 bis 1945*, ed. Bradley F. Smith and Agnes F. Peterson (Frankfurt am Main: Propyläen, 1974), 159.

38. Longerich, *Politik*, 488. See also Christopher Browning, 'A Final Hitler Decision for the "Final Solution"? The Riegner Telegram Reconsidered', *Holocaust and Genocide Studies* 10 (1996), 3–10. For an example of accelerated killing in the eastern territories from the end of May 1942 through July, Dieter Pohl, 'Schauplatz Ukraine', in Norbert Frei, Sybille Steinbacher, and Bernd Wagner (eds), *Ausbeutung, Vernichtung, Öffentlichkeit* (Munich: Saur, 2000), 135–73, here 172.

39. Dieter Pohl, *Von der 'Judenpolitik' zum Judenmord: Der Distrikt Lublin des Generalgouvernements 1939–1944* (Frankfurt am Main: Lang, 1993), 125.

40. *Der Dienstkalendar Heinrich Himmlers 1941/1942*, ed. Peter Witte et al. (Hamburg: Christians, 1999), 493, 495.

41. Wildt, *Generation*, 688–93. On Himmler's personal role, Pohl, *Lublin*, 179.

42. Dieter Pohl, 'Die Ermordung der Juden im Generalgouvernement', in Ulrich Herbert (ed.), *Nationalsozialistische Vernichtungspolitik 1939–1945: Neue Forschungen und Kontroversen* (Frankfurt am Main: Fischer, 1998), 98–121, here 98–9; Christopher Browning, *The Path to Genocide: Essays on Launching the Final Solution* (Cambridge: Cambridge University Press, 1992), p. ix.

43. Nuremberg Document NO–5574.

44. See the chapter on the Generalgouvernement in Christian Gerlach, *Krieg, Ernährung, Völkermord: Forschungen zur deutschen Vernichtungspolitik im Zweiten Weltkrieg* (Hamburg: Hamburger Edition, 1998).

45. *Faschismus—Ghetto—Massenmord*, 438–9, 444–6, 450–1.

46. e.g. Felicja Karay, *Death Comes in Yellow: Skarzysko-Kamienna Slave Labor Camp* (Amsterdam: Hardwood Academic, 1997).

47. Pohl, *Lublin*, 162–3; Thomas Sandkühler, 'Das Zwangsarbeitslager Lemberg-Janowska 1941–1944', in Ulrich Herbert et al. (eds), *Die nationalsozialistischen Konzentrationslager. Entwicklung und Struktur* (Göttingen: Wallstein, 1998), 607–35.

48. Pohl, 'Die Ermordung', 106.

49. Dieter Pohl, 'Die grossen Zwangsarbeitslager der SS- und Polizeiführer für Juden im Generalgouvernement 1942–1945', in Herbert et al. (eds), *Die nationalsozialistischen Konzentrationslager*, 415–38. here 415.

50. *Faschismus—Ghetto—Massenmord*, 296.

51. *Dienstkalendar*, 479, 483. See also 499–500.

52. Angrick and Klein, *Riga*.

53. Figures from Raul Hilberg, 'Auschwitz and the Final Solution', in Michael Berenbaum and Yisrael Gutman (eds), *Anatomy of the Auschwitz Death Camp* (Bloomington: Indiana University Press, 1998), 81–92.

54. *Das dritte Reich und die Juden: Dokumente und Aufsätze*, ed. Léon Poliakov and Joseph Wulf (Berlin: Fourier Verlag 1989), 97.

55. As the chief Foreign Office representative for Jewish affairs, Martin Luther, put it to the Bucharest Embassy on 9 January 1943, in reference to a Romanian agreement to allow Jews to emigrate to British-controlled Palestine, the transaction had to be stopped because 'given the large numbers involved [the emigration] would mean not only a significant strengthening of the immediate fighting potential of the enemy, but also a morale and propaganda . . . advantage to him. . . . The enemy would inevitably try to construe this measure as indicating a lack of unity amongst the Axis Powers' (Nuremberg Document NG–2200).

56. Yehuda Bauer, 'On the Place of the Holocaust in History', *Holocaust and Genocide Studies* 2 (1987), 209–20, here 210.

57. Griffioen and Zeller, 'France and the Netherlands', 452.

58. Ibid. *passim*. For the Himmler decisions, *Vichy-Auschwitz: La 'solution finale' de la Question Juive en France*, ed. Serge Klarsfeld (Paris: Fayard, 2001), 194–6, 210–20. On conditions in France, Bernd Kasten, 'Zwischen Pragmatismus und exzessiver Gewalt. Die Gestapo in Frankreich 1940–1944', in Gerhard Paul and Klaus-Michael Mallmann (eds), *Die Gestapo im Zweiten Weltkrieg: 'Heimatfront' und besetztes Europa* (Darmstadt: Primus Verlag, 2000), 362–82.

59. Wildt, *Generation*, 693–728.

60. Michael R. Marrus and Robert O. Paxton, *Vichy France and the Jews* (New York: Basic Books, 1981), Ch. 1.

61. Martin Broszat, 'Das dritte Reich und die rumänische Judenpolitik', and *idem*, 'Das deutsch-ungarische Verhältnis und die ungarische Judenpolitik in der Jahren 1938–41', both in *Gutachten des Instituts für Zeitgeschichte* 1 (1958), 102–83, 183–200 respectively.
62. Longerich, *Politik*, 491 ff.
63. Nuremberg Document NG–1800, Martin Luther, 'Notes on Discussion' with Hungarian Ambassador, 6 October 1942.
64. Nuremberg Document NG–2586, Luther to Foreign Minister's Field Quarters Feldmark, 21 August 1942, points 5–6.
65. Ibid. point 7. Generally on Germany's dealings with these states, see Browning, *Foreign Office*, Chs. 6 and 7.
66. Best to Foreign Office, 2 October 1943, repr. in *Dänemark in Hitlers Hand*, 302. On the context, see Hans Kirchhoff, 'Denmark: A Light in the Darkness of the Holocaust? A Reply to Gunnar S. Paulsson', *Journal of Contemporary History* 30 (1995), 465–79.
67. Reprinted in Jeremy Noakes and Geoffrey Pridham (eds), *Nazism 1919–1945*, vol. iii: *Foreign Policy, War and Racial Extermination* (Exeter: University of Exeter Press, 1988), 1199–200.
68. *Himmler. Geheimreden*, 169.
69. Goebbels, *Tagebücher*, part II, x, 72.
70. For the incident, which is not linked to 'operation harvest festival' by the authors, see Angrick and Klein, *Riga*, 401.
71. International Military Tribunal, *Trial of the Major War Criminals before the International Military Tribunal*, 42 vols (Nuremberg: IMT, 1947–9), i, 303. *Der Stürmer*, 4 November 1943, p. 2.
72. Michael R. Marrus and Robert O. Paxton, 'The Nazis and the Jews in Occupied Western Europe, 1940–1944', *Journal of Modern History* 54 (1982), 687–714, here 688.
73. See below: the 'violence of the endphase'. Also Tim Mason, 'The Third Reich and the German Left: Persecution and Resistance', in Hedley Bull (ed.), *The Challenge of the Third Reich* (Oxford: Oxford University Press, 1986), 100.
74. Much of the narrative detail here is taken from Christian Gerlach and Götz Aly, *Das letzte Kapitel: Der Mord an den ungarischen Juden* (Stuttgart: DVA, 2002), and to a lesser degree from Randolph L. Braham, *The Politics of Genocide: The Holocaust in Hungary* (New York: Columbia University Press, 1994). My analysis differs somewhat from Gerlach and Aly, however, particularly on the level of Hungarian enthusiasm for

genocide instead of segregation, and on the comparison with France and Denmark. On Hungarian attitudes towards ghettoization, and the changes wrought by the German invasion, Tim Cole, *Holocaust City: The Making of a Jewish Ghetto* (New York/London: Routledge, 2003). For statistics cited in this section, see Cole, and Randolph L. Braham, 'Hungarian Jews' in Berenbaum and Gutman (eds), *Anatomy*, 456–68.

75. On Auschwitz death tolls, F. Piper, *Die Zahl der Opfer von Auschwitz* (Oswięçim: Pánstwowe Muzeum, 1993).

76. The narrative of slave labour here is substantially culled from my article, to which I refer the reader for more detailed references: 'A Survey of Jewish Slave Labour in the Nazi System', *Journal of Holocaust Education* 10:3 (2001), 25–59

77. Franciszek Piper, *Arbeitseinsatz der Häftlinge aus dem KL Auschwitz* (Auschwitz: State Museum, 1995), 230–1.

78. On incorporation in similar projects, Hans Brenner, 'Der "Arbeitseinsatz" in den Außenlagern des KZs Flossenbürg', in Herbert et al. (eds), *Die nationalsozialistischen Konzentrationslager*, 682–706, here 691–6. On compromises on joint accommodation, Hermann Kaienburg, 'Wie konnte es soweit kommen?', in *idem* (ed.), *Konzentrationslager und deutsche Wirtschaft* (Opladen: Leske und Budrich, 1996), 265–78, here 276–7.

79. Karin Orth, *Das System der nationalsozialistischen Konzentrationslager* (Munich: Pendo, 1999), 242.

80. Rainer Fröbe, 'Der Arbeitseinsatz von KZ-Häftlingen und der Perspektive der Industrie, 1943–1945', in Hamburger Stiftung zur Förderung von Wissenschaft und Kultur (ed.), *'Deutscher Wirtschaft': Zwangsarbeit von KZ-Häftlingen für Industrie und Behörden* (Hamburg: VSA Verlag, 1991), 33–78, here 49; Orth, *Das System*, 240.

81. Statistics from US Holocaust Memorial Museum online encyclopedia: http://www.ushmm.org/wlc/en/.

82. Daniel Blatman, 'The Death Marches: Who Was Responsible for What?', *Yad Vashem Studies* 28 (2000), 155–201.

83. *Himmler. Geheimreden*, 169.

84. Klein, ' "Litzmannstadt" '.

85. Alexa Stiller, 'Reichskommissar für die Festigung deutschen Volkstums', in Ingo Haar and Michael Fahlbusch (eds), *Handbuch der völkischen Wissenschaften* (Munich: KG Saur, 2008) 531–40.

86. Henry Friedlander, *The Origins of Nazi Genocide* (Chapel Hill: University of North Carolina Press, 1995), Chs. 7–8; Götz Aly, 'Medizin gegen Unbrauchbare', in *idem* (ed.), *Aussonderung und Tod*, 9–74.

Chapter 7—Why Did They Kill?

1. Stephan Lehnstaedt, 'Das Reichsministerium des Innern unter Heinrich Himmler 1943–1945', *Vierteljahrshefte für Zeitgeschichte* 4 (2006), 639–72, here 656.

2. Jürgen Matthäus, 'Ausbildung zum Judenmord? Zum Stellenwert der "weltanschaulichen Erziehung" von SS und Polizei im Rahmen der "Endlösung" ', *Zeitschrift für Geschichtswissenschaft* 47 (1999), 677–99.

3. Michael Wildt, *Generation des Unbedingten: Das Führungskorps des Reichssicherheitshauptamtes* (Hamburg: Hamburger Edition, 2003); Herbert F. Ziegler, *Nazi Germany's New Aristocracy: the SS Leadership, 1925–1939* (Princeton, NJ: Princeton University Press, 1989). Lehnstaedt, 'Das Reichsministerium', 643–6, on the ideal Nazi bureaucrat.

4. Though not on the equivalent of the 'shop floor', where Taylorist principles are often still seen as desirable.

5. Irmtrud Wojak, *Eichmanns Memoiren: Ein kritischer Essay* (Frankfurt am Main: Campus, 2001).

6. Bernward Dörner, *Die Deutschen und der Holocaust. Was niemand wissen wollte, aber jeder wissen konnte* (Berlin: Propyläen Verlag, 2007).

7. Zygmunt Bauman, *Modernity and the Holocaust* (Ithaca, NY: Cornell University Press, 1989).

8. Michael Herzfeld, *The Social Production of Indifference: Exploring the Symbolic Roots of Western Bureaucracy* (Chicago: University of Chicago Press, 1992), 80–1.

9. Neil Gregor, 'Nazism—A Political Religion? Rethinking the Voluntarist Turn', in *idem* (ed.), *Nazism, War and Genocide: Essays in Honour of Jeremy Noakes* (Exeter: University of Exeter Press, 2005), 1–21.

10. Jean Hatzfeld, *Une saison de machettes* (Paris: Seuil, 2003); the analysis, with which I agree entirely, is from Luke Fletcher, 'Turning Interahamwe: Individual and Community Choices in the Rwandan Genocide', *Journal of Genocide Research* 9:1 (2007), 25–48, here 29.

11. Jack Katz, *Seductions of Crime* (New York: Basic Books, 1988), 40.

12. Max Weber, *Economy and Society*, vol. i (New York: Oxford University Press, 1947); *idem*, 'Politics as a Vocation', in H. H. Gerth and C. Wright Mills (eds), *From Max Weber: Essays in Sociology* (New York: Oxford University Press, 1946), 77–129. Charles E. Larmore, *Patterns of Moral Complexity* (Cambridge: Cambridge University Press, 1987), xiv, Ch. 6. For an expansion of the arguments here, see Donald Bloxham, 'Organized

Mass Murder: Structure, Participation, and Motivation in Comparative Perspective', *Holocaust and Genocide Studies* 22 (2008), 203–45.

13. Claudia Steur, 'Eichmanns Emissäre. Die "Judenberäter" in Hitlers Europa', in Gerhard Paul and Klaus-Michael Mallmann (eds), *Die Gestapo im Zweiten Weltkrieg: 'Heimatfront' und besetztes Europa* (Darmstadt: Primus Verlag, 2000), 403–36.

14. Christopher R. Browning, *Ordinary Men: Reserve Police Battalion 101 and the Final Solution in Poland* (New York: HarperCollins, 1993); and see below.

15. Nicolas Werth, 'The Mechanism of a Mass Crime: The Great Terror in the Soviet Union, 1937–1938', in Robert Gellately and Ben Kiernan (eds), *The Specter of Genocide: Mass Murder in Historical Perspective* (Cambridge: Cambridge University Press, 2003), 215–39, here 230–1; and Gabór T. Rittersporn, 'Soviet Officialdom and Political Evolution: Judiciary Apparatus and Penal Policy in the 1930s', *Theory and Society* 13 (1984), 211–37, here 227. On the character of some of the new NKVD men arriving as a result of purges, see Robert Conquest, *The Great Terror: The Great Purge of the Thirties* (Harmondsworth: Penguin, 1971), 728–9. On the role of fear and careerism together, Alex Nove, 'Stalin and Stalinism—Some Introductory Thoughts', in *idem* (ed.), *The Stalin Phenomenon* (London: Weidenfeld & Nicholson, 1993).

16. Donald Cameron Watt, *Succeeding John Bull: America in Britain's Place* (Cambridge, Cambridge University Press, 1984), 7. On Imperial Japan, see the early chapters of Chalmers Johnson, *MITI and the Japanese Miracle: The Growth of Industrial Policy, 1925–1975* (Stanford, CA: Stanford University Press, 1982).

17. Robert K. Merton et al. (eds), *Bureaucracy* (New York: Free Press, 1952), 282–97.

18. Herzfeld, *Social Production of Indifference*, 5, quoting Gerald Britan.

19. Lehnstaedt, 'Das Reichsministerium', 669.

20. Christopher R. Browning, 'The Government Experts', in Henry Friedlander and Sybil Milton (eds), *The Holocaust: Ideology, Bureaucracy, and Genocide* (Millwood, NY: Kraus International, 1980), 189.

21. Nikolaus Wachsmann, *Hitler's Prisons: Legal Terror in Nazi Germany* (New Haven, CT: Yale University Press, 2004), 380; Diemut Majer, *'Non-Germans' under the Third Reich* (Baltimore: Johns Hopkins University Press, 2003), 32.

22. Contra Hans Mommsen's depiction in his 'Der Nationalsozialismus: Kumulative Radikalisierung und Selbstzerstörung des Regimes', in *Meyers*

Enzyklopädisches Lexikon (Mannheim, Germany: Bibliographisches Institut, 1976), xvi, 785–90.

23. Rüdiger Hachtmann and Winfried Süss (eds), *Hitlers Kommissare: Sondergewalten in der nationalsozialistischen Diktatur* (Göttingen: Wallstein Verlag, 2006).

24. Hans Safrian, *Eichmann und seine Gehilfen* (Frankfurt am Main: Fischer, 1995), 137.

25. On the commissars, see the opening two essays in Hachtmann and Süss (eds), *Hitlers Kommissare*; Diemut Majer, 'Führerunmittelbare Sondergewalten in den besetzten Ostgebieten', in Dieter Rebentisch and Karl Teppe (eds), *Verwaltung contra Menschenführung im Staat Hitlers. Studien zum politisch-administrativen System* (Göttingen: Vandenhoeck und Ruprecht, 1986), 374–94.

26. 'Editorial', in Wolf Gruner and Armin Nolzen (eds), *'Burokratien'. Initiative und Effizienz* (Berlin: Assoziation A, 2001), 12.

27. Pim Griffioen and Ron Zeller, 'Anti-Jewish Policy and Organization of the Deportations in France and the Netherlands, 1940–1944: A Comparative Study', *Holocaust and Genocide Studies* 20:3 (2006), 437–73, conclusion.

28. e.g. Yaacov Lozowick, *Hitlers Bürokraten: Eichmann, seine willigen Vollstrecker und die Banalität des Bösen* (Munich: Pendo, 2000), 48. For different levels of commitment within SS–Police units, see Alexander V. Prusin, 'A Community of Violence: The SiPo/SD and Its Role in the Nazi Terror System in Generalbezirk Kiew', *Holocaust and Genocide Studies* 21 (2007), 1–30.

29. Jan Erik Schulte, *Zwangsarbeit und Vernichtung: Das Wirtschaftsimperium der SS. Oswald Pohl und das SS-Wirtschafts-Verwaltungshauptamt, 1933–1945* (Paderborn: Schöningh, 2001), 459–60.

30. Ian Kershaw, *Hitler 1889–1936: Hubris* (London: Penguin, 1999), Ch. 13.

31. Wendy Lower, ' "Anticipatory Obedience" and the Nazi implementation of the Holocaust in the Ukraine: A case study of central and peripheral forces in the Generalbezirk Zhytomyr, 1941–1944', *Holocaust and Genocide Studies* 16 (2002), 1–22.

32. David Rieff, *At the Point of a Gun* (New York: Simon and Schuster, 2005), 197.

33. Mark Tushnet, 'Evaluating Congressional Constitutional Interpretation: Some Criteria and Two Informal Case Studies', *Duke Law Journal* 50 (2001), 1395–425, here 1400.

34. Gabór T. Rittersporn, 'Zynismus, Selbsttäuschung und unmögliches Kalkül: Strafpolitik und Lagerbevölkerung in der UdSSR', in Dittmar

Dahlmann and Gerhard Hirschfeld (eds), *Lager, Zwangsarbeit, Vertreibung und Deportation* (Essen: Klartext Verlag, 1999), 291–316, here 311.

35. Robert Conquest, *The Soviet Police System* (London: Bodley Head, 1968), 42–3.

36. For the consensus on the role of Stalin and other senior leaders in approving execution lists, see for example Martin McCauley, *Stalin and Stalinism* (London: Longman, 1995), 39.

37. Alison Palmer, *Colonial Genocide* (Adelaide: Crawford House, 2000), 209.

38. For structural and contextual similarities between war and genocide, see Martin Shaw, *War and Genocide* (Cambridge: Polity Press, 2005) and those sections concerned with counterinsurgency warfare in Benjamin Valentino, *Final Solutions: Mass Killing and Genocide in the Twentieth Century* (Ithaca, NY: Cornell University Press, 2004).

39. Stathis Kalyvas, *The Logic of Violence in Civil War* (Cambridge: Cambridge University Press, 2006).

40. Of course this depends on definition, but see Dieter Pohl, *Holocaust: Die Ursachen, das Geschehen, die Folgen* (Freiburg: Herder, 2000), cf. Scott Straus, *The Order of Genocide: Race, Power, and War in Rwanda* (Ithaca, NY: Cornell University Press, 2006), 117–18 for approximately similar estimates in absolute numbers. Rwanda's population was about one tenth of Germany's. Other scholarship on Rwanda suggests hundreds of thousands more Hutus were involved than Straus's estimate of around 200,000.

41. On the details of the administration of the genocide that follow, see Allison des Forges, *Leave None to Tell the Story: Genocide in Rwanda* (New York: Human Rights Watch, 1999), 4–12, 180–594; Gérard Prunier, *The Rwanda Crisis 1959–1994: History of a Genocide* (London: Hurst, 1995), 237–55 and *passim*; Mahmood Mamdani, *When Victims Become Killers: Colonialism, Nativism, and the Genocide in Rwanda* (Oxford: James Currey, 2001), Ch. 7; and Straus, *The Order of Genocide*.

42. On which, see the conclusion below.

43. Fletcher, 'Turning Interahamwe', 34–8; Linda Melvern, *Conspiracy to Murder: The Rwandan Genocide* (London: Verso, 2004), 27–32, 63, 174–5.

44. Fletcher, 'Turning Interahamwe', 39; Straus, *The Order of Genocide*, 89, 120.

45. Fuat Dündar, *Ittihat ve Terakki'nin Müslümanları Iskân Politikası (1913–1918)* (Istanbul: Isis, 2001); on Talât as micromanager, see Uğur Ü. Üngör, ' "A Reign of Terror": CUP Rule in Diyarbekir Province, 1913–1918', MA thesis, University of Amsterdam, 2005.

46. Vahakn N. Dadrian, 'The Complicity of the Party, the Government and the Military. Select Parliamentary and Judicial Documents', *Journal of Political and Military Sociology* 22 (1994), 29–96, here 59–60.

47. Taner Akçam, 'The Ottoman Documents and the Genocidal Policies of the Committee of Uniono and Progress toward the Armenians in 1915', *Genocide Studies and Prevention* 1:2 (2006), 127–48.

48. James J. Reid, 'Militarism, Partisan War and Destructive Inclinations in Ottoman Military History: 1854–1918', *Armenian Review* 39: 3 (1986), 1–21, here 6–11; Arnold J. Toynbee, *The Western Question in Greece and Turkey: A Study in the Contact of Civilizations* (London: Constable, 1923), 278–80.

49. Donald Bloxham, *The Great Game of Genocide: Imperialism, Nationalism, and the Destruction of the Ottoman Armenians* (Oxford: Oxford University Press, 2005), 42, 70, 93; Jaques Semelin, 'Analysis of a Mass Crime: Ethnic Cleansing in the Former Yugoslavia, 1991–1999', in Gellately and Kiernan (eds), *The Specter of Genocide*, 353–70, here 366–7. James Ron, *Frontiers and Ghettos: State Violence in Israel and Serbia* (Berkeley: University of California Press, 2003).

50. For which insight I thank Uğur Üngör.

51. Raymond Kévorkian, *Le Génocide des Arméniens* (Paris: Odile Jacob, 2006), 797.

52. Vahakn N. Dadrian, 'The Documentation of the World War I Armenian Massacres in the Proceedings of the Turkish Military Tribunal', *Journal of Political and Military Sociology* 22 (1994), 97–132, here 98.

53. Annette Höss, 'Die türkischen Kriegsgerichtsverhandlungen 1919–1921', PhD dissertation, University of Vienna, 1991, on the postwar trial of these 'responsible secretaries'; Dadrian, 'Documentation'; also Akçam, 'The Ottoman Documents', 140.

54. On the Gauleiter, Peter Hüttenberger, *Die Gauleiter: Studie zum Wandel des Machtgefüges in der NSDAP* (Stuttgart: Deutsche Verlags-Anstalt, 1969), 173–4.

55. Hilmar Kaiser, *At the Crossroads of Der Zor: Death, Survival, and Humanitarian Resistance in Aleppo, 1915–1917* (Princeton, NJ: Gomidas Institute, 2001), 15–16.

56. Bloxham, 'Organized Mass Murder', 232–3.

57. Peter Longerich, *'Davon haben wir nichts gewusst!' Die Deutschen und die Judenverfolgung 1933–1945* (Munich: Siedler, 2006).

58. Paul du Gay, *In Praise of Bureaucracy: Weber, Organization, Ethics* (New York: Oxford University Press, 1947), 7, 12.

59. Paul and Mallmann (eds), *Die Gestapo*; Robert Gellately, *The Gestapo and German Society* (Oxford: Clarendon Press, 1990).

60. Wendy Lower, 'A New Ordering of Space and Race: Nazi Volksdeutsche Experiments in Zhytomyr, Ukraine, 1941–1944', *German Studies Review* 25 (2002), 227–54, here 236.

61. Readers will note my debt on the concept of exception (though my application varies) to Carl Schmitt's notion of the 'State of Exception', addressed and given its own theorization in Giorgio Agamben, *State of Exception* (Chicago: University of Chicago Press, 2005)

62. Michael Thad Allen, *The Business of Genocide: The SS, Slave Labor, and the Concentration Camps* (Chapel Hill: University of North Carolina Press, 2002).

63. Bernd Kasten, 'Zwischen Pragmatismus und exzessiver Gewalt. Die Gestapo in Frankreich 1940–1944', in Paul and Mallmann (eds), *Die Gestapo*, 362–82.

64. This analysis represents a synthesis of the positions of Thomas Kühne, *Kameradschaft: Die Soldaten nationalsozialistischen Krieges und das 20. Jahrhundert* (Göttingen: Vandenhoeck and Ruprecht, 2006); Omer Bartov, *Hitler's Army. Soldiers, Nazis and War in the Third Reich* (Oxford: Oxford University Press, 1992); and Ben Shepherd, *War in the Wild East: The German Army and the Soviet Partisans* (Cambridge, MA: Harvard University Press, 2004).

65. Emmanuel Levinas, 'Peace and Proximity', in *Emmanuel Levinas: Basic Philosophical Writings* (Bloomington: Indiana University Press, 1996), 161–9. On killers becoming 'cold-blooded' by killing, Katz, *Seductions of Crime*, 301.

66. On the anthropological side, Christopher C. Taylor, *Sacrifice as Terror: The Rwandan Genocide of 1994* (Oxford: Berg, 1999), Ch. 3; on the psychological side, Alexander Laban Hinton, 'Agents of Death: Explaining the Cambodian Genocide in Terms of Psychosocial Dissonance', *American Anthropologist* 98:4 (1996), 818–31.

67. Dale T. Miller, 'Pluralistic Ignorance: When Similarity Is Interpreted as Dissimilarity', *Journal of Personality and Social Psychology* 53 (1987), 298–305; E. Aronson, 'The Theory of Cognitive Dissonance: A Current Perspective', in L. Berkowitz (ed.), *Advances in Experimental Social Psychology*, vol. iv (New York: Academic Press, 1969), 1–34. On sadism, Roy F. Baumeister and W. Keith Campbell, 'The Intrinsic Appeal of Evil: Sadism, Sensational Thrills, and Threatened Egotism', *Personality and Social Psychology Review* 3 (1999), 210–21, here 210–13. For

the breadth of applicability of studies on the social impact on human behaviour, F. D. Richard, C. F. Bond, and J. J. Stokes-Zoota, 'One Hundred Years of Social Psychology Quantitatively Described', *Review of general psychology* 7 (2003), 331–63. For applications to the Holocaust, including reference to the famous Milgram and Zimbardo experiments, which are also relevant to the discussion of group pressures and deference to authority figures, see most famously Browning, *Ordinary Men*. On the Holocaust and other genocides, Harald Welzer, *Täter. Wie aus ganz normalen Menschen Massenmörder werden* (Frankfurt am Main: S. Fischer, 2005); James Waller, *Becoming Evil: How Ordinary People Commit Genocide and Mass Killing* (Oxford: Oxford University Press, 2002).

68. Erich Kosthorst, *Die Geburt der Tragödie aus dem Geist des Gehorsams* (Bonn: Bouvier, 1998).

69. For this and other examples, H. C. Kelman and V. L. Hamilton, *Crimes of Obedience: Toward a Social Psychology of Authority and Responsibility* (New Haven, CT: Yale University Press, 1989).

70. Donald Bloxham, *Genocide on Trial: War Crimes Trials and the Formation of Holocaust History and Memory* (Oxford: Oxford University Press, 2001), Ch. 4.

71. Ibid.

72. Moishe Postone, 'The Holocaust and the Trajectory of the Twentieth Century', in Moishe Postner and Eric Santner (eds), *Catastrophe and Meaning* (Chicago: University of Chicago Press, 2003), 81–114, here 87.

73. Christian Gerlach, *Kalkulierte Morde: Die deutsche Wirtschafts- und Vernichtungspolitik im Weißrußland* (Hamburg: Hamburger Edition, 1999); *idem*, 'Deutsche Wirtschaftsinteressen, Besatzungspolitik und der Mord an den Juden in Weißrußland', in Ulrich Herbert (ed.), *Nationalsozialistische Vernichtungspolitik 1939–1945: Neue Forschungen und Kontroversen* (Frankfurt am Main: Fischer, 1998), 263–91, here 291. Joseph-Pierre Proudhon, *Système des Contradictions Economiques, ou Philosophie de la Misere* (Paris: Marcel Riviere, 1923), i, 286.

74. On profile, Straus, *The Order of Genocide*.

75. Mamdani, *When Victims Become Killers*, 204–7, 219–20; Straus, *The Order of Genocide*, Chs. 4–5; Fletcher, 'Turning Interahamwe', 39.

76. See Part I of Henry Rousso (ed.), *Stalinism and Nazism: History and Memory Compared* (Lincoln: University of Nebraska Press, 2004). On legitimacy and WWII, Amir Weiner, *Making Sense of War: The Second World War and*

the Fate of the Bolshevik Revolution (Princeton, NJ: Princeton University Press, 2002).

77. Herzfeld, *Social Production of Indifference*, 15, 19–20.

78. Examples cited by Lower, ' "Anticipatory Obedience" ', 14, and Prusin, 'A Community of Violence', 20, seem to support this analysis.

79. I am using here an analogy from Katz, *Seductions of Crime*, 15, in which he talks of two criminals who expected indulgence in the courtroom as follows: if 'both experienced an exceptional moment of temporary insanity, they were rational in claiming that their irrationality would be understood by others as righteously inspired.'

80. *The Concept of Dread*, cited in Jean-Paul Sartre, *War Diaries: Notebooks from a Phoney War 1939–40* (London: Verso, 1999), 131–2.

Chapter 8—Locating Genocide in the Human Past

1. Friedrich Meinecke, *Die deutsche Katastrophe* (Wiesbaden: Brockhaus, 1947), 64. For a similar latter-day approach, see Rainer Zitelmann, 'Die totalitäre Seite der Moderne', in Michael Prinz and Rainer Zitelmann (eds), *Nationalsozialismus und Modernisierung* (Darmstadt: Wissenschaftliche Buchgesellschaft, 1991), 1–20.

2. Theodor Adorno and Max Horkheimer, *Dialectic of Enlightenment* (Stanford: Stanford University Press, 2002, orig. 1947); Hannah Arendt, *The Origins of Totalitarianism* (New York: Harcourt, Brace, 1951).

3. Robert Eaglestone, *The Holocaust and the Postmodern* (Oxford: Oxford University Press, 2004).

4. Norbert Frei, *Vergangenheitspolitik: Die Anfänge der Bundesrepublik und die NS-Vergangenheit* (Munich: Beck, 1996); Robert G. Moeller, *War Stories: The Search for a Usable Past in the Federal Republic of Germany* (Berkeley: University of California Press, 2001); David Bankier, 'Responses of Exiled German Socialists in the USA and the UK to the Holocaust', *Journal of Holocaust Education*, 10, 1 (2001), 1–20.

5. Donald Bloxham, *Genocide on Trial: War Crimes Trials and the Formation of Holocaust History and Memory* (Oxford: Oxford University Press, 2001), 84, on the early political uses of the resistance. For a later, selective account of the resistance, see Joachim Fest, *Plotting Hitler's Death: The Story of the German Resistance* (New York: Henry Holt, 1997).

6. Gerald Reitlinger, *The Final Solution* (London: Vallentine, Mitchell, 1953).

7. David Cesarani (ed.), *After Eichmann: Collective Memory and the Holocaust after 1961* (Cambridge, MA: Routledge, 2005), 2.

8. Léon Poliakov, *Breviaire de la haine: le. IIIe Reich et les Juifs* (Paris: Calman-Levy, 1951); *idem, The History of Anti-Semitism* (London: Routledge & Kegan Paul, 1974); *idem, The Aryan Myth: A History of Racist and Nationalist Ideas in Europe* (New York: Basic Books, 1974).

9. David Thompson, *Europe since Napoleon* (London: Longmans, 1958). On military memoirs, Bloxham, *Genocide on Trial*, 131–3.

10. Karl Jaspers, *Die Schuldfrage: von der Politischen Haftung Deutschlands* (Munich: Piper, 1965); Bloxham, *Genocide on Trial*, 143–5.

11. For much more substantial treatments, Dan Stone, *Constructing the Holocaust* (London: Valentine, Mitchell, 2003); Gunnar Heinsohn, *Warum Auschwitz? Hitler's Plan und die Ratlosigkeit der Nachwelt* (Hamburg: Rowohlt, 1995); Michael R. Marrus, *The Holocaust in History* (Hanover, NH: University Press of New England, 1989).

12. Frederick Elwyn Jones, *In My Time: An Autobiography* (London: Futura, 1983), 129.

13. Franz Neumann, *Behemoth: The Structure and Practice of National Socialism 1933–1944* (New York: Oxford University Press, 1942).

14. Czesław Madajczyk, 'General Plan East: Hitler's Master Plan for Expansion', *Polish Western Affairs*, 3:2 (1962), 391–442. The work of Kurt Pätzold is a good instance of critical scholarship from behind the Iron Curtain on Nazism and its policies.

15. Adam Tooze, *The Wages of Destruction: The Making and Breaking of the Nazi Economy* (London: Viking, 2007); Christian Gerlach, *Kalkulierte Morde: Die deutsche Wirtschafts- und Vernichtungspolitik im Weißrußland* (Hamburg: Hamburger Edition, 1999).

16. Maria Mitchell, 'Materialism and Secularism: CDU Politicians and National Socialism, 1945–1949', *Journal of Modern History* 67 (1995), 278–308.

17. Meinecke, *Katastrophe*, 125.

18. Ernst Wiechert, *Der Totenwald, Ein Bericht* (Rascher Verlag Zuerich, 1946), 19; on British anti-Slavism, Bloxham, *Genocide on Trial*, 173–8.

19. See Tom Lawson, 'The Anglican Understanding of Nazism 1933–1945: Placing the Church of England's Response to the Holocaust in Context', *Twentieth Century British History* 14 (2003), 112–37.

20. e.g. Carl Friedrich and Zbigniew Brzezinski, *Totalitarian Dictatorship and Autocracy* (Cambridge, MA: Harvard University Press, 1956). On thinking about totalitarianism in the early Cold War period, Abbott Gleason, *Totalitarianism: The Inner History of the Cold War* (Oxford: Oxford University Press, 1995), 72–89; Benjamin Alpers, *Dictators, Democracy, and American Public Culture: Envisioning the Totalitarian*

Enemy, 1920s–1950s (Chapel Hill: University of North Carolina Press, 2003).

21. Peter Baldwin (ed.), *Reworking the Past: Hitler, the Holocaust, and the Historian's Debate* (Boston: Beacon Press, 1990).

22. Robert S. Wistrich, 'Totalitarian Anti-Semitism. A Global Menace', *Anti-Semitism International* (2003), 13–22; William D. Rubinstein, *Genocide* (London: Longman, 2004). On the trend, Anson Rabinbach, 'Totalitarianism Revisited', *Dissent*, summer 2006.

23. Donald Bloxham, 'Britain's Holocaust Memorial Days: Reshaping the Past in the Service of the Present', *Immigrants and Minorities* 21 (2003), 41–62; Tim Cole, 'Nativization and Nationalization: A Comparative Landscape Study of Holocaust Museums in Israel, the US and the UK', in Cesarani (ed.), *After Eichmann*, 130–45.

24. Jeffrey Herf, *Reactionary Modernism: Technology, Culture, and Politics in Weimar and the Third Reich* (London: Cambridge University Press, 1986).

25. Hans-Ulrich Wehler, in works such as *The German Empire*, is perhaps the best known *Sonderweg* proponent. For an overview of his and other scholarship, embedded in their own trenchant critique, see David Blackbourn and Geoff Eley, *The Peculiarities of German History* (Oxford: Oxford University Press, 1984).

26. Vincent P. Pecora, 'Habermas, Enlightenment and Anti-Semitism', in Saul Friedländer (ed.), *Probing the Limits of Representation: Nazism and the 'Final Solution'* (Cambridge, MA: Harvard University Press, 1992), 155–70; Ralf Dahrendorf, *Society and Democracy in Germany* (London: Weidenfeld & Nicolson, 1968).

27. On the German historiography, see Ulrich Herbert, 'Vernichtungspolitik', in *idem* (ed.), *Nationalsozialistische Vernichtungspolitik 1939–1945: Neue Forschungen und Kontroversen* (Frankfurt am Main: Fischer, 1998), 9–66, here 13–15.

28. Helmut Krausnick et al., *Anatomie des SS-Staates*, 2 vols (Freiburg im Bresgau: Walker, 1965).

29. Nicolas Berg, *Der Holocaust und die westdeutschen Historiker: Erforschung und Erinnerung* (Göttingen: Wallstein, 2003).

30. Devin Pendas, *The Frankfurt Auschwitz Trial, 1963–1965: Genocide, History and the Limits of the Law* (Cambridge: Cambridge University Press, 2006).

31. Geoff Eley, 'Hitler's Silent Majority? Conformity and Resistance under the Third Reich', *Michigan Quarterly Review* 42 (2003), 389–425, here

390–1; Jill Stephenson, 'Generations, Emotion and Critical Enquiry: A British View of Changing Approaches to the Study of Nazi Germany', *German History* 26 (2008), 272–83.

32. Raul Hilberg, *The Destruction of the European Jews* (Chicago: Quadrangle, 1961), p. v.

33. Krausnick's essay in *idem* et al., *Anatomie*; Andreas Hillgruber, 'Die Endlösung und das deutsche Ostimperium als Kernstück des rassenideologischen Programms des Nationalsozialismus', *Vierteljahreshefte für Zeitgeschichte* 20 (1972), 133–53; Uwe Dietrich Adam, *Judenpolitik im dritten Reich* (Düsseldorf: Athenaum Verlag, 1979); Karl Schleunes, *The Twisted Road to Auschwitz* (Urbana: University of Illinois Press, 1972); Martin Broszat, 'Hitler und die Genesis der "Endlösung". Aus Anlass der Thesen von David Irving', *Vierteljahreshefte für Zeitgeschichte* 25 (1977), 739–75; Hans Mommsen, 'Die Realisierung des Utopischen: Die "Endlösung der Judenfrage" im "Dritten Reich"', *Geschichte und Gesellschaft* 9 (1983), 381–420. For an overview of the debate, Ian Kershaw, *The Nazi Dictatorship: Problems and Perspectives of Interpretation* (London: Arnold, 1985), 82–105.

34. Eberhard Jäckel and Jürgen Rohwer (eds), *Der Mord an den Juden im Zweiten Weltkrieg. Entschlussbildung und Verwirklichung* (Stuttgart: Deutsche Verlags-Anstalt, 1985); Yehuda Bauer, *A History of the Holocaust* (New York: F. Watts, 1982); Gerald Fleming, *Hitler and the Final Solution* (Berkeley: University of California Press, 1984); Lucy S. Dawidowicz, *The War against the Jews, 1933–1945* (New York: Holt, Rinehart, and Winston, 1975).

35. Saul Friedländer, *Nazi Germany and the Jews:* vol. i: *The Years of Persecution 1933–1939* (New York: HarperCollins, 1997).

36. *Center Magazine* 14:4 (1981), 56–64.

37. Yehuda Bauer, 'The Place of the Holocaust in Contemporary History', *Studies in Contemporary Jewry* 1 (1984), 201–24; Marrus, *The Holocaust in History*; see also the sources detailed in S. Katz, *The Holocaust in Historical Context*, vol. i: *The Holocaust and Mass Death before the Modern Age* (New York: Oxford University Press, 1994), 27.

38. Peter Novick, *The Holocaust in American Life* (New York: Houghton Mifflin, 1999), 9, 14.

39. Richard Rubinstein, *After Auschwitz: Radical Theology and Contemporary Judaism* (Indianapolis: Bobbs-Merrill, 1966); E. Fackenheim, 'Why the Holocaust is unique', *Judaism* 5 (2001), 438–47.

40. Zachary Braiterman, *(God) After Auschwitz: Tradition and Change in Post-Holocaust Jewish Thought* (Princeton: Princeton University Press, 1998), 13.

41. Katz, *The Holocaust in Historical Context*, i, 580.

42. Moishe Postone, 'The Holocaust and the Trajectory of the Twentieth Century', in Moishe Postner and Eric Santner (eds), *Catastrophe and Meaning* (Chicago: University of Chicago Press, 2003), 81–114, here 84–6. Dan Diner, 'Varieties of Narration: The Holocaust in Historical Memory', in Jonathan Frankel (ed.), *Studies in Contemporary Jewry: The Fate of the European Jews, 1939–1943* (Oxford: Oxford University Press, 1997), 84–100, here 89–92.

43. A. Dirk Moses, 'Conceptual Blockages and Definitional Dilemmas in the "Racial Century": Genocides of Indigenous Peoples and the Holocaust', *Patterns of Prejudice* 36:4 (2002), 7–36, here 18.

44. Zygmunt Bauman, *Modernity and the Holocaust* (Ithaca, NY: Cornell University Press, 1989).

45. Bloxham, 'Britain's Holocaust Memorial Days', 42–3.

46. Novick, *American Life*; Norman G. Finkelstein, *The Holocaust Industry: Reflections on the Exploitation of Jewish Suffering* (London: Verso, 2003).

47. Edited by Harry James Cargas (Lexington, KY: University Press of Kentucky, 1999).

48. *NRC Handelsblad*, 26 March 1994, 11, opinion. Translation by Rob van Gerwen.

49. Stone, *Constructing*, 41.

50. e.g. Christopher Browning, *The Path to Genocide: Essays on Launching the Final Solution* (Cambridge: Cambridge University Press, 1992); *Nazi Policy, Jewish Workers, German Killers* (Cambridge: Cambridge University Press, 2000); *idem* and Jürgen Matthäus, *The Origin of the Final Solution: The Evolution of Nazi Jewish Policy, September 1939–March 1942* (Lincoln: University of Nebraska Press, 2004).

51. These include but are not limited to the contributors to Herbert (ed.), *Nationalsozialistische Vernichtungspolitik*.

52. Götz Aly and Karl Heinz Roth, *Die Restlose Erfassung: Volkszählen, Indentifizieren, Aussondern im Nationalsozialismus* (Berlin: Rotbuch Verlag, 1984); Aly (ed.), *Aussonderung und Tod. Die klinische Hinrichtung des Unbrauchbaren* (Berlin: Rotbuch, 1985); Aly and Suzaanne Heim, *Vordenker der Vernichtung: Auschwitz und die deutschen Pläne für eine neue europäischen Ordnung* (Frankfurt am Main: Fischer, 1993); Aly, *'Final Solution': Nazi Population Policy and the Murder of the European Jews* (London: Arnold,

1999); *idem, Hitlers Volkstaat: Raub, Rassenkrieg und nationaler Sozialismus* (Frankfurt am Main: Fischer, 2005).

53. Ulrich Herbert, *Fremdarbeiter: Politik und Praxis des 'Auslander-Einsatzes' in der Kriegswirtschaft des Dritten Reiches* (Berlin: Verlag Dietz Nachf., 1985); *idem, Best: Biographische Studien über Radikalismus, Weltanschauung und Vernunft 1903–1989* (Bonn: Dietz, 1996); Michael Wildt, *Generation des Unbedingten: Das Führungskorps des Reichssicherheitshauptamtes* (Hamburg: Hamburger Edition, 2003).

54. Wolf Gruner's work on the role of mid- and low-level German administrators in domestic discrimination should also be mentioned here. See his *Öffentliche Wohlfahrt und Judenverfolgung: Wechselwirkung lokaler und zentraler Politik im NS-Staat (1933–1942)* (Munich: Oldenbourg, 2002)and *Der geschlossene Arbeitseinsatz deutscher Juden: Zur Zwangsarbeit als Element der Verfolgung 1938–1943* (Berlin: Metropol, 1997).

55. The best example of this general tendency is Levene's two-volume *Genocide in the Age of the Nation-State*—though Levene had, usually, begun elaborating his thesis before the end of the Cold War. I eagerly await the third volume of the series, which incorporates the Holocaust into Levene's general model. Moses' 'Conceptual Blockages' is a compelling manifesto.

56. For example Woodruff D. Smith, *The German Colonial Empire* (Chapel Hill, NC: University of North Carolina Press, 1978); *idem, The Ideological Origins of Nazi Imperialism* (New York: Oxford University Press, 1989); Aimé Césaire, *Discourse on Colonialism* (New York: Monthly Review Press, 1972). A. Dirk Moses (ed.), *Empire, Colony, Genocide* (New York: Berghahn, 2008), is a superb state-of-the-art collection.

57. Alison Palmer, *Colonial Genocide* (Adelaide: Crawford, 2000).

58. 'Internal colonization' is an expression I myself have gladly used. See Donald Bloxham, 'Internal Colonization, Inter-imperial Conflict and the Armenian Genocide', in Moses (ed.), *Empire, Colony, Genocide*, 325–42.

59. Jürgen Zimmerer's, *Deutsche Herrschaft über Afrikaner: Staatlicher Machtanspruch und Wirklichkeit im kolonialen Namibia* (Münster/Hamburg: LIT Verlag, 2002), which should be read in conjunction with his chapter in A. Dirk Moses (ed.), *Genocide and Settler Society* (New York: Berghahn Books, 2004).

60. Hannah Arendt, *Origins; Eichmann in Jerusalem: A Report on the Banality of Evil* (Harmondsworth: Penguin, 1994).

61. Amir Weiner (ed.), *Landscaping the Human Garden: Twentieth-Century Population Management in a Comparative Framework* (Stanford: Stanford University Press, 2003).

62. Michael Mann, *The Dark Side of Democracy: Explaining Ethnic Cleansing* (Cambridge: Cambridge University Press, 2005).
63. See Stone, *Constructing*, 71, summarizing Aimé Césaire's position.
64. Gavin Langmuir, *History, Religion, and Anti-Semitism* (Berkeley: University of California Press, 1990), 275.
65. Christopher Probst, 'Protestant Responses to Martin Luther's "Judens-chriften" in Germany, 1929–1945', PhD dissertation, University of London, 2008.
66. John Stuart Mill cited in S. H. Rigby, 'Historical Causation: Is One Thing More Important than Another?', *History* 80 (1995), 226–42, here 234.
67. Bauman, *Modernity*, 13: 'Modern civilization was not the Holocaust's *sufficient* condition; it was, however, most certainly its *necessary* condition.'
68. Rigby, 'Historical Causation', 236.
69. E. P. Thompson, *Persons and Polemics: Historical Essays* (London: Merlin Press, 1994), 213.
70. To adopt the title of a forthcoming series of monographs on different regions of the world that I am co-editing with Mark Levene for Oxford University Press: *Zones of Violence*.

SELECT BIBLIOGRAPHY

PRIMARY SOURCES

Arad, Yitzhak, et al. (eds) *Documents on the Holocaust* (Lincoln: University of Nebraska Press, 1999).

Benz, Wolfgang, Konrad Kwiet, and Jürgen Matthäus (eds), *Einsatz im 'Reichskommissariat Ostland': Dokumente zum Völkermord im Baltikum und in Weissrussland* (Berlin: Metropol, 1998).

Berenstein, Tatiana, et al. (eds), *Faschismus—Ghetto—Massenmord: Dokumentation über Austrottung und Widerstand der Juden in Polen während des zweiten Weltkrieges* (Berlin: Rütten and Loening, 1960).

Deutsche Geschichte im 20. Jahrhundert Online. Nationalsozialismus, Holocaust, Widerstand und Exil 1933–1945. Online-Datenbank, ed. K. G. Saur Verlag

Domarus, Max (ed.), *Hitler. Reden und Proklamationen 1932–1945*, 2 vols (Neustadt: Schmidt, 1962).

Friedman, Tuviah (ed.), *Die drei verantwortlichen SS-Führer für die Durchführung der Endlösung der Judenfrage in Europa waren: Heydrich—Eichmann—Müller: eine dokumentarische Sammlung von SS- und Gestapo-Dokumenten über die Vernichtung der Juden Europas 1939–1945* (Haifa: Institute of Documentation in Israel, 1993).

Goebbels, Joseph, *Die Tagebücher von Joseph Goebbels*, ed. Elke Fröhlich. (Munich: K. G. Saur, 1996).

Gruner, Wolf (ed.), *Die Verfolgung und Ermordung der europäischen Juden durch das nationalsozialistische Deutschland 1933–1945* (Munich: Oldenbourg, 2008).

Himmler, Heinrich, *Geheimreden 1933 bis 1945*, ed. Bradley F. Smith and Agnes F. Peterson (Frankfurt Am Main: Propyläen, 1974).

Hoess, Rudolf, *Commandant of Auschwitz: The Autobiography of Rudolf Höss* (London: Phoenix Press, 1961).

International Military Tribunal, *Trial of the Major War Criminals before the International Military Tribunal*, 42 vols (Nuremberg: IMT, 1947–9).

Jäckel, Eberhard, and Axel Kuhn (eds), *Hitler. Sämtliche Aufzeichnungen 1905–1924* (Stuttgart: Deutsche Verlags-Anstalt, 1980).

Jochmann, Werner (ed.), *Adolf Hitler: Monologe im Führerhauptquartier, 1941–1945. Die Aufzeichnungen Heinrich Heims* (Hamburg: Albrecht Knaus, 1980).

Klarsfeld, Serge (ed.), *Vichy-Auschwitz: La 'solution finale' de la Question Juive en France* (Paris: Fayard, 2001).

Mallmann, Klaus-Michael, Jochen Böhler, and Jürgen Matthäus (eds) *Einsatzgruppen in Polen. Darstellung und Dokumentation* (Darmstadt: Wissenschaftliche Buchgesellschaft, 2008).

Matlok, Siegfried (ed.), *Dänemark in Hitlers Hand. Der Bericht des Reichsbevollmächtigten Werner Best über seine Besatzungspolitik in Dänemark* (Husum: Husum Verlag, 1988).

Noakes, Jeremy, and Geoffrey Pridham (eds), *Nazism 1919–1945*, vol. iii: *Foreign Policy, War and Racial Extermination* (Exeter: University of Exeter Press, 1988).

Nuremberg documents, available in numerous archival repositories.

Pätzold, Kurt, and Erika Schwarz (eds), *Tagesordnung, Judenmord: Die Wannsee-Konferenz am 20. Januar 1942: eine Dokumentation zur Organisation der 'Endlosung', Reihe Dokumente, Texte, Materialien* (Berlin: Metropol, 1992).

Poliakov, Léon, and Joseph Wulf (eds), *Das dritte Reich und die Juden: Dokumente und Aufsätze* (Berlin: Fourier Verlag 1989).

Der Stuermer (1943).

Walk, Joseph (ed.), *Das Sonderrecht für die Juden im NS-Staat Eine Sammlung der gesetzlichen Maßnahmen und Richtlinien—Inhalt und Bedeutung* (Heidelberg: UTB Uni-Taschenbücher Verlag, 1996).

Wildt, Michael (ed.), *Die Judenpolitik des SD 1935–1938: Dokumentation* (Munich: Oldenbourg, 1995).

Witek, Hans, and Hans Safrian, *Und keiner war dabei. Dokumente des alltäglichen Antisemitismus in Wien 1938* (Vienna: Picus, 1988).

Witte, Peter, et al. (eds), *Der Dienstkalender Heinrich Himmlers 1941/1942* (Hamburg: Christians, 1999).

SECONDARY SOURCES

Abramson, Henry, *A Prayer for the Government: Ukrainians and Jews in Revolutionary Times, 1917–1920* (Cambridge, MA: Harvard University Press, 1999).

Adam, Uwe Dietrich, *Judenpolitik im dritten Reich* (Dusseldorf: Athenaum Verlag Dusseldorf, 1979).

Agamben, Giorgio, *State of Exception* (Chicago: University of Chicago Press, 2005).

Alberti, Michael, *Die Verfolgung und Vernichtung der Juden im Reichsgau Wartheland 1939–1945* (Wiesbaden: Harrassowitz, 2006).

Allen, Michael Thad, *The Business of Genocide: The SS, Slave Labor, and the Concentration Camps* (Chapel Hill: University of North Carolina Press, 2002).

Allen, William Sheridan, 'The Appeal of Fascism and the Problem of National Disintegration', in Henry A. Turner (ed.), *Reappraisals of Fascism* (New York: New Viewpoints, 1975), 44–68.

Aly, Götz (ed.), *Aussonderung und Tod. Die klinische Hinrichtung des Unbrauchbaren* (Berlin: Rotbuch, 1985).

—— and Suzanne Heim, *Vordenker der Vernichtung: Auschwitz und die deutschen Pläne für eine neue europäischen Ordnung* (Frankfurt am Main: Fischer, 1993).

Anderson, Benedict, *Imagined Communities* (London: Verso, 1991).

Angrick, Andrej, and Peter Klein, *Die 'Endlösung' in Riga: Ausbeutung und Vernichtung 1941–1944* (Darmstadt: Wissenschaftliche Buchgesellschaft, 2005).

Arendt, Hannah, *The Origins of Totalitarianism* (New York: Harcourt, Brace and World, 1951).

Bajohr, Frank, and Dieter Pohl, *Der Holocaust als offenes Geheimnis: Die Deutschen, die NS-Führung und die Alliierten* (München: C. H. Beck, 2006).

Bankier, David, *The Germans and the Final Solution: Public Opinion under Nazism* (Oxford: Blackwell, 1992).

Bartov, Omer, *Hitler's Army: Soldiers, Nazis and War in the Third Reich* (Oxford: Oxford University Press, 1992).

Bauman, Zygmunt, *Modernity and the Holocaust* (Ithaca, NY: Cornell University Press, 1989).

Bell, David A., *The First Total War: Napoleon's Europe and the Birth of Warfare as We Know It* (New York: Houghton Mifflin, 2007).

Berkhoff, Karel C., *Harvest of Despair: Life and Death in Ukraine under Nazi Rule* (Cambridge, MA: Harvard University Press, 2004).

Bessel, Richard, *Germany after the First World War* (Oxford: Oxford University Press, 1993).

Birn, Ruth Bettina, *Die Höheren SS-und Polizeiführer* (Düsseldorf: Droste, 1986).

Blackbourn, David, and Geoff Eley, *The Peculiarities of German History* (Oxford: Oxford University Press, 1984).

Blasius, Dirk, *Weimars Ende: Bürgerkrieg und Politik 1930–1933* (Göttingen: Vandenhoeck and Ruprecht, 2005).

Blatman, Daniel, 'The Death Marches: Who Was Responsible for What?', *Yad Vashem Studies* 28 (2000), 155–201.

Bloxham, Donald, *The Great Game of Genocide: Imperialism, Nationalism, and the Destruction of the Ottoman Armenians* (Oxford: Oxford University Press, 2005).

—— 'Organized Mass Murder: Structure, Participation, and Motivation in Comparative Perspective', *Holocaust and Genocide Studies* 22 (2008), 203–45.

Bloxham, Donald, 'Britain's Holocaust Memorial Days: reshaping the past in the service of the present', *Immigrants and Minorities*, 21 (2003), 41–62.

Bock, Gisela, 'Racism and Sexism in Nazi Germany: Motherhood, Compulsory Sterilization, and the State', *Signs* 8 (1983), 400–21.

Boyer, John W., *Political Radicalism in Late Imperial Vienna: Origins of the Christian Social Movement, 1848–1897* (Chicago: University of Chicago Press, 1981).

Braham, Randolph L., *The Politics of Genocide: The Holocaust in Hungary* (New York: Columbia University Press, 1994).

Brandes, Detlef, *Der Weg zur Vertreibung 1938–1945* (Munich: Oldenbourg Verlag, 2002).

Brayard, Florent, *La 'Solution Finale de la question juive': La technique, le temps et les catégories de la décision* (Paris: Fayard, 2004).

Brechtken, Magnus, *'Madagaskar für die Juden': antisemitische Idee und politische Praxis 1885–1945* (Munich: Oldenbourg, 1997).

Broszat, Martin, *The Hitler State: The Foundation and Development of the Internal Structure of the Third Reich* (London: Longman, 1981).

Browning, Christopher R., *The Final Solution and the German Foreign Office: A Study of Referat D III of Abteilung Deutschland, 1940–43* (New York: Holmes and Meier, 1978).

—— *The Path to Genocide: Essays on Launching the Final Solution* (Cambridge: Cambridge University Press, 1992).

—— *Ordinary Men: Reserve Police Battalion 101 and the Final Solution in Poland* (New York: HarperCollins, 1993).

—— *Nazi Policy, Jewish Workers, German Killers* (Cambridge: Cambridge University Press, 2000).

—— and Jürgen Matthäus, *The Origins of the Final Solution: The Evolution of Nazi Jewish Policy, September 1939–March 1942* (Lincoln: University of Nebraska Press, 2004).

Bryant, Chad, 'Either German or Czech: Fixing Nationality in Bohemia and Moravia, 1939–1946', *Slavic Review* 61 (2002), 683–706.

Burrows, Susanna, *Distorting Mirrors: Visions of the Crowd in Late Nineteenth-Century France* (New Haven, CT: Yale University Press, 1981).

Chary, Frederick B., *The Bulgarian Jews and the final solution, 1940–1944* (Pittsburgh: University of Pittsburgh Press, 1972).

Chiari, Bernhard, *Alltag hinter der Front: Besatzung, Kollaboration und Widerstand in Weissrussland 1941–1944* (Düsseldorf: Droste, 1998).

Cohn, Norman, *Warrant for Genocide: The Jewish World Conspiracy and the Protocols of the Elders of Zion* (London: Serif, 1996).

Cole, Tim, *Holocaust City: The Making of a Jewish Ghetto* (New York/London: Routledge, 2003).

Cüppers, Martin, *Wegbereiter der Shoah: Die Waffen-SS, der Kommandostab Reichsführer-SS und die Judenvernichtung 1939–1945* (Darmstadt: Wissenschaftliche Buchgesellschaft, 2005).

Curp, T. David, *A Clean Sweep? The Politics of Ethnic Cleansing in Western Poland, 1945–1960* (Rochester, NY: University of Rochester Press, 2006).

Dean, Martin, *Collaboration in the Holocaust: Crimes of the Local Police in Belorussia and Ukraine, 1941–44* (New York: St. Martin's Press, 2000).

Deutscher, Isaac, *The Non-Jewish Jew and Other Essays* (Oxford: Oxford University Press, 1968).

Dieckmann, Christoph, Christian Gerlach, and Wolf Gruner (eds), *Kooperation und Verbrechen: Formen der Kollaboration im östlichen Europa 1939–1945* (Göttingen: Wallstein, 2003).

Diner, Dan, 'Epistemics of the Holocaust Considering the Question of "Why?" and of "How?"', *Zeitschrift für deutsch-jüdische Literatur und Kulturgeschichte* 1: 2 (2008), 195–213.

Dörner, Bernward, *Die Deutschen und der Holocaust. Was niemand wissen wollte, aber jeder wissen konnte* (Berlin: Propyläen Verlag, 2007).

Dündar, Fuat, *Ittihat ve Terakki'nin Müslümanları Iskân Politikası (1913–1918)* (Istanbul, 2001).

Ehrenreich, Eric, *The Nazi Ancestral Proof: Genealogy, Racial Science, and the Final Solution* (Bloomington: Indiana University Press, 2007).

Eley, Geoff, *Reshaping the German Right: Radical Nationalism and Political Change after Bismarck* (Ann Arbor: University of Michigan Press, 1990).

Essner, Cornelia, *Die 'Nürnberger Gesetze' oder Die Verwaltung des Rassenwahns 1933–1945* (Paderborn: Schöningh, 2002).

Farrar, L. L., Jr., 'Realpolitik versus Nationalpolitik: Rethinking Nationalism during the Eastern Crisis, 1875–1878', *Eastern European Quarterly* 30 (1996).

Fink, Carole, ' "Defender of Minorities": Germany in the League of Nations, 1926–1933', *Central European History* 5 (1972), 330–57.

Finney, Patrick, ' "An Evil for All Concerned": Great Britain and Minority Protection after 1919', *Journal of Contemporary History* 30 (1995), 533–51.

Fischer, Fritz, *Germany's Aims in the First World War* (New York: Norton, 1967).

Fischer, Rolf, *Entwicklungsstufen des Antisemitismus in Ungarn, 1867–1939: Die Zerstörung der magyarischen-jüdischen Symbiose* (Munich: Oldenbourg, 1988).

Fleischhauer, Ingeborg, *Das Dritte Reich und die Deutschen in der Sowjetunion* (Stuttgart: DVA, 1983).

Fletcher, Luke, 'Turning Interahamwe: Individual and Community Choices in the Rwandan Genocide', *Journal of Genocide Research* 9:1 (2007), 25–48.

Frei, Norbert, *Vergangenheitspolitik: Die Anfänge der Bundesrepublik und die NS-Vergangenheit* (Munich: C. H.Beck, 1996).

Frei, N., S. Steinbacher, and B. Wagner (eds), *Ausbeutung, Vernichtung, Öffentlichkeit* (Munich: Saur, 2000).

Friedlander, Henry, *The Origins of Nazi Genocide* (Chapel Hill: University of North Carolina Press, 1995).

Friedländer, Saul, *Nazi Germany and the Jews:* vol. i: *The Years of Persecution 1933–1939* (New York: HarperCollins, 1997).

——— *The Years of Extermination: Nazi Germany and the Jews, 1939–1945* (New York: HarperCollins, 2007).

Gaunt, David, *Massacres, Resistance, Protectors: Muslim-Christian Relations in Eastern Anatolia during World War I* (Piscataway, NJ: Gorgias Press, 2006).

Geiss, Imannuel, *Der polnische Grenzstreifen 1914–1918. Ein Beitrag zur deutschen Kriegszielpolitik im Ersten Weltkrieg* (Hamburg: Lübeck, 1960).

Gellately, Robert, *The Gestapo and German Society* (Oxford: Clarendon Press, 1990).

——— *Backing Hitler: Consent and Coercion in Nazi Germany* (Oxford: Oxford University Press, 2001).

Gellner, Ernst, *Nations and Nationalism* (Oxford: Blackwell, 1993).

Gerlach, Christian, *Kalkulierte Morde: Die deutsche Wirtschafts- und Vernichtungspolitik im Weißrußland* (Hamburg: Hamburger Edition, 1999).

——— and Götz Aly, *Das letzte Kapitel: Der Mord an den ungarischen Juden* (Stuttgart: DVA, 2002).

——— 'The Wannsee Conference, the Fate of German Jews, and Hitler's Decision in Principle to Exterminate All European Jews', *Journal of Modern History* 70 (1998), 759–812.

Gerwarth, Robert, 'The Central European Counter-Revolution: Paramilitary Violence in Germany, Austria, and Hungary after the Great War', *Past and Present* 200:1 (2008), 175–209.

Gilroy, Paul, *The Black Atlantic: Modernity and Double Consciousness* (London: Verso, 1993).

Griffioen, Pim, and Ron Zeller, 'Anti-Jewish Policy and Organization of the Deportations in France and the Netherlands, 1940–1944: A Comparative Study', *Holocaust and Genocide Studies* 20:3 (2006), 437–73.

Gross, Jan T., *Neighbors: The Destruction of the Jewish Community in Jedwabne, Poland* (Princeton, NJ: Princeton University Press, 2001).

Gruner, Wolf, *Der geschlossene Arbeitseinsatz deutscher Juden: Zur Zwangsarbeit als Element der Verfolgung 1938–1943* (Berlin: Metropol, 1997).

——— and Armin Nolzen (eds), *'Bürokratien'. Initiative und Effizienz* (Berlin, 2001).

——— *Öffentliche Wohlfahrt und Judenverfolgung: Wechselwirkung lokaler und zentraler Politik im NS-Staat (1933–1942)* (Munich: Oldenbourg, 2002).

Haberer, Erich, *Jews and Revolution in Nineteenth-Century Russia* (New York: Cambridge University Press, 1995).

Hachtmann, Rüdiger, and Winfried Süss (eds), *Hitlers Kommissare: Sonderge-walten in der nationalsozialistischen Diktatur* (Göttingen: Wallstein Verlag, 2006).

Hausleitner, Mariana, *Deutsche und Juden in Bessarabien 1841–1941. Zur Mind-erheitenpolitik Russlands und Grossrumaniens* (Munich: IKGS Verlag 2005).

Hayes, Bascom Barry, *Bismarck and Mitteleuropa* (Madison, NJ: Fairleigh Dickinson University Press, 1994).

Heer, Hannes, and Klaus Namann (eds), *War of Extermination: The German Military in World War II 1941–1944* (New York: Berghahn Books, 2000).

Heinemann, Isabel, *'Rasse, Siedlung, deutsches Blut': Das Rasse- und Siedlung-shauptamt der SS und die rassenpolitische Neuordnung Europas* (Göttingen: Wallstein Verlag, 2003).

Herbert, Ulrich, *Best: Biographische Studien über Radikalismus, Weltanschauung und Vernunft 1903–1989* (Bonn: Dietz, 1996).

—— (ed.), *Nationalsozialistische Vernichtungspolitik 1939–1945: Neue Forschun-gen und Kontroversen* (Frankfurt am Main: Fischer, 1998).

Herf, Jeffery, *The Jewish Enemy: Nazi Propaganda during World War II and the Holocaust* (Cambridge, MA: Harvard University Press, 2008).

Hilberg, Raul, The D*estruction of the European Jews*, 3 vols (New York: Holmes and Meier, 1985).

Hirschon, René (ed.), *Crossing the Aegean: An Appraisal of the 1923 Compulsory Population Exchange between Greece and Turkey* (New York, 2003).

Hsia, R. Po-chia, *The Myth of Ritual Murder: Jews and Magic in Reformation Germany* (New Haven, CT: Yale University Press, 1988).

Hüttenberger, Peter, *Die Gauleiter: Studie zum Wandel des Machtgefüges in der NSDAP* (Stuttgart: Deutsche Verlags-Anstalt, 1969).

Ioanid, Radu, *The Sword of the Archangel* (New York: Colombia University Press, 1990).

—— *The Holocaust in Romania: The Destruction of Jews and Gypsies under the Antonescu Regime, 1940–1944* (New York: Ivan R. Dee, 2000).

Johnson, Eric, *Nazi Terror: the Gestapo, Jews and Ordinary Germans* (London: John Murray, 2000).

Kallis, Aristotle A., 'The Jewish Community of Salonica under Siege: The Antisemitic Violence of the Summer of 1931', *Holocaust and Genocide Studies* 20 (2006), 34–56.

Kalyvas, Stathis, *The Logic of Violence in Civil War* (Cambridge: Cambridge University Press, 2006).

Kann, R. A., B. K. Kiraly, and P. S. Fichtner (eds), *The Hapsburg Empire in World War I* (New York: Columbia University Press, 1977).

Katz, Steven T., *The Holocaust in Historical Context*, vol. i: *The Holocaust and Mass Death before the Modern Age* (New York: Oxford University Press, 1994).

Kershaw, Ian, *Hitler 1889–1936: Hubris* (London: Penguin, 1999).

—— 'Improvised Genocide? The Emergence of the "final Solution" in the. "Warthegau"', *Transactions of the Royal Historical Society* 6th ser., 2 (1992), 51–78.

Kévorkian, Raymond, *Le Génocide des Arméniens* (Paris: Odile Jacob, 2006).

Kirchhoff, Hans, 'Denmark: A Light in the Darkness of the Holocaust? A Reply to Gunnar S. Paulsson,' *Journal of Contemporary History* 30 (1995), 465–79.

Klee, Ernst, *'Euthanasie' im NS-Staat: Die 'Vernichtung lebensunwerten Lebens'* (Frankfurt am Main: Fischer, 1983).

Klein, Peter (ed.), *Die Einsatzgruppen in der besetzten Sowjetunion 1941/42. Die Tätigkeits- und Lageberichte des Chefs der Sicherheitspolizei und des SD* (Berlin: Wannsee-Haus, 1997).

Knox, MacGregor, 'Das faschistische Italien und die "Endlösung", 1942/43', *Vierteljahrshefte für Zeitgeschichte* 55:1 (2007), 53–92.

Koonz, Claudia, *The Nazi Conscience* (Cambridge, MA: Harvard Belknap, 2003).

Krausnick, Helmut, and Hans-Heinrich Wilhelm, *Die Truppe des Weltanschauungs krieges. Die Einsatzgruppen der Sicherheitspolizei und des SD 1938–1942* (Stuttgart: Deutsche Verlags-Anstalt, 1981).

Kühl, Stefan, *The Nazi Connection: eugenics, American racism, and German National Socialism* (New York: Oxford University Press, 1994).

Kühne, Thomas, *Kameradschaft: Die Soldaten nationalsozialistischen Krieges und das 20. Jahrhundert* (Göttingen: Vandenhoeck and Ruprecht, 2006).

Ladas, Stephen P., *The Exchange of Minorities: Bulgaria, Greece and Turkey* (New York: Macmillan, 1932).

Langmuir, Gavin I., *History, Religion, and Antisemitism* (Berkeley, CA: University of California Press, 1990).

Larmore, Charles E., *Patterns of Moral Complexity* (Cambridge: Cambridge University Press, 1987).

Lehnstaedt, Stephan, 'Das Reichsministerium des Innern unter Heinrich Himmler 1943–1945', *Vierteljahrshefte für Zeitgeschichte* 4 (2006), 639–72.

Lemkin, Raphael, 'Genocide as a Crime under International Law', *American Journal of International Law* 41:1 (1947), 145–51.

Levene, Mark, *Genocide in the Age of the Nation-State*, 2 vols (London: Tauris, 2005).

Lindemann, Albert, *Esau's Tears: Modern Antisemitism and the Rise of the Jews* (Cambridge: Cambridge University Press, 1997).

Liulevicius, Vejas, *War Land on the Eastern Front: Culture, National Identity, and German Occupation in World War I* (New York: Cambridge University Press, 2001).

Lohr, Eric, *Nationalising the Russian Empire: the Campaign against Enemy Aliens during World War One* (Cambridge, MA: Harvard University Press, 2003).

Longerich, Peter, *Politik der Vernichtung: Eine Gesamtdarstellung der national-alsozialistischen Judenverfolgung* (Munich: Piper Verlag, 1998).
—— *'Davon haben wir nichts gewusst!' Die Deutschen und die Judenverfolgung 1933–1945* (Munich: Siedler, 2006).
Lower, Wendy, *Nazi Empire-Building and the Holocaust in Ukraine* (Chapel Hill: University of North Carolina Press, 2005).
McCarthy, Justin, *Death and Exile: The Ethnic Cleansing of Ottoman Muslims, 1821–1922* (Princeton, NJ: Darwin Press, 1995).
MacQueen, Michael, 'Polen, Litauer, Juden und Deutsche in Wilna 1939–1944', in Wolfgang Benz and Marion Neiss (eds), *Judenmord in Litauen: Studien und Dokumente* (Berlin: Metropol, 1999), 51–68.
Madajczyk, Czesław, *Vom Generalplan Ost zum Generalsiedlungsplan* (Munich: Sauer, 1994).
Mallmann, Klaus-Michael, and Bogdan Musial (eds), *Genesis des Genozids: Polen 1939–1941* (Darmstadt: Wissenschaftliche Buchgesellschaft, 2004).
Mann, Michael, *The Dark Side of Democracy: Explaining Ethnic Cleansing* (Cambridge: Cambridge University Press, 2005).
Manoschek, Walter, *'Serbien ist Judenfrei': Militärische Besatzungspolitik und Judenvernichtung in Serbien 1941/42* (Munich: Oldenbourg, 1993).
Marrus, Michael R., *The Holocaust in History* (Hanover, NH: University Press of New England, 1989).
—— and Robert O. Paxton, *Vichy France and the Jews* (New York: Basic Books, 1981).
Martin, Terry, 'The Origins of Soviet Ethnic Cleansing,' *Journal of Modern History* 70 (1998), 813–61.
Marx, Anthony, *Faith in Nation: The Exclusionary Origins of Nationalism* (Oxford: Oxford University Press, 2003).
Mason, Tim, *Social Policy in the Third Reich: the Working Class and the 'National Community'* (Oxford: Berghahn, 1993).
Matthäus, Jürgen, ' "Reibungslos und planmäßig": Die zweite Welle der Judenvernichtung im Generalkommissariat Weißruthenien (1942–1944)', *Jahrbuch für Antisemitismusforschung* 4 (1995), 254–74.
—— 'Ausbildung zum Judenmord? Zum Stellenwert der "weltanschaulichen Erziehung" von SS und Polizei im Rahmen der "Endlösung" ', *Zeitschrift für Geschichtswissenschaft* 47 (1999), 677–99.
—— 'Controlled Escalation: Himmler's Men in the Summer of 1941 and the Holocaust in the Occupied Soviet Territories', *Holocaust and Genocide Studies* 21(2007), 218–42.
Michlic, Joanna, *Poland's Threatening Other: The Image of the Jew from 1880 to the Present* (Lincoln: University of Nebraska Press, 2006).
Mommsen, Hans, *Beamtentum in Dritten Reich* (Stuttgart: Oldenbourg, 1966).
Moore, R. I., *The Formation of a Persecuting Society: Power and Deviance in Medieval Europe 950–1250* (Oxford: Oxford University Press, 1987).

Moses, A. Dirk (ed.), *Empire, Colony, Genocide* (New York: Berghahn, 2008).

Musial, Bogdan, *Deutsche Zivilverwaltung und Judenverfolgung im Generalgouvernement: Eine Fallstudie zum Distrikt Lublin 1939–1944* (Leipzig: Harrassowitz, 1999).

Olzak, Susan, *The Dynamics of Ethnic Competition and Conflict* (Stanford, CA: Stanford University Press, 1992).

Orth, Karin, *Das System der nationalsozialistischen Konzentrationslager* (Munich: Pendo, 1999).

Palmer, Alison, *Colonial Genocide* (Adelaide: Crawford House, 2000),

Paul, Gerhard, and Klaus-Michael Mallmann (eds), *Die Gestapo im Zweiten Weltkrieg: 'Heimatfront' und besetztes Europa* (Darmstadt: Primus Verlag, 2000).

Pavlowitch, Stevan, *Hitler's New Disorder: The Second World War in Yugoslavia* (New York: Columbia University Press, 2008).

Pendas, Devin, *The Frankfurt Auschwitz Trial, 1963–1965: Genocide, History and the Limits of the Law* (Cambridge: Cambridge University Press, 2006).

Petersen, Roger, *Understanding Ethnic Violence: Fear, Hatred, and Resentment in Twentieth Century Eastern Europe* (Cambridge: Cambridge University Press, 2002).

Pohl, Dieter, *Von der 'Judenpolitik' zum Judenmord: Der Distrikt Lublin des Generalgouvernements 1939–1944* (Frankfurt am Main: Lang, 1993).

—— *Nationalsozialistische Judenverfolgung in Ostgalizien 1941–1944: Organisation und Durchführung eines staatlichen Massenverbrechens* (Munich: Oldenbourg, 1997).

Polian, Pavel, *Against Their Will: The History and Geography of Forced Migrations in the USSR* (New York: Central European University Press, 2004).

Postone, Moishe, 'The Holocaust and the Trajectory of the Twentieth Century', in Moishe Postner and Eric Santner (eds), *Catastrophe and Meaning* (Chicago: University of Chicago Press, 2003), 81–114.

Prusin, Alexander Victor, *Nationalizing a Borderland: War, Ethnicity, and Anti-Jewish Violence in East Galicia, 1914–1920* (Tuscaloosa: University of Alabama Press, 2005).

Przyrembel, Alexandra, *'Rassenschande': Reinheitsmythos und Vernichtungslegitimation im Nationalsozialismus* (Göttingen: Vandenhoeck und Ruprecht, 2003).

Pulzer, Peter, *The Rise of Political Antisemitism in Germany and Austria* (London: Halban, 1988).

Rebentisch, Dieter, and Karl Teppe (eds), *Verwaltung contra Menschenführung im Staat Hitlers. Studien zum politisch-administrativen System* (Göttingen: Vandenhoeck und Ruprecht, 1986).

Römer, Felix, ' "Im alten Deutschland wäre solcher Befehl nicht möglich gewesen": Rezeption, Adaption und Umsetzung des Kriegsgerichtsbarkeitserlasses im Ostheer 1941/42', *Vierteljahrshefte für Zeitgeschichte* 56 (2008), 53–99.

Ron, James, *Frontiers and Ghettos: State Violence in Israel and Serbia* (Berkley: University of California Press, 2003).

Rozenblit, Marsha L., *Reconstructing a National Identity: The Jews of Habsburg Austria during World War I* (Oxford: Oxford University Press, 2001).

Safrian, Hans, *Eichmann und seine Gehilfen* (Frankfurt am Main: Fischer, 1995).

Sandkühler, Thomas, *'Endlösung' in Galizien: Der Judenmord in Ostpolen und die Rettungsinitiativen von Berthold Beitz 1941–1944* (Bonn: J. H. W Dietz, 1996).

Shepherd, Ben, *War in the Wild East: The German Army and the Soviet Partisans* (Cambridge, MA: Harvard University Press, 2004).

Slezkine, Yuri, *The Jewish Century* (Princeton, NJ: Princeton University Press, 2006).

Snyder, Timothy, *The Reconstruction of Nations: Poland, Ukraine, Belarus, 1569–1999* (New Haven, CT: Yale University Press, 2004).

Steigman-Gall, Richard, *The Holy Reich: Nazi Conceptions of Christianity, 1919–1945* (Cambridge: Cambridge University Press, 2004).

Steinweis, Alan, *Studying the Jew: Scholarly Antisemitism in Nazi Germany* (Cambridge, MA: Harvard University Press, 2006).

Stern, Fritz, *The Politics of Cultural Despair: A Study in the Rise of Germanic Ideology* (Berkeley: University of California Press, 1974).

Stone, Dan (ed.), *The Historiography of the Holocaust* (London: Palgrave, 2004).

Straus, Scott, *The Order of Genocide: Race, Power, and War in Rwanda* (Ithaca, NY: Cornell University Press, 2006).

Streit, Christian, *Keine Kameraden: Die Wehrmacht und die sowjetischen Kriegsgefangenen 1941–1945* (Bonn: J. H. W. Dietz, 1991).

Sutcliffe, Adam, *Judaism and Enlightenment* (Cambridge: Cambridge University Press, 2003).

Ther, Philipp, and Ana Siljak (eds), *Redrawing Nations: Ethnic Cleansing in East-Central Europe, 1944–1948* (Lanham, MD: Rowman & Littlefield, 2001).

Tönsmeyer, Tatjana, *Das Dritte Reich und die Slowakei 1939–1945* (Paderborn: Schöningh, 2003).

Tooze, Adam, *The Wages of Destruction: The Making and Breaking of the Nazi Economy* (London: Viking, 2007).

Vital, David, *A People Apart: The Jews in Europe 1789–1939* (Oxford: Oxford University Press, 1999).

Volkov, Shulamit, *Germans, Jews, and Antisemites: Trials in Emancipation* (Cambridge: Cambridge University Press, 2006).

Wachsmann, Nikolaus, *Hitler's Prisons: Legal Terror in Nazi Germany* (New Haven, CT: Yale University Press, 2004).

Wagner, Patrick, *Volksgemeinschaft ohne Verbrecher: Konzeption und Praxis der Kriminalpolizei in der Zeit der Weimarer Republik und des Nationalsozialismus* (Hamburg: Christians, 1996).

Waller, James, *Becoming Evil: How Ordinary People Commit. Genocide and Mass Killing* (Oxford: Oxford University Press, 2002).

Weinberg, Gerhard L., *Germany, Hitler, and World War II: Essays in Modern German and World History* (New York: Cambridge University Press, 1995).

Weindling, Paul, *Health, Race, and German Politics between National Unification and Nazism 1870–1945* (Cambridge: Cambridge University Press, 1989).

Welzer, Harald, *Täter. Wie aus ganz normalen Menschen Massenmörder werden* (Frankfurt am Main: S. Fischer, 2005).

Westermann, Edward B., *Hitler's Police Battalions: Enforcing Racial War in the East* (Lawrence: University Press of Kansas, 2005).

Wildt, Michael, *Generation des Unbedingten: Das Führungskorps des Reichssicherheitshauptamtes* (Hamburg: Hamburger Edition, 2003).

—— *Volksgemeinschaft als Selbstermächtigung. Gewalt gegen Juden in der deutschen Provinz 1919 bis 1939* (Hamburg: Hamburger Edition, 2007).

Zimmerer, Jürgen, *Deutsche Herrschaft über Afrikaner: Staatlicher Machtanspruch und Wirklichkeit im kolonialen Namibia* (Münster; Hamburg: LIT Verlag, 2002).

Zimmermann, Michael, *Rassenutopie und Genozid: Die nationalsozialistische 'Lösung der Zigeunerfrage'* (Hamburg: Christians, 1996).

INDEX